For Dummies™

BESTSELLING
BOOK SERIES

New M_____ies,®

D0982163

Cheat Sheet

New Mexico Food Guide

One of the great delights of visiting New Mexico is eating your way through the state's delectable cuisine. This handy list explains the most common New Mexican food items on menus throughout the Land of Enchantment. So pull up a chair, pour yourself a margarita, and dig in!

- **Burrito:** A flour tortilla wrapped around beans and meat or vegetables, baked, and usually topped with lots of red or green chile.
- **Carne adovada:** Pork marinated with red chile.
- **Chalupa:** A deep-fried corn tortilla shaped into a bowl, usually filled with beans and vegetables.
- **Chile:** In New Mexico, the word *chile* refers to a sauce made of red or green chili peppers, often cooked in a chicken, beef, or pork broth, with plenty of garlic. New Mexico is chile central, and the most common question you'll be asked in this state's restaurants is "red or green?" meaning "Would you prefer red or green chile as a sauce with your meal?" If you can't make up your mind, just say "Christmas," which means a combination of the two. If you're not used to chile, order some on the side so you can taste it first.
- **Chile relleno:** A chile pepper stuffed with cheese, breaded, and fried.
- **Chimichanga:** A deep-fried burrito.
- **Chipotle:** A smokey-flavored red chile.
- **Chorizo:** Spicy sausage.
- **Enchilada:** A corn tortilla (often made with blue corn) that is rolled or served flat; filled with meat, chicken, beans, or cheese; and baked.
- **Fajitas:** Grilled beef, chicken, or seafood — often prepared at your table — served with tortillas to wrap it all in.
- **Flauta:** A rolled-up, flute-shaped tortilla filled with meat or cheese and fried.
- **Frijoles:** Beans.
- **Guacamole:** A dip of mashed-up avocado, usually combined with tomatoes, onions, garlic, and chiles.
- **Huevos rancheros:** Fried eggs on a corn tortilla, usually served with refried beans and lots of chile.
- **Posole:** A stew made from green chile, pork, hominy, and chile.
- **Quesadilla:** A folded tortilla that is filled with cheese, meat, or vegetables and baked.
- **Salsa:** Well-chopped chiles, peppers, onions, garlic, and spices, often served as a condiment.
- **Sopaipillas:** Puffy, deep-fried breads usually served with a meal or filled with ice cream for dessert. You usually find honey on your table to go with them.
- **Taco:** A small flour or corn tortilla served soft or crispy; filled with meat, seafood, chicken, or beans; and topped with lettuce, tomatoes, onions, and cheese.
- **Tamale:** A steamed and folded corn husk stuffed with cornmeal and meat or vegetables.
- **Tortilla:** A round, thin bread made from flour or corn, baked, and served as a bread or part of the meal.

New Mexico Driving Times & Distances

RED NUMBERS *indicate distances in miles.*

BLUE NUMBERS *indicate driving times.*

In this schematic we assume 100 miles will take an average of 1 hour, 49 minutes (excluding stops) at an average speed of 55 miles per hour.

Hungry Minds™

For Dummies: Bestselling Book Series for Beginners

New Mexico

FOR

DUMMIES®

1ST EDITION

by Lesley S. King
with Granville Green

Hungry Minds™

Best-Selling Books • Digital Downloads • e-Books • Answer Networks
e-Newsletters • Branded Web Sites • e-Learning

New York, NY ◆ Cleveland, OH ◆ Indianapolis, IN

New Mexico For Dummies,® 1st Edition

Published by:
Hungry Minds, Inc.
909 Third Avenue
New York, NY 10022
www.hungryminds.com
www.dummies.com

Library of Congress Control Number: 2001092931

ISBN: 0-7645-6527-3

ISSN: 1534-9071

Printed in the United States of America

10 9 8 7 6 5 4 3 2 1

1B/QR/RR/QR/IN

Distributed in the United States by Hungry Minds, Inc.

Distributed by CDG Books Canada Inc. for Canada; by Transworld Publishers Limited in the United Kingdom; by IDG Norge Books for Norway; by IDG Sweden Books for Sweden; by IDG Books Australia Publishing Corporation Pty. Ltd. for Australia and New Zealand; by TransQuest Publishers Pte Ltd. for Singapore, Malaysia, Thailand, Indonesia, and Hong Kong; by Gotop Information Inc. for Taiwan; by ICG Muse, Inc. for Japan; by Intersoft for South Africa; by Eyrolles for France; by International Thomson Publishing for Germany, Austria and Switzerland; by Distribuidora Cuspide for Argentina; by LR International for Brazil; by Galileo Libros for Chile; by Ediciones ZETA S.C.R. Ltda. for Peru; by WS Computer Publishing Corporation, Inc., for the Philippines; by Contemporanea de Ediciones for Venezuela; by Express Computer Distributors for the Caribbean and West Indies; by Micronesia Media Distributor, Inc. for Micronesia; by Chips Computadoras S.A. de C.V. for Mexico; by Editorial Norma de Panama S.A. for Panama; by American Bookshops for Finland.

For general information on Hungry Minds' products and services please contact our Customer Care department; within the U.S. at 800-762-2974, outside the U.S. at 317-572-3993 or fax 317-572-4002.

For sales inquiries and resellers information, including discounts, premium and bulk quantity sales and foreign language translations please contact our Customer Care department at 800-434-3422, fax 317-572-4002 or write to Hungry Minds, Inc., Attn: Customer Care department, 10475 Crosspoint Boulevard, Indianapolis, IN 46256.

For information on licensing foreign or domestic rights, please contact our Sub-Rights Customer Care department at 650-653-7098.

For information on using Hungry Minds' products and services in the classroom or for ordering examination copies, please contact our Educational Sales department at 800-434-2086 or fax 317-572-4005.

Please contact our Public Relations department at 212-884-5174 for press review copies or 212-884-5000 for author interviews and other publicity information or fax 212-884-5400.

For authorization to photocopy items for corporate, personal, or educational use, please contact Copyright Clearance Center, 222 Rosewood Drive, Danvers, MA 01923, or fax 978-750-4470.

Hungry Minds™ is a trademark of Hungry Minds, Inc.

About the Authors

Lesley S. King grew up on a ranch in northern New Mexico, where she still returns on weekends to help work cattle. A freelance writer, editor, and photographer, she's a contributor to *The New York Times, Audubon Magazine,* United Airlines *Hemispheres* magazine, and the *Santa Fe Institute Bulletin,* a publication for which she also serves as managing editor. She is writer and host of *Written on the Wind,* a television documentary series. She is also the author of *Frommer's Santa Fe, Taos & Albuquerque, Frommer's New Mexico,* and *Frommer's Great Outdoor Guide to Arizona & New Mexico.*

Granville Greene is a freelance writer based in Santa Fe, New Mexico. He has written for *Outside, Mountainfreak, Condé Nast Traveler, American Way, Bride's, New York Press, Skin Diver,* Travelocity, and many other publications. He studied writing at The Johns Hopkins University.

Dedications

To my family: Barbara, Elbert, Brian, Nicole, Brenda, and Amy, who are responsible for me living and working in this enchanted land.

—Lesley S. King

I would like to dedicate my half of this book to my dog Elroy, who never treats me like a Dummy . . . as far as I can tell.

—Granville Greene

Authors' Acknowledgments

It's not possible in this space for me to thank all the tourism agencies, restaurant and hotel owners and managers, and attraction public relations people, but I'd like to. Thank you for your patience and generosity. Others who have been helpful in many ways of support include Garji, Barbara Doolittle, Elbert King, Michael Rafter, Julie Zimber, Claire Romero, Robert Stivers, Memphis Barbree, and Lex Weimer. Above all, I thank our editor Lisa Torrance, whose excellent work with refining prose made the book read smoothly, and whose patience got it into print.

—Lesley S. King

A big thank you to Elspeth Bobbs, and to everyone else who helped me with the book.

—Granville Greene

Publisher's Acknowledgments

Some of the people who helped bring this book to market include the following:

Editorial

Editors: Joan Friedman, Lisa Torrance

Copy Editor: Billie A. Williams

Cartographer: Roberta Stockwell

Editorial Manager: Christine Meloy Beck

Editorial Assistant: Jennifer Young

Senior Photo Editor: Richard Fox

Assistant Photo Editor: Michael Ross

Front Cover Photo: © Joe Viesti/Viesti Collection

Back Cover Photo: © Donovan Reese/ Tony Stone Images

Production

Project Coordinator: Ryan Steffen

Layout and Graphics: Amy Adrian, Julie Trippetti, Erin Zeltner

Proofreaders: Laura Albert, TECHBOOKS Production Services

Indexer: Maro Riofrancos

Hungry Minds Consumer Reference Group

Business: Kathleen Nebenhaus, Vice President and Publisher; Kevin Thornton, Acquisitions Manager

Cooking/Gardening: Jennifer Feldman, Associate Vice President and Publisher; Anne Ficklen, Executive Editor; Kristi Hart, Managing Editor

Education/Reference: Diane Graves Steele, Vice President and Publisher

Lifestyles: Kathleen Nebenhaus, Vice President and Publisher; Tracy Boggier, Managing Editor

Pets: Kathleen Nebenhaus, Vice President and Publisher; Tracy Boggier, Managing Editor

Travel: Michael Spring, Vice President and Publisher; Brice Gosnell, Publishing Director; Suzanne Jannetta, Editorial Director

Hungry Minds Consumer Editorial Services: Kathleen Nebenhaus, Vice President and Publisher; Kristin A. Cocks, Editorial Director; Cindy Kitchel, Editorial Director

Hungry Minds Consumer Production: Debbie Stailey, Production Director

Contents at a Glance

Cartoons at a Glance

By Rich Tennant

"Oh, it's okay if you're into neo-romanticist art. Personally, I prefer the soaring perspectives of David Hockney or the controlled frenzy of Gerhard Richter."

page 85

"Of all the stuff we came back from New Mexico with, I think these adobe bathrobes were the least well thought out."

page 53

"I'll have a peanut butter sandwich without the chiles, a glass of iced tea without the chiles, and a bowl of vanilla ice cream without the chiles."

page 7

TRUTH OR CONSEQUENCES, NM - 7 mi
JUDGE OR BE JUDGED, NM - 25 mi
SPEAK OR LOOK DUMB, NM - 100 mi
SING OR SHUT UP, NM - 48 mi

page 227

Just for the record, it was your idea to book the Yoga/Meditation package tour.

page 331

Cartoon Information:
Fax: 978-546-7747
E-Mail: richtennant@the5thwave.com
World Wide Web: www.the5thwave.com

Maps at a Glance

Table of Contents

Introduction

• •

*H*aving grown up here, I can't imagine what it would be like *not* to know New Mexico. The state is as much a part of my psyche as my parents. But over the years, in my worldly travels, I have come to know that, for those unfamiliar with the Land of Enchantment, misconceptions abound.

I remember as a child traveling to the Midwest, where people thought my home state lacked such basics as bubble gum and sidewalks. But the biggest misconception is that this state resembles any other. In fact, New Mexico is a unique animal, combining exotic cultures and landscapes more evocative of a foreign country than a southwestern U.S. state.

That's why the only way to get a sense of New Mexico is to come here. I designed this book to help you make important choices before you step into this wonderfully foreign land, and to act as your guide and translator while you're here.

About This Book

If you're like me, you may not be much for reading all the directions before diving into a project. (In fact, I'm known not to read them at all.) Or, maybe you do like to read the directions but you want them to cut to the chase and give you what you need *now*. Either way, you'll find this book useful. Rather than having a textbook format where you have to begin at the beginning and wade your way to deeper water, this book is like a reference book — or one of those great encyclopedias on your computer that let you go directly to the information you want. Best of all, this book is to-the-point, highlighting the best of the best, so you don't have too much extraneous information to wade through or remember.

Here's how the book works. Maybe you want to find a cozy inn in Santa Fe, and then you want to book one of their best rooms at a good price. No problem. Simply go to the "Staying in style" section for Santa Fe in Chapter 13 to find a hotel, and then flip to Chapter 8 for tips on getting a great hotel deal. Or, maybe you're traveling with kids, and you're following the kid-friendly itinerary outlined in Chapter 3. You want your kids' eating adventures to be as delectable as the rest of their trip. That's easy. Simply consult the "Dining out" sections in the chapters mentioned in the itinerary, and look for the Kid Friendly icon. (Later in this introduction, I tell you the significance of each of the funny little icon symbols.)

Please be advised that travel information is subject to change at any time — this is especially true of prices. I therefore suggest that you write or call ahead for confirmation when making your travel plans. The authors, editors, and publisher cannot be held responsible for the experiences of readers while traveling. Your safety is important to us, however, so we encourage you to stay alert and be aware of your surroundings. Keep a close eye on cameras, purses, and wallets, all favorite targets of thieves and pickpockets.

Conventions Used in This Book

Throughout the book, I include abbreviations for commonly accepted credit cards. Take a look at the following list for an explanation of each:

AE	American Express
CB	Carte Blanche
DC	Diners Club
DISC	Discover
MC	MasterCard
V	Visa

I divide the hotels into two categories — my personal favorites and those that don't quite make my preferred list but still get my hearty seal of approval. Don't be shy about considering these runner-up hotels if you're unable to get a room at one of my favorites or if your preferences differ from mine. The amenities that the runners up offer and the services that each provides make all of these accommodations good choices to consider as you determine where to rest your head at night.

I also include some general pricing information to help you decide where to unpack your bags or dine on the local cuisine. I use a system of dollar signs to show a range of costs for one night in a hotel or a meal at a restaurant. The hotel price refers to a double-occupancy room during high season; the cost of the meal refers to the main course (at dinner) with its side dishes, not including dessert, coffee, or alcohol (the cost refers to lunch or breakfast if those are the only meals offered). Check out the following table to decipher the dollar signs:

Cost	Hotel	Restaurant
$	$75 or less	$6 or less
$$	$76–$125	$7–$12
$$$	$126–$175	$13–$16
$$$$	$176 or more	$17 and up

Foolish Assumptions

As I wrote this book with Granville Greene, we made some assumptions about you and what your needs might be as a traveler. Here's what we assume about you:

- ✔ You may be an inexperienced traveler looking for guidance when determining whether to take a trip to New Mexico and how to plan for it.

- ✔ You may be an experienced traveler who hasn't had much time to explore New Mexico and wants expert advice when you finally do get a chance to enjoy this particular locale.

- ✔ You're not looking for a book that provides all the information available about New Mexico or that lists every hotel, restaurant, or attraction available to you. Instead, you're looking for a book that focuses on the places that will give you the best or most unique experience in New Mexico.

If you fit any of these criteria, then *New Mexico For Dummies* gives you the information you're looking for!

How This Book Is Organized

With its simple and logical organization, I'd wager that even a smart breed of dog (like my Australian cattle dog!) could follow this book. First, I divide the book into five parts, each one covering a major aspect of your trip. I further subdivide these parts into chapters that cover more specific topics, so you can head directly to the one that most interests you. The parts break down as follows:

Part I: Getting Started

This part contains the basic recipe for preparing a delicious travel feast. I include information about when to travel to the Land of Enchantment and a calendar of special festivals and events. I also offer some fully drawn itinerary options, budgeting tips, and pointers for travelers with special needs and interests.

Part II: Ironing Out the Details

This part gets down to the nitty-gritty of how to make your trip actually happen — sort of the baking instructions, if you will. I tell you how to get here and how to get around when you arrive. I also provide tips on how to find accommodations to fit your needs; how to deal with money and health matters; and how to manage all of those other little details, such as travel insurance and packing.

Part III: Exploring the Most Popular Cities

Because most people come to New Mexico to see culture, they head to Albuquerque, Santa Fe, and Taos, cities where culture and beauty are concentrated. This part recommends hotels, restaurants, sights, tours, activities, shops, and nightlife in three of New Mexico's most exciting spots. I've pared down the recommendations to the very best, and, within each review, I tell you why you would want to stay, eat, or go there. Two additional chapters in this part present fun side trips that you can take from Albuquerque and Santa Fe.

Part IV: Discovering the Outback: New Mexico's Regions

This section takes you out of the Rio Grande corridor, the location of the three major cities (Albuquerque, Santa Fe, and Taos), and into the deserts and mountains of New Mexico. I include the same types of recommendations that I give in Part III, including only the very best options to make your trip a total blast.

Part V: The Part of Tens

This is my "best of" section — the place to go to find out the essence of the state. Here I tell you how to find your way in the land of coyotes, lone buttes, and Southwestern culture. Topics include the top ten ways to act like a New Mexican, the top ten ways to be friendly with the Native Americans, and the top ten New Mexican arts and crafts.

Quick Concierge

You also find two other elements near the back of this book. I include a helpful Appendix — your Quick Concierge — containing lots of handy information that you may need when traveling in New Mexico, such as phone numbers and addresses for emergency personnel or area hospitals and pharmacies, contact information for babysitters, lists of local newspapers and magazines, protocol for sending mail or finding taxis, and so on. Check out this feature when searching for answers to lots of little questions that may come up as you travel.

You also find a bunch of worksheets to make your travel planning easier. Among other things, you can determine your travel budget, create specific itineraries, and keep a log of your favorite restaurants so you can hit them again next time you're in town. You can find these worksheets easily because they're printed on yellow paper.

Icons Used in This Book

We all know how many words a picture is worth. Well, the little icons presented throughout this book may not quite top the 1,000-word mark, but they do give you a quick flash on a few bonuses that the accommodations, restaurants, and attractions listed in this book offer. Here's the encryption key:

Find out useful advice on things to do and ways to schedule your time when you see the Tip icon.

Watch for the Heads Up icon to identify annoying or potentially dangerous situations, such as tourist traps, unsafe neighborhoods, budgetary rip-offs, and other things to beware.

Look to the Kid Friendly icon for attractions, hotels, restaurants, and activities that are particularly hospitable to children or people traveling with kids.

Keep an eye out for the Bargain Alert icon as you seek out money-saving tips and/or great deals.

Watch for the New Mexico Flavor icon to cue you in on the hotels, restaurants, and attractions that most embody the qualities of this state — a richness and spiciness of culture found nowhere else.

Look to the Far Out icon to find attractions that are out there (or just plain weird) in only a way that New Mexico can offer. From spaceship landing sites to mysteriously constructed staircases, these places just may make you consider whether or not we're alone.

Where to Go from Here

From here, you hit the road, or the air, or the rails, and find your way to this enchanted state. As you go, and when you arrive, flip your way merrily through these pages to find your own route around this seemingly foreign land. You may find that with the friendliness of the people and the brightness of the sunshine, you're as comfortable in New Mexico as in your own home.

Part I
Getting Started

The 5th Wave   By Rich Tennant

"I'll have a peanut butter sandwich without the chiles, a glass of iced tea without the chiles, and a bowl of vanilla ice cream without the chiles."

In this part . . .

So, New Mexico is calling you to its pink buttes, piñon-studded hills, and ancient Native American dwellings, but you don't quite know what to expect? This part of *New Mexico For Dummies, 1st Edition* answers many of your primary questions. Chapter 1 clues you in on the must-see and must-do happenings in the Land of Enchantment. Chapter 2 gives you pointers on when to visit and provides a roundup of the cities and regions covered in this book. Chapter 3 outlines key itineraries — some of the best ways to see the state. Finally, Chapters 4 and 5 get down to business, helping you figure out what your stay in New Mexico will cost and advising you on topics such as adventuring with kids, taking advantage of senior discounts, and ensuring that a disability won't hamper your enjoyment.

Chapter 1

Discovering the Best of New Mexico

· ·

In This Chapter

▶ Exploring Native America and natural wonders

▶ Meandering through museums

▶ Finding the best food and beds

▶ Shopping indoors and playing outdoors

· ·

*W*arning: A trip to New Mexico can give you an attitude problem. You may return home and find that your response to the world is completely different from the way it used to be. (That is, if you return at all.) When you enter the Land of Enchantment, you find few customary points of reference. Rather than sharp-cornered buildings, you find adobes made of mud bricks. Rather than hearing a single language on the street, you hear many, from Navajo and the Pueblo Tiwa and Tewa to Spanish and English. The pace here is slow, and the objectives are less obvious than in most places.

New Mexico casts a certain lost-and-not-caring-to-be-found spell that's akin to some kind of magic. When you're here, wildly foreign images cross your vision and stay there: Pilgrims walking for days to a church where magical dirt may heal them; Native Americans dancing for hours in the summer heat while curtains of rain pound across the plains; towering mountain ranges giving way suddenly to stark, sandy deserts.

So here you'll stand amid the dust or sparkling light, not sure whether to speak Spanish or English, until some switch clicks in you. You'll settle under a portal and drink margaritas all afternoon, or get in your car and drive into history, through ruins abandoned hundreds of years ago.

And when you return home, you'll find yourself gazing about with a new clarity. You may look askance at your suit and tie or your heels and nylon stockings. And the next time you climb in the car in your own state or country, you may just head down a road you've never taken before and hope that it goes nowhere.

A Trip to the Ancient: New Mexico's Native American Culture

Native American culture is the big draw for many visitors to New Mexico, and it's no wonder. Nowhere in the United States is so much ancient culture so readily available. The big kahuna is **Chaco Culture National Historic Park** (Chapter 19), where as many as 5,000 ancestral Puebloans (once called *Anasazi*) previously lived amid huge ceremonial rooms, called *kivas*, set in a stunning canyon. **Bandelier National Monument** (Chapter 14), situated in a lush canyon, also offers a glimpse into the mysterious past of a people who lived almost a millennium ago. Many of their descendents still live in much the same manner, and the two best places to encounter today's Puebloan culture are at **Acoma Pueblo** (Chapter 19), an adobe "sky city" perched atop a mesa, and **Taos Pueblo** (Chapter 15), a sculpted adobe mountain, where some residents still live without electricity and running water.

Caves, Beaches, Canyons, and Volcanoes: New Mexico's Natural Wonders

If you like to imbibe in nature's outlandish wonders, you can get your fill at places such as **Carlsbad Caverns National Park** (Chapter 16), one of the world's largest and most complex cave systems, and **White Sands National Monument** (Chapter 16), the world's largest gypsum dune field. Other Oz-like destinations in the Land of Enchantment include the **Rio Grande Gorge** (Chapter 15), which displays millions of years of geologic history; **Capulin Volcano National Monument** (Chapter 18), a volcano active 60,000 years ago; and **El Malpais National Monument** (Chapter 19), with 115,000 acres of cinder cones, arches, and ice caves, one of the outstanding examples of lava flows in the United States.

Climb Every Mountain, Ford Every Stream: New Mexico Outdoors

With just over a million people scattered around New Mexico, which is the fifth largest state in the United States (encompassing more than 120,000 square miles), you can't help but enjoy the outdoors here. There's just so darn much of it!

One of the biggest draws to New Mexico is the **skiing,** especially at the world-renowned Taos Ski Valley (Chapter 15), with its rustic Bavarian feel and its steep mogul runs, but also at neighboring spots, such as Red River and Angel Fire (I discuss both in Chapter 15), where families rule and **snowboarding** is allowed.

If your vision of the Southwest involves animals, you'll want to saddle yourself a steed and head to the hills. Plenty of places offer a taste of the Old West while **horseback riding,** especially in the Santa Fe area (Chapter 13) as well as in the southwest in the Silver City and Gila Wilderness areas (Chapter 17).

Maybe you're tired of being reined in and want to let your tethers loose and float free. If so, a **balloon ride** is in order. You can book flights in Albuquerque and Taos (Chapters 11 and 15, respectively), but the biggest spectacle of the hot-air globes takes place each October when 1,000 balloons descend on the Kodak Albuquerque International Balloon Fiesta (Chapter 11).

Every region of the state has alluring **hiking** trails. Check out trails traversing the pristine desertscape of White Sands (Chapter 16) in the south, the lava flow badlands of El Malpais in the west (Chapter 19), the hauntingly sculpted rock formations in Abiquiu (Chapter 14) near Santa Fe, or the pristine mountains around Santa Fe and Taos (Chapters 13 and 15, respectively).

So you like hiking but don't want to carry your stuff? Here's a unique way to surrender your life load for a few hours: **Llama trekking.** Docile llamas help you make your way on long or short outings in the Taos area, often including a gourmet meal or two (Chapter 15).

If you'd rather cruise than walk, the state makes a great destination for **biking.** Cyclists can peddle the renowned South Boundary Trail in the areas around Santa Fe and Taos (Chapter 15). Others rave about the trails in Silver City (Chapter 17) and Cloudcroft (Chapter 16) to the south.

If biking doesn't fulfill your need for an adrenaline rush, maybe **rafting** and **kayaking** on New Mexico's rivers will. Half- or full-day whitewater rafting trips down the Rio Grande and Rio Chama originate in Taos (Chapter 15).

Although you more leisurely types won't exactly find Pebble Beach here, you do find some pretty impressive **golf** courses, particularly in Albuquerque (Chapter 11) and Santa Fe (Chapter 13).

With the San Juan River, a world-class catch-and-release **fishing** spot in the northwestern part of the state, New Mexico rates for anglers (Chapter 19). Other rivers in New Mexico provide a less challenging but equally beautiful experience. Head to north central New Mexico for the most variety (Chapter 15).

Bird watchers find plenty to fill their binoculars at the **Bosque del Apache National Wildlife Refuge** (Chapter 17), where some 300 species visit, at times in great quantity (try 45,000 snow geese or 18,000 sandhill cranes annually — count 'em!). Other birdy spots include the Rio Grande Nature Center in Albuquerque (Chapter 11) and the Gila wilderness area (Chapter 17).

Bizarre Bazaar: New Mexico's Far-Out Sights

This land of lizards with horns (horned toads) and running birds (road-runners) can probably outdo most places in the category of sheer weirdness. New Mexico is the place to come if you thrive on the bizarre.

The **Lightning Field** (Chapter 17) is an enormous outdoor sculpture consisting of 400 metal poles arranged in a giant grid in the middle of nowhere. Lightning doesn't have to strike to enjoy the piece, but if you want to increase your odds, prime thunderstorm season is from July to September. Ground zero for X-Filers, **Roswell** (Chapter 16) rose to fame after an "incident" in 1947 when a spaceship allegedly crash-landed in the area. Jodie Foster helped land the **Very Large Array National Radio Astronomy Observatory** (Chapter 17) on the map in the 1997 film *Contact*. You may not *hear* aliens here, but you do see 27 *very* giant dish-shaped antennae. And if that's not enough bang for you, head to **Los Alamos** (Chapter 14), home of the A-bomb, where museums show you what such a destructive creature looks like and how humans can use atomic power in calmer ways. A more lighthearted view of mankind's wanton waste and destruction is **Stonefridge** (Chapter 13), a recreation of Stonehenge built from discarded refrigerators.

If you're after miracles, look to New Mexico's churches. First, head to the **San Francisco de Asis Church** (Chapter 15), where a painting reveals an Escher-like oddity in an image of Christ. Meanwhile, the **Loretto Chapel** (Chapter 13) in Santa Fe has a miraculous staircase, which is sturdy without revealing any means of support. Finally, **El Santuario de Nuestro Señor de Esquipulas** (Chapter 14) in Chimayo has dust in a hole in the anteroom floor that has allegedly cured many a hurting pilgrim.

Indoor Discoveries: New Mexico's Museums

Even if you're not a museum lover, you can't deny that New Mexico has an interesting selection from which to choose. If space is your kinda place, you can visit the **International UFO Museum and Research Center** in Roswell or the **New Mexico Museum of Space History** in

Alamogordo (both in Chapter 16). Contemporary art lovers will appreciate **SITE Santa Fe** and the **Museum of Fine Arts** (both in Chapter 13). If you enjoy history, check out the **Taos historic museums** (Chapter 15) and the **Palace of the Governors** (Chapter 13).

You can find Native American art in Santa Fe at the **Wheelwright Museum of the American Indian** and **Museum of Indian Arts and Culture** (both in Chapter 13). The **Museum of International Folk Art** (Chapter 13) brings out the kid in everyone. The **Georgia O'Keeffe Museum** (Chapter 13) has the world's largest collection of the modernist painter's work, along with changing exhibits.

From Haciendas to Cattle Ranches: New Mexico's Best Beds

New Mexico has arrived kicking and screaming into the 21st century, which is good news for travelers who like ambience, and bad news for those in e-commerce and other efficiency-dependent businesses. If you're looking to sip margaritas in a Spanish hacienda, you're in luck in this state, where you can also take lazy horseback rides toward bold sunsets or stare at bullet holes in the ceilings of Wild-West hotels.

In Santa Fe, **Dos Casas Viejas** (Chapter 13) offers up plenty of atmospheric old Spanish flavor, as do **Hacienda Antiqua** (Chapter 11) in Albuquerque and **Casa de las Chimineas** (Chapter 15) in Taos. Down south, the **Ellis Store Country Inn** (Chapter 16) in historic Lincoln does the trick. If you want a more traditional hotel with Western flair, head to **La Fonda** (Chapter 13), Santa Fe's first inn (from the era of the Santa Fe Trail), or to the **St. James Hotel** in Cimarron, where Western novelist Zane Grey wrote (Chapter 18). The **Lodge at Cloudcroft** (Chapter 16) fulfills any Victorian fantasies you may have.

If the open range is calling, you can saddle up and eat some dust at some of the state's few dude ranches: **Bishop's Lodge** (Chapter 13) will have you riding in style through the Sangre de Cristo Mountain foothills. If you're in the mood to stay put and hunker down for some pampering, settle in to **La Posada de Santa Fe Resort & Spa** in Santa Fe or **Vista Clara Ranch Resort and Spa** in Galisteo (both in Chapter 13), which have spa facilities on their premises.

Eating the Past and the Future: Food as Legacy and Innovation

Where else but New Mexico can you find such delicacies as blue bread (I'm not talkin' refrigerator science experiments, either), red corn (not breakfast cereal), and "chili" spelled with an "e" on the end?

Fortunately, this state is known not only for its unique food, but also for its incredible flavors, many derived from Puebloan and Spanish ingredients. For one of the best enchiladas in the state (and on Earth), head to **The Shed** or **La Choza** in Santa Fe (Chapter 13) or **Sadie's** (Chapter 11) in Albuquerque. For a nouveau spin on Southwestern flavors, head to the **Coyote Café** (Chapter 13) in Santa Fe, or if you want to add a little Asian flavor to the mix, try **Santacafé** (Chapter 13). For new American flavors, check out **Joseph's Table** and the **Trading Post Café** in Taos (Chapter 15) and **Diane's Restaurant and Bakery** in Silver City (Chapter 17).

P.S.: Blue bread is paper-thin Zuni piki bread, a multi-layered bread made of blue corn. The red corn just grows that way (but don't tell the Green Giant). As for the "e" on the end of "chile," that's the Spanish spelling, which, like the Spanish language itself, holds boundless romantic allusions.

The Retail Scene: From Art to Exotica

The bewitching, ever-changing light of New Mexico has stirred the soul of many an artist, and sometimes it seems as if everyone you talk to here has an artistic bent of one kind or another, even if they don't make a living selling their creations. Because so many artists inhabit each square inch of the state, the shopping scene centers around fine art and crafts. **Santa Fe** (Chapter 13) claims to be the third largest art market in the United States, after New York and Los Angeles. **Taos** (Chapter 15) has been a bastion for free-spirited artists — everyone from D.H. Lawrence to Dennis Hopper — for well more than a century. You can easily spend your entire trip wandering the stylish galleries in both towns, where you find everything from big-ticket paintings by Western masters to more affordable pieces by emerging local artists.

Second to art is an enormous array of exotic goods from around the world (often with exotic prices to match), which are displayed in high-end boutiques found mostly in **Santa Fe** (Chapter 13) and **Taos** (Chapter 15). You can usually find cheaper prices at the **Pueblo of Tesuque Flea Market** (Chapter 13), where you can buy everything from African drums to Afghan rugs. **Jackalope,** in Santa Fe, is an enormous store filled with handicrafts from all over the world, mostly from Mexico, and it has a huge selection of pottery. You can find some good deals at Jackalope, too.

If you're interested in taking home some locally made traditional items, such as Spanish-Colonial or Native American handicrafts, **Taos** (Chapter 15) is a great place to pick up handmade moccasins and drums. **Chimayo** (Chapter 14) is the place to head for weavings, and **Cordova** (Chapter 14) is a good place to find woodcarvings. Every summer, serious collectors jet in to Santa Fe for the **Traditional Spanish Market** (Chapter 2) and **Indian Market** (Chapter 2) to haggle with local artisans who often save their best work for these events.

Chapter 2

Deciding When and Where to Go

*T*his book isn't exactly the genome project for the state of New Mexico — I don't map the DNA of the entire place. Instead, I pick the most crucial pleasure cells within the state — places unique to New Mexico.

If you're one of those all-inclusive types, you may feel sorry for spots I neglect, such as Clovis and Hobbs over on the eastern Plains. The truth is that I doubt you'd find a lot to *do* in those places, unless you like to watch oil wells pump.

Of course, I include the major cities, and the minor ones as well. I also include many incredible hot spots in between and some in pretty remote areas. My intention is to make your trip like an espresso — all the best condensed down to an intense shot that will fuel your passions long after your traveling has ended.

The Cities

Most people who visit New Mexico concentrate their adventuring efforts on Albuquerque, Santa Fe, and Taos, ground zero for much of the Native American, Hispanic, and Anglo culture. Although these cities vary broadly in size and temperament, they share one characteristic: All are quite spread out, requiring wheels and a good map in order to negotiate them. Of the three, Albuquerque has the mildest climate and is the most like a traditional Western city, with lots of strip malls and

New Mexico

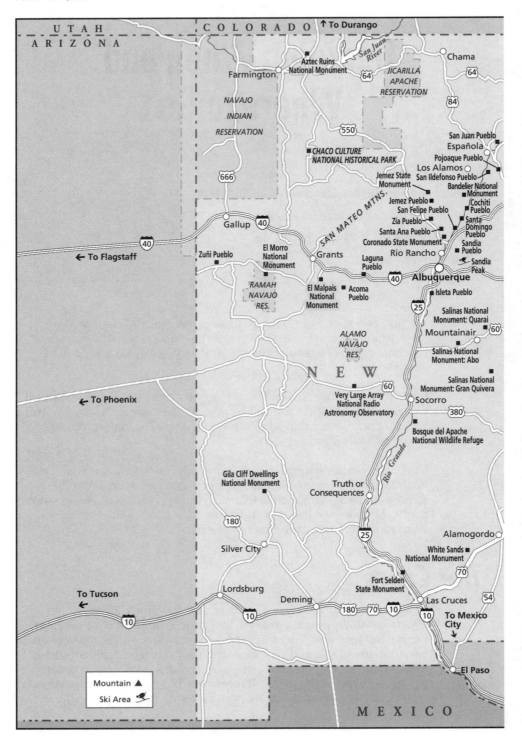

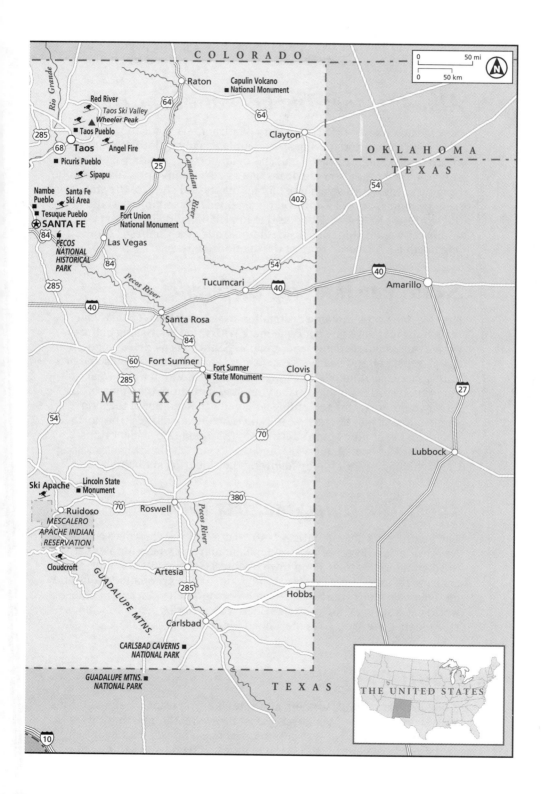

freeway traffic. Santa Fe and Taos share a high elevation around 7,000 feet, so they're cooler, both in terms of temperature and temperament. Santa Fe and Taos are two of the hippest towns on the planet — just ask people like Julia Roberts and Tom Cruise, who hang out in them.

Albuquerque: The Enchantment Hub

New Mexico's largest city has plenty of attractions but is most often used as a landing and leaving spot: People usually fly into Albuquerque International Sunport, rent a car, and head north or south from there. A spread-out city that New Mexicans use as a shopping spot, Albuquerque has one of the Southwest's most intact plazas and some of the state's best museums, as well as one of the most visually stunning events in the world — the Kodak Albuquerque International Balloon Fiesta. In addition, two fun side trips from Albuquerque (see Chapter 12) take you north to the state's hottest destination, Santa Fe.

Santa Fe: The City Different

New Mexico's most notable destination has so much flavor that your taste buds just might be overwhelmed. With three flourishing cultures — Native American, Hispanic, and Anglo — Santa Fe is as rich as a gourmet six-course meal, and nearly as expensive. World-class museums and arts, atmospheric accommodations, trend-setting restaurants, and wear-out-your-credit-cards shopping make your stay here more than memorable. When you're ready for something new, you can head out of town on some journeys into the past — to Native American villages (the northern Pueblos), the atomic bomb's birthplace (Los Alamos), ancient ruins (Bandelier National Monument), and traditional Hispanic villages (along the High Road to Taos) — by following the side trips in Chapter 14.

Taos: The renegade arts town

The Southwest's favorite little arts town is a funky place where Native Americans have lived for at least a millennium and where hippies set the contemporary tone. For a town of only 5,000 inhabitants, Taos offers amazing richness, from great arts and food, to fine accommodations and incredible outdoor sports. The town has an inhabited ancient pueblo, a world-class ski area, funky streets lined with galleries, and a rebellious attitude that will keep you entertained for days.

The Regions

If you're after natural wonders and rural life, you want to take a serious look at some of New Mexico's regions. Be aware, though, that this is a big state with lots of desert between sights, so buckle your seat belt, set your cruise control, slip in some tunes, and enjoy the ride.

The Southeast: Cave and sand country

Two of the world's major wonders live in this part of New Mexico, both well worth the hours of driving to get there: Carlsbad Caverns National Park, one of the most intricate cave systems ever discovered; and White Sands National Monument, the world's largest gypsum dune field. Although both of these sights sit on vast desert lands, don't be deceived: This part of the state has lush mountains too, as well as vast plains where the notorious Billy the Kid once rampaged.

The Southwest: Wilderness country

Think wildness when you think of this part of New Mexico. The Southwest has the first designated wilderness area in the United States — part of the Gila National Forest — which was once inhabited by the ancient Mogollon people. It also has one of the nation's best bird refuges — the Bosque del Apache National Wildlife Refuge. The region also includes oddities such as the Very Large Array National Radio Astronomy Observatory, which houses the world's most powerful radio telescope, and one of the state's most interesting desert towns, Las Cruces.

The Northeast: High plains country

Northeastern New Mexico is the land of long silences — you may find them when talking to the area's short-winded ranchers and in the distances between sights on these broad plains. The plains are also a Wild-West place with a raucous history still visible on the land, from the towering Capulin Volcano, which erupted some 60,000 years ago, to the Pecos and Fort Union National Monuments, which mark important dates on the frontier calendar. Other more subtle reminders of the region's history remain as well, such as bullet holes left by notorious gunslingers Jesse James and Butch Cassidy, and ruts forged by wagons on the Santa Fe Trail.

The Northwest: Native American country

Self-proclaimed "Indian Capital of the World," this region is rich with culture. From its heart in Gallup, with some of the Southwest's best shopping; to Chaco Culture National Historical Park, with hundreds of ruins; to Acoma's "Sky City," an inhabited ancient village perched on a mesa top, Native American culture is ubiquitous here. The Northwest is also a place rich with natural beauty, including El Malpais National Monument with its 115,000 acres of lava badlands and the Chama area, rich with forests and high-mountain meadows — best traversed via the Cumbres and Toltec Scenic Railroad.

The Secret of the Seasons

As a rule, you almost always find gorgeous weather in at least some part of New Mexico, where the skies are typically blazing blue and the sun seems to shine every day. When considering the best time of year for your visit, you may want to keep in mind the pros and cons of each season.

New Mexico has the highest incidence of people being struck by lighting in the United States, something to keep in mind before running around a bare mountaintop while waving a metal tent stake.

Rainfall year-round is sparse except in the higher mountains, where afternoon thunderstorms can be common in summer. See Table 2-1 for average temperatures and precipitation across the state. (Temperatures are given in degrees Fahrenheit.)

Table 2-1 New Mexico Temperatures and Precipitation

	January (High–Low)	April (High–Low)	July (High–Low)	October (High–Low)	Annual Rainfall in inches
Alamogordo	57–28	78–40	95–65	79–42	7.5
Albuquerque	47–28	70–41	91–66	72–45	8.9
Carlsbad	60–28	81–46	96–67	79–47	13.5
Chama	33–3	54–22	73–37	52–18	9.3
Cloudcroft	41–19	56–33	73–48	59–36	25.8
Farmington	44–16	70–36	92–58	70–37	7.5
Las Cruces	56–26	79–45	95–66	82–47	8.6
Roswell	56–24	78–42	91–65	75–45	12.7
Ruidoso	50–17	65–28	82–48	67–31	21.4
Santa Fe	40–18	59–35	80–57	62–38	14.0
Taos	40–10	62–30	87–50	64–32	12.1
Truth or Consequences	54–27	75–44	92–66	75–47	8.5

Springtime in the Southwest

Aficionados of New Mexico will tell you that spring and fall are the best times to visit the state. Some of spring's selling points include:

- ✔ The weather is particularly pleasant.
- ✔ Tourist traffic is sparse.
- ✔ Room rates are generally lower.
- ✔ With snow often falling as late as May, you can enjoy some excellent spring skiing — don't be surprised to see many of your fellow skiers wearing t-shirts and shorts as they cruise the slopes.

But keep in mind these springtime pitfalls:

- ✔ Cold snaps can still snag you.
- ✔ You're too early for the performing arts events of summer.

Summer in the Land of Enchantment

Summer is the busiest time of year in New Mexico, particularly in the tourist towns of the north. RVs clog the already busy arteries of downtown Santa Fe and wealthy patrons of the arts jet in for opera season. The crowds enjoy the following:

- ✔ Temperatures generally cool down at night, particularly in the higher elevations.
- ✔ You find more cultural activities than at any other time of year.

But keep in mind:

- ✔ The days can get very hot throughout the state, but especially in the south.
- ✔ Tourist traffic is at its peak.
- ✔ Rooms rates are generally high.

Fall in New Mexico

Like spring, fall is a wonderful time to visit the Land of Enchantment. Autumn bonuses include:

- ✔ The weather is pleasant.
- ✔ Tourist traffic is light.

> ✔ Room rates are among the year's lowest.
>
> ✔ In the higher elevations, early fall is prime time for aspen viewing, when the trees' leaves change from green to golden.

Some things to look out for include:

> ✔ Cold snaps can turn your fall fiesta into a winter war.
>
> ✔ The sun usually shines all day, but daylight hours become fewer and fewer.

Winter in the West

Winters tend to be on the mild side in the south and harsher in higher altitudes up north, where snowfall is common from November through March, and sometimes even as late as May. The points that make winter wonderful include:

> ✔ There's nothing like a desert snowfall, let alone seeing the white stuff on adobe — you feel like you're in a land of gingerbread houses.
>
> ✔ The weather is crisp and clear.

However, the cons of the seasons include:

> ✔ The winter wonderland can entrap you as well as enchant you.
>
> ✔ The ski slopes can be crowded during holidays.

New Mexico's Calendar of Events

There's always something fun to do in New Mexico, and aside from the holidays that everyone else celebrates, the Land of Enchantment has many cultural events that are unique to the state. In the fall and around Christmastime, many of the pueblos hold ceremonial dances. If you're interested in attending, call the Indian Pueblo Cultural Center (☎ 800-766-4405 or 575-843-7270) for a schedule. Before you visit the pueblos, be sure to read Chapter 21 of this book.

January

On **New Year's Day,** festivities at most pueblos include the transfer of canes to new officials and various dances. The Turtle Dance is held at Taos Pueblo (no photography allowed). For information, call ☎ 800-793-4955 or 505-852-4265. January 1.

On **Three Kings' Day,** when residents fête new tribal officers with cere-
monies, dances are held at all eight northern pueblos. For information,
call ☎ **800-793-4955** or 505-852-4265. January 6.

At the **Winter Wine Festival** in the Taos Ski Valley, you can taste a variety of wines and foods prepared by local chefs. Call ☎ **505-776-2291.**
Mid-January.

February

Winter Fiesta at the Santa Fe ski area features ski races, the Great
Santa Fe Chile Cookoff, snow-sculpture contests, and snowshoe races.
For details, call ☎ **800-777-2489** or 505-955-6200. The first weekend in
February.

March

Albuquerque's **Fiery Food Show,** an annual trade show, features chiles
and a wide array of chile-related products. Call ☎ **505-873-8680.** Early
March.

The **Rio Grande Arts and Crafts Festival,** an annual juried show at
Albuquerque's State Fairgrounds, features 200 artists and craftspeople
from around the country. Call ☎ **505-292-7457.** March 8–10.

Gems, jewelry, tools, and crafted items are displayed and sold at the
Rockhound Roundup. Events take place at the Southwest New Mexico
State Fairgrounds in Deming. Call ☎ **505-546-9281.** Second weekend in
March.

April

Easter Weekend Celebrations at Nambé, San Juan, and San Ildefonso
Pueblos include church Masses, parades, corn dances, and other traditional dances such as the Bow and Arrow Dance at Nambé. For information, call ☎ **800-793-4955** or 505-852-4265. Late March or early April.

Acclaimed as one of the best film festivals in the world, the **Taos
Talking Pictures Festival** lures film buffs from all corners of the globe.
For schedules, call ☎ **505-751-0637** or check the Internet at www.
ttpix.org. April 11–14.

Dance competitions, arts-and-crafts exhibitions, and the Miss Indian
World contest are held in conjunction with the **Gathering of Nations
Powwow** at the University Arena in Albuquerque. Call ☎ **505-836-2810**
or check the Internet at www.gatheringofnations.com. Late April.

May

Statewide **Cinco de Mayo Fiestas** celebrating the restoration of the Mexican republic (from French occupation in 1867) take place in many places, including Hobbs (☎ **800-658-6291** or 505-397-3202); Las Cruces at Old Mesilla Plaza (☎ **800-FIESTAS** or 505-524-8521); and Truth or Consequences (☎ **800-831-9487** or 505-894-3536). First weekend in May.

The **Taos Spring Arts Festival** features gallery openings, studio tours, performances by visiting theatrical and dance troupes, live musical events, traditional ethnic entertainment, a film festival, literary readings, and more. For details, call ☎ **800-732-TAOS** or 505-758-3873, or check the Internet at www.taos.chamber.com. First two weeks in May.

June

The annual eight-day **Taos Poetry Circus** draws poetry aficionados from all parts. The festival describes itself as "a literary gathering and poetry showdown among nationally known writers," and includes performances, seminars, workshops, and a main event called the **World Heavyweight Championship Poetry Bout.** Call ☎ **505-758-1800** or check the Internet at www.poetrycircus.org. Mid-June.

The four-day **Rodeo de Santa Fe** typically features a Western parade, rodeo dance, and five rodeo performances featuring bronc riding, calf roping, and other cowboy fare. Kids can tap into their inner cowpoke at this fun-filled summer event. Call ☎ **505-471-4300.** Late June.

You can catch national touring acts at the **Taos Solar Music Festival** celebrating the summer solstice. A tribute to solar energy, this outdoor event has a stage powered by a solar generator. Events take place at Kit Carson Municipal Park. Call ☎ **505-758-9191** or check the Internet at www.solarmusicfest.com. Late June.

The second-largest event of its type in the United States, the **New Mexico Arts and Crafts Fair,** at the New Mexico State Fairgrounds in Albuquerque, features more than 300 artisans exhibiting and selling their crafts. Call ☎ **505-884-9043.** Last weekend in June.

July

Opera lovers jet in from all parts to catch performances at the world-class **Santa Fe Opera.** The season runs from the beginning of July to the end of August. Call ☎ **800-280-4654** or 505-986-5900, or check the Internet at www.santafeopera.org for details.

The annual **Fiestas de Santiago y Santa Ana** begins with a Friday night mass at Our Lady of Guadalupe Church, where a fiesta queen is crowned, and is followed by a weekend of candlelight processions, special masses, music, dancing, parades, crafts and food booths at Taos Plaza, and Corn Dances at Taos Pueblo. Call ☎ **800-732-8267** or 505-758-3873, or check the Internet at www.taos.chamber.com. Third weekend in July.

Hundreds of Hispanic artists from New Mexico and southern Colorado exhibit and sell their work at Santa Fe's **Traditional Spanish Market,** and collectors come from all over to snap it up. Call ☎ **505-983-4038** or check the Internet at www.spanishcolonial.org. Last weekend in July.

August

Come to the **Bat Flight Breakfast** at Carlsbad Caverns National Park to chow down on an early morning buffet breakfast while watching Count Dracula's friends return to the cave. No reservations accepted. Call ☎ **505-785-2232** or check the Internet at www.nps.gov/cave. Second Thursday in August.

Lincoln's **Old Lincoln Days and Billy the Kid Pageant** features reenactments of Billy the Kid's escape from jail amid late 19th-century pageantry. Most kids delight in the Old West lore. Call ☎ **505-653-4025** or check the Internet at www.zianet.com\lpfc. First full weekend in August.

The **Intertribal Indian Ceremonial** happens in Red Rock State Park near Gallup. Fifty tribes from the United States and Mexico participate in rodeos, parades, dances, athletic competitions, and an arts and crafts show. The town fills up, so reserve early. Call ☎ **800-233-4528** or 505-863-3896, or check online at www.ceremonial.org. Second week in August.

Santa Fe's **The Indian Market,** the largest all–Native American market in the country, features about 1,000 artisans displaying their wares in the Plaza and De Vargas Mall. Sales are brisk, so arrive early. The market is free, but hotels are booked months in advance of this event. Call ☎ **505-983-5220,** or go online to www.swaia.com. Third weekend in August.

Deming's **Great American Duck Race** invites you to slap down your greenbacks on this quacky race devised in a bar in 1979. You can also enjoy a parade, tortilla toss, outhouse race, and ballooning. The *Duck Downs* takes place on the courthouse lawn. Call ☎ **888-345-1125** or check the Internet at www.swnm.com/gadr. Fourth weekend in August.

September

New Mexicans celebrate their favorite fiery food at the **Chile Festival** in Hatch, "Chile Capital of the World." Call ☎ **505-267-5050.** Labor Day weekend.

One of America's top ten state fairs, the **New Mexico State Fair and Rodeo** at Albuquerque's State Fairgrounds features horse racing, a rodeo, country singing, Native American and Spanish villages, a midway, and livestock shows. Dial ☎ **505-265-1791,** or check online at www.nmstatefair.com. Early September.

The City Different hosts **La Fiesta de Santa Fe,** which features the burning of Zozobra (old man gloom), a pet parade, mariachi concerts, and food booths. This is the oldest community celebration in the United States. Call ☎ **505-988-7575.** The weekend after Labor Day.

Arts-and-crafts exhibitions and competitions, studio tours, and gallery openings are just a few of the happenings at the oh-so-artsy **Taos Fall Arts Festival.** Call ☎ **800-732-8267** or check online at www.taos chamber.com. Mid-September to the first week in October.

October

The **Rio Grande Arts and Crafts Festival** in Albuquerque features artists and craftspeople from around the country. Events take place near the intersection of I-25 and Paseo del Norte (near Balloon Fiesta grounds). Call ☎ **505-292-7457,** or check the Internet at www.rio grandefestivals.com. First and second weekend in October.

Albuquerque's **Kodak Albuquerque International Balloon Fiesta,** in Balloon Fiesta Park, is the world's largest balloon rally. This nine-day festival brings together more than 1,000 colorful balloons and includes races and contests. Book your hotel *early;* many fill up a year in advance. Dial ☎ **800-733-9918** or check online at www.balloonfiesta.com. Second week in October.

November

During the **Festival of the Cranes,** some 18,000 cranes fill the sky as they return to Bosque del Apache National Wildlife Refuge near Socorro, their winter home. Events include four days of guided hikes, lectures, and birding workshops. Call ☎ **505-835-0424** or look online at www.friendsofthebosque.com. Third weekend of November.

No Scrooges are allowed at **Yuletide in Taos,** which celebrates northern New Mexican traditions and cultures with *farolito* (candle lantern) tours, candlelight dinners, and Native American dance performances in Taos Plaza. Call ☎ **800-732-8267** or check the Internet at www.taos chamber.com. Late November to New Year's Day.

December

You can ride a pontoon boat past brilliant displays of Christmas lights on riverside homes and businesses during **Christmas on the Pecos** in Carlsbad. Call ☎ **800-221-1224** or check the Internet at www.chamber@caverns.com. Thanksgiving to New Year's Eve (except December 24).

The village of Madrid lights up for **Christmas in Madrid Open House.** Attractions include strolling carolers and Santa Claus. Call ☎ **505-471-1054,** or check online at www.turquoisetrail.org/madrid. First two weekends in December.

An awe-inspiring display of ceremony takes place at Picuris, Tesuque, Nambé, and Taos Pueblos during the **Sundown Torchlight Procession of the Virgin.** Call ☎ **800-793-4955** or 505-852-4265. December 24.

For the **Canyon Road Farolito Walk,** locals and visitors bundle up and stroll Santa Fe's Canyon Road, where streets and rooftops are lined with *farolitos.* Musicians play and carolers sing around *luminarias* (little fires) and sip cider. If you don't like crowds, head out early or not at all. Call ☎ **505-955-6200** or check the Internet at www.santafe.org. December 24.

Chapter 3

Five Great Itineraries

*Y*ou may already have an idea of how you want to spend your vacation time in the Land of Enchantment — power shopping, maybe, or culture cruising at a world-class opera, symphony, and museums. If these are your tastes, you probably want to head straight to the state's cultural center, Santa Fe. Or maybe you want to check out some primo skiing in Taos Ski Valley, or white-water rafting in the notorious Taos Box Canyon. But if you're like most people, you may be scratching your scalp wondering how best to spend your time. Though exploration is the height of adventure, when you're on a limited time schedule, it can also be the pinnacle of frustration.

So, in this chapter I offer some itineraries. All that's required of you is an automobile (which you can rent if you need to), some decent walking shoes, and a good bit of energy.

For each itinerary, I assume that you're flying into the Albuquerque International Sunport, the air transportation hub of the state. (See Chapter 6 for information on flying into Albuquerque.)

La Crema de la Crema: Northern New Mexico in One Week

Most visitors to New Mexico keep their compass pointed to the north, because that's where the greatest concentration of culture and beauty resides. With elevations upwards of 7,000 feet, the region can be cold in winter, but its beauty resonates through all four seasons (although spring is, well . . . bring your windbreaker). And usually, winter days are warm enough to convince you that you're still on a Southwestern vacation. If, however, you just can't stand the idea of cold, consider the next itinerary, "Family Time: New Mexico for Kids and the Young at Heart in One Week," which takes you south into the warmer lands.

If you arrive in Albuquerque on **Day One** and have some energy after traveling, head to **Old Town,** where you can wander the **plaza,** peruse some shops, and, if you have time, head over to the **Albuquerque Museum** and the **New Mexico Museum of Natural History and Science.** Finish the day with one of New Mexico's premier treats — an enchilada — at either **Sadie's** or **La Hacienda.** (See Chapter 11 for information on the attractions I list in this paragraph.)

For **Day Two,** start out at the **Indian Pueblo Cultural Center,** and then head to the **Albuquerque Biological Park,** both in the vicinity of the Old Town Plaza. Next, head out to **Petroglyph National Monument,** west of town. In the late afternoon, find your way to Central Avenue, just south of Old Town, and drive east on **Route 66.** This takes you right through downtown, to the Nob Hill district, and the Sandia Mountains foothills, respectively. Finish your day with a ride up the **Sandia Peak Tramway.** After you reach the top, you may want to hike along the crest. Ideally, you should ride up during daylight and ride down at night for a view of the city lights. You may even want to dine at **High Finance Restaurant and Tavern** at the top. (See Chapter 11.)

On **Day Three,** strike out for the ghost towns and other sights along the **Turquoise Trail** to Santa Fe (see Day Trip Two in Chapter 12). If you rode the Sandia Peak Tramway yesterday, you won't need to drive up to Sandia Crest. After you complete the rest of the Turquoise Trail trip, you'll arrive in Santa Fe in time to do some sightseeing. Head straight to the **Plaza** and the **Palace of the Governors.** Next, make your way over to the **Georgia O'Keeffe Museum,** followed by the nearby **St. Francis Cathedral.** Finish your day with an enchilada at **The Shed.** In the evening, depending on the season, you may want to take in some of Santa Fe's excellent arts, such as the **Santa Fe Opera, Santa Fe Chamber Music Festival,** or **Shakespeare in Santa Fe.** (See Chapter 13 for information on attractions in this paragraph.)

On **Day Four,** head out to the **Museum of International Folk Art,** the **Museum of Indian Arts and Crafts,** and the **Wheelwright Museum of the American Indian.** En route back to the Plaza, take a stroll and do some shopping on **Canyon Road.** After you're back at the Plaza, head to the **Loretto Chapel Museum.** In the warmer months, you can enjoy a cocktail from atop the bell tower of the historic **La Fonda** hotel. Eat dinner at the **Coyote Café** or its **Rooftop Cantina.** You may want to head over to the **Cowgirl Hall of Fame** bar and restaurant or the **Paramount** nightclub for some live music and dancing, or maybe check out the piano bars at **Vanessie's** or the **Palace.** (See Chapter 13.)

On **Day Five,** head out of town to **Bandelier National Monument** and **Los Alamos** and follow Day Trip Two in Chapter 14. After completing that trip, continue north to Taos. On the way into Taos, stop at the **San Francisco de Asis Church** and shop the **Ranchos de Taos Plaza.** If you like music, head out to the **Sagebrush Inn** for some country-and-western music or to **Momentitos de la Vida** to hear some jazz. (See Chapter 15 for information.)

For **Day Six,** spend your morning at **Taos Pueblo,** the **Millicent Rogers Museum,** and the **Rio Grande Gorge Bridge.** You can then ditch your car for the afternoon and step out on foot. Do some shopping around the **Taos Plaza.** Within walking distance is the **Kit Carson Home & Museum.** At cocktail hour, head to the **Adobe Bar** at the Historic Taos Inn. (Check out Chapter 15.)

On your last day, **Day Seven,** start the day with a leisurely morning. After relaxing, head south by following, in reverse, Day Trip Three in Chapter 14, The High Road to Taos. Though most people drive this route from Santa Fe to Taos, the views are actually most spectacular heading south from Taos to Santa Fe. You may want to spend the night at a bed-and-breakfast (B&B) in **Chimayo** along the way, or, depending on your flight time the next morning, stay the night in Santa Fe or Albuquerque.

Family Time: New Mexico for Kids and the Young at Heart in One Week

Although wonderful, northern New Mexico is not the most suitable vacationland for kids — unless they already have a credit card and a precocious interest in history and architecture. The museum/pueblo type of sightseeing the north offers may bore some adults as well. Some hearts are better suited to Wild West action and natural wonders than to gourmet food and history. If you prefer a more active vacation, this one-week trip is for you, whatever your age.

The climate in this region is fairly mild, but summers in the south can be quite hot.

After you arrive in Albuquerque on **Day One,** devote some time to wandering around the **Old Town Plaza.** Head to the **New Mexico Museum of Natural History and Science** and, if you have time, visit the **Albuquerque Biological Park.** Finish the day with an enchilada. Or, if you have time and energy, ride the **Sandia Peak Tramway.** (See Chapter 11 for information on these attractions.)

On **Day Two,** head west, visiting the **Petroglyph National Monument** (see Chapter 11) on your way out of town. From there, continue west about 70 miles to **Acoma Pueblo** (see Chapter 19). Stop for lunch in Grants and visit the **New Mexico Museum of Mining** (see Chapter 19), where your kids can go underground in a simulated mine. After leaving the Museum of Mining, head south on N.M. 117 to **El Morro and El Malpais National Monuments** (see Chapter 19), where you can stretch your legs on a short or long hike. Continue south through Quemado, and then turn east and drive to Socorro, where you can spend the night, or continue just south to San Antonio, which has a nice B&B, Casa Blanca (see Chapter 17).

On **Day Three,** if it's wintertime, wake before dawn and head out to **Bosque del Apache National Wildlife Refuge** (see Chapter 17), where you can watch thousands of cranes and snow geese take flight. (Even if it's not winter, you can still tour the refuge to see birds and wildlife and stretch your legs on a hike.) From the refuge, head east on U.S. 380 to the **Valley of Fires Recreation Area** (Chapter 16), an amazing lava field. Your next stop is Carrizozo, where you can have New Mexico's best green chile cheeseburger at the **Outpost.** Continue east to **Capitan** and **Smokey Bear Historical State Park.** (See Chapter 16 for more on these attractions.) Farther east along the **Lincoln Loop,** you come to Lincoln, where you can walk in Billy the Kid's footsteps while touring **Lincoln State Monument** (Chapter 16). You may want to spend the night there. Both of the excellent B&Bs rent *casitas* ("little houses") for families. You may need to get dinner in one of the cafes in Capitan, about 10 miles away. If you'd rather stay the night in Ruidoso, you can start the Day Four itinerary.

On **Day Four,** drive the rest of the Lincoln Loop, stopping at the **Hurd–La Rinconada Gallery** and then cruising into the mountains of **Ruidoso.** If you like to hike, stop at the Lincoln National Forest Ranger Station for directions to the many trails in the area. Otherwise, you may want to shop a little. If it's winter, you can ski at **Ski Apache.** Or, if your kids have any interest in horses, head over to the **Hubbard Museum of the American West.** By now the kids may have had their fill of sights and want to simply play. If that's the case, head to **Funtrackers Family Fun Center,** where they can race cars and boats and make mischief. In the evening, head to the **Flying J Ranch** for a chuck-wagon dinner and an Old-West show. Spend the night in Ruidoso. (See Chapter 16 for information on the attractions in this paragraph.)

Day Five takes you south out of Ruidoso through the **Mescalero Apache Indian Reservation** on U.S. 70 and N.M. 244. Just outside the reservation, you arrive in **Cloudcroft,** a darling mountain town with some good hiking and mountain biking. Next, head down a spectacularly scenic pass on N.M. 244 into **Alamogordo** to visit the **New Mexico Museum of Space History** and, one of the stars of this trip, **White Sands National Monument.** Spend the night in Alamogordo. (Chapter 16 gives you more information on these attractions.)

On **Day Six,** head east to **Carlsbad** to visit the **Living Desert Zoo and Gardens State Park.** Have lunch in Carlsbad, and then head out to the most spectacular sight in New Mexico, **Carlsbad Caverns National Park,** where you want to *walk* down into the cave, rather than riding the elevator (trust me). Or, you may want to call ahead and schedule one of the guided tours. If it's summer when you visit, you may want to end your hot day at your hotel pool, or alternately, at the **Riverwalk,** where the kids can swim and peddle paddleboats. (See Chapter 16 for more information.)

Spend your last day, **Day Seven,** taking a long cruise north to Albuquerque. Take U.S. 285 to Roswell, where your kids can stock up on little-green-men stickers and see the **International UFO Museum and Research Center.** (The drive takes you across fairly barren plains.) History buffs may want to detour to Fort Sumner to see **Billy the Kid's grave,** but more importantly to see the tragedy presented at **Fort Sumner State Monument,** once an internment camp for Navajos who survived the "Long March." If you take this option, afterward, stop for a bite at **Joe's** in Santa Rosa. (See Chapter 16 for information on these attractions, except Joe's, which is included in Chapter 19.)

Parents who are first-time visitors to New Mexico may want to trade the Day One schedule for a trip north to **Santa Fe** (see Chapter 13) to take in the cultural sights there. You can then skim down I-25 and resume the itinerary in Albuquerque on the morning of Day Two.

The Whole Enchilada: The Best of New Mexico in Two Weeks

If you're fortunate enough to spend two weeks in New Mexico, you're in for a treat. The itinerary that I suggest is a counter-clockwise loop that incorporates most of the two preceding itineraries. But, because you don't have to return to Albuquerque between the two, you have an added bonus.

For **Days One through Four,** follow the itinerary "La Crema de la Crema: Northern New Mexico in One Week," earlier in this chapter.

On **Day Five,** travel the High Road to Taos following Day Trip Three in Chapter 14. On the way into Taos, stop at the **San Francisco de Asis Church** and shop the **Ranchos de Taos Plaza.** If you like music, head out to the **Sagebrush Inn** for some country-and-western music or to **Momentitos de la Vida** to hear some jazz (see Chapter 15).

Spend the morning of **Day Six** at **Taos Pueblo,** the **Millicent Rogers Museum,** and the **Rio Grande Gorge Bridge.** During the afternoon, do some shopping around the **Taos Plaza,** and then visit the **Kit Carson**

Home & Museum. At cocktail hour, head to the **Adobe Bar** at the Historic Taos Inn. (See Chapter 15 for information on these attractions.)

On **Day Seven,** get up very early and head west on a scenic drive to Chama, where you can spend the day riding the **Cumbres and Toltec Scenic Railroad** (Chapter 19). Make sure to check departure times for the train. Spend the night in Chama. On **Day Eight,** head to the **Chaco Culture National Historic Park** (see Chapter 19), and spend the night in Grants.

On **Days 9 through 14,** follow Day Two through Day Seven in the "Family Time: New Mexico for Kids and the Young at Heart in One Week" itinerary, earlier in this chapter, which concludes in Albuquerque.

Historical Delights: The Pueblo and Conquistador Trail

If you come to the Land of Enchantment with an agenda — to visit Native America and taste the tragic history that their conquest wrought — you're in luck. This one-week trip is one of the best in the Southwest, filled with a contrast of ancient and contemporary culture.

When you arrive in Albuquerque, spend what's left of **Day One** visiting the **Pueblo Cultural Center** and the **Albuquerque Museum,** which serves as a primer for the rest of your trip. Finish the day at the **Old Town Plaza,** where you may want to eat dinner. (See Chapter 11 for information on these attractions.)

On **Day Two,** head west to **Petroglyph National Monument** (see Chapter 11), then to **Acoma Pueblo,** and later to **El Morro National Monument** (for information on both sights, see Chapter 19). Stay the night in Grants.

Early the next day, **Day Three,** drive to **Chaco Culture National Historic Park** (Chapter 19). Be sure to check road conditions before going into the park. From there head to **Jemez Springs** (Chapter 12) or **Los Alamos** (Chapter 14) to spend the night. If you stay in Los Alamos, visit the **Jemez State Monument** (Chapter 12) before driving to your hotel.

On **Day Four,** begin at the Jemez State Monument if you stayed in Jemez Springs. Otherwise, set off for the **Bradbury Science Museum,** in Los Alamos, and the **Bandelier National Monument** (see Chapter 14 for information on both). From there, stop in at **San Ildefonso Pueblo** Chapter 14). In the afternoon, make your way north to Taos, stopping at the **San Francisco de Asis Church** and **La Hacienda de los Martinez**

(Chapter 15). If you like to swing at night, head out to the **Sagebrush Inn** for some country-and-western dancing, or go to **Momentitos de la Vida** to hear some jazz.

For **Day Five,** spend the morning touring **Taos Pueblo,** the **Millicent Rogers Museum,** and the **Rio Grande Gorge Bridge.** You can then strike out on foot downtown. Do some shopping around the **Plaza,** and then walk to the **Kit Carson Home & Museum.** For a little local flavor, have a cocktail at the **Adobe Bar** at the Historic Taos Inn. (See Chapter 15 for information on the attractions in this paragraph.)

On **Day Six,** take the **High Road to Taos** (see Chapter 14) south to Santa Fe, visiting all the sights along the way. When you arrive in the City Different (one of Santa Fe's nicknames), head straight to the **Plaza** and the **Palace of the Governors.** Then, visit the nearby **St. Francis Cathedral.** Finish your day with an enchilada at **The Shed.** In the evening, depending on the season, you may want to take in some of Santa Fe's excellent arts, such as the **Santa Fe Opera, Santa Fe Chamber Music Festival,** or **Shakespeare in Santa Fe** (see Chapter 13).

On **Day Seven,** visit the **Museum of International Folk Art,** the **Museum of Indian Arts and Crafts,** and the **Wheelwright Museum of the American Indian.** Have lunch at one of the restaurants on **Canyon Road** (see Chapter 13). In the afternoon, head east out of town to **Pecos National Monument** (see Chapter 18). Return to Santa Fe for the night, where you'll definitely want to have a good meal, and maybe take in some art or theater.

Energy Bar Express: The Best of New Mexico's Outdoors

Including all New Mexico's major outdoor adventures in one trip is impossible, so I chose the route that allows for the most unique outdoor experiences. However, in this trip, I don't include three major adventures: Skiing at Taos Ski Valley, rafting the Taos Box Canyon, and fly-fishing the San Juan River. (See Chapter 15 for the first two adventures and Chapter 19 for the last.) The reason? The first two experiences are seasonal, and the last is a trip in itself, because it's located in the far northwestern part of the state.

For this itinerary, I send you south, to the world's first officially recognized forest, the Gila National Forest. During this one-week trip you can hike badlands; climb upon odd rock formations; and visit a rejuvenated mining town, a waterless beach at White Sands National Monument, and a fathomless cave at Carlsbad Caverns National Park.

If you're set on heading north instead of south, you can follow the "La Crema de la Crema: Northern New Mexico in One Week" itinerary, earlier in this chapter, but instead of focusing on museums, focus on activities in the "Keeping Active" sections of Chapters 11, 13, and 15. By doing so, you can find a good mix of history and outdoor adventure.

When you arrive in Albuquerque on **Day One,** you may want to head to the **Old Town Plaza** for some relaxed strolling and a visit to the **New Mexico Museum of Natural History and Science.** In the evening, ride the **Sandia Peak Tramway** to the top of Sandia Crest, where you can hike along the rim. (See Chapter 11 for more on these attractions.)

Head west to **Petroglyph National Monument** (see Chapter 11) on **Day Two.** If you want to experience a bit of Native America, spend a few hours at **Acoma Pueblo** (Chapter 19). Have lunch in Grants, and then head to **El Malpais National Monument** (Chapter 19), where you can spend as long as you wish hiking. Also, spend time at **El Morro National Monument** (Chapter 19) before you stay the night in Grants.

On **Day Three,** head south early through the village of Quemado and into the spectacular **Gila National Forest.** Take a side trip to the **Mogollon** ghost town, and then take the **Catwalk National Recreation Area** hike near Glenwood. In the evening, arrive in Silver City. (See Chapter 17 for the attractions in this paragraph.)

On **Day Four,** head into the heart of the Gila Wilderness to the **Gila Cliff Dwellings National Monument.** Near the monument is the trailhead for the **West Fork of the Gila River,** which makes for a great day hike or backpacking trip. Spend the afternoon wandering Silver City, biking one of the many trails in the area or horseback riding with one of the outfitters. (See Chapter 17.)

Head south on **Day Five** to the odd formations at the **City of Rocks State Park.** If you like to collect rocks, detour farther south to **Rock Hound State Park.** Next, find your way to Las Cruces, where you can spend the afternoon exploring the spectacular **Organ Mountains.** (Check out Chapter 17 for more information.)

On **Day Six,** head northeast to **White Sands National Monument,** where you find some amazing hiking trails. The rest of the trip separates the power travelers from the more relaxed. If you have energy for more, continue east to Carlsbad, where you can spend the night and devote the morning of **Day Seven** to touring **Carlsbad Caverns National Park.** If you choose this option, you have a long drive back to Albuquerque that night. (See Chapter 16 for more on the attractions in this paragraph.)

If you don't feel like pushing yourself, here's an easier last-day option: Head up to the **Cloudcroft** area, where you may want to do some hiking, to finish up **Day Six.** Spend the night in Alamogordo. On **Day Seven,** head north through the Tularosa Valley, visiting **Three Rivers National Recreation Site** and, if you want to see another lava flow, the **Valley of Fires National Recreation Area.** Spend the early evening at **Bosque del Apache National Wildlife Refuge.** Truck on in to Albuquerque for your last night. (See Chapter 16.)

Chapter 4

Planning Your Budget

· ·

In This Chapter

▶ Estimating your trip costs

▶ Ferreting out the sneaky charges

▶ Cutting expenses without cutting corners

· ·

*L*et's face it, you started paying for your trip when you bought this book. (But I'm confident that the handy advice in these pages will help save you more than the book's cost.) This is the first of many expenses that go along with taking a vacation, and if you don't plan ahead, those expenses can easily become overwhelming.

To really enjoy yourself in New Mexico, you have to feel a sense of control over how much you're going to spend and what you're going to get for your money. This chapter is dedicated to helping you get a handle on the dollars and cents of your trip.

Adding Up the Elements

Planning a budget for a trip to New Mexico is easy, and using the yellow budget worksheet at the end of this book will help you approximate your trip's costs. Keep in mind, however, that even the most carefully planned trip can have surprise expenses — everything from car repairs to that piece of (ahem) "art" you just had to have. But if you accept this before you leave home (and factor some wiggle room into your budget), a few extra costs here and there won't ruin your trip. And if you're lucky, you may even end up spending less than you budgeted.

Your trip ca-chings will begin before you even walk out the front door, so start adding them up from the get go. Begin with your pre–New Mexico expenses: transportation to your home airport or airport parking fees, plus flight costs (see Chapter 6 for tips on how to fly for less); the cost of a ticket on a bus or train; or all the on-the-road expenses that you'll face if you drive here. Then, add up all your in–New Mexico expenses — car rental, gas, hotel rates, meals (except breakfast, if included in the hotel rate), admission prices to attractions, and the cost of activities you're interested in (rafting trips, ski lift tickets, or seats at the opera, for example). If you absolutely have to bring home a woodcarving of a howling pink coyote, a smiling ceramic sun, or some other New Mexico icon, put the cost of this souvenir in the budget. If you decide you don't want this trinket once you're actually in New Mexico, you'll be able to afford another round of margaritas.

Transportation

Getting to New Mexico and traveling around the state will consume a large part of your trip budget. Unless you're just coming to Albuquerque or Santa Fe for a couple of days and staying downtown, renting a car is the best way to get around the state. When you calculate your rental-car costs, don't forget to add taxes and gas costs to the daily rental fee. (To approximate gas expenses for a rental or your own car, divide your estimated mileage by the car's miles per gallon. Then multiply the resulting figure by the cost of gasoline per gallon.) Also, make sure that you get a rental-car package with unlimited mileage. Certainly, you can fly between certain destinations within New Mexico, but this adds significant costs, and you'd very likely need to rent a car in each destination anyway. See Chapter 7 for information on car rentals or flying within the state.

Lodging

New Mexico offers a wide range of accommodations to suit every budget. You find everything from tired Western motels to swanky resorts with New-Age spas, so take your pick. Bear in mind that rooms in Santa Fe and Taos are generally more expensive than in most parts of the state, so a room at a budget, chain motel in these tourist towns often costs a bit more than elsewhere. Summer and winter are the high seasons in northern New Mexico, so you can usually save some money if you visit there in fall or spring. In the rest of the state, prices fluctuate only slightly throughout the year. See Chapter 8 for specifics on lodging types and the price ratings used throughout this book.

Dining

In New Mexico, you can feast on everything from green chile cheeseburgers at local drive-thru joints to dramatically prepared elk steaks in internationally acclaimed restaurants. In almost every part of the state, you can find an unpretentious, inexpensive meal for under $10 or $12 a person, excluding alcohol. In the more populated areas, plenty of midrange restaurants offer meals for $20 or so per person, and in the less populated areas, you'd have a hard time spending that much money. The really expensive restaurants are mostly clustered in Santa Fe, Taos, and Albuquerque, where you can easily drop $100 for a dinner for two with wine. See the Introduction for specifics on the restaurant price ratings used throughout this book.

What things cost in Santa Fe

This list gives you a rundown of some basic costs:

Double room in high season at La Posada de Santa Fe Resort & Spa	$279
Double room in high season at Santa Fe Motel and Inn	$114
Dinner for two at Geronimo, without drinks, tax, or tip	$94
Dinner for two at La Choza, without drinks, tax, or tip	$25
An imported Mexican beer at the Dragon Room	$3.50
A half-hour Swedish or deep-tissue massage at Ten Thousand Waves Japanese Health Spa	$40
Adult admission to the Museum of International Folk Art	$5

Attractions

You don't have to spend a lot of money to visit New Mexico's attractions. White Sands National Monument, for example, costs $3 per person, and in Santa Fe you can buy a four-day pass to visit the Museum of New Mexico System, which includes four attractions, for $10. And that gorgeous view out your window is free.

Activities and tours

This is one area of your budget where you can really drop some bucks. Before you come to New Mexico, try to decide how many greens you want to golf, rivers you want to raft, slopes you want to ski, art classes you want to take, or operas you want to see (just to name a few examples of what you can spend your money on). Then try to narrow the choices down to what you can reasonably afford.

Shopping

Shopping is really the gravy part of your budget, so if you need to cut corners, do it here. Particularly in Santa Fe, you can blow tons of cash on pricey art and exotic goods from around the world. Most of us can't afford any of it. On the other hand, you may just want to take home a pair of charmingly weathered antique cowboy boots from a local flea market or some cheap but cute-and-functional Mexican ceramics. At the end of the day, enjoying yourself is more important than stressing out about a bunch of doo-dads you can't afford to buy — maybe you can pick 'em up on your next trip.

What things cost in Las Cruces

This list gives you a rundown of some basic costs:

Double room in high season at the Las Cruces Hilton	$79
Double room in high season at Best Western Mission Inn	$59
Dinner for two at the Double Eagle, without drinks, tax, or tip	$66
Dinner for two at Nellie's, without drinks, tax, or tip	$18
An imported Mexican beer at Way Out West	$3.25
Hiking in the Organ Mountains	Free
Adult admission to New Mexico Farm and Ranch Heritage Museum	$3

Nightlife

A good rule for gauging the costs of a town is to check the drink prices at the local watering holes. In Santa Fe, domestic beers typically cost between $3 and $4 apiece, but they tend to run a bit cheaper in the rest of the state. In general, tickets for concerts and performing arts events will cost you a pretty penny, as will dinners in fancy restaurants, but you can still have a good time dancing to live music in bars where the cover charge, if any, is rarely above $5. And hey, you can always gaze at the stars for free. If you're buying tickets for an event and don't mind weary feet and/or the risk of not getting a ticket at all, always ask if standby or standing room-only tickets are available.

Keeping a Lid on Hidden Expenses

When budgeting for travel, you should always factor in some wiggle room for unexpected expenses. Here are some below-the-radar expenses to keep in mind.

Tipping tips

Tipping in New Mexico is similar to tipping everywhere else. Expect to shell out about 20% for good service at a fine dining establishment. Anything from 15 to 20% is acceptable in a regular joint. For spa treatments, guide services, or other special services, expect to leave a tip of 10 to 15%. If you're on an Indian reservation and photography is allowed, you should always ask permission before taking someone's picture, and then offer him or her a dollar or two if they pose for you.

Dialing away dollars

Hotels can really get you with charges for outgoing phone calls. Before you let your fingers do the walking, find out the fee for the talking. Some high-end hotels and resorts charge as much as $1 per call, even if you're dialing a toll-free number — so watch out. If you have a cell phone with no roaming fees and unlimited minutes, bring the phone with you.

Watching out for costly room perks

If you stumble down to the check-out desk after an evening spent with your best new buddy, Mr. Minibar, you'll be presented with a hefty bill for all that camaraderie. In case your mother never told you, minibars are always, always major rip-offs, so use them to chill your own sodas, water bottles, and fruit from the local market. Also, that inviting welcome basket in the room may be added to your bill, so check with the front desk before diving into it.

Cutting Costs

So you want to save a few dollars but not skimp on your vacation fun? No problem. What follows are cost-saving tips that you can use for any vacation, as well as some specific tips for New Mexico:

- **Go in the off-season.** If you can travel at non-peak times (September to November or April to June, for example), you find hotel prices that are as little as half the cost as during peak months.

- **Travel midweek.** If you can travel on a Tuesday, Wednesday, or Thursday, you may find cheaper flights to your destination. When you inquire about airfares, ask if you can obtain a cheaper rate by flying on a different day.

- **Try a package tour.** For many destinations, you can book airfare, hotel, ground transportation, and even some sightseeing just by making one call to a travel agent or packager for a lot less than if you tried to put the trip together yourself. (See Chapter 6 for more on package tours.)

- **Reserve a room with a kitchen.** Doing your own cooking and dishes may not be your idea of a vacation, but you save a lot of money by not eating in restaurants three times a day. Even if you only make breakfast and pack an occasional bag lunch, you save in the long run. And you'll never be shocked by a hefty room service bill.

- **Always ask for discount rates.** Membership in AAA, frequent flyer plans, trade unions, AARP, or other groups may qualify you for savings on car rentals, plane tickets, hotel rooms, and even meals. Ask about everything; you may be pleasantly surprised.

✓ **Ask if your kids can stay in the room with you.** A room with two double beds usually doesn't cost any more than one with a queen-size bed. And many hotels won't charge you the additional person rate if the additional person is pint-sized and related to you. Even if you have to pay $10 or $15 extra for a rollaway bed, you save hundreds by not taking two rooms.

✓ **Try expensive restaurants at lunch instead of dinner.** Lunch tabs are usually a fraction of what dinner would cost at a top restaurant, and the menu often boasts many of the same specialties.

✓ **Walk a lot.** A good pair of walking shoes can save you time and gas money because you'll be sightseeing instead of seeking parking spots. As a bonus, you get to know your destination more intimately, because you explore at a slower pace.

✓ **Skip the souvenirs.** Your photographs and your memories should be the best mementos of your trip. If you're concerned about money, you can do without the chile ristras, scorpion paperweights, jars of salsa, dream catchers, and other trinkets.

✓ **Invest in a cheap cooler.** You quickly recover the costs if you buy large bottles of water and six-packs of soft drinks instead of purchasing single items at more expensive roadside convenience stores. Give the cooler away to someone you like at the end of the trip, or to the clerk at the car rental company; almost everyone in this state can use an extra ice chest.

✓ **Don't rent a gas guzzler.** Renting a smaller car is cheaper, and you save money on gas to boot. Unless you travel with kids and need lots of space, there's no reason to go beyond economy size. (And hey, if you ever use a valet parking guy, he'll be less inspired to take your car for a spin.)

Chapter 5

Planning Ahead for Special Travel Needs and Interests

In This Chapter

▶ Traveling with kids

▶ Putting your age to work

▶ Traveling with disabilities

▶ Discovering resources for gay and lesbian travelers

▶ Flying solo: advice for singles on the move

▶ Exploring special interests

*Y*ou want your vacation to be special, of course, and with a little advance preparation, you can tailor your travels to meet your special interests and needs.

Bringing the Brood: Advice for Families

With its robust mix of outdoorsy activities and cultural attractions that conveniently appeal to kids and adults alike, New Mexico lends itself to family vacations. That said, the drives between the activities and attractions can be rather long, and they don't lead to the sort of juicy theme-park treats that you find in other states. Sure, you may stumble across a water park or a video arcade here and there, but the real attractions are the natural ones — and the adventurous ways you can experience them: whitewater rafting down the Rio Grande, climbing a wooden ladder up to a cliff dwelling, skiing the slopes above Taos, trekking through the wilderness on a llama, or sledding on the dunes at White Sands National Monument, to name just a few examples.

If you're not traveling with an adventure-oriented brood, no worries. Many of the hotels and resorts listed in this book have inviting pools to laze around or on-site activities planned especially for kids. But keep in mind that New Mexico can truly offer your children a new perspective on the United States by exposing them to ancient ruins, Southwestern cuisine, and Hispanic and Native American cultures that they may not experience elsewhere.

Travel-with-kids tips

To take the stress out of your family road trip, and to avoid the proverbial "Are we there yet?", keep the following tips in mind:

✔ **Take along your kids' favorite music, books, and toys.** Even if they add bulk to your luggage, you won't regret it. Going to unfamiliar places can be hard on even the most outgoing youngsters, and security blankets of all sorts help.

✔ **Hot kids can mean hot tempers.** Bring lots of protective gear — hats, sunglasses, and sunscreen (although you won't have trouble finding these items in New Mexico). And don't leave your kids locked in a hot car, even for a moment — temperatures can rise to dangerously high levels before you know it.

✔ **Don't try to do too much.** You run the risk of overwhelming your kids with back-to-back activities. Your personal agenda to see and do absolutely everything may not be the best agenda for your kids. Gear activities to your child's age, physical condition, and attention span.

✔ **Look for the Kid Friendly icon as you flip through this book.** This icon highlights hotels, restaurants, and attractions that families will find particularly welcoming. Zeroing in on these listings will help you plan your trip more efficiently.

Kid- and family-oriented publications

The Santa Fe–based free bimonthly tabloid **New Mexico Kids!,** 6392 Entrada de Milagro, Santa Fe, NM 87505 (☎ **505-473-5189;** Internet: www.newmexico-kids.com; home delivery: $20/year), is packed with information on activities in the Albuquerque and Santa Fe areas, and it includes calendars for the two cities as well. The publication is distributed at around 400 locations in northern New Mexico.

Another useful publication is the Santa Fe quarterly **Tumbleweeds,** 369 Montezuma #191, Santa Fe, NM 87501 (☎ **505-984-3171;** e-mail: tumbleweeds@trail.com; subscription: $10/year), which offers useful articles on family-oriented subjects in the Santa Fe area.

Likewise, you can order Lynnell Diamond's **New Mexico for Kids** (Otter Be Reading Books), a learning activity guidebook for young people, online at www.Amazon.com.

Going Gray: Suggestions for Seniors

More people over the age of 60 are traveling than ever before. And why not? Being a senior citizen entitles you to some terrific travel bargains. If you're not a member of **AARP (American Association of Retired Persons),** 601 E St. NW, Washington, DC 20049 (☎ **800-424-3410** or 202-434-AARP; Internet: www.aarp.org), do yourself a favor and join. You'll get discounts on car rentals and hotels.

In addition, most of the **major domestic airlines,** including American, United, Continental, US Airways, and TWA, all offer discount programs for senior travelers — be sure to ask whenever you book a flight. In most cities, people over the age of 60 get reduced admission at theaters, museums, and other attractions, and they can often get discount fares on public transportation. Carrying identification with proof of age can pay off in all of these situations.

The Mature Traveler, a monthly newsletter on senior citizen travel, is a valuable resource. The publication is available by subscription ($30 a year); for a free sample send a postcard with your name and address to GEM Publishing Group, Box 50400, Reno, NV 89513, or send an e-mail request to maturetrav@aol.com. GEM also publishes **The Book of Deals,** a collection of more than 1,000 senior discounts on airlines, lodging, tours, and attractions around the country; the book is available for $9.95 by calling ☎ **800-460-6676.** Another helpful publication is **101 Tips for the Mature Traveler,** available from Grand Circle Travel, 347 Congress St., Suite 3A, Boston, MA 02210 (☎ **800-221-2610;** Internet: www.gct.com).

Grand Circle Travel is also one of the literally hundreds of travel agencies that specialize in vacations for seniors. But beware: Many of these senior vacations are of the tour-bus variety, with free trips thrown in for those who organize groups of 20 or more. Seniors seeking more independent travel should probably consult a regular travel agent. **SAGA International Holidays,** 222 Berkeley St., Boston, MA 02116 (☎ **800-343-0273**), offers inclusive tours and cruises for those 50 and older.

The Albuquerque-based monthly tabloid **Prime Time,** P.O. Box 7104, Albuquerque, NM 87194 (☎ **505-880-0470;** Internet: www.primetime-nm.com), publishes a variety of articles aimed at New Mexicans 50 years and older.

Transcending Limitations: Tips for Travelers with Disabilities

These days, a disability shouldn't stop anybody from traveling. More options and resources are available than ever before. **A World of Options,** a 658-page book of resources for disabled travelers, covers everything from biking trips to scuba outfitters. The publication costs $35 and is available from **Mobility International USA,** P.O. Box 10767, Eugene, OR, 97440 (☎ **541-343-1284** voice and TTY; Internet: www. miusa.org). Another place to try is **Access-Able Travel Source** (Internet: www.access-able.com), a comprehensive database of travel agents who specialize in disabled travel; the Web site serves as a clearinghouse for information about accessible destinations around the world.

To make sure that a particular hotel, restaurant, or attraction is accessible for your special needs, always call in advance.

National resources

Many of the major car-rental companies now offer hand-controlled cars for disabled drivers. **Avis** (☎ **800-831-2874;** Internet: www.avis.com) can provide such a vehicle at any of its locations in the U.S. with 48-hour advance notice; **Hertz** (☎ **800-654-3131;** Internet: www.hertz. com) requires between 24 and 72 hours of advance reservation at most of its locations. **Wheelchair Getaways** (☎ **800-536-5518** or 606-873-4973; Internet: www.wheelchair-getaways.com) rents specialized vans with wheelchair lifts and other features for the disabled in more than 35 states, plus the District of Columbia and Puerto Rico.

Travelers with disabilities may also want to consider joining a tour that caters specifically to them. One of the best operators is **Flying Wheels Travel,** P.O. Box 382, Owatonna, MN 55060 (☎ **800-535-6790;** fax 507-451-1685; Internet: www.flyingwheelstravel.com), which offers various escorted tours and cruises, as well as private tours in minivans with lifts. Another good company is **FEDCAP Rehabilitation Services,** 211 W. 14th St., New York, NY 10011. Call ☎ **212-727-4200** or fax 212-727-4373 for information about membership and summer tours.

Vision-impaired travelers should contact the **American Foundation for the Blind,** 11 Penn Plaza, Suite 300, New York, NY 10001 (☎ **800-232-5463**), for information on traveling with Seeing Eye dogs.

New Mexico resources

Measures have been taken throughout New Mexico to provide access for the disabled. For more information, contact the **Information Center**

for New Mexicans with Disabilities, 435 St. Michael's Dr., Bldg D, Santa Fe, NM 87505 (☎ **800-552-8195**), for free information about traveling with disabilities in New Mexico. A statewide guide published by the Governor's Committee on Concerns of the Handicapped, **Access New Mexico,** lists accessible hotels, attractions, and restaurants throughout New Mexico (☎ **505-827-6465;** Internet: www.state.nm.us/gcch). Throughout the state, chambers of commerce can answer questions regarding accessibility in their areas. (However, calling on your own to insure the accessibility of your destination is a good idea.)

If you need to rent a wheelchair-accessible van, contact **Wheelchair Getaways,** P.O. Box 93501, Albuquerque, NM 87199 (☎ **800-408-2626** or 505-247-2626).

Stepping Out: Resources for Gay and Lesbian Travelers

New Mexico has an active gay and lesbian population, particularly in Santa Fe. A useful Web site, **GayNM.com** (www.gaynm.com), offers local news and event listings. Keep an eye out for **Out! Magazine,** P.O. Box 27237, Albuquerque, NM 87125 (☎ **505-243-2540;** Internet: www.out magazine.com; home delivery: $30/year), a free monthly containing news, features, and an events calendar. You can find *Out! Magazine* at coffee shops, clubs, and selected businesses in Albuquerque and Santa Fe. **Common Bond** (☎ **505-891-3647**) provides information and outreach services for Albuquerque's gay and lesbian community, as well as referrals for other New Mexico cities.

Flying Solo: Tips for Travelers on Their Own

 Solo travelers, especially women, should be cautious when venturing out alone at night in urban areas, but in general, New Mexico is a perfectly safe place to travel alone, as long as you take the same precautions you would take anywhere else in the United States.

Traveling alone has its pros and cons. The solo experience can be lonely and more expensive at times, but on the other hand, single travelers get to call all the shots. If you're reluctant to travel on your own, a resource worth checking out is the **Travel Companion Exchange,** P.O. Box 833, Amityville, NY 11701 (☎ **800-392-1256** or 631-454-0880; Internet: www.travelcompanions.com). A six-month membership costs $99 and includes a newsletter packed with useful travel tips for seniors and singles on the go, as well as contact information for other members.

Finding Your Niche: Special-Interest Tours

The Land of Enchantment is a great place to test your limits and expand your horizons — you can arrange everything from photographic motorcycle tours to writing workshops. An excellent place to start researching travel ideas is at the official Web site of the **New Mexico Department of Tourism** (www.newmexico.org), an informative site with links to tons of Web sites representing a wide variety of activities.

Adventure

New Mexico is an outdoors mecca, with a mind-boggling array of adventure options from which to choose. From biking to backpacking, you can easily plan an adventure on your own, but if you want some guidance, contact the **New Mexico Guides Association,** P.O. Box 2463, Santa Fe, NM 87504 (☎ **505-466-4877;** Internet: www.nmguides.com), a nonprofit organization for professional tour guides in New Mexico.

New Mexico is a popular fly-fishing destination, especially in the northern part of the state. An excellent resource for up-to-date info is **High Desert Angler,** 435 S. Guadalupe, Santa Fe, NM 87051 (☎ **505-988-7688;** Internet: www.highdesertangler.com), which offers fly-fishing services and instruction, equipment rental, and permit information.

Golfers will find **Golf New Mexico** magazine, 308 Enchanted Valley Circle NW, Albuquerque, NM 87107 (☎ **505-342-1563;** Internet: www.golfnew mexico.com), a useful resource for information about the local greens.

For statewide ski information, click on **Ski New Mexico** (www.skinew mexico.com), an informative Web site covering all of New Mexico.

Hikers and backpackers may want to check out the Web site of the **Public Lands Information Center** (www.publiclands.org), which includes information on New Mexico's diverse and vast public lands. You can find three-dimensional topological maps of the Southwestern states at **Topo 3D** (www.topo3d.com).

Arts

Santa Fe and Taos in particular are well known as arts meccas, and many visitors come to New Mexico specifically for arts-related forays. An excellent, regularly updated resource for statewide cultural information is **New Mexico CultureNet** (www.nmcn.org), an organization whose mission is to increase access to cultural information relating to New Mexico. The site includes information on crafts, language, and folkways, as well as the literary, visual, performing, media, and applied arts in New Mexico.

Native American culture

Exploring New Mexico's Native American culture can open your eyes to another world. You can find plenty of information in this book to discover this unique culture on your own, but you may also consider joining a cultural tour with a company such as **Aventura Artistica,** P. O. Box 25671, Albuquerque, NM 87125 (☎ **800-808-7352;** Internet: www. newmexicotours.com), which offers small group tours featuring New Mexico's history, culture, and natural wonders.

Part II
Ironing Out the Details

The 5th Wave   By Rich Tennant

"Of all the stuff we came back from New Mexico with, I think these adobe bathrobes were the least well thought out."

In this part . . .

You're ready to visit New Mexico, and you have an idea of where and how you want to be enchanted. Chapters 6 and 7 help you get to New Mexico and get around while you're there. Chapter 8 fills you in on the types of lodgings available and how much they cost, and Chapter 9 helps you plan other financial matters as well. Chapter 10 presents assorted flotsam and jetsam, from packing and planning to dressing like a local. (Here's a hint: Don't bother bringing an iron with you.)

Chapter 6

Getting to New Mexico

- -

In This Chapter

▶ Talking with a travel agent

▶ Exploring the escorted and package tour routes

▶ Going it alone

▶ Riding the wheels and rails

- -

*B*efore you burn pavement to get to New Mexico, you need to decide on the best travel strategy for you. Your big decision at this point is whether to plan your own trip, let someone else (besides me, of course) in on the action, or use a combo of the two.

Consulting a Travel Agent: A Good Idea?

The best way to find a good travel agent is the same way you find a good plumber, mechanic, or doctor — through word of mouth.

Any travel agent can help you find a bargain airfare, hotel, or rental car. A good travel agent stops you from ruining your vacation by trying to save a few dollars. The best travel agents can tell you how much time you should budget in a destination and how to find a cheap flight that doesn't require you to change planes in Atlanta and Chicago. They can also get you a better hotel room for about the same price, arrange for a competitively priced rental car, and even give recommendations on restaurants.

To get the most out of your travel agent, do a little homework. Read up on your destination (you've already made a sound decision by buying this book) and pick out some accommodations and attractions that appeal to you. If you have access to the Internet, check prices on the Web (see the section "Making Your Own Arrangements," later in this chapter, for ideas) to get a sense of ballpark figures. Then take your guidebook and Web information to your travel agent and ask him or her to make the arrangements for you. Because travel agents can access more resources than even the most complete travel Web site, they generally can get you better prices than you can get by yourself, and they can issue your tickets and vouchers in the agency's office. In addition, your travel agent can recommend an alternative if he or she can't get you into the hotel of your choice.

Travel agents work on commissions. The good news is that *you* don't pay the commissions — the airlines, accommodations, and tour companies do. The bad news is that an unscrupulous travel agent may try to persuade you to book the vacation that nabs him or her the most money in commissions. Over the past few years, however, some airlines and resorts have limited or eliminated these commissions altogether. The immediate result is that travel agents don't bother booking certain services unless the customer specifically requests them. Additionally, some travel agents have started charging customers for their services.

Considering Escorted and Package Tours

I'll get right to the point: New Mexico isn't exactly the land of tours. Sure, companies offer both package and escorted tours (see the next two sections to understand the difference), but here you don't want to chisel your vacation plans in stone as you would in such places as Arizona or California, where you find really BIG tourist attractions such as the Grand Canyon and Disneyland. New Mexico is a subtler place, with many of the adventures requiring flexibility and a more personal touch than tours generally offer. Fortunately, tour companies are changing with the times, and some are sophisticated enough to tackle places such as the Land of Enchantment and do a good job of both saving you money and showing you a good time.

Joining an escorted tour versus traveling on your own

Do you like letting a bus driver worry about traffic while you sit in comfort and listen to a tour guide explain everything? Or do you prefer renting a car and following your nose, even if you don't catch all the highlights? Do you like having events planned for each day, or would you rather improvise as you go along? The answers to these questions determine whether you should choose the guided tour or travel a la carte.

Some people love escorted tours. The tour company takes care of all the details and tells you what to expect at each attraction. You know your costs up front, and there aren't many surprises. Escorted tours can take you to the maximum number of sights in the minimum amount of time with the least amount of hassle.

Other people need more freedom and spontaneity. They prefer to discover a destination by themselves and don't mind getting caught in a thunderstorm without an umbrella or finding that a recommended restaurant is no longer in business — that's just part of the adventure.

If you decide to go with an escorted tour, I strongly recommend purchasing travel insurance, especially if the tour operator asks you to pay up front. But don't buy insurance from the tour operator! If the tour operator doesn't fulfill its obligation to provide you with the vacation you paid for, you have no reason to think it'll fulfill its insurance obligations either. Get travel insurance through an independent agency. (I give you more about the ins and outs of travel insurance in Chapter 10.)

When choosing an escorted tour, along with finding out whether you need to put down a deposit and when final payment is due, ask a few simple questions before you buy, such as the following:

- ✔ **What is the cancellation policy?** How late can you cancel if you can't go? Do you get a refund if you cancel? Do you get a refund if the operator cancels?

- ✔ **How jam-packed is the schedule?** Does the tour schedule try to fit 25 hours into a 24-hour day, or does it give you ample time to relax by the pool or shop? If getting up at 7 a.m. every day and not returning to your hotel until 6 or 7 p.m. sounds like a grind, certain escorted tours may not be for you.

- ✔ **How big is the group?** The smaller the group, the less time you spend waiting for people to get on and off the bus. Tour operators may be evasive about this, because they may not know the exact size of the group until everybody has made their reservations, but they should be able to give you a rough estimate.

- ✔ **Does the tour require a minimum group size?** Some tour operators require a minimum group size and may cancel the tour if they don't book enough people. If a quota exists, find out what it is and how close they are to reaching it. Again, tour operators may be evasive in their answers, but the information may help you select a tour that's sure to take place.

- ✔ **What exactly is included?** Don't assume anything. You may be required to get yourself to and from the airports at your own expense. A box lunch may be included in an excursion, but drinks may be extra. Beer may be included, but not wine. How much flexibility does the tour offer? Can you opt out of certain activities or does the bus leave once a day, with no exceptions? Are all of your meals planned in advance? Can you choose your entree at dinner or does everybody get the same chicken cutlet?

Choosing a package tour

Package tours are not the same as escorted tours. They're simply a way of buying your airfare and accommodations at the same time.

For popular destinations like Santa Fe and Albuquerque, package tours can be a smart way to go. In many cases, a package that includes airfare, hotel, and transportation to and from the airport costs less than just the hotel alone if you booked it yourself, because packages are sold in bulk to tour operators, who resell them to the public. The process is kind of like buying your vacation at a buy-in-bulk store — except the tour operator is the one who buys the 1,000-count box of garbage bags and then resells them, 10 at a time, at a cost that undercuts the local supermarket.

The cost of package tours can vary as much as those garbage bags, too. Shop around and ask a lot of questions when you book your trip. Prices vary according to departure city, hotel, and extras, such as car rental and optional tours. Timing is as important as other options in determining price. Adjusting your travel dates by a week (or even a day) can yield substantial savings.

The following companies offer package tours to New Mexico:

- ✔ **Southwest Airlines Vacations** (☎ **800-243-8372;** Internet: www. swavacations.com) offers packages to Albuquerque, Santa Fe, Taos, and Angel Fire with reasonable prices.

- ✔ **Liberty Travel** (☎ **888-271-1584;** Internet: www.libertytravel. com), one of the biggest packagers in the northeastern United States, offers reasonably priced packages, particularly for skiers bound for Taos.

- ✔ **Amtrak Vacations** (☎ **800-654-5748;** Internet: www.amtrak vacations.com) offers all-inclusive packages to Albuquerque and surrounding sights, with a day-trip to Santa Fe.

Good places to look for additional package tours include:

- ✔ **Online at www.vacationpackager.com.** At this Web site, you can plug in your destination and interests, and the site will make many suggestions of companies that you can contact on your own or through a travel agent.

- ✔ **Local newspaper.** Look in the travel section of your local Sunday newspaper for advertisements. One reliable packager that you may see is **American Express Vacations** (☎ **800-346-3607;** Internet: http://travel.americanexpress.com/travel/).

- ✔ **National travel magazines.** Check the ads in the back of magazines such as *Arthur Frommer's Budget Travel, Travel & Leisure, National Geographic Traveler,* and *Condé Nast Traveler.*

> ✔ **Hotel chains, casinos, and resorts.** If you already know where you
> want to stay, call the hotel or resort and ask if they offer land/air
> packages.

Making Your Own Arrangements

You may want to be totally independent, whether because you're a
control freak and can't stand even a single detail being out of your
hands; because you're into spontaneity and hate having anything pre-
arranged outside of what's absolutely essential (like, say, your flight);
or because you just like to do your own thang. Whatever your reason,
I'm happy to supply some basic transportation data.

Finding out who flies where

The recently expanded and renovated **Albuquerque International
Sunport** (☎ **505-842-4366** for the administrative offices; Internet:
www.cabq.gov/airport/welcome.html) is the hub for travel to most
parts of New Mexico. Nine major airlines and one minor airline serve
it (as do three commuter airlines) with nonstop flights to and from 28
U.S. cities. Although the airport doesn't provide nonstop international
flights, it does offer nonstop connections to international hubs such as
Los Angeles, Houston, Dallas, Chicago, and Seattle. A secondary hub
for southern New Mexico is **El Paso International Airport** (☎ **915-
780-4700**) in western Texas, which has nonstop international service
to Mexico via Aeromexico.

In conjunction with United Airlines, **United Express** offers commuter
flights to and from **Santa Fe Municipal Airport** (☎ **505-955-2900**) via
Denver. Additionally, **America West** serves Santa Fe from Phoenix.

Table 6-1 indicates which airlines service Albuquerque and El Paso,
Texas. See the Appendix for the airlines' toll-free numbers and Web sites.

Table 6-1	Airlines Serving Albuquerque and El Paso	
Airline	*Flies to Albuquerque*	*Flies to El Paso*
Aeromexico	No	Yes
American Airlines	Yes	Yes
America West Airlines	Yes	Yes
Continental Airlines	Yes	Yes
Delta Air Lines	Yes	Yes
Frontier Airlines	Yes	Yes

(continued)

Table 6-1 *(continued)*

Airline	Flies to Albuquerque	Flies to El Paso
Mesa Airlines	Yes	No
Northwest Airlines	Yes	No
Southwest Airlines	Yes	Yes
TWA	Yes	No
United Airlines	Yes	No
United Express	Yes	No

Snagging the best airfare

If you need flexibility, be ready to pay for it. Full-price fare usually applies to last-minute bookings, sudden itinerary changes, and round trips that get you home before the weekend. On most flights, even the shortest routes, full-price fare can approach $1,000.

You pay far less than full fare if you book well in advance, can stay over Saturday night, or can travel on Tuesday, Wednesday, or Thursday. A ticket bought as little as 7 or 14 days in advance costs only 20 to 30% of the full fare. If you can travel with just a couple days' notice, you may also get a deal (usually on a weekend fare that you book through an airline's Web site — see the section "Getting away on the weekend," later in this chapter, for more).

Airlines periodically lower prices on their most popular routes. Restrictions abound, but the sales translate into savings. For instance, a flight across the United States may cost as little as $400. You may also score a deal when an airline introduces a new route or increases service to an existing one.

Watch newspaper and television ads and airline Web sites, and when you see a good price, grab it. These sales usually run during slow seasons (for New Mexico, this includes mid-October to Thanksgiving and January and February). Sales rarely coincide with peak travel times such as summer vacation and the winter holidays, when people must fly, regardless of price.

Cutting ticket costs by using consolidators

Consolidators, also known as bucket shops, are good places to find low fares. Consolidators buy seats in bulk and resell them at prices that undercut the airlines' discounted rates. Be aware that tickets bought this way are usually nonrefundable or carry stiff cancellation penalties (as much as 75% of the ticket price). **Important:** Before you pay, ask the consolidator for a confirmation number, and then call the airline to confirm your seat. Be prepared to book your ticket through a different consolidator if the airline can't confirm your reservation.

Consolidators' small ads usually appear in major newspapers' Sunday travel sections at the bottom of the page. **Council Travel** (☎ 800-226-8624; Internet: www.counciltravel.com) caters to young travelers but offers bargain prices to people of all ages. **Travel Bargains** (☎ 800-247-3273; Internet: www.1800airfare.com) offers deep discounts with a four-day advance purchase. Other reliable consolidators include **1-800-FLY-CHEAP** (☎ 800-359-2432; Internet: www.1800flycheap.com); **TFI Tours International** (☎ 800-745-8000 or 212-736-1140), which serves as a clearinghouse for unused seats; and *rebaters* such as **Travel Avenue** (☎ 800-333-3335 or 312-876-1116; Internet: www.travelavenue.com), which rebates part of its commissions to you.

Snaring a deal on the Web

Use the Internet to search for deals on airfare, hotels, and car rentals. Among the leading sites are **Arthur Frommer's Budget Travel Online** (www.frommers.com), **Travelocity** (www.travelocity.com), **Lowestfare** (www.lowestfare.com), **Microsoft Expedia** (www.expedia.com), **The Trip** (www.thetrip.com), **Smarter Living** (www.smarterliving.com), and **Yahoo!** (http://travel.yahoo.com).

Each site provides roughly the same service, with variations that you may find useful or useless. Enter your travel dates and route, and the computer searches for the lowest fares. Several other features are standard, and periodic bell-and-whistle updates make occasional visits worthwhile. You can check flights at different times or on different dates in hopes of finding a lower price, sign up for e-mail alerts that tell you when the fare on a route you specify drops below a certain level, and gain access to databases that advertise cheap packages and fares for those who can get away at a moment's notice.

Remember that you don't have to book online; you can ask your flesh-and-blood travel agent to match or beat the best price you find.

Getting away on the weekend

Airlines make great last-minute deals available through their Web sites once a week, usually on Wednesday. Flights generally leave on Friday or Saturday (that is, only two or three days later) and return the following Sunday, Monday, or Tuesday. Some carriers offer hotel and car bargains at the same time.

You can sign up for e-mail alerts through individual Web sites or all at once through **Smarter Living** (www.smarterliving.com). If you already know what airline you want to fly, consider staying up late on Tuesday and checking the site until the bargains for the coming week-end appear. Book right away and avoid losing out on the limited number of seats.

Arriving by Other Means

Though flying is the most common way to get to New Mexico, you have a few other options.

By car

Road tripping to New Mexico can be fun from anywhere in the U.S., but is most convenient if you live in Arizona, Nevada, Utah, Colorado, Oklahoma, or Texas. Driving saves money on car rental fees and allows you to bring along essential equipment such as a cooler or maybe a bicycle or kayak. If you drive, you can easily connect onto I-40, which follows the path of the old Route 66 east–west through Tucumcari, Albuquerque, and Gallup, and I-25, which traverses north–south across the center through Las Vegas, Santa Fe, Albuquerque, and Las Cruces. I-10 from San Diego crosses southwestern New Mexico until intersecting I-25 in Las Cruces.

Albuquerque is 811 miles from Los Angeles, 437 miles from Denver, 458 miles from Phoenix, 604 miles from Salt Lake City, and for you true road-trippers, a whopping 1,997 miles from New York City.

By train or bus

Two **Amtrak** (☎ **800-USA-RAIL;** Internet: www.amtrak.com) trains run through the state. The *Southwest Chief,* which makes its way between Chicago and Los Angeles, passes through New Mexico once daily in each direction, with stops in Gallup, Grants, Albuquerque, Lamy (for Santa Fe), Las Vegas, and Raton. A second train, the *Sunset Unlimited,* skims through the southwest corner of the state three times weekly in each direction — between Los Angeles and New Orleans — with stops in Lordsburg, Deming, and El Paso, Texas.

Greyhound/Trailways (☎ **800-231-2222** for schedules, fares, and information; Internet: www.greyhound.com, www.trailways.com) bus lines provide through-ticketing (meaning, your bus ticket is also good for the train) for Amtrak between Albuquerque and El Paso. You can get a copy of Amtrak's National Timetable from any Amtrak station, from travel agents, or by contacting Amtrak.

Chapter 7

Getting Around New Mexico

· ·

In This Chapter

▶ Cruising the state by land yacht

▶ Landing deals on rented wheels

▶ Getting around by other means, including telephone

· ·

*O*key dokey, so you're in New Mexico, but how do you get around these here parts? By far the best way to navigate the state is via car. In fact, quite often that's the *only* way to get around the Land of Enchantment, so you'd better get used to driving. If you're willing to shell out the beans, you can also fly between a few cities and towns, or even cover some of the major routes on buses. Train routes, however, are extremely limited and hardly worth considering. Most folks fly in to either Albuquerque or Santa Fe, rent themselves a vehicle, and put the pedal to the metal — yessirree.

Driving in the Land of Enchantment

If you drive your own vehicle to New Mexico, then you'll probably arrive via either the east–west running I-40 or the north–south running I-25, which together divide the state into four quadrants. You'll be ahead of the game, because you won't have to rent a car to get around. For any exploration of New Mexico beyond the downtown areas of the major cities and towns, a car is essential. For this reason, most of this chapter is devoted to the subject of getting around by car and how to rent one if necessary.

Navigating highways and byways

For the most part, New Mexico's roads are modern and well maintained, particularly I-40 and I-25, where the speed limit is 75 miles per hour. However, when you stray from the interstates, two-lane highways are the norm, where the speed limits are much lower and you can expect to find a lot more twists and turns — particularly up in the mountains. Dirt roads are also quite common, even within the city proper of Santa Fe.

The flower-adorned crosses along the sides of the roads here are not part of a highway beautification project — they are memorials to people who have lost their lives in accidents. New Mexico has one of the highest incidences of drunk-driving fatalities in the United States, so staying extra alert to the behavior of other drivers is very important. Some drivers here keep their headlights on during the day to be more visible to other drivers. If you see someone weaving around the road and suspect that person may be drunk, you can report the driver by calling a toll-free number on your cell phone: Press the star symbol, then 3-9-4 (or star-D-W-I).

Aside from other drivers, some other road hazards to consider are floods, blizzards, and dust storms, as well as animals such as deer, elk, coyotes, cows, or horses wandering into the road in rural areas (which means most of the state). At certain times of the year, you may also see tarantulas crossing a road in large numbers, and migrating cranes (some have been hit by drivers) on I-25 near the Bosque del Apache National Wildlife Refuge (see Chapter 11).

Gas stations and convenience stores can be few and far between, so keep an eye on your gas tank and other fluid levels, and keep extra water in your vehicle — for both you and your car — if you're driving in the desert. For estimated driving times and distances between destinations in New Mexico, see the Cheat Sheet at the beginning of this book.

Renting a car

The good news is that just about every major car rental company is represented in New Mexico, so you can shop around for the best deal. The bad news is that they all know you need a car to get around New Mexico, so their prices can be higher than in other states. Because Albuquerque is the transportation hub for New Mexico, you're likely to rent a car at the Albuquerque International Sunport, the city's airport. See the Appendix for the toll-free numbers of the major rental-car companies, almost all of which serve Albuquerque. See Chapters 13 and 15 for information on rental-car agencies in Santa Fe and Taos, respectively.

Car-rental rates vary even more than airline fares. The price depends on a host of factors, including the size of the car, the length of time you keep it, where and when you pick it up and drop it off, and how far you drive it. Asking a few key questions can save you hundreds of dollars. What follows are factors to keep in mind when you speak with a rental-car agent:

- ✔ Weekend rates may be lower than weekday rates.

- ✔ For a weekend rental, the rate for pickup Thursday night may be cheaper than for pickup Friday morning.

- ✔ The rate may be cheaper if you pick up the car at the airport or at a location in town.

✔ If you keep the car for five or more days, a weekly rate may be cheaper than the daily rate.

✔ Some companies may assess a drop-off charge if you don't return the car to the same renting location; others, notably National, do not.

✔ If you see an advertised price in your local newspaper, be sure to ask for that specific rate; otherwise, you may be charged the standard (higher) rate.

✔ Don't forget to mention membership in AAA, AARP, frequent flyer programs, and trade unions. These usually entitle you to discounts ranging from 5% to 30%. Ask your travel agent to check any and all of these rates.

✔ Most car rentals are worth at least 500 miles on your frequent flyer account.

On top of the standard rental prices, other **optional charges** apply to most car rentals. The Collision Damage Waiver (CDW), which requires you to pay for damage to the car in a collision, is covered by many credit card companies. Check with your credit card company before you go so you can avoid paying this hefty fee (as much as $15/day).

The car-rental companies also offer **additional liability insurance** (if you harm others in an accident), **personal accident insurance** (if you harm yourself or your passengers), and **personal effects insurance** (if your luggage is stolen from your car). If you have insurance on your car at home, you're probably covered for most of these unlikelihoods. If your own insurance doesn't cover you for rentals, or if you don't have auto insurance, you should consider these additional coverages (the car rental companies are liable for certain base amounts, depending on the state). But weigh the likelihood of getting into an accident or losing your luggage against the cost of these coverages (as much as $20/day combined), which can significantly add to the price of your rental.

Some companies also offer **refueling packages,** in which you pay for an entire tank of gas up front. The price is usually fairly competitive with local gas prices, but you don't get credit for any gas remaining in the tank. If you reject this option, you pay only for the gas you use, but you have to return the car with a full tank or face charges of $3 to $4 a gallon for any shortfall. If you think that a stop at a gas station on the way back to the airport will make you miss your plane, then by all means take advantage of the fuel purchase option. Otherwise, skip it.

You are most likely to rent a car at the airport in Albuquerque, where added costs include a **state tax** (10.8%), a **state surcharge** ($2), a **customer facility charge** ($1.53 per day), and a **concession-recovery fee** (9.89%) — the extra charge for renting at the airport.

As with other aspects of planning your trip, using the Internet can make comparison-shopping for a rental car much easier. All the major booking sites — **Travelocity** (www.travelocity.com), **Expedia** (www.expedia.com), **Yahoo Travel** (www.travel.yahoo.com), and **Cheap Tickets** (www.cheaptickets.com), for example — have search engines that can dig up discounted car-rental rates. Just enter the size of the car you want, the pickup and return dates, and the city where you want to rent, and the server returns a price. You can even make the reservation through these sites.

Flying and Riding Around New Mexico

If you don't have a car and don't want to rent one, your options for getting around New Mexico are very limited. Two airlines fly between a selected number of cities and towns: **Rio Grande Air** (☎ 877-435-9742) flies between Albuquerque, Santa Fe, Farmington, Ruidoso, and Taos; and **Mesa Airlines** (☎ 800-637-2247) flies between Albuquerque, Farmington, Gallup, Carlsbad, Clovis, Roswell, Alamogordo, and Hobbs.

Want to ride some rails around the state? Fuggedaboudit — the railway routes are extremely limited. If you want someone else to do the driving, take the bus. Call **Greyhound/Trailways** (☎ 800-231-2222; Internet: www.greyhound.com or www.trailways.com) or **TNM&O Coaches** (☎ 505-243-4435) for schedules, fares, and information. Refer to the appropriate city and regional chapters in this book for information about shuttle bus services between airports and tourist destinations.

Getting Around by Telephone

Although New Mexico has for years lived blissfully with the simplicity of one area code — 505 — the state's Zen-like phone existence will likely change in the upcoming years. If the 505 area code doesn't work for you, call the **New Mexico Department of Tourism** at ☎ 800-733-6396 or log onto www.newmexico.org to find out if the change has taken place.

Chapter 8

Booking Your Accommodations

● ●

In This Chapter

▶ Choosing the right bed in New Mexico

▶ Reserving a room

▶ Paying the best price for a room

● ●

*O*ne thing New Mexico has in abundance, besides chiles, cacti, and sunny days, is beds. They come in a pretty broad variety of types, with an even broader range of prices. This chapter sketches your bunking options and then suggests ways to secure a good deal.

Finding the Place That's Right for You

No two travelers are alike; fortunately, New Mexico has a broad enough range of accommodations to satisfy even the most eccentric adventurer. Maybe your goal is to spend as much time as possible out in the world exploring sights. If this is the case, your accommodation needs may be simple: a good bed and a shower. Or maybe you're longing to sink into a luxury escape and stay there, in which case you're looking for a full-service resort. Many people fall in between these extremes.

In this chapter, I discuss what you find at each type of accommodation available in the state and how much you can expect to pay. For a list of the beds I recommend most, see Chapter 1. If you have special needs in regard to your accommodations, see Chapter 5. You Girl and Boy Scout–types are the only ones out of luck with this book — I don't discuss camping options. If you're interested in a back-to-nature adventure in New Mexico, check out my two other books, *Frommer's Great Outdoor Guide to Arizona & New Mexico* and *Frommer's New Mexico* (both published by Hungry Minds, Inc.).

I list the different accommodations types in descending price order based on their *rack rate,* which is the maximum rate a hotel charges for a room (see "Revealing the Truth about Rack Rates," later in this chapter). Here and throughout the book, dollar signs give you an idea of prices. The $ ratings for the hotels are based on the nightly rack rate for two people in a double room in high season, which is March through Easter, June through September, and Thanksgiving through New Year's Day (see Chapter 2 for more on high and low season). The $ ratings represent the following price ranges:

$	$75 or less
$$	$76–$125
$$$	$126–$175
$$$$	$176 or more

Be aware that some lodgings, particularly in Albuquerque, Santa Fe, and Taos, add a steep lodgers tax (generally around 10%) to all hotel bills. You may also encounter other added costs, such as gratuities, so make sure you ask before reserving a room. (See Chapters 11, 13, and 15 for specific details on tax rates in Albuquerque, Santa Fe, and Taos, respectively.)

Sleeping in luxury: Resorts

Longing to be pampered, to get away from the rigor of daily life? Or maybe you have some extra bucks that you want to sink into your vacation. If so, one of New Mexico's few resorts may be for you. Unfortunately, the only resorts at this time are in the Santa Fe area, but the City Different (Santa Fe's nickname) is a good jumping off point for many adventures.

Though New Mexico isn't known for its resorts, recent years have brought some pretty swanky digs to the state and spruced up some older ones. Duffers won't find golf resorts in New Mexico, but those of you with other interests will find plenty of amenities to keep you busy (and spending money) on resort grounds. You usually find a pool complex and exercise facilities, whereas some resorts offer activities such as tennis and horseback riding. Spa treatments are the latest trend in resort life. Some resorts offer a full range of treatments, from massages to salt rubs, as well as facilities such as steam rooms and hot tubs. The pampering includes the palate: All the resorts serve excellent food in atmospheric settings.

If you're vacationing with kids, you're in luck in the Santa Fe area, where **Bishop's Lodge** offers a full children's program, with activities for adults as well (see Chapter 13).

Competition among Santa Fe's top resorts has led to real refinement in the rooms themselves. All have the latest decor, high-quality bath amenities, and other luxuries available, such as fireplaces, robes, and in-room safes.

Naturally, none of this comes cheap. Rack rates for most resort rooms start at about $180 a night during high season. However, you may be able to get a package deal that includes spa treatments, horseback riding, or some meals if you're willing to spend two nights or more. If your schedule is flexible, you may also be able to get special deals on weekdays. And during the slower seasons, such as mid-winter, late spring, and late fall, you can definitely find lower prices.

Sleeping with history: Hotels, lodges, and inns

The Land of Enchantment has very few glossy high-rise hotels. Like New Mexico's cities, the lodgings tend to s-p-r-e-a-d o-u-t across the vastness of the Southwestern desert. What's great is the *way* they've spread, in such a variety of styles that you may be hard-pressed to pigeonhole a true "New Mexico inn." Probably the closest you can come is the *hacienda-style* inn, an adobe one- or two-story structure often built around a courtyard. If possible, try to schedule at least one night in one of these gems. Many of the hotels have a distinctive pueblo architectural style, meaning they're patterned after the hand-rubbed adobes of the Rio Grande Pueblo tribes, often with multiple stories stacked one on top of another to mimic the shape of a mountain. You can also find some Victorian inns that have a frontier flavor. Within this variety of architecture, the amenities vary, from places with antique but workable plumbing and no televisions, to those with hot tubs and dataports in the rooms (and many variations in between). Don't fret, though; I tell you what to expect in my descriptions of the individual properties in Parts III and IV of this book.

One novelty unique to the Southwest is *casitas* (little houses). These freestanding units are often more expensive than regular rooms but offer benefits, such as private entrances and spaces between you and your neighbors — an ideal set-up for light sleepers and families.

All the hotels and inns that I discuss in this book are clean, safe, and comfortable, but the quality and perks tend to increase with the price. In fact, in New Mexico you generally pay extra for the history, so you find very few (non-franchise) hotels in the single $ category. Hotels, lodges, and inns fall into the other price categories as follows: a rustic small-town Victorian hotel or renovated lodge is in the $$ range; the chic inn or hotel with classy in-room amenities and modern facilities falls into the $$$ category; and the full-on luxury hotel, with primo amenities and services, is in the $$$$ price slot.

Sleeping with novelty: Bed-and-breakfasts

In recent years, bed-and-breakfasts (B&Bs) have proliferated in New Mexico — good news for travelers who like a little adventure in their stay. Though you can find traditional Victorian-style B&Bs here (and some lovely ones at that), complete with lacy bedding and elaborately carved accents, you also find more traditional New Mexican B&Bs in a variety of styles. You can choose from old hacienda-style homes that once housed outlaws (in Lincoln, see Chapter 16) to tiered adobe struc-tures that were once home to authors (in Taos, see Chapter 15), and a cave carved out of the side of a cliff (in Farmington, see Chapter 19). You find B&Bs all over the state, but the greatest number are in Albuquerque, Santa Fe, and Taos (see Chapters 11, 13, and 15, respectively). All are comfortable, and a few (in Santa Fe and Taos) are luxurious. All the ones listed in this book serve tasty, full breakfasts, some outstanding. Prices run from the $$ to the $$$ range, with a few in Santa Fe running in the $$$$ category. The most expensive B&Bs offer designer bedding and bath amenities as well as spa treatments (at an extra charge).

Though space limits my ability to include all the great B&Bs in the state, if you're especially interested in this type of lodging, contact the **New Mexico Association of Bed & Breakfast Inns** (☎ **800-661-6649** or 505-766-5380; Internet: www.nmbba.org). With strict guidelines for membership, the association helps assure a comfortable stay in more than 40 B&Bs.

Sleeping with assurance: Franchise hotels

We all know those nights when only predictability will do. Maybe you've pulled into town late and all you want to do is fall into bed, or maybe you're traveling on a budget or with children; in these cases, you need a chain hotel. You may already have your favorites, places so familiar they feel like home. Well, you find them all in New Mexico, though not quite everywhere. Some places, such as Chama and Lincoln, still shun the presence of such cookie-cutter establishments, but most every-where else you can find them along the highways or even in the center of town. See the Appendix for the toll-free numbers for those hotels rep-resented in the state. Rooms are generally in the $ or $$ price range.

With so many brand-new chain hotels opening up, you may expect rooms to look the same here as they do in Peoria, but that's not always the case. Becoming a franchise may only mean that a hotel complies with the standards of that chain. So you may find that your Best Western is a pink stucco adobe-style hotel here, rather than the farmhouse style to which you're accustomed. Don't fret; you'll likely find the same amenities inside, though the room size may be different than your usual. Do, however, check out the room before you unpack your car.

Making a Reservation: Necessary or Not?

Because the state isn't generally overrun by vacation crowds (except in Santa Fe during peak seasons), New Mexico lends itself well to the road-tripping mentality in which you cruise through the day and don't worry about where to stay until night comes creeping in. If that's your mode of travel, you'll probably do fine in the Land of Enchantment, but you may not get to sleep in some of the choice digs available to those who plan ahead. If you're looking for a really atmospheric stay, book in advance. The next question, I know, is how *far* in advance.

Rooms are in the most demand during high season, the period from March through Easter, June through September, and Thanksgiving through New Year's Day (see Chapter 2 for more on high and low season). However, don't rely simply on the high- or low-season designation as your guide to when to reserve. Variations exist even within those time periods. For example, hotel rooms are most expensive and most quickly booked in Santa Fe during summer, but even without advance reservations, you still may be able to find a chain hotel room or even a more upscale room somewhere in town during that time. However, for a trip in August, during Indian Market, you may have to book even a chain hotel room up to a year in advance. A similar situation happens in Albuquerque. Overall, October is a slow month for Albuquerque's hotels, but in order to get a room during the week of the Kodak Albuquerque International Balloon Fiesta, you may have to book a year in advance.

In general, reserving a room as soon as you have some idea of your plans is a good idea. In most cases, you can do no harm booking six months in advance. You usually need to put down a credit card number to secure your room, but if you decide to cancel, you usually aren't held responsible for the price of the room. However, ask before you make a reservation to make sure this is the case; some B&Bs, in particular, hold you responsible for room costs if you cancel too close to the time you've booked (usually within a month).

If you find yourself in a New Mexican city and can't find an available room, try contacting the local tourism office or chamber of commerce (see the Quick Concierge section in each city or regional chapter for telephone numbers). These folks can probably find you a last-minute bed for the night.

Revealing the Truth about Rack Rates

The *rack rate* is the standard amount that a hotel charges for a room. If you walk in off the street and ask for a room for the night, you pay the rack rate. You sometimes see this rate printed on the emergency exit diagrams on the back of your hotel room door.

You don't have to pay the rack rate. Hardly anybody does. Perhaps the best way to avoid paying it is surprisingly simple: Ask for a cheaper or discounted rate.

In all but the smallest accommodations, room rates depend on many factors, not the least of which is how you make your reservation. For example, a travel agent may be able to negotiate a better deal with certain hotels than you can get by yourself. (That's because hotels sometimes give agents discounts in exchange for steering business their way.)

Prices also fluctuate with the seasons and the occupancy rate. If a hotel is nearly full, it's less likely to offer you a discount. If it's nearly empty, the reservations staff may be willing to negotiate. These circumstances can change from day to day, so if you're willing to be flexible, say so.

Getting the Best Room at the Best Rate

Finding the best rate may require some digging. For example, reserving through the hotel's toll-free number may result in a lower rate than if you call the reservations desk directly. On the other hand, the central reservations number may not know about discounts at specific locations. For example, local franchises may offer a special group rate for a wedding or family reunion but may neglect to tell the central booking line. Your best bet is to call both the local hotel number and the central number and see which one offers you a better deal.

Be sure to mention your membership in AAA, AARP, frequent flyer programs, and any other corporate rewards program to which you belong when you make your reservation. You never know when a membership may be worth a few dollars off your room rate.

After you know where you're staying, asking a few more questions can help you land the best possible room:

✔ **Ask for a corner room.** They're usually larger, quieter, and brighter, and may cost a bit more.

✔ **Request a room on a high floor.** Being farther away from the street or an outdoor pool area means your room may be quieter. Plus, a higher room may give you the added bonus of a better view. Make sure to ask for the highest standard floor, as some upper floors contain "club" or "concierge" level rooms that cost a little extra for such features as complimentary breakfasts, afternoon snacks, and newspapers.

✔ **Ask if the hotel is renovating.** If the answer is yes, request a room away from the renovation work, and make sure you ask again when you check in.

✔ **Inquire about the location of restaurants, bars, and meeting facilities, which can be noisy.**

✔ **If you aren't happy with your room when you arrive, return to the front desk right away.** If another room is available, the staff should be able to accommodate you, within reason.

If you need a room where you can smoke, be sure to request one when you reserve. If you can't bear the lingering smell of smoke, tell everyone who handles your reservation that you need a smoke-free room.

Surfing the Web for Hotel Deals

Many Web sites allow you to gather information about New Mexico–area hotels. The Internet is an invaluable resource, allowing you to compare various properties' features and to see hotels before you book. Reserving online can save not just time but also money — Internet-only deals can represent substantial savings.

Subpar travel arrangements can cost you time and money. Choosing the wrong hotel based on incomplete information can drag down your whole trip. If you're not satisfied with the information you gather via the Internet, pick up the phone and call the hotel directly. The extra time that you spend on a single phone call may help you confirm that the hotel meets your expectations.

Although the major travel Web sites (Travelocity, Microsoft Expedia, The Trip, and Yahoo!; see Chapter 6 for details) offer hotel booking, a better option is to use a site devoted primarily to lodging. Some lodging sites specialize in a particular type of accommodation, such as B&Bs, which you may not find on the more mainstream sites. Others, such as TravelWeb (see the following bullet list), offer weekend deals on major chain properties, which cater to business travelers and have more empty rooms on weekends.

Among the reputable Web sites listing hotels and B&Bs in New Mexico are the following:

- **New Mexico Hotels** (www.leisurelodgingonline.com/ink/new_mexico.htm) connects Internet users to many of the New Mexico Lodging Association's 300 members, with links to individual sites. What's best about this site is its lodging search engine. You plug in requirements such as "traveling with a pet" or "looking for a kitchenette," and the site helps you find a hotel or inn that can accommodate you. You can also book most accommodations online.

- Although the name **All Hotels on the Web** (www.all-hotels.com) is something of a misnomer, the site does have tens of thousands of listings throughout the world. Bear in mind that each hotel pays a small fee ($25 and up) to be listed, so the list is less like an objective reference and more like a book of online brochures.

- **hoteldiscount!com** (www.180096hotel.com) lists bargain room rates at hotels in more than 50 U.S. and international cities. Select a city, input your dates, and you get a list of best prices for a selection of hotels. This site is notable for delivering deep discounts in cities where hotel rooms are expensive. Call the toll-free number ☎ **800-96-HOTEL** if you want more options than are listed online.

- **InnSite** (www.innsite.com) has B&B listings in more than 50 countries around the globe. Find an inn at your destination, see pictures of the rooms, and check prices and availability. This extensive directory of B&Bs includes a listing only if the proprietor submitted one. (Listing an inn is free.) The innkeepers write the descriptions, and many listings link to the inns' own Web sites. If you're interested in B&Bs, see also the **Bed-and-Breakfast Channel** (www.bedandbreakfast.com).

- **TravelWeb** (www.travelweb.com) lists more than 26,000 hotels in 170 countries, focusing on chains such as Hyatt and Hilton. You can book almost 90% of these online. TravelWeb's Click-It Weekends, updated each Monday, offers weekend deals at many leading hotel chains.

Chapter 9

Minding Money Matters

*H*ow are you going to pay for your New Mexico excursion when you're on the road? For your answer, you must ponder the traveler's eternal question: Do I use cash, plastic, traveler's checks, or a combo? But that's not all. You also need to face the traveler's second eternal question: What do I do if all my funds get (gulp) stolen?

Choosing a Money Mode

Paying cash or credit is a capitalist's quandary, one that, come vacation time, can cause many people to lose sleep. Do you cram your wallet with big bills, follow a pay-as-you-go philosophy, and chance having your cash lost or stolen? Or should you reach for the plastic and hope the bill that greets you at home doesn't bankrupt you? Some folks carry little cash and prefer instead to test their credit card limit — and their self-restraint. Others hate plastic and prefer cash, traveler's checks, and conservatism. The approach you take depends on what you're comfortable with. But keep in mind that you'll be spending more money than you usually spend on a daily basis, so you'll need to have access to more of the green stuff. Plus, if your mind slips into vacation mode, you may not be as vigilant of your personal belongings as you are when you're on your own turf.

Toting traveler's checks

Traveler's checks are something of an anachronism from the days when people wrote personal checks instead of going to an ATM. Because traveler's checks can be replaced if lost or stolen, they were a sound alternative to stuffing your wallet with cash at the beginning of a trip. If you still prefer the safety of using traveler's checks, go for it. Piece of mind, however achieved, is crucial to any vacation.

You can get traveler's checks at almost any bank. **American Express** offers checks in denominations of $20, $50, $100, $500, and $1,000. You pay a service charge ranging from 1% to 4%, although AAA members can obtain checks without a fee at most AAA offices. You can also get American Express traveler's checks over the phone by calling ☎ **800-221-7282.**

Visa (☎ **800-227-6811**) also offers traveler's checks, available at Citibank locations across the country and at several other banks. The service charge ranges between 1½% and 2%; checks come in denominations of $50, $100, $500, and $1,000. **MasterCard** also offers traveler's checks; call ☎ **800-223-9920** for a location near you.

Carrying cash and using ATMs

If you generally like to pay for all of your day-to-day expenses with cash to keep from melting your credit card, you don't need to abandon this practice on vacation. Just don't leave your wallet in your room or on the dashboard of your car. You should also consider carrying just enough cash for a few days' expenses rather than all the cash you may need for your entire vacation. As you go, you can refill your wallet from the many ATMs around the state.

Most cities have 24-hour ATMs linked to a national network that almost always includes your bank at home. **Cirrus** (☎ **800-424-7787;** Internet: www.mastercard.com/atm/) and **Plus** (☎ **800-843-7587;** Internet: www.visa.com/atms) are the two most popular networks; check the back of your ATM card to see which network your bank belongs. The 800 numbers and Web sites can give you specific locations of ATMs where you can withdraw money while on vacation. (You can also check the "Quick Concierge" sections of the city and regional chapters in this book for ATM locations.)

One important reminder: Many banks now charge a fee ranging from 50¢ to $3 whenever a non-account holder uses their ATMs. Your own bank may also assess a fee for using an ATM that's not one of their branch locations. This means you may get charged *twice* just for using your ATM card when you're on vacation. Given these sneaky tactics, reverting back to traveler's checks may be cheaper in some cases, although certainly less convenient.

Doting on debit cards

Another way of working with your money — as opposed to the theoretical money of credit cards — is by using a debit card. You can use a debit card with a major credit card logo anywhere that accepts the credit card. The difference is that the money comes directly out of your checking account. As long as you record all your debit-card purchases, just as you would record any purchases made with checks, debit cards are a great way to go. Not only do you not need to carry cash, but the receipts also provide a convenient record of all your travel expenses.

Charging ahead with credit cards

Credit cards are a good and a bad thing. They afford the advantages of a debit card — they're accepted in most places, you don't need to carry cash, and you receive receipts of all your purchases. However, there is one important disadvantage: They allow you to spend money that you don't have. You can charge as much as your credit limit allows (which may relate little to your actual financial resources). With a credit card, you can indulge in more impulse buying than with any other form of payment.

But credit cards also have an important advantage. If you suddenly need extra cash, a credit card comes in handy. You can get cash advances off your credit card at any ATM if you know your PIN (personal identification number). If you've forgotten the number or didn't even know you had one, call the phone number on the back of your credit card and ask the bank to send it to you. Your new PIN should arrive in five to seven business days, although some banks will give it to you over the phone if you tell them your mother's maiden name or some other security clearance.

Personally, I would never get a cash advance from my credit card unless it was an emergency. Interest rates for cash advances are often significantly higher than rates for credit-card purchases. More importantly, you start paying interest on the advance the *minute you receive the cash.* On an airline-affiliated credit card, a cash advance does not earn frequent-flyer miles.

Coping with Loss or Theft

Sometimes, no matter how careful you are, you can lose your wallet. This mishap is not the greatest thing that can happen to you, but it's not the end of the world either (though it may seem like it). In fact, if you don't let your emotions take over, your loss may only put a small crimp in your trip.

So what happens if your belongings somehow escape? Take a deep breath and get to a phone. Almost every credit card company provides an emergency 800 number that you can call if your wallet or purse is lost or stolen. The company may be able to wire you a cash advance off of your credit card immediately; in many places, they can get you an emergency credit card within a day or two. The issuing bank's 800 number is usually on the back of the credit card, but that doesn't help much if your card is gone. Write down the number before you leave for your trip and keep it in a safe place (um, not your wallet or purse).

For **Citicorp Visa,** the U.S. emergency number is ☎ **800-645-6556.** **American Express** cardholders and traveler's check holders should call ☎ **800-221-7282** for all money emergencies. **MasterCard** holders should call ☎ **800-307-7309.**

If you opt to carry traveler's checks, keep a record of their serial numbers — in the same, separate place in which you keep your emergency credit card numbers — so you can handle this emergency, too.

If your wallet is stolen, you've probably seen the last of it, and the police won't likely recover it for you. However, after you realize that your wallet is gone and you've canceled your credit cards, call the local police to report the incident. You're likely to need the police report number for credit card and insurance purposes later.

Finally, although this may not be much solace at the time, federal law restricts your liability for unauthorized charges if your card is stolen and you immediately report it; you generally won't be required to pay more than $50. Fraud protection also includes debit cards. Check with your bank for the specific limits.

Chapter 10

Tying Up Loose Ends

• •

In This Chapter

▶ Buying travel insurance

▶ Dealing with sickness on the road

▶ Making (or not making) reservations

▶ Packing for the trip

▶ Looking like a local

• •

*M*ost of the other chapters in this book help you answer the big travel questions: Where to go in New Mexico and how to get there. In this chapter, I show you how to tackle the smaller, yet important, odds and ends that can make or break your trip.

Considering Travel Insurance

Having insurance is kind of like carrying around an umbrella; if you carry it, you won't need it. However, buying insurance can be expensive. So should you or shouldn't you invest in travel insurance?

Of the three primary kinds of travel insurance — **trip cancellation, medical,** and **lost luggage** — the only one I recommend is trip cancellation insurance, which is a good idea if you have to pay a large portion of your vacation expenses up front. Trip cancellation insurance covers three emergencies — if a death or sickness prevents you from going, if a tour operator or airline goes out of business, or if some kind of disaster prevents you from getting to your destination. Medical and lost luggage insurance don't make sense for most travelers. Your existing health insurance should cover you if you get sick while on vacation (although if you belong to an HMO, check to see whether you are fully covered when away from home). Homeowner's insurance policies cover stolen luggage if they include off-premises theft. Check your existing policies before you buy any additional coverage.

If you fly, you should be aware of coverage that you already have:

✔ Airlines are responsible for $2,500 on domestic flights (and $9.07 per pound, up to $640, on international flights) if they lose your luggage. If you plan to carry anything more valuable than what the airline covers, keep it in your carry-on bag.

✔ Some credit cards (American Express and certain gold and platinum Visa and MasterCards, for example) offer automatic flight insurance against death or dismemberment in case of an airplane crash.

If you decide to purchase additional insurance, be careful not to buy more than you need. If you need only trip cancellation insurance, don't buy coverage for lost or stolen property. Trip cancellation insurance should cost approximately 6% to 8% of the total value of your vacation.

The following companies are reputable issuers of trip cancellation, medical, and lost luggage insurance:

✔ **Access America,** 6600 W. Broad St., Richmond, VA 23230 (☎ **800-284-8300;** Fax: 800-346-9265; Internet: www.accessamerica.com).

✔ **Travelex Insurance Services,** 11717 Burt St., Ste. 202, Omaha, NE 68154 (☎ **800-228-9792;** Internet: www.travelex-insurance.com).

✔ **Travel Guard International,** 1145 Clark St., Stevens Point, WI 54481 (☎ **800-826-1300;** Internet: www.travel-guard.com).

✔ **Travel Insured International, Inc.,** P.O. Box 280568, 52-S Oakland Ave., East Hartford, CT 06128-0568 (☎ **800-243-3174;** Internet: www.travelinsured.com).

Finding Medical Care on the Road

Illness can not only ruin your vacation, but it can be scary. Finding a doctor that you trust isn't always easy when you're away from home. The best defense against illness is a good offense: Bring all of your medications with you, as well as a prescription for more if you worry that you'll run out. Also, be sure to carry an identification card, and pack items such as an extra pair of contact lenses, in case you lose one, and medication for common travelers' ailments like upset stomach or diarrhea.

If you have health insurance, check with your provider to find out the extent of your coverage outside of your home area. And if your existing policy isn't sufficient, get more medical insurance for comprehensive coverage (see the list of issuers in the preceding section). If you suffer from a chronic illness, talk to your doctor before taking the trip. For illnesses such as epilepsy, diabetes, or a heart condition, wearing a

Medic Alert identification tag will immediately alert any doctor to your condition and give him or her access to your medical records through Medic Alert's 24-hour hotline. Membership is $35, with a $15 annual renewal fee. Contact the Medic Alert Foundation, 2323 Colorado Ave., Turlock, CA 95382 (☎ **800-432-5378;** Internet: www.medicalert.org).

If you do get sick, ask the concierge at your hotel to recommend a local doctor — even his or her own doctor if necessary. This is probably a better recommendation than any national consortium of doctors available through an 800 number. If you can't get a doctor to help you right away, try the emergency room at the local hospital. Many hospital emergency rooms have walk-in-clinics for emergency cases that are not life threatening. You may not get immediate attention, but you won't pay the high price of an emergency room visit (usually a minimum of $300 just for signing your name, on top of whatever treatment you receive).

Making Reservations and Getting Tickets

New Mexico has no major-league sports teams or theme parks, so aside from booking hotel rooms, making reservations for special tours at Carlsbad Caverns, and buying tickets to the Santa Fe Opera and the Santa Fe Chamber Music Festival (all of which you should do well in advance), you don't need to fret about other reservations in this state. Certainly, to dine at the finer restaurants that I mention in later chapters, calling a couple days ahead for a weekend table at dinner (particularly in high season) can be a good idea. Otherwise, relax.

Although you don't need to buy tickets to visit a pueblo, you should always call before heading out, because many pueblos close for feast days and other tribal activities.

Packing for New Mexico

When you're ready to pack, start by assembling enough clothing and accessories to get you through the trip and piling it all onto the bed. Now put half of it into your suitcase and return the other half to your dresser.

Pack light, not because you can't take everything you want on the plane — you can, with some limits — but because spraining your back in an attempt to lift your whole wardrobe is no way to start a vacation.

What to bring

So what are the bare essentials when traveling in New Mexico? Comfortable walking shoes, a camera, a versatile sweater and/or jacket, a belt, toiletries and medications, and something to sleep in. Unless you plan on attending a board meeting, wedding, or one of the city's finest restaurants, you probably won't need a suit or a fancy dress. You'll get more use out of a pair of jeans or khakis and a comfortable sweater.

Here are a few points to keep in mind when assembling your vacation supplies:

- ✔ A day or fanny pack and a refillable water bottle may be the most useful items you bring on your trip (aside from this guidebook, of course).

- ✔ Don't forget to bring along sunglasses and plenty of sunscreen — the UV rays at high altitudes can be fierce.

- ✔ Remember that New Mexico is in the desert and you'll very likely move through a variety of elevations and, therefore, temperatures.

- ✔ In summer you should dress in layers with T-shirts, light sweaters, and jackets so you can easily transition from hot days to chilly nights.

- ✔ Although not the North Pole, New Mexico can get quite cold in winter (particularly up in the mountains), so you should dress in layers and come prepared for ice and snow.

- ✔ Because you never know when rain will fall, bring a rain jacket to protect yourself from sudden downpours. You can also use an umbrella, but because of the wind that often accompanies New Mexico's rain, those crumply, packable rain jackets make much more sense (and you won't have to carry around an umbrella all day).

How to select a suitcase

When choosing your suitcase, think about the kind of traveling you'll be doing. If you'll be walking with your luggage on hard floors, a bag with wheels makes sense. If you'll be carrying your luggage over uneven roads or up and down stairs, wheels won't help much. A fold-over garment bag will help keep dressy clothes wrinkle-free, but it can be a nuisance if you'll be packing and unpacking a lot. Hard-sided luggage protects breakable items better but weighs more than soft-sided bags.

How to pack

When packing, start with the biggest, hardest items (usually shoes) and then fit smaller items in and around them. Pack breakable items in between several layers of clothes, or keep them in your carry-on bag. Put things that can leak, such as shampoos or suntan lotions, in plastic bags. Lock your suitcase with a small padlock (available at most luggage stores, if your bag doesn't already have one), and put a distinctive identification tag on the outside so your bag is easy to spot on the baggage carousel.

Most airlines allow each passenger two pieces of carry-on luggage, but some allow just one (see the sidebar "Learn the limits of carry-on luggage" in this chapter). Airlines enforce the limit strictly, especially on crowded flights. The exact dimensions vary, so be sure you know what your carrier allows. In a carry-on bag that you know will get through, pack valuables, prescription drugs, vital documents, return tickets, and other irreplaceable items. Add a book or magazine, anything breakable, and a snack. Leave room for the sweater or light jacket you pull off after a few minutes of hauling bags through the overheated terminal.

Learn the limits of carry-on luggage

Because the reports of lost luggage are at an all-time high, consumers are trying to divert disaster by bringing their possessions onboard. In addition, planes are more crowded with passengers than ever, and overhead compartment space is at a premium. Because of these factors, some domestic airlines have started cracking down, imposing size restrictions on the bags you can bring onboard and sometimes limiting you to a single carry-on when the flight is crowded. The dimensions vary, but the strictest airlines say that carry-ons must measure no more than 22 × 14 × 9 inches, including wheels and handles, and weigh no more than 40 pounds. Many airports are already furnished with X-ray machines that literally block any carry-ons bigger than the posted size restrictions.

These measures may sound drastic, but they are important to follow to avoid overcrowding the cabin. Look on the bright side. For example, you may only carry on a small bag with your essentials, but your fellow traveler may try to carry on a bag big enough to hold a piano. Without the carry-on restrictions, the Liberace wannabe may take up all the space in the overhead bin, leaving you to check your wee bag or allow it to be flattened like a pancake.

Keep in mind that many of these regulations are enforced only at the discretion of the gate attendants. If you plan to bring more than one bag aboard a crowded flight, be sure your medications, documents, and valuables are consolidated in one bag in case you are forced to check the second one.

Words for the wise

Reading a book set in a place where you're traveling is one of the finest ways to gain insights to your destination. New Mexico has a long and great tradition of writers (D.H. Lawrence and Willa Cather, for example) who use the state as a subject. Among many New Mexico books, three excellent reads worth checking out are *The Milagro Beanfield War,* by John Nichols; *Death Comes to the Archbishop,* by Willa Cather; and *Cities of Gold,* by Douglas Preston.

Most visitors to New Mexico end up doing a fair amount of driving, so consider bringing along some recorded books to make the road less tiresome. You can borrow recorded books free from many local libraries, or contact **Books on Tape** (☎ **800-88-BOOKS**; Internet: www.booksontape.com) or **Recorded Books Inc.** (☎ **800-638-1304**; Internet: www.recordedbooks.com).

Dressing Like the Locals

New Mexico has long been a bastion for free spirits, and the local dress reflects the local attitude: ultracasual. Truly anything goes here — from black tie at charity events to jeans and cowboy boots at fancy restaurants. On rare occasions, a gentleman may be expected to wear a jacket in a fine dining establishment, but that is truly a rare occasion. More common are large numbers of women looking like Stevie Nicks on a bad hair day. (This doesn't mean that you need to add to their numbers.)

Although ultracasual dress is the norm, that self-conscious "relaxed" look isn't always ultra cheap — great care often goes into the carefully weathered cowboy boots and artfully-holed jeans you see around town. Bottom line: Sloppy can still be expensive, but dress as nice as you want and you won't feel out of place. However, slip into a get-up that has been festering in your laundry basket for six months, and you'll receive the same disdainful glances you would anywhere else.

Part III
Exploring the Most Popular Cities

"Oh, it's okay if you're into neo-romanticist art. Personally, I prefer the soaring perspectives of David Hockney or the controlled frenzy of Gerhard Richter."

In this part . . .

Welcome to New Mexico's central cities, the core of the state's cultural and natural attractions. When most travelers come to the Land of Enchantment, they head for these three gems: Albuquerque (New Mexico's gateway), Santa Fe (the state's cultural center), and Taos (the funky little art town). For each of these hot spots, I give you everything you need to know, from basics such as how to get there to recommendations of the best places to stay and the most fun ways to spend your time. This part also provides some excellent ways to get *out* of town — side trips to natural and human-made wonders.

Chapter 11

Albuquerque

. . . .

In This Chapter

▶ Finding your way to and around Albuquerque

▶ Locating a crib: Where to stay

▶ Filling your *boca:* Where to dine

▶ Exploring the sights on your own or with a guide

▶ Getting outdoors

▶ Shopping to oblivion

▶ Finding your way by the light of the moon: Where to go at night

. . . .

*O*n first glance, New Mexico's largest city appears like one giant strip mall sandwiched between a spectacular mountain range, the Sandias, and the lifeblood of the state, the mighty Rio Grande. But this city offers much more than Walgreens and Wal-Mart. Its historic center, Old Town, is an 18th-century village, complete with an enchanting plaza. Cruising by Old Town is Route 66, where you find 1950s signage and period motels and diners, some still operating, though with a bit of rust tarnishing the edges. En route to Old Town, the *Mother Road,* as Route 66 is known, also cruises straight through the University of New Mexico campus (where the state's literati and hippies drink too much coffee) and on to downtown Albuquerque, a place that's mostly suits and heels during the day but knows how to rock at night. The *Road to Freedom,* yet another nickname for Route 66, also leads to some of New Mexico's most incredible museums and attractions, such as the New Mexico Museum of Natural History, where you can travel back in time some 12 billion years and scratch dinosaur chins en route. Add some of the state's best and cheapest crafts stores, incredible hiking trails, and, best of all, the world's largest balloon event — the Kodak Albuquerque International Balloon Fiesta — and you have a major fun city.

For locations of the accommodations, restaurants, and attractions mentioned in this chapter, see the corresponding downtown maps of central Albuquerque.

Getting There

Because Albuquerque is the transportation hub for New Mexico, you're likely to start your New Mexico exploration here. For the lowdown about airlines that fly into Albuquerque, see Chapter 6. If you fly in, you'll definitely want to rent a car. The spaces are broad in the West, and most people are happiest if they can steer their own spaceship, or horse, or car, for that matter.

Flying in

The **Albuquerque International Sunport** is in the south-central part of the city, about 5 miles from downtown, between I-25 on the west and Kirtland Air Force Base on the east, just south of Gibson Boulevard. Sleek and efficient, the airport is served by most national airlines and three local ones, Mesa Airlines, America West Express, and Rio Grande Air. (See the Appendix for the toll-free numbers of airlines.)

Most hotels have courtesy vans to meet their guests and take them to their respective destinations. In addition, **Checker Airport Express** (☎ **505-765-1234**) runs vans to and from city hotels (fares to downtown hotels cost $11 one-way, to Journal Center area hotels $20 one-way). **Sun Tran** (☎ **505-843-9200**), Albuquerque's public bus system, also makes airport stops (see "Getting Around," later in this chapter, for info on public transportation). Efficient taxi services and numerous car-rental agencies also provide transport to and from the airport. Your best bet for a taxi is **Yellow Cab** (☎ **505-247-8888**), which always has taxis waiting at the airport; a trip downtown costs about $12. (See the Appendix for the toll-free numbers of major car-rental agencies.)

Driving in

If you're in a car, you'll probably arrive via either the east–west running I-40 or the north–south running I-25. Exits are well marked.

Riding in

If you enjoy letting someone else do the driving, you have the following options:

  ✔ **Riding the rails. Amtrak's** "Southwest Chief" arrives and departs daily to and from Los Angeles and Chicago. The station is at 214 First St. SW, two blocks south of Central Avenue (☎ **800-USA-RAIL** or 505-842-9650; Internet: www.amtrak.com).

> ✔ **Taking the bus.** Greyhound/Trailways (☎ **800-231-2222** for schedules, fares, and information; Internet: www.greyhound.com, www.trailways.com) and **TNM&O Coaches** (☎ **505-243-4435**) arrive and depart from the Albuquerque Bus Transportation Center, 300 Second St. SW (at the corner of Lead and Second, near the train station).

Orienting Yourself

Except for the traffic that can, at times, clog I-25 and I-40 (watch out during the morning and evening rush hours), Albuquerque is easy to get around. This section helps you find your way to this sprawling city's neighborhoods.

Strolling (er, driving) the neighborhoods

When you look at a map of Albuquerque (see any of the Albuquerque maps in this chapter), the first thing you notice is that it lies at the crossroads of I-25, which runs north–south, and I-40, which runs east–west. Getting this big X in your psyche helps you find your way to what tend to be more like regions than actual neighborhoods. When looking for an address, it is helpful to know that Central Avenue divides the city into north and south, and the railroad tracks — which run just east of First Street downtown — comprise the dividing line between east and west. A direction — NE, NW, SE, or SW — follows street names. The Albuquerque Convention and Visitors Bureau distributes the most comprehensive Albuquerque street map; see "Finding information after you arrive," later in this chapter, for the bureau's location.

Southwest: Downtown and Old Town

Because most of the city's museums lie in this region, southwest Albuquerque is a tourist magnet. Downtown Albuquerque is the recent recipient of all the love this city has to offer in the form of major renovation and building projects, making it fun to wander as well as to attend events at the Civic Plaza. Lomas Boulevard and Central Avenue (the old Route 66) flank downtown on the north and south. They come together 2 miles west of downtown near the Old Town Plaza, where oodles of shops await travelers' greenbacks. In the vicinity of Old Town are some of Albuquerque's most fun sights, such as the Rio Grande Zoo, the Biological Park, the Albuquerque Museum, and the Indian Pueblo Cultural Center (see "Discovering the top attractions," later in the chapter).

University of New Mexico and Nob Hill

From downtown, Lomas and Central cruise east across I-25, staying about half a mile apart as they pass by the University of New Mexico and the New Mexico State Fairgrounds. From the University eastward on Central Avenue is a great place to browse for hip restaurants and shops. The Nob Hill district is where the city's literati, hippies, and professors hang, drinking coffee and ruminating about life. The airport is directly south of the UNM campus, about 3 miles via Yale Boulevard. Kirtland Air Force Base — site of Sandia National Laboratories and the National Atomic Museum — is an equal distance south of the fairgrounds on Louisiana Boulevard.

Northeast Heights

Roughly paralleling I-40 to the north is Menaul Boulevard, the focus of midtown and uptown shopping as well as the hotel districts. As Albuquerque expands northward, the Journal Center office park, about 4½ miles north of the freeway interchange, is growing; more and more business offices are inhabiting the place, although it offers little for visitors to enjoy. Nearby are the **Kodak Albuquerque International Balloon Fiesta** grounds, where the annual event is held each October. East of Eubank Boulevard lie the Sandia Foothills, where the alluvial plain slants a bit more steeply toward the mountains — an excellent place to hike and mountain bike.

West Mesa

Coors Boulevard is the main thoroughfare on the west side of the Rio Grande. This rapidly expanding region is home to New Mexico's largest shopping mall, the Cottonwood Mall. Its greater fame, though, is as a sacred land and hunting ground for ancient Puebloan people who left their marks on the rock there in the form of *petroglyphs* (paintings on rock), which now lie within Petroglyph National Monument.

Finding information after you arrive

The main office of the **Albuquerque Convention and Visitors Bureau** is at 20 First Plaza NW, Suite 601 (☎ **800-284-2282** or 505-842-9918; Internet: www.abqcvb.org). Hours are Monday to Friday from 8 a.m. to 5 p.m. You can find information centers at the airport, on the lower level at the bottom of the escalator, open daily from 9:30 a.m. to 8 p.m.; and in Old Town at 303 Romero St. NW, Suite 107, open daily from 9 a.m. to 5 p.m.

Getting Around

If you took a bunch of marbles and let them fall on the floor, you'd have the equivalent of city planning in Albuquerque. The place is v-e-r-y s-p-r-e-a-d o-u-t, without a lot of forethought as to how a person might get from one corner to the other. My mother tells me that years ago, a city planner mentioned the notion of putting in a freeway loop around the city, but he probably ended up emptying trash cans for such a brilliant idea. So today, you have to do your best with what's there — a big cross of two major interstates and lots of traffic lights elsewhere. But don't despair. Thanks to its wide thoroughfares and grid layout, combined with its efficient transportation systems, Albuquerque is easy to get around.

Exploring by car

Behind the wheel of your own car or a rental, figuring out the way is easy, but the going can be slow. With two main freeways forming a cross upon the city, you can often move quickly until you have to turn off and take the scenic route through neighborhoods and business districts the rest of the way. The good news is that many travelers' destinations, such as Old Town and downtown, are not far off I-40 and I-25. Except in downtown (where you find many one-way streets), most of Albuquerque's streets are spacious, well marked, and dual-direction. The most important streets for visitors are east–west running Central Avenue (Route 66), Lomas Avenue, and Paseo del Norte and north–south running Rio Grande, San Mateo, and Tramway boulevards.

Finding **parking** is generally not difficult in Albuquerque. Meters operate weekdays from 8 a.m. to 6 p.m. and are not monitored at other times. Only the large downtown hotels charge for parking. **Traffic** is a problem only at certain hours. Avoid I-25 and I-40 at the center of town during morning (8 to 9 a.m.) and evening (4 to 6 p.m.) rush hours.

 Most New Mexicans think that turn signals are optional, so don't expect to always see them before the car in front of you slams on its brakes and screams around a corner. In fact, this little driving oddity and Northern New Mexico's New Age penchant have prompted the oft-seen bumper sticker "Visualize Turn Signal Use." (See Chapter 20 for more on the state's New-Age tendencies.)

Calling a taxi

If you want to hail a cab on the street in Albuquerque, you may have to wave your arm until around 2050. If you need a cab, call for one. Because the distances in the city are so far, the ride won't come cheap. A good idea is to ask for an estimate in advance. Your best bet is **Yellow Cab** (☎ 505-247-8888), which serves the city and surrounding area 24 hours a day.

Riding the bus

Sun Tran of Albuquerque (☎ 505-843-9200) serves the city with its bus network. If you're not in a hurry to get to where you want to go, it can be a good resource. Buses operate daily from 6 a.m. to 10 p.m., depending on the route. Fares run 75¢ for adults and 25¢ for students or children; ages 5 and under ride free. You need exact change, and you should request a free transfer when boarding. Call for information on routes.

Moving those feet

My sister-in-law once decided to walk a few blocks from her home to a shopping mall in Albuquerque, and twice people stopped their cars to ask if she needed a ride. In a sense, Albuquerque is like Los Angeles; nobody walks here, except in three places: Old Town, downtown, and the University/Nob Hill area. All three are good places to stroll and see the sights. Keep in mind, however, that you shouldn't stroll around any area of Albuquerque by yourself late at night.

Staying in Style

Joseph and Mary would've been in luck in Albuquerque. The city's hotel glut assures even the most wayward travelers a night's sleep, except during very specific times: the New Mexico Arts and Crafts Fair (late June), the New Mexico State Fair (September), and the Kodak Albuquerque International Balloon Fiesta, known simply as the Balloon Fiesta (early October). If you're one of those cheap (or bold) kind of bargainers, you may even try your hand at haggling for a lower-priced room during all but the previously-mentioned months.

The listings that follow include rack rates as well as a price category shown in $ symbols for each lodging — see Chapter 8 for an explanation of both. Only a few of the places listed here make you pay to park your car; where a fee is required, I note it.

A tax of almost 11% is added to every hotel bill. All hotels listed offer rooms for nonsmokers and travelers with disabilities; the B&Bs offer the same.

The top hotels and B&Bs

Böttger-Koch Mansion

$$–$$$ Old Town

You may find yourself trilling your r's like a true Spaniard if you stay in this Spanish/Victorian B&B set just off the Old Town Plaza. In a recent

Central Albuquerque Accommodations

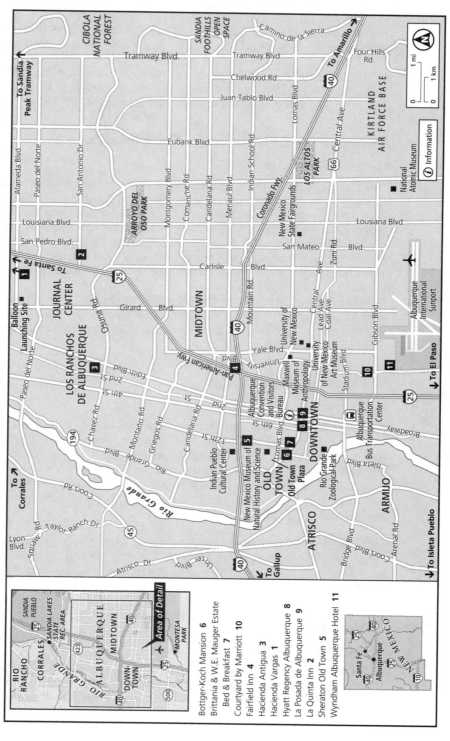

Bottger-Koch Mansion 6
Brittania & W.E. Mauger Estate
Bed & Breakfast 7
Courtyard by Marriott 10
Fairfield Inn 4
Hacienda Antigua 3
Hacienda Vargas 1
Hyatt Regency Albuquerque 8
La Posada de Albuquerque 9
La Quinta Inn 2
Sheraton Old Town 5
Wyndham Albuquerque Hotel 11

stunning makeover, innkeeper Yvonne Koch capitalized on the history of this 1912 mansion while adding hints of elegance in the form of fine bedding and bath goods. Breakfasts are large and scrumptious. Fortunately, here you're within walking distance of many of the city's best sights — a good incentive to work off that crispy French toast with sautéed apples.

110 San Felipe NW (just off Central Ave. on the south side of Old Town). ☎ *800-758-3639 or 505-243-3639. Internet:* www.bottger.com. *Parking: $2–$6 per day. Rack rates: $99–$179 double. Rates include full breakfast. AE, DC, MC, V.*

Brittania & W. E. Mauger Estate Bed & Breakfast

$$–$$$$ Downtown

If you like the intimacy of a B&B and want to be downtown, this restored Queen Anne–style inn constructed in 1897 will serve you well. Wonderfully atmospheric, the place has decor ranging from Tuscany to Africa. Each room has a coffeemaker, refrigerator stocked with complimentary beverages, snack basket, and hair dryer, as well as satellite dish TV, voice mail telephones, and data ports. Indulge in complimentary culinary treats in the evenings and a full breakfast each morning.

701 Roma Ave. NW (at 7th St.). ☎ *800-719-9189 or 505-242-8755. Fax: 505-842-8835. Internet:* www.maugerbb.com. *Rack rates: $109–$209 double. Rates include full breakfast. AE, DC, DISC, MC, V. Children welcome ($25 extra person charge), as are dogs by prior arrangement ($30).*

Courtyard by Marriott

$$ Airport

Full-on consistency and plenty of amenities await you at this four-story hotel with a village feel built on lots of green grass with scatterings of native plants. Though business travelers frequent the place most, families and other travelers alike enjoy in-room coffee and tea service, on-command movie channels, desks, irons, and hair dryers, as well as an indoor pool (great for kids) and whirlpool. A coffee shop is open daily for breakfast and dinner.

1920 Yale Blvd. SE (from I-25 take exit 222-A; follow Gibson Blvd. east to the second light). ☎ *800-321-2211 or 505-843-6600. Fax: 505-843-8740. Internet:* www.marriott.com. *Rack rates: $108 double. Weekend rates available. AE, DC, DISC, MC, V.*

Fairfield Inn

$ Northeast Heights

If you like a clean, centrally located room at a decent price, check into this hotel, owned by Marriott. Ask for an east-facing room to avoid the noise from (and view of) the highway. Rooms are medium-size, and each has a balcony or terrace. Amenities include an indoor/outdoor swimming pool, a sauna, and a Jacuzzi.

1760 Menaul Rd. NE (at University Blvd. where I-40 and I-25 meet). ☎ *800-228-2800 or 505-889-4000. Fax: 505-872-3094. Internet:* www.fairfieldinn.com. *Rack rates: $69 double. Extra person $10. Children age 18 and under stay free in parent's room. Rates include continental breakfast. AE, DC, DISC, MC, V.*

Hacienda Antigua (Bed & Breakfast)

$$–$$$$ **North Valley**

Two hundred years ago, stagecoach travelers used to enter the court-yard of this hacienda and find safety from marauders. Today you can bar the gates and relax in luxury. Set around an artistically landscaped court-yard, each room fulfills some kind of historical fantasy, from La Capilla, the home's former chapel, with a sacred feel and bedside fireplace, to the La Sala Suite, with a two-person hot tub that looks out upon the Sandia Mountains. Light sleepers beware — trains pass by this inn during the night.

6708 Tierra Dr. (from I-25 head west on Osuna Rd. 2.5 miles, cross the railroad tracks, and turn right on Tierra Dr.). ☎ *800-201-2986 or 505-345-5399. Fax: 505-345-3855. Internet:* www.haciendantigua.com. *Rack rates: $99–$229 double. Extra person $25. Rates include breakfast. AE, DISC, MC, V. Small dogs accepted by prior arrangement, $30 fee.*

Hyatt Regency Albuquerque

$$–$$$$ **Downtown**

This is the place for those of you who like a cosmopolitan feel. Located right smack downtown, this $60-million hotel, which opened in 1990, is pure shiny gloss and Art Deco. The rooms have plenty of space and big views of the mountains. If you want to taste Albuquerque's nightlife, as well as all the events at Civic Plaza, this hotel's location makes it easy. McGrath's restaurant serves three meals daily, and Bolo Saloon is the place to go for a shot. The Hyatt has major amenities, including an out-door pool, sauna, concierge, and valet parking.

330 Tijeras NW (downtown between 3rd and 4th Sts.). ☎ *800-233-1234 or 505-842-1234. Fax: 505-766-6710. Internet:* www.hyatt.com. *Parking: $8–$11 self-parking; $15 valet. Rack rates: weekdays $155–$199 double; weekends $89–$119 double. AE, DC, DISC, MC, V.*

La Posada de Albuquerque

$$–$$$ **Downtown**

If you find yourself sipping a glass of red wine within a 19th-century plaza, you aren't dreaming of being in old Spain; you're sitting in the La Posada lobby. Built in 1939 by famed hotelier Conrad Hilton, the inn is on the

National Register of Historic Places. A major remodelling in 1996 brought new furnishings to the place but kept the ambiance of old Spain, with such touches as a Moorish fountain and high archways in the lobby. Handcrafted furniture gives the spacious rooms a cozy feel. On site is Conrad's Downtown, a restaurant featuring Southwestern cuisine. The Lobby Bar is where you find a glass of wine, as well as entertainment Thursday through Saturday evenings.

125 Second St. NW (at Copper Ave.). ☎ *800-777-5732 or 505-242-9090. Fax: 505-242-8664. Internet:* www.laposada-abq.com. *Valet parking $5. Rack rates: $90–$140 double. AE, DISC, MC, V.*

La Quinta Inn

$–$$ Northeast Heights

If you come to Albuquerque to attend the Balloon Fiesta, this is the place to stay. It's not far from the launch site, which means that you have to reserve as much as a year in advance if you're coming for that event. (The rest of the year, reservations are more readily available.) These fairly spacious rooms seem to have all a traveler could want: a comfortable bed, table and chairs where you need them, and a bathroom in which you can move around. A bean-shaped heated pool, open May to October, offers respite from Albuquerque's hot summers.

5241 San Antonio Dr. NE (exit 231 off I-25). ☎ *800-531-5900 or 505-821-9000. Fax: 505-821-2399. Internet:* www.laquinta.com. *Rack rates: $70–$76 double (higher during Balloon Fiesta). Rates include continental breakfast. Children age 18 and under stay free in parent's room. AE, DC, DISC, MC, V. Pets welcome.*

Sheraton Old Town

$$$ Old Town

If you're one of those people who likes to put in minimum effort for maximum pleasure, you can appreciate this hotel, the closest one to Albuquerque's best attractions. Five minutes from Old Town Plaza, the Museum of Natural History, and the Museum of Albuquerque, its location can please shopaholics as well as nostalgics. Rooms have nice Southwestern flair, with such amenities as handcrafted *trasteros* (armoires) and furnishings. With two restaurants on-site, grub is readily available.

800 Rio Grande Blvd. NW (I-40 west, Rio Grande exit, near Old Town). ☎ *800-325-3535 or 505-843-6300. Fax: 505-842-8426. Internet:* www.sheraton.com\oldtownalbuquerque. *Rack rates: $149–$169 double. Children stay free in parent's room. AE, DC, DISC, MC, V.*

The runner-up hotels and B&Bs

Wyndham Albuquerque Hotel

$$$ **Near airport** The easiest airport access in town and a Southwestern feel with lots of sandstone and pine make this a good choice for travelers, especially those business people who are accustomed to plenty of amenities. *2910 Yale Blvd. SE. ☎ 800-227-1117 or 505-843-7000. Internet:* www.wyndham.com. *Small pets welcome with prior approval.*

Hacienda Vargas

$$ **Algodones**   If you plan to visit both Albuquerque and Santa Fe and you like a country setting, this inn, located on old Route 66 between the two cities, offers suites with Jacuzzis and fireplaces, making it a perfect spot for a getaway. Light sleepers, take note: A train passes near the inn during most nights. *El Camino Real (30 minutes north of Albuquerque). ☎ 800-261-0006 or 505-867-9115. Internet:* www.haciendavargas.com.

Dining Out

Although Albuquerque doesn't have the quality of food that Santa Fe and Taos have, a few really good restaurants do exist in town (Artichoke Café and The Range, for instance). The good news is that food is less expensive here than in Santa Fe, and the atmosphere in most cases is casual. Even though Albuquerque has the ancestry of Route 66 diners, its food crosses many ethnic lines. You find everything from Continental to French to Native American.

The top restaurants

Artichoke Café

$$$–$$$$ **Downtown**   CONTINENTAL

I've always wondered who the brave soul was that first bit into the spiny artichoke fruit. That question isn't answered at this artsy downtown eatery, but many more are. For example, how many ways can you eat an artichoke? The answer is "an infinite number" as far as these folks are concerned. Try yours steamed with three dipping sauces or in ravioli. But don't stop with the artichokes. Entrees include pasta dishes, as well as fish, chicken, and beef dishes prepared with equal imagination and flair. Set in three rooms with paintings and sculptures against azure walls, this place encourages you to linger and question away.

424 Central Ave. SE. ☎ 505-243-0200. Reservations recommended. Main courses: $5.95–$12.95 lunch, $12.95–$23.95 dinner. AE, DISC, MC, V. Open: Mon–Fri lunch; Mon–Sat dinner.

Central Albuquerque Restaurants

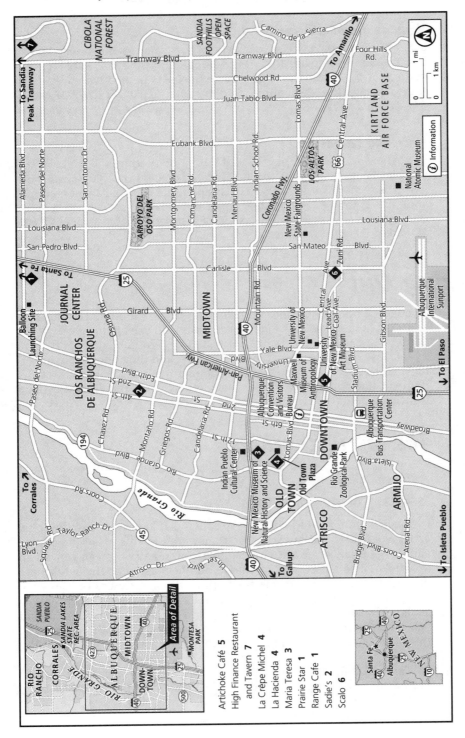

Artichoke Café **5**
High Finance Restaurant
and Tavern **7**
La Crêpe Michel **4**
La Hacienda **4**
Maria Teresa **3**
Prairie Star **1**
Range Cafe **1**
Sadie's **2**
Scalo **6**

High Finance Restaurant and Tavern

$$$–$$$$ Atop Sandia Peak   STEAK/SEAFOOD

Here's a great way to get "high" without breaking any laws or even having a hangover. Ride the Sandia Peak Tramway (see "Exploring Albuquerque," later in this chapter) to the 10,678-foot top of the Sandia Mountains and dine with views across the Rio Grande Valley and hundreds of miles to the west. The decor follows the restaurant's high-finance theme, with lots of shiny brass and carved woodwork. Though the food isn't the most notable in the state, you can find tasty dishes such as tenderloin beef flambé, rack of ribs, or chicken penne pasta (in a white cream sauce). Drinks from a full bar may enhance the high, and the ride down after dark is, well, probably the closest you will ever get to owning a 15-mile-wide bowl of diamonds.

40 Tramway Rd. NE (from I-25 or I-40, take Tramway exit and follow the signs; the restaurant is accessible only by tram). ☎ *505-243-9742. Dinner reservations required. Main courses: $14.95–$39.95. Tramway $10 with dinner reservations ($14 without). AE, DC, DISC, MC, V. Open: Daily lunch and dinner.*

La Crêpe Michel

$$–$$$$ Old Town   COUNTRY FRENCH

Though your eyes tell you that you're just digging into another burrito, your taste buds have a different take on one of the many varieties of crepes at this casual French restaurant down a quaint alley in Old Town. Chef Claudie Zamet-Wilcox from France serves up a variety of the delectable rolled concoctions, from the *crepe aux fruits de mer* (blend of sea scallops, bay scallops, and shrimp in a velouté sauce with mushrooms) to a *crepe aux fraises* (with strawberries) for dessert. For those who have had their fill of stuffed pancakes, a variety of fish, chicken, and beef specials show up daily. The previously dry restaurant recently acquired a beer and wine license.

400 San Felipe NW, C2 (just off Old Town Plaza). ☎ *505-242-1251. Reservations accepted. Main courses: $5.95–$12.50 lunch; $7.50–$19.95 dinner. MC, V. Open: Tues–Sun lunch; Tues–Sat dinner.*

Maria Theresa

$$$–$$$$ Old Town   AMERICAN/NEW MEXICAN

Can a person eat the past? Well, if it were possible, this would be the place to chomp down on some delectable Victorian Old West, but without the dust. The dining tables are set within the seven rooms of this 1840s house, once the home of Salvador Armijo, an early Albuquerque landholder. Your best bets are the chicken fajitas, the bacon-wrapped tenderloin, or the pasta Maria Theresa (boneless chicken sautéed with mushrooms, green chile, and spinach in a fontina–New York cheddar sauce) served over egg *tagliatelle* (wide, flat noodles). During the warm months, spend some time languishing on the lovely patio near a fountain and sipping some of the best margaritas in town.

618 Rio Grande Blvd. NW. ☎ 505-242-3900. Reservations recommended. Main courses: $8–$12 lunch; $13–$26 dinner. AE, DC, MC, V. Open: Daily lunch and dinner.

Range Cafe

$$–$$$$ Bernalillo   AMERICAN/NEW MEXICAN

James Beard meets Wyatt Earp at this contemporary American cafe set in an Old West drugstore on the main drag of Bernalillo about 15 minutes from Albuquerque. Food here ranges from hearty down-home meals, such as meatloaf with roasted garlic mashed potatoes, to refined selections, such as scallops in a lime cream sauce with red bell and poblano peppers tossed with *farfalle* (bowtie pasta). It can be a busy place, with locals, families, and travelers filling the tables and chairs that are hand-painted with whimsical stars and clouds. This is a primo spot to stop en route to Santa Fe.

925 Camino del Pueblo (take I-25 north to Bernalillo). ☎ 505-867-1700. Reservations not accepted. Internet: www.rangecafe.com. *Main courses: $4–$8.95 lunch; $6.50–$19.95 dinner. AE, DISC, MC, V. Open: Daily lunch and dinner.*

Sadie's

$$ North Valley   NEW MEXICAN

Although this restaurant's main dining room is a little too big and the atmosphere's a little too bright, something here draws crowds: the food. It's simply some of the best in New Mexico, with tasty sauces and large portions. I recommend the enchilada, either chicken or beef. The stuffed *sopaipilla* (a deep-fried, puffed pastry) dinner is also delicious and is one of the restaurant's signature dishes. All meals come with chips and salsa, beans, and sopaipillas. A kids' menu offers both American and New Mexican options. Sadie's has a full bar, with excellent margaritas (and TV screens for sports lovers).

6230 Fourth St. NW. (at Solar Rd. between Osuna Rd. and Montaño Rd.). ☎ 505-345-5339. Reservations accepted only for parties of eight or more. Main courses: $7–$12. AE, DC, DISC, MC, V. Open: Daily lunch and dinner.

Scalo

$$–$$$$ Nob Hill   NORTHERN ITALIAN

Looking for a little Italian urban adventure? Albuquerque locals find it at this Nob Hill restaurant. The decor is simple and elegant, with white tablecloths set off by a black marble floor. A good way to start is with the *calamaretti fritti* (fried baby squid served with a spicy marinara and lemon *aioli* — a kind of mayonaisse). From there, your best bet is one of the daily specials. You can also find a selection of pastas (including excellent ravioli) for lunch and dinner, as well as meat, chicken, and fish dishes.

3500 Central Ave. SE. (at Carlisle Blvd.). ☎ *505-255-8782. Reservations recommended. Main courses: $8–$16 lunch; $9–$25 dinner. AE, DC, DISC, MC, V. Open: Mon–Sat lunch; dinner daily.*

The runner-up restaurants

Albuquerque's primo restaurant district is the Nob Hill area, where you can find everything from pizza to Pacific Rim cuisine. Old Town has a few restaurants on its plaza that serve decent but not great New Mexican food, as well as a number of decent cafes tucked into alleys. Here are a couple of other options.

La Hacienda

$$ Old Town   If you're strolling around Old Town and want to sample some New Mexican food, this restaurant gives you a good taste in a festive Old Spain atmosphere, although the food isn't as good as Sadie's. Former President Clinton ate here during a 1998 visit. *302 San Felipe St. NW (at North Plaza).* ☎ *505-243-3131.*

Prairie Star

$$$$ Bernalillo   Easily blending new and old, this restaurant serves nouveau cuisine, such as rock shrimp rell.os (stuffed peppers) with a Japanese curry aioli, while maintaining a traditional ambiance in a 1940s mission style adobe complete with vigas (log beams) and thick walls. *255 Prairie Star Rd. (travel north of town for 15 miles on I-25, take exit 242, travel west 2 miles past Jemez Dam Rd. to Tamaya Blvd., and turn right).* ☎ *505-867-3327. Internet:* www.santaanagolf.com.

Exploring Albuquerque

Albuquerque's original town site, known today as Old Town, is where you can spend much of your sightseeing time. Here, grouped around the plaza, are the venerable Church of San Felipe de Neri and numerous restaurants, art galleries, and crafts shops. Several important museums are situated close by. Within a few blocks are the Museum of Natural History and the recently completed Albuquerque Biological Park (near Central Avenue and Tingley Drive NW). But don't get stuck in Old Town. Elsewhere you find the Sandia Peak Tramway, Kirtland Air Force Base and the National Atomic Museum, the University of New Mexico with its museums, and a number of natural attractions. Within day-trip range are several pueblos (Native American villages) and a trio of significant monuments (see Chapter 12).

Central Albuquerque Attractions

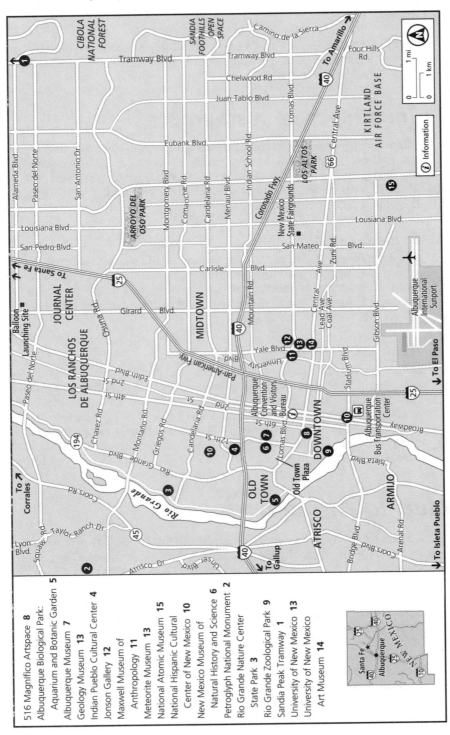

516 Magnifico Artspace **8**
Albuquerque Biological Park:
    Aquarium and Botanic Garden **5**
Albuquerque Museum **7**
Geology Museum **13**
Indian Pueblo Cultural Center **4**
Jonson Gallery **12**
Maxwell Museum of
    Anthropology **11**
Meteorite Museum **13**
National Atomic Museum **15**
National Hispanic Cultural
    Center of New Mexico **10**
New Mexico Museum of
    Natural History and Science **6**
Petroglyph National Monument **2**
Rio Grande Nature Center
    State Park **3**
Rio Grande Zoological Park **9**
Sandia Peak Tramway **1**
University of New Mexico **13**
University of New Mexico
    Art Museum **14**

Discovering the top attractions

Albuquerque Biological Park: Aquarium and Botanic Garden

Old Town

Are you brave enough to face off a sand-tiger shark or a moray eel? This park tests your courage, a little. After all, you are separated from the beasts by plenty of glass. The self-guided aquarium tour takes you from a touch pool, where at certain times of day children can gently touch hermit crabs and starfish, to a bold walk under an arched eel tank. The culminating show consists of a 285,000-gallon shark tank, where many species of fish and 15 to 20 sand-tiger, brown, and nurse sharks swim around looking ominous. Next door, in a football-stadium-sized conservatory, is an elaborate botanical garden. Allow at least two hours to see both parks. A restaurant is on the premises.

2601 Central Ave. NW (from I-40, take the Rio Grande Blvd. exit to Central Ave.; head west to the first light at New York Ave.). ☎ *505-764-6200. Admission: $4.50 for adults, $2.50 for children 3–12 and for seniors age 65 and over, free for children under 3. Open: Tues–Sun 9 a.m.–5 p.m.; Sat–Sun during June, July, and Aug 9 a.m.–6 p.m. Ticket sales stop at 4:30 p.m. Closed: New Year's Day, Thanksgiving, and Christmas.*

Albuquerque Museum

Old Town

Catch up on the latest in conquistador fashion or the hottest 18th-century interiors at this excellent museum near Old Town. You see the real thing: Don Quixote–style helmets, swords, even horse armor — all part of the largest collection of Spanish-colonial artifacts in the United States. You can wander through an 18th-century house with an adobe floor and walls and see gear used by *vaqueros,* the original cowboys who came to the area in the 16th century. A weaving exhibition allows kids to try spinning wool, and a trapping section provides them with pelts to touch. A gift shop sells books and jewelry and has a nice selection of Navajo dolls. Allow one to two hours to see the museum.

2000 Mountain Rd. NW (east of the intersection with Rio Grande Blvd.). ☎ *505-243-7255. Free admission, but donations are appreciated. Open: Tues–Sun 9 a.m.–5 p.m. Closed: Major holidays.*

Indian Pueblo Cultural Center

Old Town

Here's your crash course on New Mexico's Native American culture. Owned by the 19 pueblos of New Mexico, this museum is modeled after Pueblo Bonito, a spectacular ninth-century ruin in Chaco Culture National Historic Park. You journey through the evolution of the Pueblo people from prehistory to the present. Kids can learn with hands-on exhibits. At various times, Native American dancers perform, and artists demonstrate their crafts expertise. Allow one to two hours to see the museum.

2401 12th St. NW (at Menaul Blvd.). ☎ *800-766-4405 or 505-843-7270. Admission: $4 adults, $3 seniors, $1 students, free for children age 4 and under. Open: Daily 9 a.m.– 5:30 p.m.; restaurant 7:30 a.m.–3:30 p.m. Closed New Year's Day, Thanksgiving, and Christmas.*

National Atomic Museum

Southeast of Nob Hill on Kirtland Air Force Base

Few places in the world have a contemporary history as resonant as New Mexico, home of the first atomic bomb. This museum offers the next-best introduction to the nuclear age after the Bradbury Science Museum in Los Alamos, making for an interesting one- to two-hour perusal. You find full-scale models of the "Fat Man" and "Little Boy" bombs, as well as displays and films on the peaceful application of nuclear technology. Other exhibits deal with the use and development of robotics, with plenty of strange R2-D2 types moving around for kids to enjoy.

Wyoming Blvd. and K St. (on Kirtland Air Force Base). ☎ *505-284-3243. Internet:* www.atomicmuseum.com. *Admission: $3 adults, $2 children age 7–18 and seniors, free for children age 6 and under. Visitors must obtain passes (and a map) at the Wyoming or Gibson Gate of the base. Open: Daily 9 a.m.–5 p.m. Closed: New Year's Day, Easter, Thanksgiving, and Christmas.*

National Hispanic Cultural Center of New Mexico

South of Old Town

Built in *Az-tech* style — a melding of ancient and high-tech — this hot new museum celebrates the world's Hispanic roots by showcasing historic and contemporary Hispanic arts, humanities, and achievements from the past 400 years. The $50 million facility, located on 22 acres near the Rio Grande, has Spanish and Latin American architectural roots, with courtyards, plazas, and *portals* (covered porches) throughout. At press time, the highlights were in the visual arts arena, with other areas to open up in the future. A restaurant on-site serves Hispanic, New Mexican, and American food.

1701 Fourth St. SW (follow Fourth St. south from downtown for 1 mile to Avenida Cesar Chavez). ☎ *505-246-2261. Internet:* www.nmmnh-abq.mus.nm.us/hcc/ hcc.html. *Admission: Free at press time. Open: Tues–Sun 10 a.m.–5 p.m.*

New Mexico Museum of Natural History and Science

Old Town

Talk about time traveling — even Captain Kirk would be impressed with this museum's journey through 12 billion years of natural history, from the formation of the universe to the present day. You experience such highlights as a simulated volcano and the Evolator (kids love this!), a time-travel ride that moves and rumbles, taking you 2,000 meters up (or down) and through 38 million years of history. Be sure to check out the newest addition to the museum, the LodeStar Astronomy Center, a sophisticated planetarium with a Virtual Voyages Simulation theater. Those exhibits, as well as the Dynamax Theater, which surrounds you with images and sound, cost an additional fee. A gift shop on the ground floor sells imaginative nature games and other curios.

1801 Mountain Rd. NW (two blocks east of Rio Grande Blvd.). ☎ *505-841-2800. Admission: $5 adults, $4 seniors, $2 children age 3–12, free for children under 3. Planetarium, Virtual Voyages, and Dynamax cost extra, each with prices in the $6 range for adults and $3 range for children. Buying ticket combinations qualifies you for discounts. Open: Daily 9 a.m.–5 p.m. Closed: Non-holiday Mondays Jan and Sept.*

Old Town

Northeast of Central Ave. and Rio Grande Blvd. NW

Created in 1780, the Old Town Plaza once served as the central business district for the region. Today, the charming, tree-shaded square hearkens back to those old days, with its bandstand and Pueblo-style and Territorial-style buildings. (Territorial style is a mixture of Midwestern and New Orleans styles, incorporating a broad range of elements, from brick facades and cornices to Victorian bric-a-brac.) A maze of cobbled courtyard walkways leads from the plaza to hidden patios and gardens, where many of Old Town's 150 galleries and shops are located. Pueblo and Navajo artisans often display their pottery, blankets, and silver jewelry on the sidewalks lining the plaza. The most notable structure is the **Church of San Felipe de Neri,** which faces the plaza on its north side. It's a cozy church with wonderful stained-glass windows and vivid *retablos* (altar paintings). This house of worship has been in almost continuous use for about 290 years. Many other historical structures, once residences, adorn Old Town. To see them you may want to take the excellent Old Town historic **walking tour** which originates at the Albuquerque Museum (described earlier in this section) at 11 a.m. Tuesday through Sunday during spring, summer, and fall. If this time isn't convenient, the museum publishes a brochure for a self-guided walking tour of Old Town. Allow one to two hours to tour Old Town. Shops are generally open from 10 a.m. to 5 p.m.

Petroglyph National Monument

West Mesa

Come here to discover volcanoes covered with ancient symbols — wow, does that sound exotic or what? The lava flows are covered with some 15,000 petroglyphs left etched on the dark basalt. All you have to do is stroll through, and you not only get a great historic hit, but if you're in tune with the heavens, you may get a spiritual one as well. The site, which was once a hunting and gathering area for prehistoric Native Americans, is considered sacred to their descendents, the area Pueblo tribes. You should stop at the visitor center to get a map and directions to the best sites. Allow about one hour.

6001 Unser Blvd. NW (3½ miles north of I-40 on Unser Blvd.). ☎ 505-899-0205. Admission: $1 per vehicle weekdays, $2 weekends. Open: Visitor Center and Boca Negra area daily 8 a.m.–5 p.m.; other sites open during daylight hours. Closed: New Year's Day, Thanksgiving, and Christmas.

Rio Grande Nature Center State Park

Old Town

Looking to do the Walden thing in the midst of your sightseeing hustle? Here's the fast track to nature (oh, wouldn't Thoreau hate that notion?). The center, located just a few miles north of Old Town, spans 270 acres of riverside forest and meadows that include stands of century-old cottonwoods, a three-acre pond, and two marsh wetlands. Located on the Rio Grande Flyway, it's an excellent place for bird-watching — more than 260 species have landed here at various times.

2901 Candelaria Rd. NW (at the western end of Candelaria). ☎ 505-344-7240. Admission: $1 adults, 50¢ children age 6 and older, free for children under age 6. Open: Daily 10 a.m.–5 p.m. Closed: New Year's Day, Thanksgiving, and Christmas.

Rio Grande Zoological Park

Old Town

If I had to be an animal in captivity, I'd call this zoo home. Most of the 1,200 animals have plenty of room (the zoo is spread across 60 acres) and lots of shade (it's nestled under a riverside *bosque* — Spanish for "forest"). The polar bears and sea lions (both with underwater viewing) make you and the kids laugh until your sides cramp, as do the gorillas and orangutans, with their hauntingly human antics. Numerous snack bars dot the zoo grounds, and La Ventana Gift Shop carries film and souvenirs. Allow about two hours.

903 10th St. SW (from I-25 take the Lead and Coal aves. exit; take Lead Ave. west to 10th St., and head south to the zoo). ☎ 505-764-6200. Admission: $4.50 adults, $2.50 for seniors and children ages 3–12, free for children under age 3. Open: Tues–Sun 9 a.m.–5 p.m., and on summer weekends until 6 p.m. Ticket sales stop at 4:30 p.m. Closed: New Year's Day, Thanksgiving, and Christmas.

Sandia Peak Tramway

Northeast Heights

If you like a thrill with little consequence, you may appreciate a ride on this tramway to the top of Sandia Peak, 10,678 feet above sea level. This is a fun and exciting half-day or evening outing, allowing for incredible views of the Albuquerque landscape and wildlife. Several hiking trails are available on Sandia Peak, and one of them — La Luz Trail — takes you on a steep and rigorous trek from base to summit. The views in all directions are extraordinary. *Note:* The trails on Sandia may not be suitable for children.

A popular and expensive restaurant, High Finance Restaurant and Tavern, awaits at Sandia's summit (see "Dining Out," earlier in this chapter). Special tram rates apply with dinner.

10 Tramway Loop NE (take I-25 north to Tramway Rd. Exit 234, then proceed east about 5 miles on Tramway Rd.; or take Tramway Blvd., Exit 167 north of I-40 approximately 8½ miles. Turn east the last half mile on Tramway Rd.). ☎ *505-856-7325. Internet:* www.sandiapeak.com. *Admission: $14 adults, $10 seniors 62 and over and children age 5–12, free for children under age 5. Open: Summer daily 9 a.m.–10 p.m.; spring and fall Sun–Tues and Thurs 9 a.m.–8 p.m., Wed 5–8 p.m., Fri–Sat 9 a.m.–9 p.m.; ski season (Dec–Mar) Thurs–Tues 9 a.m.–8 p.m., Wed noon–8 p.m.*

University of New Mexico Museums

University District

I can hardly stand to be on a campus anymore (all those nightmarish memories of tests), but this is one campus that's capable of luring me in. With five excellent museums, the state's largest institution of higher learning has exhibits for many interests. The best way to see the museums and parts of the campus is on a walking tour, which can make for a nice two- to three-hour morning or afternoon outing. I won't go into the details of each here, but I do include phone numbers so that you can find your way on your own. You can obtain a campus map at the Student Service Center, located north of the University of New Mexico Art Museum. Begin at the **Maxwell Museum of Anthropology** (☎ 505-277-4404,** situated on the west side of the campus on Redondo Dr., south of Las Lomas Blvd.). You can find parking meters there. Next, head to the **Geology Museum** (☎ 505-277-4204) and **Meteorite Museum** (☎ 505-277-1644) in Northrup Hall. From there, walk over to the **University of New Mexico Art Museum** (☎ 505-277-4001), and finish up at the **Jonson Gallery,** at 1909 Las Lomas Blvd. NE (☎ 505-277-4967). If you can't do all the museums, focus on the Maxwell Museum of Anthropology, the Meteorite Museum, and the University of New Mexico Art Museum.

University of New Mexico main address and phone number: Yale Blvd. NE (about 2 miles east of downtown Albuquerque, north of Central Ave. and east of University Blvd.). ☎ *505-277-0111. Internet:* www.unm.edu. *Most museums open Tues–Fri 9 a.m.–4 p.m. and Tues evening 5–8 p.m., though you should call for exact times.*

Finding more cool things to see and do

If you're saturated with sights, you may be ready for some other diversions. Here are a few possibilities:

A mini downtown art walk

The **516 Magnífico Artspace** (☎ 505-242-8244), at 516 Central Ave. SW, is a great place to wander while you explore Route 66 (see Chapter 18) and the Civic Plaza. Here you see some excellent art shows as well as art events, from performance art to poetry to exhibit tours for kids. Admission is free. Hours are Tuesday through Saturday, from 12 a.m. to 5 p.m. After you leave there, step next door to **Skip Maisel's** (see "Shopping 'til You Drop," later in the chapter), where murals painted in 1933 by notable Navajo painter Harrison Begay and Pueblo painter Pablita Velarde adorn the outside of the store.

✔ **Cook an enchilada.** So you're afraid that when you head back home, you'll go through chile withdrawal? Believe it or not, New Mexican food isn't *that* hard to make — how complex can recipes be that are almost all different combinations of chile, beans, corn, and meat? Embark on a culinary adventure by calling Jane Butel, a leading Southwestern cooking authority and author of 14 cookbooks. At **Jane Butel's Cooking School,** 125 Second St. NW (La Posada de Albuquerque; ☎ **800-472-8229** or 505-243-2622; Internet: www.janebutel.com), you learn the history and techniques of Southwestern cuisine and have your chance to burn your own enchilada if you please. Call or check out her Web site for current schedules and fees.

✔ **Catch some hoops.** The University of New Mexico basketball team (☎ **505-925-5626**), nicknamed **"The Lobos"** (and in bad years the "Slowbos"), plays an average of 16 home games from late November to early March. Capacity crowds cheer the team at the 18,018-seat University Arena (seductively called "The Pit") at University and Stadium boulevards. Tickets range in price from about $13 to $18. UNM also has a **football** team which plays from September to November. You can purchase football tickets at the Lobos number.

Keeping active

Albuquerque's mild climate makes for year-round sports fun. Just remember to always bring a jacket and water, and don't talk to snakes and scorpions.

Ballooning

So you don't enjoy just *watching* all those colorful globes fly through the air? Me neither. To explore the Albuquerque skies first-hand, hook up with one of the many balloon operators in town. Rates start at about $135 per person per hour. Contact **Rainbow Ryders,** 11520 San Bernardino NE (☎ **505-823-1111;** Internet: www.rainbowryders.com), or **World Balloon Corporation,** 4800 Eubank Blvd. NE (☎ **505-293-6800**).

The annual **Kodak Albuquerque International Balloon Fiesta** is held the first through second weekends of October. See Chapter 2 for details.

Biking

The best of Albuquerque's bike-friendly areas, the **Foothills Trail,** runs along the base of the Sandia Mountains. Actually a whole network of trails accessed off Tramway Boulevard, this single-track heaven is fun for riders of all levels. Allow two hours to traverse back and forth on this trail that runs 7 miles one-way. For access from downtown, head east on Montgomery Boulevard past the intersection with Tramway Boulevard. Go left on Glenwood Hills Drive and head north for about half a mile before turning right onto a short road that leads to the Embudito Trailhead.

A great family biking destination is **Rio Grande Nature Center State Park** (see listing under "Discovering the top attractions," earlier in this chapter). Along the riverside bosque, this easy 2- to 10-mile round-trip journey takes you along century-old cottonwoods to a view of the mighty Rio Grande (which is not quite so mighty any more, because so many people use its water to grow crops and quench thirsts). Allow one to three hours. From I-40, take the Rio Grande Boulevard exit and travel north to Candelaria Road. Turn left and drive to the road's end, where you see the parking lot at 2901 Candelaria Rd. NW.

If you didn't bring your bike with you, head over to **Rio Mountain Sport,** 1210 Rio Grande NW (☎ **505-766-9970**); they can also hook you up with helmets, maps, and locks. For information about other mountain-biking areas, contact the **Albuquerque Convention and Visitors Bureau** (☎ **800-284-2282** or 505-842-9918; Internet: www.abqcvb.org).

Bird-watching

The **Rio Grande Nature Center State Park** (see listing under "Discovering the top attractions," earlier in this chapter) occupies 270 acres of riverside land and is smack in the way of the Rio Grande Flyway, an important migratory route for many birds, so it's an awesome place to see sandhill cranes, Canada geese, and quail. At **Bosque del Apache National Wildlife Refuge** (☎ **505-835-1828**) you won't have to crane your neck to see cranes. Just look in any direction and, in winter, you can see thousands of them (and their Canada geese friends too). The refuge is located 90 miles south of Albuquerque on I-25 and is well worth the drive. For details, see Chapter 17.

Golfing

Although Albuquerque isn't exactly a golf destination, the city has many courses — some that can even flaunt a few accolades. These include:

- **Public courses.** The **Championship Golf Course** at the University of New Mexico, 3601 University Blvd. SE (☎ 505-277-4546), is one of the best in the Southwest and was rated one of the country's top-25 public links by *Golf Digest*. **Paradise Hills Golf Course,** 10035 Country Club Lane NW (☎ 505-898-7001), is a popular 18-hole golf course that was recently renovated.

  Other Albuquerque courses to check with for tee times are **Ladera,** 3401 Ladera Dr. NW (☎ 505-836-4449); **Los Altos,** 9717 Copper Ave. NE (☎ 505-298-1897); **Puerto del Sol,** 1800 Girard Blvd. SE (☎ 505-265-5636); and **Arroyo del Oso,** 7001 Osuna Rd. NE (☎ 505-884-7505).

  Greens fees for these public courses range from $16 to $67.

- **Pueblo courses.** If you're willing to drive a short distance just outside Albuquerque, you can play at the **Santa Ana Golf Club** at Santa Ana Pueblo, 288 Prairie Star Rd., Bernalillo (☎ 505-867-9464), which was rated by *The New York Times* as one of the best public golf courses in the country. Rentals are available (call for information), and greens fees range from $30 to $38. In addition, **Isleta Pueblo,** 4001 Highway 47, has recently completed building an 18-hole golf course (☎ 505-869-0950); greens fees range from $34 to $40.

Hiking

Even though the Sandia Mountains look like one big face with a thinning hairline of blinking radio towers, they're actually an intricate series of mountains, which make up part of the 1.6-million-acre Cíbola National Forest. Within town, the best hike is the **Embudito Trail,** which heads up into the foothills with spectacular views down across Albuquerque. The 5½-mile one-way hike is moderate to difficult. Allow one to eight hours, depending on how far you want to go. Access is off Montgomery Boulevard and Glenwood Hills Drive. The premier Sandia Mountain hike is **La Luz Trail,** a very strenuous journey from the Sandia foothills to the top of the Crest. It's a 15-mile round-trip jaunt, half that if you take the Sandia Peak Tramway (see "Discovering the top attractions," earlier in this chapter) either up or down. Allow a full day for this hike. Access is off Tramway Boulevard and Forest Service Road 333. For more details about trails and sites, contact **Sandia Ranger Station,** Highway 337 south toward Tijeras (☎ 505-281-3304).

Horseback riding

Sometimes I just have to get in a saddle and eat some trail dust. If you get similar hankerings, call **Turkey Track Stables, Inc.,** 1306 U.S. 66 E. Tijeras (☎ 505-281-1772). Located about 15 miles east of Albuquerque, the outfit offers rides on trails in the Manzano foothills. Rides run about $25 per person for two hours; a kid's gentle horse ride is $10.

Skiing

Believe it or not, there's snow in them thar hills in winter. Most years, the **Sandia Peak Ski Area** (☎ **505-242-9133**) gets dusted enough to make for some nice family skiing. Plenty of beginner and intermediate runs line the slopes. However, if you're looking for bumps or an adrenaline rush, head north to Santa Fe or Taos. At Sandia Peak, you find 30 runs above the day lodge and ski-rental shop. Four chairs and two ground lifts accommodate 3,400 skiers an hour. All-day lift tickets are $36 for adults, $26 for children and seniors (age 62 and over), and free for those ages 72 and over. The season runs mid-December to mid-March. You can access Sandia Peak Ski Area either by riding the Sandia Peak Tramway (see "Discovering the top attractions," earlier in this chapter) or by driving east on I-40 to N.M. 14. Follow N.M. 14 to N.M. 536, which takes you to Sandia Crest.

Tennis

Albuquerque has 29 public parks with courts perfect for whacking balls. Because of the city's vast size, your best bet is to call the **Albuquerque Convention and Visitors Bureau** (☎ **800-284-2282**) to find out which park is closest to your hotel.

Seeing Albuquerque by guided tour

Although I'm not much for the cow sensibility, being herded from place to place by a tour guide, sometimes I find that a city tour gives me a good sense of a place so that I can further explore. Specialized tours are often less crowded than general tours, and they're full of information I'd have to search years to find on my own. Here are some of my favorite tour picks.

General tours

Gray Line/Coach USA (☎ **800-256-8991** or 505-242-3880; Internet: www.rt66.com/grayline) has a fun city tour that covers Kirtland Air Force Base and Route 66 through downtown and Old Town. The tour costs $23 for adults and $11.50 for children. This company also offers a tour to Acoma Pueblo's Sky City ($35 for adults and $17.50 for children), as well as a Balloon Fiesta tour that takes you from your hotel to the balloon park, helps you through the crowds, and, for an additional cost, gets you on a short balloon ride. The tour runs $25 per person, with an additional $10 per person for the balloon ride.

Special-interest tours

Aventura Artistica (☎ **800-808-7352** or 619-350-9321; Internet: www.newmexicotours.com) offers a broad range of weeklong tours with unique themes, such as their Soothing Tour (which includes a night at the Santa Fe Opera and stays in New Mexico spas) and their Artistic Adventure (which includes hands-on work with artists and a visit to the home of artist Georgia O'Keeffe). They also have photography and golf tours. All tours last one week and average $1,150 per person, double occupancy.

Following one- or two-day itineraries

For me, the perfect Albuquerque day has a good mix of indoor and outdoor activities. Fortunately, Albuquerque has a mild enough climate so that you can be fairly comfortable outdoors during any season. Many of the outdoor activities are on the outskirts, though, so if you don't care to drive much, you may want to stay close to Old Town for your sightseeing. Unless otherwise mentioned, for details on all the sights and restaurants that I mention in these itineraries, see the related sections in this chapter.

One-day itinerary

If you have just a single day in Albuquerque, start out early at the **Indian Pueblo Cultural Center.** Spend a few hours there, then drive to **Old Town,** about five minutes away. Wander around the Old Town Plaza, and if it's Tuesday through Sunday in the spring, summer, or fall, take in the historic walking tour. If you'd rather shop, be sure to check out the jewelry and pottery that the Native Americans spread on blankets under the portal. Also, wander into some of the narrow side streets to get a feel for the neighborhood. Old Town Plaza is a good place to have lunch. Either before or after you eat, take a five-minute walk to the **Albuquerque Museum,** where you can spend about an hour getting a feel of New Mexico history. Across the street from the Albuquerque Museum is the **New Mexico Museum of Natural History and Science,** where you may want to spend two hours. In the late afternoon, find your way to Central Avenue just south of Old Town and drive east on **Route 66.** This takes you right through downtown (where you can note plenty of Mother Road–era signage — see Chapter 18), through Nob Hill, and into the Northeast Heights. Finish your day with a ride up the **Sandia Peak Tramway.** After you reach the top, you may want to hike a little along the crest. Ideally, you should ride up during daylight and ride down at night. You may even want to dine at **High Finance Restaurant and Tavern** at the top.

Two-day itinerary

During your first day, follow the one-day itinerary I just described. On day two, start early at the **National Atomic Museum,** where you can spend about an hour and a half. Then work your way west to a place bent on preserving nature rather than blowing it up, **Albuquerque Biological Park: Aquarium and Botanic Garden,** where you can spend two hours or maybe more. If you want to see more wildlife, head over to the **Rio Grande Zoo.** In the afternoon, continue driving west out to **Petroglyph National Monument.** There you can spend about 15 minutes in the visitor center and then head out to the Mesa Point Trail for a half-hour hike through the petroglyphs. In the evening, if you like cultural activities, check into the schedule for the **New Mexico Ballet Company** or the **New Mexico Symphony Orchestra.** Better yet, go to **Sadie's** for a margarita and an enchilada or to the **Martini Grille** for a you-know-what and a burger.

Shopping 'til You Drop

If you hope to linger in glossy, hiply lit malls, you're out of luck in this city. Though three of New Mexico's largest malls inhabit Albuquerque, the city is not a shopping destination like Scottsdale, Arizona, or Dallas, Texas. Much of the available shopping is the old fashioned kind, in shops with plenty of character, often with the owner presiding.

Business hours vary, but shops are generally open Monday to Saturday from 10 a.m. to 6 p.m.; many have extended hours; some have reduced hours; and a few, especially in shopping malls or during the high tourist season, are open on Sunday.

Best shopping areas

By far, the greatest concentration of **galleries** is in Old Town; others are spread around the city, with smaller groupings in the University District and the Northeast Heights. You find some interesting shops in the Nob Hill area, which is just west of the University of New Mexico. That whole area has an Art Deco feel. What follows are some recommendations for the greater Albuquerque area.

Old Town

Though you encounter a lot of trinket-like junk in Old Town, you also find beautiful buys at the many worthwhile **galleries.** Here you can find everything from fudge with chiles in it to Spanish birdcages, and maybe even a few practical things that you can wear. The bonus to shopping in Old Town is the beauty of the place — much like an 18th-century village.

Downtown

For years now, Albuquerque has been in the midst of major revitalization, turning the downtown into a fun place to wander among Route 66 memorabilia and find some good deals on Native American and Hispanic arts and crafts. While in the area, stick your head into **516 Magnífico Artspace** for a little art hit. (See the box "A mini downtown art walk," earlier in this chapter, for information on this place.)

Nob Hill

Albuquerque's hippest shopping district has a lot of variety, from good furnishings to one-of-a-kind jewelry. An added bonus is the number of cafes where you can rest your feet and gear up for more exhausting cash handling.

Getting mall'd

Albuquerque has three of the largest shopping malls in New Mexico. Two are within two blocks of each other on Louisiana Boulevard just north of I-40: **Coronado Center** (☎ 505-881-4600) and **Winrock Center** (☎ 505-888-3038). The other is **Cottonwood Mall** at 10,000 Coors Blvd. NW (☎ 505-899-SHOP). Though none are shopping destinations in their own rights, they can provide some fun. If you have higher taste (or like to pretend you do!), a nice boutique mall is **The Courtyard,** 1500 San Mateo Blvd. NE (no phone number available). Shops at The Courtyard are open Monday to Saturday from 10 a.m. to 5 p.m. The other three malls are open approximately Monday through Saturday from 10 a.m. to 9 p.m. and Sunday from 12 a.m. to 6 p.m., with hours varying during holidays.

What to look for and where to find it

Albuquerque is a good place to shop for Southwestern goods, from Navajo blankets to squash-blossom necklaces. Though you won't find the variety that you do in Santa Fe, the prices in Albuquerque tend to be lower. The best items to buy in Albuquerque are traditional Native American and Hispanic works.

If you're into art galleries, consult the brochure published by the Albuquerque Gallery Association, "A Select Guide to Albuquerque Galleries," or Wingspread Communications' annual *The Collector's Guide to Albuquerque,* both widely distributed at shops. Once a month, usually from 5 to 9 p.m. on the third Friday, the Albuquerque Art Business Association (☎ 505-244-0362 for information) sponsors an **ArtsCrawl** to dozens of galleries and studios, providing a great way to meet the artists.

Arts and crafts

If you're in Old Town and want to really peruse a broad range of art, head to the **Amapola Gallery,** 2045 S. Plaza St. NW (☎ 505-242-4311). Fifty artists and craftspeople show their talents at this lovely cooperative gallery off a cobbled courtyard. You find pottery, paintings, textiles, carvings, baskets, jewelry, and other items. Another good Old Town spot is **La Piñata,** No. 2 Patio Market (☎ 505-242-2400). This shop features (what else?) piñatas, in shapes from dinosaurs to parrots to pigs, as well as paper flowers, puppets, toys, and crushable bolero hats decorated with ribbons. Also in Old Town, **Tanner Chaney**

Galleries, 323 Romero NW (☎ **800-444-2242** or 505-247-2242), has been in business since 1875 and has fine jewelry, pottery, and rugs.

Mariposa Gallery, 3500 Central Ave., SE (☎ **505-268-6828**), has moved away from Old Town but is still worth a visit. Consistently voted the best gallery in Albuquerque by the *Alibi,* a weekly magazine, the store has fine contemporary crafts, including fiber arts, jewelry, clay works, sculptural glass, and other media. If you want a real bargain in Native American arts and crafts, head to **Skip Maisel's,** 510 Central Ave. SW (☎ **505-242-6526**; Internet: www.skipmaisels.com). Here you find a broad range of quality and price in goods such as pottery, weavings, and *kachinas* (ceremonial dolls).

Books

Bookstar, 2201 Louisiana Blvd. NE (☎ **505-883-2644**), has 18,000 square feet of floor space covered with bookcases. **Bound to Be Read,** 6300 San Mateo Blvd. NE (☎ **505-828-3502**), is an especially good place to find books on New Mexico and the outdoors. The store has a coffee bar that features live entertainment on Friday and Saturday nights. **Bookworks,** 4022 Rio Grande Blvd. NW (☎ **505-344-8139**), sells both new and used books and has one of the most complete Southwestern nonfiction and fiction sections in the region. The shop also carries CDs, cassettes, and books on tape.

Crafts

Bien Mur Indian Market Center, I-25 at Tramway Rd. NE (☎ **800-365-5400** or 505-821-5400), is Sandia Pueblo's crafts market on its reservation, just beyond Albuquerque's northern city limits. The market sells turquoise and silver jewelry, pottery, baskets, and other arts and crafts. **Gallery One,** in the Nob Hill Shopping Center, 3500 Central SE (☎ **505-268-7449**), features folk art, jewelry, contemporary crafts, and natural fiber clothing. If you want some great buys on Native American crafts, check out **Ortega's Indian Arts and Crafts,** 6600 Menaul Blvd. NE, #53 (☎ **505-881-1231**), the sister store to the notable Ortega's in the western New Mexico city of Gallup.

Fashions

Albuquerque Pendleton, 1100 San Mateo Blvd. NE, Suite 4 (☎ **505-255-6444**), is the place to cuddle up with a large selection of blankets and shawls and haul them away in a handbag. **Western Warehouse,** 6210 San Mateo Blvd. NE (☎ **505-883-7161**), has plenty of hats and boots (8,000 pairs) to satiate any cowboy craving.

Food

The Candy Lady, 524 Romero NW, Old Town (☎ **800-214-7731** or 505-243-6239; Internet: www.thecandylady.com), has been making chocolate for more than 20 years and is especially known for 21 varieties of fudge, including jalapeño flavor.

Furniture

Ernest Thompson Furniture, 4531 Osuna NE, at the corner of I-25 and Osuna Road (☎ 800-568-2344 or 505-344-1994), has original-design, handcrafted furniture. **Strictly Southwestern,** 1321 Eubank Blvd. NE (☎ 505-292-7337), sells nice solid pine and oak Southwestern-style furniture, as well as art, pottery, and other interior items.

Gifts/Souvenirs

If you like the exotic nature of Pier One Imports, check out **Jackalope International,** 834 Highway 44, Bernalillo (☎ 505-867-9813). Even if you're not looking to buy, you can take a little trip to another land — to many lands — at this shop that sells everything from Mexican *trasteros* (armoires) to sculpture, Christmas ornaments, and Balinese puppets.

Markets

If you don't mind crowds and you enjoy sunshine, the smell of cotton candy, and a nearly overwhelming amount of stuff, come to the **Flea Market** (☎ 505-265-1791) at the New Mexico State Fairgrounds. Every Saturday and Sunday year-round (except September), the fairgrounds host this market from 8 a.m. to 5 p.m. You can find turquoise and silver jewelry and locally made crafts, as well as newly manufactured inexpensive goods like socks and T-shirts. There's no admission charge.

Living It Up After Dark

You'd probably expect a city of 700,000 people to have a fair amount to do at night, and you're right. Albuquerque has an active performing arts and nightlife scene. What's best about the night scene here is that the performing arts are multicultural, with Hispanic and (to a lesser extent) Native American productions sharing stage space with Anglo works, including theater, opera, symphony, and dance. Albuquerque also attracts many national touring companies. Rock and jazz music predominates in nightclubs, although aficionados of country and other forms of music can find offerings here as well.

You can obtain complete information on all major cultural events from the **Albuquerque Convention and Visitors Bureau** (☎ 800-284-2282). Current listings appear in the two daily newspapers, *Albuquerque Tribune* and *Albuquerque Journal;* you can find detailed weekend arts calendars in the Thursday evening *Tribune* and the Friday morning *Journal.* The monthly magazine *On the Scene* also carries entertainment listings. Your best bet for exploring the club scene is to pick up a free copy of the *Alibi,* published weekly.

Check out **Ticketmaster,** 4004 Carlisle Blvd. NE (☎ 505-883-7800), to obtain tickets for nearly all major entertainment and sporting events. Discount tickets are often available for midweek and matinee performances. Check with specific theaters or concert halls.

Nightlife

Albuquerque ranks as a landing spot for major bands touring the country, and often, particularly during the summer, you can catch world-class live music. With the recently built **Journal Pavilion** (☎ **505-452-5100,** concert hotline at 505-246-8742), an outdoor concert hall seating 12,000 with state-of-the-art sound equipment and good sight-lines throughout, the city has hit the big time. It's open May to October. Other venues for live-music performances include the **KiMo Theatre,** 423 Central Ave. (☎ **505-764-1700**) and **Popejoy Hall,** University of New Mexico, Cornell Street at Redondo Drive South (☎ **800-905-3315** or 505-277-3824).

Clientele at Albuquerque's bars and clubs tend to be amazingly diverse. You find everyone from hippies to college nerds sipping away elbow to elbow. Bars close at 2 a.m., and covers range from nonexistent to $4 to $20 for a big-name musical act.

Rock and jazz clubs

The Albuquerque club scene is constantly changing, with new hot spots opening and old ones closing. A few of the jammin' joints are near the University while a few are downtown, within walking distance of each other. **Brewsters Pub,** 312 Central Ave. SW, downtown (☎ **505-247-2533**), offers live blues, jazz, folk, or light rock entertainment in a sports bar-type setting every Tuesday to Sunday. Also on the downtown club circuit is **Burt's Tiki Lounge,** 313 Gold Ave. (☎ **505-243-BURT**), which won *Alibi's* award for the best variety of drinks. The club offers live music Thursday to Sunday and charges no cover. A favorite pub in the university area is **Oniell's,** 3211 Central NE (☎ **505-256-0564**), which serves up good pub fare as well as live local music on Saturday nights, and Celtic and bluegrass on Sunday evenings. If it's a brewpub that strikes your fancy, head to **Kelly's BYOB,** 3222 Central SE (☎ **505-262-2739**). Set in a renovated auto/body shop, the place has excellent brew specials and live music Thursday to Saturday, usually with no cover. The **Martini Grille,** 4200 Central SE (☎ **505-255-4111**), on the eastern edge of the Nob Hill district, pours more than 30 flavors of martinis in primo glasses in a seductive Batman cave atmosphere and offers live entertainment most weekends and some weeknights.

Comedy clubs/Dinner theater

Laffs Comedy Caffé, San Mateo Boulevard and Osuna Road in the Fiesta del Norte Shopping Center (☎ **505-296-5653;** Internet: www.laffscomedy.com), lures in top acts from each coast, including comedians who have appeared on *The Late Show with David Letterman* and HBO. Shows happen Wednesday, Thursday, and Sunday nights and cost $7 per person with a two-drink and/or menu-item minimum purchase. Call for show times. **Mystery Café** at the Sheraton Uptown, at Menaul and Louisiana Boulevards (☎ **505-237-1385**), stirs Albuquerque and visitors up with a little interactive dinner theater. You help the characters solve a mystery as they serve you a four-course meal.

Reservations are a must. Tickets are approximately $35. Performances are on Friday and Saturday evenings at 7:30 p.m.; doors open at 7 p.m.

Country and western music

If you like to experience the best (biggest, fastest, hippest) in life, head to **Midnight Rodeo,** 4901 McLeod Rd. NE, near San Mateo Boulevard (☎ **505-888-0100**). Though technically it can prove only one of those bests — it's the Southwest's largest nightclub of any kind — it also has a fast, fancy-dancing crowd worth watching. Open Tuesday through Saturday, the club's cover runs $4 Friday and Saturday and is lower on other nights.

The arts

Albuquerque has a broad range of high-brow and not-so-high-brow cultural events appearing at a number of venues.

Dance and classical music

The **New Mexico Ballet Company** (☎ **505-292-4245**; Internet www. mandala.net/nmballet) has been entertaining in Albuquerque since I was a kid — 1972. They do the pointed toe thing generally at Popejoy Hall. Typically, they mount a fall production such as *Dracula,* a holiday one such as *The Nutcracker* or *A Christmas Carol,* and a contemporary spring production. Tickets run $20 to $25 adults, $10 to $20 children ages 12 and under. The **New Mexico Symphony Orchestra** (☎ **800-251-6676** for tickets and information, or 505-881-9590) performs classics as well as pops, family, and neighborhood concerts from September to May. I recommend going to one of the outdoor concerts under the bandshell at the Rio Grande Zoo. Ticket prices run $14 to $20, with discounts for children.

Theater

You may find yourself surprised, even shocked, at the range of theater available in Albuquerque. Whether you're like my mother and can spend days humming songs from Broadway musicals such as *A Chorus Line,* or like me and want to be shocked by locally written productions that tackle community issues, you just may find what you want during your visit. Tickets range in price from $10 to $23 for adults; most companies offer discounts for students and seniors.

Companies worth checking out include the **Musical Theatre Southwest,** 4804 Central Ave. SE (☎ **505-262-9301**), which from February to January produces six Broadway musicals and other smaller productions in either Popejoy Hall or its own 890-seat Hiland Theater. The **Albuquerque Little Theatre,** 224 San Pasquale Ave. SW (☎ **505-242-4750**), has been offering a variety of productions ranging from comedies to dramas to musicals (plus children's productions) since 1930. Seven plays and four children's productions are presented here annually during an August-to-May season. **La Compañía de Teatro de Albuquerque** (☎ 505-242-7929) offers an exciting inside view of New Mexico's culture. One of the few major professional Hispanic companies in the United States, La Compañía stages three shows per year, a mix of bilingual comedies, dramas, and musicals. Performances are held at the KiMo Theatre and South Broadway Cultural Center, 1025 Broadway SE. The theater's office is at 415 Central Ave. NW. The **Vortex Theatre,** 2004½ Central Ave. SE, at Buena Vista Drive (☎ **505-247-8600**), is known as Albuquerque's off-Broadway theater and presents a range of plays from classic to original. Performances take place year-round on Friday and Saturday at 8 p.m. and on Sunday at 6 p.m.

Quick Concierge: Albuquerque

AAA

For roadside assistance, dial ☎ 800-222-4357 or 505-291-6600.

American Express

An American Express Travel Service office is at Atlas Travel and Cruise, 1301 Wyoming Blvd. (☎ 505-291-6575). To report lost credit cards, call ☎ 800-528-2122.

Area Code

The telephone area code for all of New Mexico is **505**, though at press time plans were rumbling to add new ones in the state. For updates, contact the New Mexico Department of Tourism (☎ 800-733-6396; Internet: www.newmexico.org).

ATMs

You can choke money from machines all over town. (Wells Fargo and Bank of America are everywhere.)

Credit Cards

For lost or stolen cards, contact the following: Visa (☎ 800-847-2911), MasterCard (☎ 800-307-7309), American Express (☎ 800-668-2639), or Discover (☎ 800-347-2683).

Doctors

You should first contact your insurance provider; then call the Greater Albuquerque Medical Association at ☎ 505-821-4583 for a referral.

Emergencies

For police, fire, or ambulance, dial ☎ **911**.

Hospitals

The major facilities are Presbyterian Hospital, 1100 Central Ave. SE (☎ 505-841-1234; 505-841-1111 for emergency services); and University of New Mexico Hospital, 2211 Lomas Blvd. NE (☎ 505-272-2111; 505-272-2411 for emergency services).

Information

The main office of the Albuquerque Convention and Visitors Bureau is at 20 First Plaza NW (☎ 800-284-2282 or 505-842-9918; Internet: www.abqcvb.org). It's open Monday to Friday from 8 a.m. to 5 p.m. Information centers are at the airport, on the lower level at the bottom of the escalator, open daily from 9:30 a.m. to 8 p.m.; and in Old Town at 303 Romero St. NW, Suite 107, open daily from 9 a.m. to 5 p.m. Tape-recorded information about current local events is available from the bureau after 5 p.m. weekdays and all day Saturday and Sunday.

Internet Access

Kinko's provides high-speed Internet access at five locations throughout the city. Two convenient ones are 6220 San Mateo Blvd. NE at Academy Blvd. (☎ 505-821-2222) and 2706 Central Ave. SE at Princeton Blvd. (☎ 505-255-9673).

Liquor Laws

The legal drinking age is 21 in New Mexico. Bars may remain open until 2 a.m. Monday to Saturday and until midnight on Sunday. Licensed supermarkets and liquor stores sell wine, beer, and spirits daily until midnight, but package sales are not allowed on election days until after 7 p.m. and on Sundays until after noon. Transporting liquor through most Native American reservations is illegal.

Maps

The Albuquerque Convention and Visitors Bureau at 20 First Plaza NW (☎ 800-284-2282 or 505-842-9918) offers decent city maps.

Newspapers & Magazines

The two daily newspapers are the *Albuquerque Tribune,* published evenings, and the *Albuquerque Journal,* published mornings.

Pharmacies

Walgreens has many locations throughout Albuquerque. To find one near you, call ☎ 800-WALGREENS. Two centrally located ones open 24 hours are 8011 Harper Dr. NE at Wyoming (☎ 505-858-3134) and 5001 Montgomery Blvd. NE at San Mateo (☎ 505-881-5210).

Police

For emergencies, call ☎ 911. For other matters, contact the Albuquerque City Police (☎ 505-242-COPS) or the New Mexico State Police (☎ 505-841-9256).

Post Office

The Main Post Office, 1135 Broadway NE (☎ 505-245-9561), is open daily from 7:30 a.m. to 6 p.m. There are 26 branch offices, with about another dozen in surrounding communities.

Restrooms

Albuquerque is not known for its public restrooms. (In fact, in researching this book, I couldn't find anyone who even knew what they were.) Find them downtown at the Convention and Visitor's Bureau, 20 First Plaza, and in Old Town on the plaza.

Road Conditions

For a road report, call ☎ 800-432-4269.

Safety

Alhough Albuquerque is a relatively friendly city, it isn't really safe at night. Stick to crowded public areas during night time, especially in the downtown area. Car break-ins are common, so beware of leaving valuables in your car.

Smoking

Most public places, such as airports and auditoriums, allow smoking only in designated areas. While most clubs allow smoking, more and more restaurants relegate the activity to smoking sections and many ban the practice altogether.

Taxes

In Albuquerque, the sales tax is 5.9%. For hotel rooms, a lodging tax of 5% is added to the sales tax to total almost 11%.

Taxis

Yellow Cab (☎ 505-247-8888) serves the city and surrounding area 24 hours a day.

Time Zone

Mountain standard time.

Transit Information

Sun Tran of Albuquerque is the public bus system. Call ☎ 505-843-9200 for schedules and information.

Weather Updates

For time and temperature, call ☎ 505-247-1611. To get weather forecasts on the Internet, check www.accuweather.com and use the Albuquerque zip code, 87104.

Chapter 12

Side Trips from Albuquerque

. . . .

In This Chapter

▶ Touring the pueblos and ruins north of Albuquerque

▶ Road tripping on the Turquoise Trail

. . . .

*I*f you really want to get a sense of Pueblo life, your first priority should be to visit Acoma Pueblo (see Chapter 19), which offers the most intact glimpse of traditional Pueblo life. However, if you want a little more variety in your day (and want to make your way to Santa Fe), this chapter outlines two ways you can do that. On the first trip, you get to see Pueblo people in their daily lives, as well as ruins left by their ancestors. If you don't mind a long day, you can also see Los Alamos, the birthplace of the atomic bomb, in the same trip. For the second side trip, I outline another great way to get to Santa Fe by touring the "ghost towns" along the Turquoise Trail.

Day Trip 1: Exploring the Jemez Mountain Trail

Some people, like my mother, can spend their entire lives walking among the dead — we've visited ruins all over the world together. As for me, I prefer spending time with people whose blood still runs in their veins. This trip satisfies us both.

The **Jemez Mountain Trail** takes you to the ancient Puebloan ancestral ruins known as Kuaua at Coronado State Monument. It then continues west to Zia Pueblo, a great place to see and buy pottery. The trip next heads north through orchards and along narrow cornfields of Jemez Pueblo. Farther north on N.M. 4, you find another archaeological site, the Jemez State Monument, which tells a tragic story of slavery. You also find Jemez Springs, where you can stop for a hot soak. The road continues to the Los Alamos area, where you can see the birthplace of the atomic bomb, as well as the spectacular ruins at Bandelier National Monument. From there you have the option of returning the way you came or continuing on to Santa Fe.

Side Trips from Albuquerque

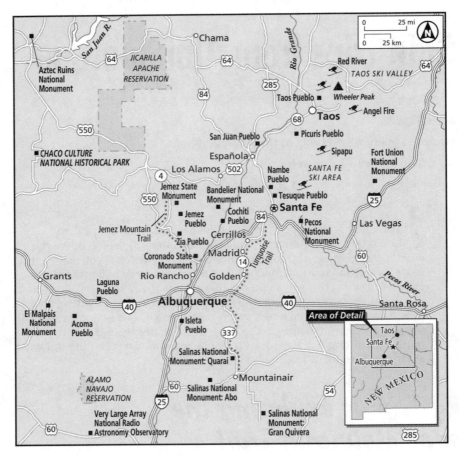

Getting there

To reach the Jemez Mountain Trail, head north from Albuquerque on I-25 for 15 miles to N.M. 550. Drive west 1 mile through Bernalillo to the Coronado State Monument. Continue west on N.M. 550 for 15 miles to Zia Pueblo. Six miles farther on N.M. 550 takes you to N.M. 4, where you turn north and drive 8 miles to Jemez Pueblo's Walatowa Visitor Center. Continue north 9½ miles to the village of Jemez Springs. Another quarter mile north is Jemez State Monument. This is a good place to turn around. If you still have some sightseeing in you, continue north on N.M. 4 for 40 miles to Bandelier National Monument, where you can see some of New Mexico's most spectacular ruins, and then to Los Alamos, where you may want to visit the Bradbury Science Museum. If you've gone this far, take N.M. 502 east from Los Alamos to U.S. 84, which leads south to Santa Fe, where you should probably stay the night.

Golden cities

In 1540, Francisco Vásquez de Coronado set out from New Spain (what is now Mexico) in search of the Seven Cities of Cíbola, also known as the Seven Cities of Gold. The myth of the cities had built over many years from a few sources, but the reality proved to be very different. Traveling with several hundred soldiers, accompanied by servants and missionaries, Coronado found only rock-and-mud pueblos. He pushed onward as far as Kansas before finally heading home, defeated. However, he brought back first-hand views of the Southwest, the Great Plains, and the Grand Canyon.

Seeing the sights

When you leave Albuquerque for this trip, you travel through Sandia Pueblo land to the village of Bernalillo, one of the oldest European towns in the United States. You pass Bernalillo en route to the **Coronado State Monument** (☎ **505-867-5351**), the closest place near Albuquerque to get a sense of the lives of the ancestral Puebloans, commonly referred to as the *Anasazi*. At the monument, you see hundreds of restored rooms as well as a *kiva* (round ceremonial room), into which you can descend. The site is named for Spanish explorer Francisco Coronado, who traveled through this region from 1540 through 1541 while searching for the Seven Cities of Cíbola and wintered here (see the "Golden cities" box in this chapter). In the small museum, you can see some multicolored murals, which were found within the kivas. The monument and museum are open daily from 8:30 a.m. to 5 p.m. and closed Easter, Thanksgiving, Christmas, and New Year's Day. Admission is $3 for adults, free for children age 16 and under.

I know that you spend sleepless nights wondering about the origins of the sun-shaped New Mexico state symbol. Well, a trip to **Zia Pueblo** (☎ **505-867-3304**) will finally win you some zzz's. About 15 miles northwest of the Coronado State Monument, the pueblo is home to 720 inhabitants and the birthplace of that official state symbol, adapted from a pottery design showing three rays going in each of the four directions from a circle. The pueblo has stood on its hill overlooking the Jemez River at least since the 17th century. Within the village stands the church of Nuestra Señora de la Asuncio de Sía, built before 1613. Our Lady of the Assumption, the pueblo's patron saint, is given a celebratory corn dance each year on her day, August 15. Admission to the pueblo, which is open year-round during daylight hours, is free. Photography is not permitted.

If you want to buy pottery, Zia Pueblo is one of the best places to get it. Zia pottery has unglazed terra-cotta coloring and is painted with traditional geometric designs and plant and animal motifs. Paintings, weavings, and sculptures are also prized products of the artists of the Zia community. You can view and purchase their work at the **Zia Cultural Center.**

Six miles farther west on N.M. 550 takes you to N.M. 4, where you turn north and drive 8 miles to **Walatowa Visitor Center** (☎ **505-834-7235**) on Jemez Pueblo. En route, if it's summer, you may encounter Jemez people sitting under *ramadas* (thatch-roofed lean-tos) selling home-baked bread, cookies, and pies. If you're lucky, they may also be making fry bread, which you can smother with honey for one of New Mexico's more delectable treats. Unfortunately, the Jemez Pueblo no longer allows visitors to walk about (except on feast days), but you can get a good sense of these people and their history at the visitor center, with its museum and shop. This pueblo of more than 3,000 natives is most known for excellent dancing and feast-making; their feast days attract residents from other pueblos, turning the celebrations into multitribal fairs. Two rectangular kivas are central points for groups of dancers. Try to attend the Feast of Our Lady of Angels on August 2, which celebrates the Pecos Bull; the Feast of San Diego on November 12, when residents perform the corn dance; or the Feast of Our Lady of Guadalupe on December 12, which includes the Matachines dance, based on a Spanish morality play.

Almost 10 miles north of the visitor center, you come to the village of **Jemez Springs.** This sleepy hamlet has seen lots of history, from sheep wars to gambling casinos. It now has a bathhouse and a decent restau-rant, a good place for a lunch break. If you want to soak in a spring *au naturalle,* ask locals to point you toward some of the natural springs in the area.

One-quarter mile north of the village lies **Jemez State Monument** (☎ **505-829-3530**), one of the Jemez people's original homesites. The highlight of this enchanting ancient pueblo is the 17th-century Mission of San José de los Jemez (founded in 1621). Its broad doorway and 6-foot-thick walls tell a story of the slave labor used to build it — slavery imposed by the Spaniards who conquered this place that the Jemez people called *Giusewa,* meaning "place of boiling waters." Admission is $3 for adults and free for children age 16 and under. The monument is open daily from 8:30 a.m. to 5 p.m. and closed on New Year's Day, Easter Sunday, Thanksgiving, and Christmas Day.

If you're out just for a day trip, Jemez Springs is a good place to turn around and head back to Albuquerque. However, if you choose to head on to Santa Fe, continue north on N.M. 4 for 40 miles to the Los Alamos area, where you should visit the Bradbury Science Museum and Bandelier National Monument (see Chapter 14 for further directions and information).

Staying in style

Your best bet for lodging in the Jemez area is **Riverdancer Retreat and Bed & Breakfast** ($$–$$$$), 16445 Scenic Hwy. 4, Jemez Springs (☎ **800-809-3262** or 505-829-3262). Set along the cottonwood-banked

Jemez River, this inn is the perfect spot to retreat from the world. The inn offers massage and body treatments, guided nature walks, art classes, yoga, tai chi, and drumming.

Dining on the road

In the middle of Jemez Springs is New Mexico's version of the Whistle Stop Café, the **Laughing Lizard Inn & Café** ($$), 17526 N.M. 4 (☎ **505-829-3108**), the center of hospitality in this modest rural town. No pretension here, just thick adobe walls painted Southwestern salmon, a wood-burning stove, and some quite eclectic eats. Try the beef stirfry burrito or the Virgin Mesa pizza (pesto, sun dried tomatoes, and feta and mozzarella cheeses). Beer guzzlers take note: No alcohol is served, though at press time the cafe was applying for a beer and wine license. Open: Summer, Tuesday through Friday lunch and dinner, Saturday and Sunday breakfast, lunch, and dinner; winter Thursday and Friday lunch and dinner, Saturday and Sunday breakfast, lunch, and dinner. Always call first, because hours vary with business flow.

Day Trip 2: Heading to Santa Fe along the Turquoise Trail

If you don't mind adding an extra hour onto the hour-long drive from Albuquerque to Santa Fe, definitely follow the state-designated scenic and historic route called the **Turquoise Trail.** It traverses the revived "ghost towns" of Golden, Madrid, and Cerrillos, where gold, silver, coal, and turquoise were once mined in great quantities. Today, artists and craftspeople have breathed life into the funky dwellings in these towns and sell their wares in small shops.

Getting there

Begin your journey by heading east from Albuquerque on I-40. Drive 16 miles from downtown Albuquerque to the Cedar Crest exit. From there, follow N.M. 14 as it winds 46 miles to Santa Fe along the east side of the Sandia Mountains. When you reach I-25, turn west and drive to Santa Fe.

Seeing the sights

Once you're on N.M. 14, you first encounter **Sandia Park,** 6 miles north of the I-40 junction. If you didn't get a chance to ride the Sandia Peak Tramway (see Chapter 11), here's your chance to take a little side trip up to 10,678-foot **Sandia Crest.** If you want to go to the Crest, turn onto N.M. 536. Follow this paved road 6 miles to the parking lot at the summit overlook.

Back at Sandia Park, drive north about 10 miles on N.M. 14 through the ghost town of **Golden.** Trucking farther along, about 12 miles north of Golden, you stumble into the thriving community of **Madrid,** the namesake of Spain's capital, although *this* Madrid is pronounced with the accent on the first syllable (*Ma*-drid). The town's roots (and that of neighboring Cerrillos) as a mining spot date back to prehistory. Today, the village seems stuck in the 1960s; full of funky ramshackle houses, it's home to "hippies," who operate several crafts stores and import shops. During Christmastime, the town presents a light show well worth catching.

History addicts may want to stop at Madrid's **Old Coal Mine Museum** (☎ 505-438-3780), which features mining and railroad relics, including antique cars, tools, workshops, and a fully restored 1900 Baldwin Steam Locomotive. The museum is open daily (weather permitting) during winter from 10 a.m. to 5 p.m. and summer from 9 a.m. to 5 p.m. Admission is $3 for adults and seniors and $1 for children age 6 to 12; children under age 6 are free.

Next door, the **Mine Shaft Tavern** (☎ 505-473-0743) is a good place to grab a burger and see some local color. It's open for dinner Wednesday and Friday through Sunday. Adjacent to the Tavern, the **Madrid Engine House Theatre** (☎ 505-438-3780) holds the claim to fame as the only theater on earth with a built-in steam locomotive on its stage. Performances take place from Memorial Day to Columbus Day on Saturdays at 3 and 8 p.m. and on Sundays (and Monday holidays) at 3 p.m. Admission is $10 adults, $8 seniors, and $4 for children under 12.

Drive just a few miles north of Madrid, and you come to **Cerrillos.** Once a bustling mining town with several hotels and two dozen saloons, Cerrillos today is a dusty spot with some fancy homes tucked among the *piñon trees* (low-growing pines). The main street includes the Cerrillos Bar, part of the original Tiffany Saloon (founded by the New York jewelry family); a dilapidated hotel; and a few shops.

Taking a tour

Outback Tours (☎ 800-800-JEEP or 505-820-6101; Internet: www. outbacktours.com) runs a "safari" along the Turquoise Trail. Their tour prices range from $65 to $95 per person.

Staying in style

If you just can't get enough of this picturesque high desert called the Galisteo Basin, plan a night or two in nearby Galisteo at the **Galisteo Inn** ($$) on N.M. 41, 15 miles from Cerrillos via the dirt County Road 42 (☎ 505-466-4000). This charming 250-year-old hacienda has plenty of shade and thick adobe walls to keep you cool in the summer. The rooms, filled with Latin art of the Americas, will charm you. With the cost of your room, you get a full breakfast, and for an extra cost, you can savor a fixed-price dinner on Wednesday to Sunday nights.

Dining on the road

If you find that you're a little saddle sore and want to take a break with some good grub, stop at **Back Road Pizza** ($$) on N.M. 14 in the center of Madrid (☎ 505-474-5555). Gourmet pizza is the order of the day here, with a unique crust rolled in cornmeal and rimmed with sesame seeds. The restaurant is open daily for lunch and dinner.

Chapter 13

Santa Fe

• •

In This Chapter

▶ Getting the Santa Fe skinny

▶ Bedding down at the end of the trail

▶ Grubalicious — eating the city's best chow

▶ Seeing the City Different's primo attractions and activities

▶ Shopping for local and exotic treasures

▶ Finding your way under the stars — Santa Fe after dark

• •

The state capital of New Mexico describes itself as the City Different, and it's easy to see why. Santa Fe's distinctive mix of Hispanic, Native American, and Anglo cultures; its adobe architecture, Southwestern dress, and cuisine; and the relaxed *mañana* (tomorrow) attitude of its often artsy residents all combine to create what has become known internationally as Santa Fe Style. Some people call the place Adobe Disneyland, but, love it or hate it, "Fanta Se" (yet another nickname) is unique.

Founded by the Spanish in the early 1600s, Santa Fe combines historic ambience with modern chic. Among its present population of approximately 70,000, you find a quirky assortment of artists, politicos, scientists, urban refugees, retirees, New Agers, and crunchy outdoors types all calling the place home. You also find golf; plenty of great restaurants; world-class opera, theater, and classical music; several fine museums; and more art galleries than you can shake a credit card at — all in an idyllic setting 7,000 feet up in the high desert foothills of the Sangre de Cristo Mountains.

For locations of the accommodations, restaurants, and attractions mentioned in this chapter, see the corresponding downtown maps or the Greater Santa Fe map, all in this chapter.

Greater Santa Fe

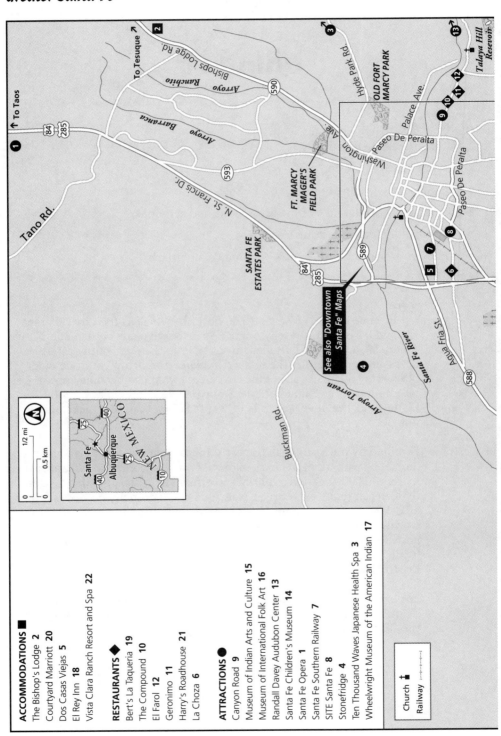

ACCOMMODATIONS ■
The Bishop's Lodge **2**
Courtyard Marriott **20**
Dos Casas Viejas **5**
El Rey Inn **18**
Vista Clara Ranch Resort and Spa **22**

RESTAURANTS ◆
Bert's La Taqueria **19**
The Compound **10**
El Farol **12**
Geronimo **11**
Harry's Roadhouse **21**
La Choza **6**

ATTRACTIONS ●
Canyon Road **9**
Museum of Indian Arts and Culture **15**
Museum of International Folk Art **16**
Randall Davey Audubon Center **13**
Santa Fe Children's Museum **14**
Santa Fe Opera **1**
Santa Fe Southern Railway **7**
SITE Santa Fe **8**
Stonefridge **4**
Ten Thousand Waves Japanese Health Spa **3**
Wheelwright Museum of the American Indian **17**

Church
Railway

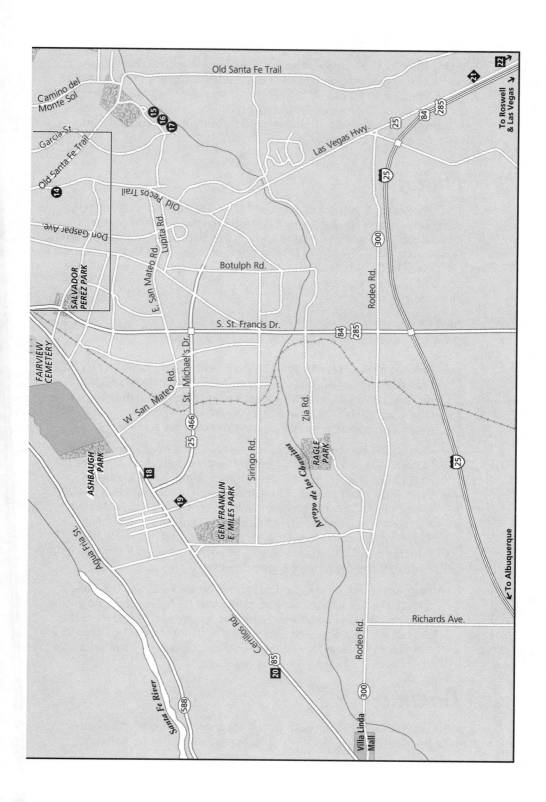

Getting There

Flying into Santa Fe's tiny airport is the nicest way to arrive (if only because you get to stroll into the cute adobe terminal), but it's usually much cheaper to fly into Albuquerque — just over an hour away by car or shuttle bus. The closest train station is 30 inconvenient miles away in Lamy, which can add logistical hassles, but you can roll right into town on a Greyhound bus.

Flying in

The tiny **Santa Fe Municipal Airport** (☎ 505-955-2900) is just outside the southwestern city limits on Airport Road and primarily services private planes. If you don't have one of your own, you can fly in on **Rio Grande Air** (☎ 877-435-9742) from Albuquerque, or on **United Express** (☎ 800-241-6522) from Denver, Colorado. The airport has a small cafe and no baggage carousel — you find your luggage with everyone else's on the curb outside.

Once at the airport in Santa Fe, you can rent a car, call a taxi, or take a shuttle to downtown. Here are the details for each one:

✔ **Renting a car. Avis** (☎ 505-471-5892) and **Hertz** (☎ 505-471-7189) both have offices in the terminal, and **Thrifty** (☎ 505-474-3365) has one just across the parking lot in the **Santa Fe Jet Center.** To ensure that a car will be available when you arrive, reserve one at least 24 hours in advance, especially during peak tourist seasons.

✔ **Catching a cab or a shuttle.** You can take the **Roadrunner Shuttle** (☎ 505-424-3367) to anywhere in the downtown Santa Fe area for $11. These shuttles meet every arriving flight, and although a reservation isn't required for the ride into town, you need one for the return trip to the airport. **Capital City Cab** (☎ 505-438-0000), Santa Fe's only taxi service, has a free hotline in the terminal. Their flagdrop charge is $2.39 (with $1.25 added for each additional person), and then you pay $2.00 per mile. They charge approximately $25 to get to the downtown area.

✔ **Hopping a bus.** The local bus system, **Santa Fe Trails** (☎ 505-955-2001), has a stop along Airport Road (at least a mile-long walk from the airport) but doesn't run all the way to the airport at this time. If you feel like hoofing it from the airport to the bus stop, the 50¢ ride is by far your cheapest option for getting to town. Call for schedules.

Driving in

If you cruise in from the south (most likely Albuquerque), you can take four-lane I-25, which slips along Santa Fe's southern limits, or alternatively take two-lane Route 14 (also known as the Turquoise Trail), which offers a longer but more scenic drive. If you come into town from the north, you can also arrive by I-25. If you travel from Colorado, the most direct (and most beautiful) route is via two-lane U.S. 84 from Durango, which passes through scenic Abiquiu (see Chapter 14) before bringing you into Santa Fe.

Riding in

Most visitors fly or drive into Santa Fe, but you can also arrive by bus or (with some extra effort) by train. Here are the details:

✔ **Shuttling in from Albuquerque.** Taking the 70-minute shuttle ride to Santa Fe from the airport in Albuquerque is easy. **Santa Fe Shuttle** (☎ **888-833-2300**) makes eight daily runs each way and costs $21 ($38 round-trip). **Sandia Shuttle Express** (☎ **505-243-3244** in Albuquerque, ☎ **505-474-5696** in Santa Fe) makes ten daily runs each way and costs $20. Gray Line also runs a shuttle service between the airport and Santa Fe, called **Express Shuttle USA** (☎ **800-256-8991**), with nine daily runs each way for $25.

✔ **Arriving by bus.** Buses for **Greyhound** (☎ **800-231-2222;** Internet: www.greyhound.com) and **Texas, New Mexico and Oklahoma Coaches, Inc.** (☎ **505-471-0008**) both stop at the **Santa Fe Bus Depot,** which is inconveniently located approximately 3 miles from downtown at 858 St. Michael's Dr.

✔ **Riding the rails.** A city with a railroad named after it surely has its own train station, right? Guess again. If you want to take the train to Santa Fe, you have to step off in dusty Lamy, a picturesque village about 20 miles south of town. Amtrak's Southwest Chief, which runs between Chicago and Los Angeles, makes two daily stops in Lamy going once in each direction. After arriving in Lamy, you can hop on the **Lamy Shuttle Service** (☎ **505-982-8829**), which takes passengers on the 25- to 30-minute drive between Lamy and Santa Fe for $16 each way. Reservations are required, and you can either book the shuttle through **Amtrak** (☎ **800-872-7245;** Internet: www.amtrak.com) when you buy your train ticket or call the shuttle directly.

Orienting Yourself

The city of Santa Fe is situated 7,000 feet up in the high desert foothills of the Sangre de Cristo Mountains. Most buildings (including gas stations) are either built of or made to look like adobe, and the tallest are only a few stories high. If you're used to navigating by landmarks, you'd better grab a map fast.

Discovering the neighborhoods

Like many popular western towns, Santa Fe has seen its share of sprawl in recent years, but the heart of the city is still its historic downtown area, and this is where you will likely spend most of your time (and money). Otherwise, you'll soon become more familiar than you may want with Cerrillos Road, a motel and fast-food strip extending several miles through the southside of town.

Downtown

As with many towns of Hispanic origin, Santa Fe radiates from its central downtown plaza. The area lends itself to walking, and because parking places can be difficult to find anyway, getting around by foot is best. Historic adobe buildings filled with art galleries, restaurants, coffee shops, and boutiques line the narrow streets around the plaza. Several of Santa Fe's museums, including the Georgia O'Keeffe Museum, the Palace of the Governors, and the Museum of Fine Arts, are all located in the area, as are many of the better hotels. The St. Francis Cathedral presides over everything, with the Sangre de Cristo Mountains looming behind it. The limits of downtown Santa Fe are demarcated on three sides by the horseshoe-shaped street called Paseo de Peralta, and on the west by St. Francis Drive, otherwise known as U.S. 84/285. Alameda Street follows the north side of the tiny Santa Fe River through downtown, with the state capitol and other federal buildings on the south side of the river, and most buildings of historic and tourist interest on the north, east of Guadalupe Street.

Eastside

As Alameda Street heads east from the Paseo de Peralta, it runs parallel to Canyon Road, a pretty street lined with art galleries and boutiques as well as a handful of restaurants. Canyon Road is best seen on foot, especially on Friday evenings, when many of the art galleries have openings from 5 to 7 p.m. A pleasant residential neighborhood surrounds Canyon Road, with cute, tree-lined streets, which lend themselves to walking. Just before Alameda Street curves round to intersect Canyon Road, you find the Patrick Smith Park, a refreshing oasis of green frequented by dogs and Frisbee players. After crossing Alameda Street, Canyon Road becomes Upper Canyon Road and ends at the leafy Randall Davey Audubon Center.

Southside

Cerrillos Road runs southwest from the downtown area, beginning opposite the state office buildings on Galisteo Avenue and eventually taking you all the way to I-25. You find just about every discount store, fast food joint, and chain motel you could ever desire alongside it. St. Francis Drive, which crosses Cerrillos Road 3 blocks south of Guadalupe Street, also runs into I-25 about 4 miles southeast of downtown. The Old Pecos Trail, on the east side of the city, links downtown and I-25, and

St. Michael's Drive connects the three arteries. A new byway, State Road 599, runs from St. Francis Drive north of town all the way to Airport Road, southwest of the city.

Northside

Santa Fe's most exclusive neighborhoods lie north of town, including Tesuque, La Tierra, and Las Campanas (a posh development built around a Jack Nicklaus golf course). You also find the open air Santa Fe Opera, which attracts aficionados from round the world during its popular summer season. Next door to the opera is the Pueblo of Tesuque Flea Market, where you can buy everything from Afghan rugs to power tools.

Finding information after you arrive

The **Santa Fe Visitor Information Center** is located across the street from the State Capitol Building at 491 Old Santa Fe Trail (☎ **800-545-2070** or 505-827-7336; Internet: www.newmexico.org). The center is open daily from 8 a.m. to 5 p.m. You can talk to information specialists here and pick up free literature about hotels, restaurants, and attractions.

You can also find a tourist information center in the **Sweeney Convention Center**, 201 W. Marcy St. (☎ **800-777-2489** or 505-955-6200).

Getting Around

Even if you live here, all that curvy brown adobe can start looking the same, and Santa Fe's hodgepodge of twisty streets makes absolutely no sense. Although locals are used to tourists asking for directions, make sure you carry a map. You can easily get around downtown on foot and by car, bus, taxi, or bicycle. However, unless you're on a sightseeing tour, traveling much beyond the city limits is difficult without your own wheels. So, if you're in Santa Fe for more than a couple of days, renting a car is a must.

Moving those feet

By far the best way to see the downtown area is by foot. A map is included in the free **Santa Fe Official Visitor's Guide,** which you can pick up at **Sweeney Convention Center** or at the **Santa Fe Visitor Information Center** (see "Finding information after you arrive" for locations).

Exploring by car

Traffic in Santa Fe has grown worse in recent years, and Santa Fe drivers are notoriously awful. The bumper stickers you see around town reading "Visualize Turn Signal Use" are no joke — local drivers often turn without warning. If you stay downtown for only a day or two, you won't necessarily need a car. However, a car is essential for explorations beyond the city limits. You can rent a car from any of the following firms in Santa Fe: **Avis,** Garrett's Desert Inn, 311 Old Santa Fe Trail (☎ **505-982-4361**); **Budget,** 1946 Cerrillos Rd. (☎ **505-984-8028**); **Enterprise,** Santa Fe Hilton, 100 Sandoval St. (☎ **505-473-3600**); and **Hertz,** Santa Fe Airport (☎ **505-471-7189**). A parking lot is available near the federal courthouse, two blocks north of the Plaza; another one is behind Santa Fe Village, a block south of the Plaza; and a third is located at Water and Sandoval streets. Street parking can be difficult to find during summer months, and parking tickets are common.

Calling a taxi

Calling ahead for a cab is best, because your odds of hailing one on the street are about as good as winning the jackpot at one of the local casinos. **Capital City Cab** (☎ **505-438-0000**) is the only taxi company in Santa Fe. Their flagdrop charge is $2.39 (plus another $1.25 for each additional person), and they charge $2.00 per mile after that.

Riding the bus

Santa Fe Trails (☎ **505-955-2001**) has eight routes, and you can go anywhere on their buses for 50¢ a ride. You can buy a day pass for $1 and a monthly pass for $10. Pick up a route map at the **Sweeney Convention Center** (see "Finding information after you arrive," earlier in the chapter). Buses operate Monday to Friday from 6:30 a.m. to 10 p.m. and Saturday from 7:30 a.m. to 7:30 p.m. There is no service on Sunday or holidays. Call for a current schedule and fare information.

Pedaling a bike

If you don't mind taking your life into your hands, bicycling can be a fun way to cruise around town. Bike lanes are rare, however, so watch out for those Santa Fe drivers and be sure to wear a cycling helmet. For bike rentals, check out **Sun Mountain Bike Company,** 107 Washington Ave. (☎ **505-820-2902**), or **Bike-N-Sport,** 1829 Cerrillos Rd. (☎ **505-820-0809**).

Staying in Style

The City Different has been masterfully fleecing tourists for years, so if quaint old Santa Fe is what you're after, don't expect to find much of it on the cheap. Lodgings run the gamut from budget chain motels to expensive, ranch-style resorts, and sometimes it seems like a cute Santa Fe style bed-and-breakfast is on every corner. Prices are highest

Downtown Santa Fe Accommodations

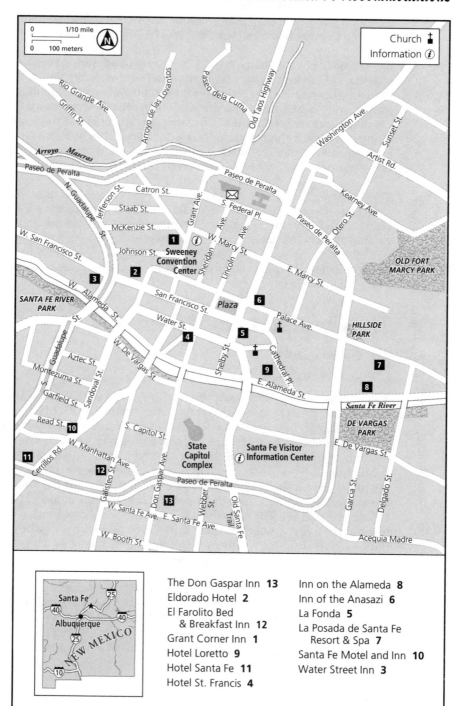

The Don Gaspar Inn **13**
Eldorado Hotel **2**
El Farolito Bed
   & Breakfast Inn **12**
Grant Corner Inn **1**
Hotel Loretto **9**
Hotel Santa Fe **11**
Hotel St. Francis **4**

Inn on the Alameda **8**
Inn of the Anasazi **6**
La Fonda **5**
La Posada de Santa Fe
   Resort & Spa **7**
Santa Fe Motel and Inn **10**
Water Street Inn **3**

downtown, so if you want to save money, Cerrillos Road is the place to look, where you find no shortage of cheapish chain and family-operated motels. If you need help finding a room, assistance is available from **Santa Fe Central Reservations** (☎ **800-776-7669** or 505-988-2800).

If you have some flexibility, it pays to shop around during the shoulder seasons of May to June and September to October. Santa Fe has more than 4,500 rooms in over 100 different establishments, but finding a room during peak tourist seasons can still be hard. Accommodations are often booked solid around Christmas and throughout the summer months, and most places raise their prices accordingly. Rates increase even more during Indian Market, the third weekend of August. During these periods, making reservations well in advance is essential.

The following listings are divided between the top resorts and spas, and the top hotels and bed-and-breakfasts. Each lodging has a $ rating (see Chapter 8 for an explanation), and unless otherwise noted, the establishments listed here have free parking.

Be forewarned: A combined city–state tax of 11.44% is added to every hotel bill in Santa Fe.

The top resorts and spas

The Bishop's Lodge
$$$–$$$$ **Northside**

A rambling, rustic resort (great for families) set on 1,000 piñon-studded acres just north of Santa Fe, this is the former retreat of Archbishop Jean-Baptiste Lamy. His tiny chapel (listed in the National Register of Historic Places) sits above the main building of the property, which houses a fine restaurant and bar. The southwestern-style guest rooms are spread throughout several lodge buildings of various shapes and ages, and despite a recent multi-million dollar overhaul, some of the rooms are much more appealing than others — it's worth looking at more than one before you commit. The lodge has an activity-packed children's program in summer, and a guided morning horseback ride with a cowboy cook-out breakfast most days. Other amenities include extensive hiking trails, an outdoor pool, tennis courts, a fitness room, and a hot tub and sauna.

Bishop's Lodge Rd. ☎ *505-983-6377. Fax: 505-989-8739. Internet:* www.bishops lodge.com. *Rack rates: Winter $129–$299 double; fall and spring $179–$249 double; summer $299 double. AE, DC, DISC, MC, V.*

La Posada de Santa Fe Resort & Spa
$$$$ **Downtown**

This expansive hotel has the feel of a secluded adobe village, but it's only three blocks from the Plaza. Its historic main building is built around a

Victorian mansion (reputedly haunted), while the rest of the hotel's pueblo-style buildings sprawl over 6 acres. Twisty walkways shaded by gnarled old fruit trees connect the newly-renovated guest rooms, which can be hit or miss, but have plenty of rustic Southwestern character. The chic Avanyu Spa, offering a full range of tempting treatments, sits in the center of the grounds next to an inviting outdoor pool and hot tub.

330 E. Palace Ave. at Paseo de Peralta. ☎ *800-727-5276 or 505-986-0000. Fax: 505-982-6850. Internet:* www.laposadadesantafe.com. *Valet parking $12 a day. Rack rates: $189–$279 double, depending on the season. Spa packages are available. AE, CB, DC, DISC, MC, V.*

Vista Clara Ranch Resort and Spa
$$$$ Galisteo

The perfect place to come for a luxurious New Age escape, Vista Clara Ranch is hidden among the low, piñon-covered hills just outside the sleepy village of Galisteo (about 25 minutes from Santa Fe). When you're not enjoying a hot-stone massage, hiking up to the local *petroglyphs* (ancient rock paintings), or indulging in a native body glow, you can soak away your troubles in the cliff-top Jacuzzi and watch the sun set over the surrounding desert where Hollywood comes to shoot its westerns (*Silverado, Wyatt Earp*). The Sunday evening sweat lodge ceremony is an absolute must — you can commune with the ancient ones while shaking rattles and beating tom-toms. The restaurant's all-organic cuisine is superb.

County Hwy. 75 (Box 111), Galisteo (about 25 minutes from downtown). ☎ *888-663-9772 or 505-466-4772. Fax: 505-466-1942. Internet:* www.vistaclara.com. *Rack rates: Summer $520 double; winter $494 double. Extensive spa packages are available. MC, V.*

The top hotels and B&Bs

The Don Gaspar Inn
$$–$$$$ Downtown

This inn is laid-back class in the South Capitol district. Rooms surround a pretty garden planted with aspen, cottonwood, and fruit trees, as well as a multitude of native and heirloom flowers. The best rooms are in a restored historic residence, where you find king-size beds, hand-carved beams, wooden floors, Navajo rugs, gas fireplaces, private patios, and sumptuous bathrooms with hot tubs for two. Breakfast is served in a sunny enclosed patio or in the garden during the warmer months.

623 Don Gaspar Ave. ☎ *888-986-8664 or 505-986-8664. Fax: 505-986-0696. Internet:* www.dongaspar.com. *Rack rates: $115–$295 double, depending on the season. Rates include breakfast. AE, MC, V.*

Dos Casas Viejas (B&B)
$$$$ Southwest of Downtown

This bed-and-breakfast offers secluded luxury a short distance from the Plaza in the Guadalupe District. A pair of restored adobe houses (*dos casas viejas* means "two old houses") offers some of the most elegant lodging in Santa Fe. Each of the beautifully-decorated guest rooms has its own enclosed patio and private entrance, *kiva fireplace* (a traditional rounded fireplace), and tasteful Southwestern antiques. The inviting library and breakfast area are in a main building next to a lap pool. You can also arrange in-room spa treatments.

610 Agua Fria St. ☎ *505-983-1636. Fax: 505-983-1749. Internet:* www.doscasas viejas.com. *Rack rates: $195–$295 single or double. Rates include breakfast. MC, V.*

El Rey Inn
$$–$$$ Southside

Loaded with retro-groovy Southwestern character, the hip El Rey transports you back to the days of getting your kicks on Route 66. Opened in the 1930s and renovated bit by bit over the years, the exteriors of the motel's quirky mission-style units are decorated with fancifully-painted trim and pretty Mexican tiles. No two rooms are alike — some have fireplaces, while others have opulently tiled bathrooms or patios. Some of the best deals in Santa Fe are the suites surrounding a Spanish colonial courtyard in back. You also find an outdoor swimming pool, two hot tubs, and a sauna.

1862 Cerrillos Rd. ☎ *800-521-1349 or 505-982-1931. Fax: 505-989-9249. Internet:* www.elreyinnsantafe.com. *Rack rates: May–Oct $85–$175 double, $155 suite; Nov–Apr $75–$165 double, $145 suite. Rates include continental breakfast. AE, CB, DC, DISC, MC, V.*

Eldorado Hotel
$$$$ Downtown

The 800-pound gorilla of Santa Fe hotels, the gigantic five-story Eldorado towers over the downtown area with great self importance. Everything's big with a capital "B" here, from the cavernous lobby to the spacious guest rooms. Although popular with the convention crowd, the hotel also attracts celebrities — Elizabeth Taylor and Mick Jagger have both spent the night in the Presidential suite. The hotel has just undergone a major makeover, and now the pleasant fifth floor suites each have their own kiva fireplaces. Other amenities include a heated rooftop swimming pool and hot tub, a fitness room with his-and-hers saunas, professional massage therapists, a business center, a beauty salon, and several boutiques. The Old House restaurant on the ground floor is excellent.

309 W. San Francisco St. ☎ *800-955-4455 or 505-988-4455. Fax: 505-995-4544. Internet:* www.eldoradohotel.com. *Valet parking $13 per night. Rack rates: Jan 1–Feb 13 $159 double; Feb 14–Apr 4 $199 double; Apr 5–Jun28 $249 double; Jun 29–Aug 24 $269 double; Aug 25–Oct 27 $249 double; Oct 28–Dec 31 $199 double. AE, CB, DC, DISC, MC, V.*

Grant Corner Inn (B&B)

$$–$$$$ **Downtown**

If you can score a room in this restored historic mansion next to the Georgia O'Keeffe Museum, you are very lucky — it's one of the most popular places to stay in Santa Fe. The second floor guest rooms have been beautifully renovated with grand marble bathrooms, enormous comfy beds, and elegant furnishings. Popular with locals, breakfast and Sunday brunch are served fireside during winter and on the front veranda in summer. You can also stay in a separate hacienda that the inn runs.

122 Grant Ave. ☎ *800-964-9003 or 505-983-6678. Fax: 505-983-1526. Internet:* www.grantcornerinn.com. *Rack rates: Nov–May (excluding holidays and Mar) $120–$180 double; Jun–Oct (and holidays and Mar) $135–$225 double. Rates include breakfast and afternoon tea. Hacienda rates for up to four people: Nov–May (excluding holidays and March) $270; Jun–Oct (and holidays and March) $310. AE, MC, V.*

Hotel Loretto

$$$$ **Downtown**

Built in 1975 in the style of the Taos Pueblo, this multi-storied hotel attracts so many picture-snapping tourists that you could easily mistake it for a historical monument. The Loretto has recently undergone a multi-million dollar renovation, and a relaxed, ranch-style decor now permeates the hotel. The rooms have been tastefully redecorated with subdued Southwestern touches, and some have views of St. Francis Cathedral or the famous Loretto Chapel next door. Amenities include a heated outdoor swimming pool, a fitness center, a decent restaurant (Nellie's), several boutiques, a lounge bar, and a coffee shop.

211 Old Santa Fe Trail (at Alameda St.). ☎ *800-727-5531 or 505-988-5531. Fax: 505-984-7988. Internet:* www.noblehousehotels.com/loretto. *Parking: $12 per night. Rack rates: $215–$309 double. AE, CB, DC, DISC, MC, V.*

Hotel Santa Fe

$$–$$$$ **Downtown**

Probably the best all-around place to stay near downtown, this is also Santa Fe's only Native American–owned hotel, and part of the fun of staying here is enjoying the Native American influence, which extends from the Taos-style guest rooms to the Picuris Pueblo dancers who perform on the patio during summer. You also find a heated outdoor pool, a teepee, a Jacuzzi, and the fine Corn Dance Café, which specializes in indigenous cuisine from around the world. The hotel has just added a new wing of luxury suites, called the Hacienda at the Hotel Santa Fe.

1501 Paseo de Peralta (at Cerrillos Rd.). ☎ *800-210-6441 or 505-982-1200. Fax: 505-955-7878. Internet:* www.hotelsantafe.com. *Rack rates: $99–$259 double, depending on the season. AE, CB, DC, DISC, MC, V.*

Inn of the Anasazi
$$$$ Downtown

Widely considered Santa Fe's finest hotel, this inn contains archaeology-chic decor, including hand-carved *vigas* (log beams) and artfully-stacked flagstone, meant to reflect the culture of the Anasazi Indians. The ancient cliff dwellers would no doubt be surprised to find stereos and VCRs in all of the (smallish) guest rooms, as well as four-poster beds with custom-made sheets, handsome rugs and furnishings, fireplaces, and fine bathrooms. A clubby-feeling library and living room are on the ground floor, along with a cozy bar and one of the best restaurants in town, the Anasazi Restaurant (see "Dining Out," later in this chapter). The Plaza is only a block away.

113 Washington Ave. (at Palace Ave.). ☎ *800-688-8100 or 505-988-3030. Fax: 505-988-3277. Internet:* www.innoftheanasazi.com. *Valet parking $12 per day. Rack rates: Mar 1–June 27, Dec 3–Jan 1 $265–$435 double; Jun 28–Dec 2 $235–$455 double. AE, CB, DC, DISC, MC, V.*

Inn on the Alameda
$$$–$$$$ Downtown

This three-story, pueblo-style adobe inn sits across the street from the wooded Santa Fe River — only a block from Canyon Road and three blocks from the Plaza. The guest rooms are comfortably decorated in somewhat unimaginative Southwestern style, but a pleasant intimacy pervades the place. Massage therapists are on call 24 hours a day, and a fitness room and two open-air hot tubs await guests. A full-service bar is open nightly.

303 E. Alameda St. (at Paseo de Peralta). ☎ *800-289-2122 or 505-984-2121. Fax: 505-986-8325. Internet:* www.inn-alameda.com. *Rack rates: July 1–Oct 15 (and major holidays year-round) $207–$347 double; Nov–Feb $157–$297 double; Mar–Apr $172–$312 double; May–June and last two weeks of Oct $187–$327 double. Rates include buffet-style breakfast. AE, DC, DISC, MC, V.*

La Fonda
$$$–$$$$ Downtown

A pueblo revival behemoth on the southeast corner of the Plaza, this hotel was built in 1920 on the site of the original, which housed such notables as Kit Carson and General Ulysses S. Grant. The standard rooms at La Fonda, nicknamed the "Inn at the End of the Trail," are by no means the finest in town, but nothing can match the place for its funky atmosphere of historic, Santa Fe kitsch. Perhaps the finest hotel rooms in Santa Fe, however, are La Fonda's extraordinary new **La Terraza** suites, located along a rooftop terrace overlooking the St. Francis Cathedral. These suites have handsome hand-carved furnishings, hardwood floors, and beautifully tiled bathrooms, as well as a balcony and living room. Among the other room choices, the economy rooms are the most basic (just a double room with bed and bath), the standard rooms are slightly larger and have a small sitting room, and the deluxe doubles have a large alcove sitting room. On the inn's ground floor, you find the swinging La Fiesta Lounge and La Plazuela restaurant, which serves so-so food in a lovely skylit patio. The Bell Tower Bar is the highest point in downtown Santa Fe — the perfect spot for sunset cocktails. Amenities include an outdoor swimming pool, hot tubs, and a shopping arcade.

100 E. San Francisco St. (at Old Santa Fe Trail). ☎ ***800-523-5002*** *or 505-982-5511. Fax: 505-988-2952. Internet:* www.lafondasantafe.com. *Parking: $7 per day. Rack rates: $139 economy; $199–$229 standard; $209–$249 deluxe double; $249–$529 suite; $329–$459 La Terraza suite. AE, CB, DC, DISC, MC, V.*

Water Street Inn (B&B)

$$$–$$$$ **Downtown**

Provence meets the Southwest in this immaculate, award-winning inn four blocks from the Plaza. The sunny, spacious rooms are beautifully-furnished and painted in muted pastel color schemes. You find some of the most inviting beds in Santa Fe here, as well as Mexican-tiled bathrooms, kiva fireplaces, VCRs, and CD players. The inn offers breakfast and a daily happy hour either in the living room or on the upstairs *portal* (covered porch) in the afternoon. Other amenities include an outdoor hot tub and twice-daily maid service. Vanessie's, an upscale piano bar and restaurant, is right next door (see "Living It Up After Dark," later in this chapter for more info).

427 Water St. ☎ ***800-646-6752*** *or 505-984-1193. Fax: 505-984-6235. Internet:* www. waterstreetinn.com. *Rack rates: $135–$225 double. Rates include breakfast. AE, DISC, MC, V.*

The runner-up hotels and B&Bs

Courtyard Marriott

$$ **Southside**   This unremarkable-looking hotel is great for families on a budget, offering clean, generic Southwestern rooms. Amenities include a nice indoor pool and two hot tubs, as well as free shuttle bus service to downtown and to and from the Santa Fe Airport. *3347 Cerrillos Rd.* ☎ ***800-777-3347*** *or 505-473-2800. Fax: 505-473-4905. Internet:* www.santafe courtyard.com.

El Farolito Bed & Breakfast Inn

$$$ **Downtown** This B&B features cute and cozy casitas (little houses) with different Southwestern themes. The owner's highly prized collection of Southwest art adorns the walls, which are beautifully polished with beeswax. The smell of baking bread greets you in the inviting breakfast/reception area. *514 Galisteo St. (at Paseo de Peralta).* ☎ *888-634-8782 or 505-988-1631. Internet:* www.farolito.com.

Hotel St. Francis

$$ **Downtown** This handsome 19th-century building reeks of Old World class, which is ironic because it was a flophouse before it was overhauled in 1986. These days, the inviting front portal makes a prime perch for people-watching and afternoon tea. *210 Don Gaspar Ave. (between Water St. and Alameda St.).* ☎ *800-529-5700 or 505-983-5700. Internet:* www.hotel stfrancis.com.

Santa Fe Motel and Inn

$ **Downtown** Here you find Santa Fe style on a budget, with cute, spacious rooms only six blocks from the Plaza. Ask for one of the well-appointed historic casitas in back for increased charm and privacy. *510 Cerrillos Rd.* ☎ *800-745-9910 or 505-982-1039. Fax: 505-986-1275. Internet:* www. santafemotelinn.com.

Dining Out

You know you're in a food-conscious town when the local newspaper uses chiles (and onions) to rate movies. A large part of Santa Fe's cachet as a chic destination derives from its famous cuisine. The competition among the higher-end restaurants is fierce, which means that locals are spoiled rotten by the selection of good eats on hand, and visitors have plenty of swell options from which to choose. Aside from establishments serving the internationally known New Southwestern grub that the city is famous for, you can also find French, Italian, and interesting hybrids of the previously mentioned. Luckily, not all the top restaurants are high-end; several hidden gems satisfy your taste buds without emptying your coffers.

Reservations are always recommended at the higher-end restaurants and are essential during peak tourist seasons. Other than the fast food chains that are amply represented along Cerrillos Road, finding a restaurant in Santa Fe that serves dinner after 9:30 or 10 p.m. is difficult, so try to book a table by 8 p.m.

Santa Fe is known for being ultra-casual, so pretty much anything goes as far as dressing up for dinner (but feel free to look as good as you want). Men appreciate that coats and/or ties are never expected here. And women find that they never *really* have to put on a skirt or heels.

Downtown Santa Fe Restaurants

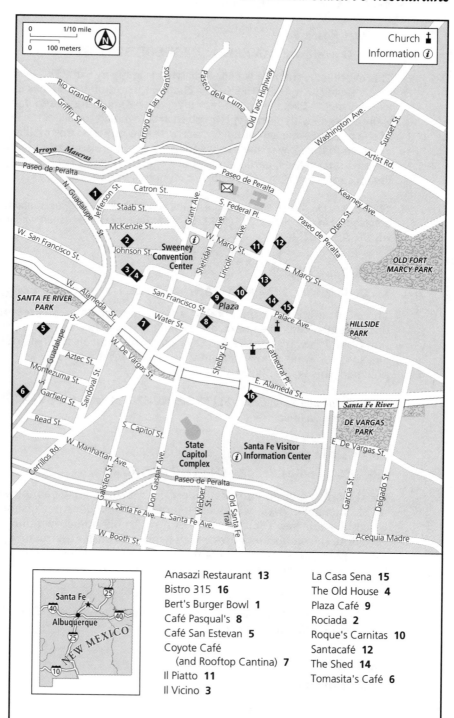

Anasazi Restaurant **13**
Bistro 315 **16**
Bert's Burger Bowl **1**
Café Pasqual's **8**
Café San Estevan **5**
Coyote Café
  (and Rooftop Cantina) **7**
Il Piatto **11**
Il Vicino **3**

La Casa Sena **15**
The Old House **4**
Plaza Café **9**
Rociada **2**
Roque's Carnitas **10**
Santacafé **12**
The Shed **14**
Tomasita's Café **6**

The top restaurants

Anasazi Restaurant
$$$$ Downtown   AMERICAN/NEW SOUTHWESTERN

This excellent restaurant is located in what is arguably Santa Fe's best hotel (see "Staying in Style," earlier in this chapter). The dining room has a warm, woodsy feel — like a great old hunting lodge — and the stacked flagstone walls adorned with petroglyph-inspired art are meant to reflect the culture of the ancient Anasazi Indians. Start with the grilled corn tortilla soup, move on to the slow-roasted venison *osso bucco* (venison stewed in white wine with tomatoes, garlic, and other vegetables), and try the tasty key lime pie for dessert. A solid wine list complements the menu.

113 Washington Ave. (in the Inn of the Anasazi). ☎ *505-988-3236. Reservations recommended. Main courses: $17.00–$32.50 Open: Daily breakfast, lunch, and dinner. AE, DC, DISC, MC, V.*

Bert's Burger Bowl
$ Downtown   NEW MEXICAN/AMERICAN

The mouth-watering aroma of Bert's sizzling green chile cheeseburgers draws Santa Feans like buzzards to roadkill, which is why this unpretentious joint is always packed. Bert's is a favorite of locals from all walks of life, so if you want a dose of homegrown, untouristy Santa Fe at its least polished, this is the place to come.

235 N. Guadalupe St. (at Catron St.). ☎ *505-982-0215. Main courses: 90¢–$2.59. AE, MC, V. Open: Daily lunch and dinner.*

Bert's La Taqueria
$$$–$$$$ Southside   AUTHENTIC MEXICAN

Local foodies rave about this nondescript restaurant in a shopping mall on St. Michael's Drive, where chef Fernando Olea does not disappoint when he promises a "culinary adventure" to his hometown of Mexico City. Both the *barbacoa* (slow-cooked lamb) and *pastor* (marinated pork) tacos make tasty appetizers, and this is one of the few places in the United States where you can try *cuitlacoche*, a Mexican delicacy also known as "corn truffles."

1620 St. Michael's Dr. ☎ *505-474-0791. Main courses: $14.95–$31.95. AE, MC, V. Open: Mon–Sat lunch and dinner.*

Bistro 315
$$$$ Downtown   FRENCH

Take a trip to provincial France in this bustling three-room restaurant, where the food and service are equally superb. The seasonal menu changes constantly, but you can't go wrong with the basil wrapped shrimp, seared duckling with dried cherries, or grilled New Zealand venison and wild berry sauce.

315 Old Santa Fe Trail. ☎ 505-986-9190. Reservations recommended. Main courses: $19–$25. AE, MC, V. Open: Summer daily lunch and dinner; winter Mon–Sat lunch and dinner.

Café Pasqual's

$$$$ Downtown   NEW SOUTHWESTERN

You almost always find a line for breakfast outside Café Pasqual's, but it's hard to find a tastier dish than their famous *huevos motuleños* (two eggs over easy on blue corn tortillas, with black beans topped with sautéed bananas, feta cheese, roasted jalapenos, and red or green salsa). Owner Katharine Kagel's Mexican-inspired restaurant has high ceilings, lively murals, and colorful paper cutouts — the closest you get to Oaxaca, Mexico in the United States. Lunch and dinner are also good, and if you travel on your own, you can sit at the communal table and make new friends.

121 Don Gaspar Ave. ☎ 505-983-9340. Reservations recommended for dinner. Main courses: $18–$29. AE, MC, V. Open: Daily breakfast, lunch, and dinner.

The Compound

$$$$ East of Downtown   NEW AMERICAN

Striving hard to be the classiest restaurant in Santa Fe, The Compound offers stellar service, exquisite cuisine, and a superb wine list. Start with the tuna tartar topped with Ostera caviar, move on to the buttermilk roast chicken with *foie gras* (goose liver) pan gravy, and for a grande finale, dig into the warm, bittersweet liquid chocolate cake. They have a cozy bar and a wine list that includes an appealing selection of 30 wines for $30. In summer, The Compound is tops with the old money set for pre-opera vittles, so book a table ahead on weekends.

653 Canyon Rd. ☎ 505-982-4353. Reservations recommended. Main courses: $19–$29. AE, MC, V. No personal checks accepted. Open: Summer Mon–Sat lunch and dinner; winter Mon–Sat dinner, Thur–Fri lunch.

Coyote Café (and Rooftop Cantina)

$$$$ Downtown   NEW SOUTHWESTERN

Superstar chef Mark Miller is world-renowned for upgrading the chile pepper to celebrity status, and you can taste how he did it at his flagship restaurant a block from the Plaza. Always packed, the Coyote Café is the most famous restaurant in New Mexico. The high-ceilinged dining room has a lively open kitchen and is decorated in groovy Santa Fe style with low benches and a zoo of quirky folk art animals. Start with the griddled corn cakes with chipotle shrimp, move on to the grilled pork chop (with a glaze made from mezcal and habañero peppers) and Cuban sweet potato mash, and try the decadent chocolate caramel hazelnut crunch bomb for dessert. In the warmer months, the more affordable adjoining outdoor **Rooftop Cantina,** serving Latino/Cuban fare, is a popular hangout for swilling *mojitos* (a Cuban drink made from lime juice, rum, sugar, and mint); the tasty duck quesadilla is fantastic.

132 Water St. ☎ 505-983-1615. Reservations highly recommended. Main courses: $18–$36. AE, DC, DISC, MC, V. Open: Daily lunch and dinner. Rooftop Cantina: Apr–Nov daily lunch and dinner.

Geronimo

$$$$ East of Downtown INTERNATIONAL/NEW SOUTHWESTERN

If you eat elk only once in your life, it should be here: The peppery elk tenderloin is outstanding. The restaurant occupies the handsomely restored Borrego House, built by Geronimo Lopez in 1756. Several intimate dining rooms surround one of the most romantic lounges in Santa Fe for enjoying an evening drink. In summer, a table under the shady front portal offers prime Canyon Road people-watching.

724 Canyon Rd. ☎ 505-982-1500. Reservations recommended. Main courses: $18–$30. AE, MC, V. Open: Daily lunch and dinner, Sunday brunch.

Il Piatto

$$–$$$ Downtown NORTHERN ITALIAN

Subdued, intimate, and reasonably priced, this is a perfect little place for a quiet romantic dinner, although it's also a very popular lunch spot for downtown executives. Try the grilled calamari with shaved fennel salad as an appetizer, and either the *pancetta* (Italian bacon) wrapped trout or the pumpkin ravioli as an entree.

96 West Marcy St. ☎ 505-984-1091. Reservations recommended. Main courses: $8–$15. AE, MC, V. Open: Mon–Fri lunch; Mon–Sun dinner.

Il Vicino

$–$$ Downtown ITALIAN

Delicious pizzas and salads, reasonable prices, and a warm, stylish atmosphere make this one of the best places in town for a casual bite to eat. The tasty thin-crust pizzas are baked to perfection in a wood-burning oven and make up the bulk of the menu. You can also order calzones, lasagna, and excellent salads. The restaurant also serves its own award-winning beer — definitely worth a try.

821 W. San Francisco St. ☎ 505-986-8700. Main courses: $4.95–$7.50. AE, DISC, MC, V. Open: Daily lunch and dinner.

La Casa Sena

$$$$ **Downtown** **AMERICAN/NEW SOUTHWESTERN**

With an unbeatable location just off the Plaza in the historic Sena compound, La Casa Sena's courtyard provides one of Santa Fe's most memorable outdoor dining experiences in summer. Once inside the casually elegant restaurant, you find chef Kelly Rogers's New Southwestern cuisine that includes imaginative treats such as tequila- and grapefruit-cured salmon nachos and pan-seared molasses duck breast. The wine cellar is the largest and best-stocked in town. You find a less expensive menu in the adjacent **La Cantina,** but don't be surprised if your server suddenly belts out *Oklahoma* in the middle of taking your order — the waitstaff double as singers here.

125 E. Palace Ave. ☎ *505-988-9232. Reservations recommended. Main courses: $23–$27. AE, DC, DISC, MC, V. Open: Daily lunch and dinner.*

La Choza

$$ **West of Downtown** **NEW MEXICAN**

You instantly feel at home in this casual Northern New Mexican eatery, which offers delicious, reasonably priced food in a rustic hacienda-like setting. Both the chicken enchiladas and blue-corn burritos are particularly tasty, but the green chile stew, chile con carne, and *carne adovada* (chile-marinated meat) are also good.

905 Alarid St. ☎ *505-982-0909. Main courses $6.95–$8.75. AE, DISC, MC, V. Open: Mon–Sat lunch and dinner.*

The Old House

$$$$ **Downtown** **NEW AMERICAN**

Located on the ground floor of the colossal Eldorado Hotel (see "Staying in Style," earlier in this chapter), the somewhat cheesy surroundings of The Old House are wildly outclassed by chef Martin Rios's beautifully presented cuisine. The atmosphere is full-on Santa Fe style, with a loud, Vegas-style carpet and lots of Southwestern art, but don't let the surroundings put you off. The food here is probably the best in Santa Fe, and the restaurant is the only one in town to receive both a AAA Four Diamond Award and a Mobil Four Star Award. Start with the sautéed escargot or the yellow fin tuna tartare, and move on to the grilled veal chop or the pan-seared sea bass. The wine list has received a *Wine Spectator* award of its own.

309 W. San Francisco St. (in the Eldorado Hotel). ☎ *505-988-4455, ext. 130. Reservations recommended. Main courses: $20–$30. AE, DISC, MC, V. Open: Daily dinner.*

Plaza Café

$$ Downtown   AMERICAN/NEW MEXICAN/GREEK

This retro-classic diner, where locals and tourists mingle on stools along the soda fountain or in red-upholstered banquettes, is always busy. You're just as likely to see the governor as your hotel housekeeper at breakfast, because this is one of the most popular places in town to start off the day.

54 Lincoln Ave. (on the Plaza). ☎ 505-982-1664. Reservations not accepted. Main courses: $7–$11. AE, DISC, MC, V. Open: Daily breakfast, lunch, and dinner.

Roque's Carnitas

$ Downtown   NEW MEXICAN

You wander around the Plaza when a mouth-watering smell begins to taunt and tantalize you — a sure sign that Roque Garcia has set up his pushcart for the warmer months. Carnitas are the name of the game here — grilled chicken or strips of beef, with onions and green chile, all wrapped in a tortilla with delicious homemade salsa. Top it off with a fresh-squeezed lemonade, and devour it on a park bench.

Washington Ave. at Palace Ave. Carnitas: $5. Open: Daily for lunch during the warmer months.

Santacafé

$$$$ Downtown   NEW SOUTHWESTERN

Modern American bistro meets the Southwest and Asia in the elegantly restored rooms of the 18th-century Padre Gallegos House. The well-presented food is considered the art here, so the walls are bare except for strategically placed antlers. In the warmer months, you can dine in the central courtyard, one of the most popular spots in town for lunch. Start with the crispy calamari, move on to the *prosciutto di Parma*–wrapped pork tenderloin, and try the Tongan vanilla bean *crème brulée* for dessert. If you eat alone, a meal at the bar is one of the best options in town.

231 Washington Ave. ☎ 505-984-1788. Reservations highly recommended. Main courses: $19–$29. AE, MC, V. Open: Daily lunch and dinner.

The Shed

$$–$$$$ Downtown   NEW MEXICAN

This is the place to introduce your tastebuds to New Mexican chiles. Don't be surprised to see lines of jones-ing chile pepper–addicts forming outside at noon. A popular luncheon institution since 1953, the restaurant occupies several gaily decorated rooms and the patio of a rambling hacienda built in 1692. The chicken enchilada verde is exemplary, as are the blue corn burritos.

113½ E. Palace Ave. ☎ 505-982-9030. Reservations accepted for dinner. Main courses: $7–$17. DC, DISC, MC, V. Open: Mon–Sat lunch, Wed–Sat dinner.

The runner-up restaurants

Café San Estevan
$$ **Downtown** The atmosphere is warm and rustic, and chef/owner Estevan Garcia's French twists on classic New Mexican dishes will have you saying oo-la-la with a local accent. Start with the cabbage salad, move on to the chile relleños (stuffed peppers), and top it all off with the flan. *428 Agua Fria (at Montezuma St.). ☎ 505-995-1996.*

Harry's Roadhouse
$$ **Westside** Harry's is a fun roadhouse restaurant serving a wide array of comfort food and delicious homemade desserts. In the warmer months, you can eat in the garden in back. *Old Las Vegas Hwy. (half a mile from the intersection of Old Pecos Trail and I-25). ☎ 505-989-4629.*

Rociada
$$$$ **Downtown** Rated by Conde Nast Traveler as one of the world's 60 best new restaurants in 2000, Rociada serves country French cuisine along with an excellent wine list. Try the traditional steak frites (steak with fries). *304 Johnson St. ☎ 505-983-3800.*

Tomasita's Café
$$ **Downtown** Occupying a former railroad station, Tomasita's is always, always busy. The atmosphere is airy '70s fern fest, and the bar is a popular hangout for margarita-swilling. The burritos and chile relleños are good, and daily blue-plate specials are available. *500 S. Guadalupe St. ☎ 505-983-5721.*

Exploring Santa Fe

One of the oldest cities in the United States, Santa Fe is also a hot bed for the creative and performing arts, so it should be no surprise to hear that most of the city's major attractions are related to art and history.

Downtown Santa Fe Attractions

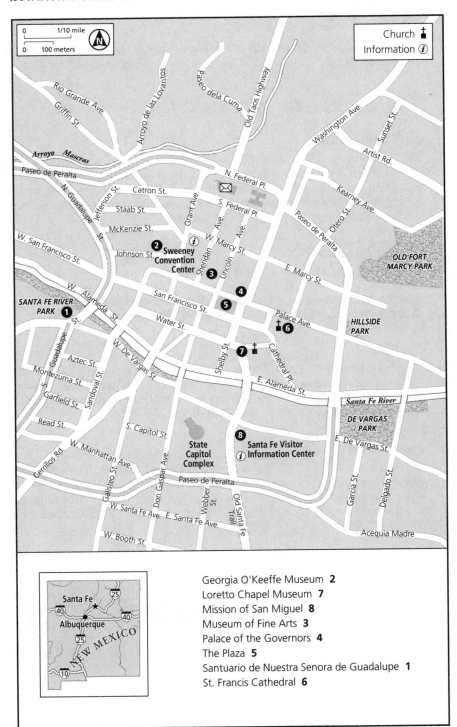

Georgia O'Keeffe Museum **2**
Loretto Chapel Museum **7**
Mission of San Miguel **8**
Museum of Fine Arts **3**
Palace of the Governors **4**
The Plaza **5**
Santuario de Nuestra Senora de Guadalupe **1**
St. Francis Cathedral **6**

Discovering the top attractions

Canyon Road
Eastside

A Canyon Road stroll is essential to any visit to Santa Fe. Aside from the multitude of galleries and boutiques, you also find **El Zaguán** at 545 Canyon Rd. (☎ **505-983-2567**), a sprawling hacienda and gardens. For more on this famous street, which I couldn't resist including among the city's top attractions, see "Shopping 'til You Drop," later in this chapter.

Canyon Rd. begins at Paseo de Peralta.

Georgia O'Keeffe Museum
Downtown

Georgia O'Keeffe (1887–1986) is internationally known for her haunting depictions of Northern New Mexico, particularly the scenic Abiquiu area, where she lived for some time. The museum contains the largest collection of works by O'Keeffe in the world (more than 120 pieces). As you wander through the handsome space, you find such well-known works as *Jimson Weed,* painted in 1932, and *Evening Star No. VII,* from 1917.

217 Johnson St. (at Grant Ave.). ☎ 505-946-1000. Admission: $5, free Fridays 5–8 p.m. Open: Nov–June Mon–Tues, Thu, and Sat–Sun 10 a.m.–5 p.m., and Fri 5–8 p.m; July–Oct Thu–Tues 10 a.m.–5 p.m., Wed noon–8 p.m., Fri 10 a.m.–8 p.m.

Loretto Chapel Museum
Downtown

Constructed from 1873 to 1878, this lovely chapel was modeled after the Eglise Sainte-Chapelle in Paris, and although no longer consecrated for worship, it's a popular spot for weddings. However, the chapel is best known for its extraordinary spiral staircase, which makes two complete turns with no visible means of support. According to legend, when the chapel was near completion in 1878, the workers realized there was no room for stairs to the choir loft. After a *novena* (a special prayer, usually used to ask for a favor) was made to St. Joseph, the Patron Saint of Carpenters, a mysterious carpenter appeared on a donkey and, using only a saw, hammer, and t-square, built a miraculous staircase without using a single nail. After completing his masterpiece, the carpenter vanished without collecting his fee.

207 Old Santa Fe Trail (between Alameda and Water Sts.). ☎ 505-982-0092. Admission: $2.50 adults, $1 children age 7–12, free for children age 6 and under. Open: Mon–Sat 9 a.m.–5 p.m., Sun 10:30 a.m.–5 p.m.

Mission of San Miguel
Downtown

Built in the early 1600s and thought to be the oldest church in the country, this colonial mission has fortress-like adobe walls with windows set up high, an elegant altar screen from 1798, and a 780-pound bell cast in Spain in 1356. Inside, you find some biblical scenes painted on buffalo hide and deerskin, which were used by 17th-century Franciscan missionaries to instruct Native Americans in the ways of the Lord. Sunday mass here is a memorable experience.

401 Old Santa Fe Trail (at E. De Vargas St.). ☎ *505-983-3974. Admission: $1 adults, free for children age 6 and under. Open: Mon–Sat 9 a.m.–5 p.m., Sun 1–4 p.m. Sunday Mass at 5 p.m.*

The Museum of New Mexico System

The **Museum of New Mexico System** consists of the **Museum of Fine Arts,** the **Museum of Indian Arts and Culture,** the **Museum of International Folk Art,** and the **Palace of the Governors,** as well as five state monuments. All of the museums are open Tuesday through Sunday from 10 a.m. to 5 p.m. Four-day passes (good at all four museums) can be purchased for $10 for adults; individual museum tickets are $5. For information, call their 24-hour hotline at ☎ **505-827-6463.**

The **Museum of Fine Arts,** 107 W. Palace at Lincoln Ave., downtown (☎ **505-476-5072**), is an excellent place to view landscapes and portraits by the Taos Masters and Los Cinco Pintores (two highly influential artistic groups from the region) from a permanent collection of more than 20,000 pieces. Temporary exhibits feature contemporary work by modern artists. The museum has two sculpture gardens.

The **Museum of Indian Arts and Culture** is at 710 Camino Lejo, about 2 miles south of the Plaza (☎ **505-476-1250**). Drive southeast on Old Santa Fe Trail, which becomes Old Pecos Trail, and look for signs pointing right onto Camino Lejo. Over 70,000 pieces of Native American basketry, pottery, clothing, carpets, and jewelry are on continual rotating display here. A permanent interactive exhibit called "Here, Now, and Always" is one of the more interesting Native American museum experiences you can find in the Southwest.

The **Museum of International Folk Art** is at 706 Camino Lejo, about 2 miles south of the Plaza (☎ **505-476-1200**). Drive southeast on Old Santa Fe Trail, which becomes Old Pecos Trail, and look for signs pointing right onto Camino Lejo. If you have time to see only one museum in Santa Fe, make it this one. The outstanding museum is home to the largest collection of folk art in the world, including some 130,000 objects from more than 100 countries. You find colorful displays of everything from Mexican tribal costumes and Brazilian folk art to African sculptures and East Indian textiles, as well as the marvelous Morris Miniature Circus. Kids love the hundreds of toys on display throughout the museum, many of them housed in a wing built for part of a collection donated by **Alexander and Susan Girard.** During their extensive travels around the world, the Girards amassed more than 100,000 pieces of folk art, 10,000 of which are now exhibited at the museum. The **Hispanic Heritage Wing** houses one of the finest collections of Spanish colonial and Hispanic folk art in the country.

The **Palace of the Governors,** 105 Palace Ave., downtown (☎ **505-827-6483**), was built in 1610 as the original capitol of New Mexico. The palace has been in continuous public use longer than any other structure in the United States. The only successful Native American uprising took place here in 1680. Inside, an engaging series of displays illustrates 400 years of New Mexico history, from 16th-century Spanish explorations, through the frontier era, and on up to modern times.

The Plaza
Downtown

When The Gap set up shop here a few years ago, it seemed to signify that the once thriving local culture that The Plaza was known for had officially died. However, the historic old square is still the official center of town where **Fiesta** and the **Indian** and **Spanish Colonial** markets are all held every summer. The obelisk in the center has caused some controversy over the years, because it commemorates the defeat of the "savages" (the word has been chiseled off). Not surprisingly, an ongoing movement persists to tear it down and erect a bandstand in its place. For now, however, evening musical performances are held on a makeshift stage to the side throughout the summer.

Between San Francisco St., Lincoln Ave., Palace Ave., Washington Ave., and Old Santa Fe Trail. Admission: Free. Open: 24 hours.

Stonefridge: Santa Fe's Stonehenge

This Stonehenge-inspired monument to consumer waste (also known as Fridgehenge) was built with more than 200 discarded refrigerators and is the wacky vision of local artist Adam Horowitz. Reporters have journeyed from all over the world to cover this unusual erection. A particularly memorable segment on *CBS Sunday Morning* featured loincloth-clad laborers dragging the refrigerators over logs. Sourpuss city officials thwarted the project for years, but Horowitz finally prevailed, and the site was officially dedicated in 2001.

Stonefridge is located at the former city landfill on Paseo de Vista Drive. From St. Francis Drive, take West Alameda to Torreon, turn right, and go to the top of the hill. Free admission. Open daily.

Santa Fe Children's Museum
South of Downtown

This interactive museum with an environmental focus was named by *Family Life* magazine as one of the 10 hottest children's museums in the nation. Exhibits focus on the arts, humanities, and science. Kids love a nifty 16-foot climbing wall that they can scale after being outfitted with helmets and harnesses. You also find a one-acre Southwestern horticulture garden, complete with animals, wetlands, and a greenhouse, which serves as an outdoor classroom for ongoing environmental educational programs.

1050 Old Pecos Trail. ☎ *505-989-8359. Internet:* www.santafechildrens museum.org. *Admission: $4 adults, $3 children under age 12. Open: Thurs–Sat 10 a.m.–5 p.m, Sun noon–5 p.m; June–Aug also Wed 10 a.m.–5 p.m.*

Santuario de Nuestra Señora de Guadalupe
Downtown

Better known as the Santuario de Guadalupe, this is believed to be the oldest shrine in the United States honoring the Virgin of Guadalupe, the Patron Saint of Mexico. Built between 1795 and 1800 by Franciscan missionaries, the shrine's massive adobe walls are nearly 3-feet thick. A famous oil painting inside, *Our Lady of Guadalupe,* was commissioned from the renowned Mexican artist José de Alzibar and brought from Mexico City by mule caravan in 1783.

100 S. Guadalupe St. ☎ *505-988-2027. Admission: Free; donations appreciated. Open: Mon–Sat 9 a.m.–4 p.m. Closed: Nov–Apr weekends.*

SITE Santa Fe
West of Downtown

This 18,000 square foot contemporary art space (housed in a former beer warehouse) was modeled after the European concept of a *kunsthalle* (an art space which is a non-collecting museum). The cutting-edge exhibitions by internationally known artists (Sigmar Polke, Agnes Martin) change every few months, and SITE also hosts a splashy biennial exhibit, most recently curated by the celebrated art critic Dave Hickey.

1606 Paseo de Peralta. ☎ *505-989-1199. Admission: $5 adults, $2.50 students and seniors, Fridays free. Open: Wed–Sun 10 a.m.–5 p.m.; Fri until 7 p.m.*

St. Francis Cathedral
Downtown

This cathedral is Santa Fe's most recognizable landmark, second only to the much-photographed Hotel Loretto. The Romanesque cathedral's twin towers stand vigil at the top of San Francisco Street (a block east of the Plaza), and you can hear their bells ring all over downtown. Archbishop

Jean–Baptiste Lamy built the cathedral, named after Santa Fe's patron saint, between 1869 and 1886. Our Lady of Peace, a wooden icon set in a niche in the north chapel, is the oldest representation of the Madonna in the United States. Also on-site is a statue of Bishop Lamy, who is buried under the main altar.

Cathedral Place (at San Francisco St.). ☎ *505-982-5619. Admission: Free; donations appreciated. Open: Daily 7 a.m.–6:30 p.m. Visitors may attend mass Mon–Sat 7 a.m. and 5:15 p.m.; Sun 8 a.m., 10 a.m., noon, and 5:15 p.m.*

Wheelwright Museum of the American Indian
Eastside

Founded in 1937 by Boston scholar Mary Cabot Wheelwright in collaboration with a Navajo medicine man, Hastiin Klah, the museum offers an esoteric collection of living arts from all Native American cultures. The eight-sided museum was inspired by the design of a traditional Navajo *hogan* dwelling, and exhibits change three times a year. The Case Trading Post gift shop was built to resemble a turn-of-the-century trading post found on the Navajo reservation. Kids love storyteller Joe Hayes, who performs in a teepee outside at dusk in July and August.

704 Camino Lejo. ☎ *505-982-4636. Admission: Free; donations appreciated. Open: Mon–Sat 10 a.m.–5 p.m., Sun 1–5 p.m.*

Finding more cool things to see and do

Are you ready to explore the outer-limits of your psyche and of this coyote-bitten town? Here are some options:

✔ **Find your muse.** If you want to include a little self-improvement in your vacation plans, you can choose from several types of classes. After touring the local galleries, you may feel inspired to take a drawing or painting class. Local artist Jane Shoenfeld, of **Sketching Santa Fe** (☎ **505-986-1108**), instructs students on how to sketch and paint the landscapes of Santa Fe and New Mexico. You can also find basic to intermediate painting and drawing classes at **Artisan Santa Fe**, 717 Canyon Road (☎ **505-988-2179**). The swanky new **Santa Fe Art Institute**, 1600 St. Michael's Dr. (☎ **505-424-5050**) on the College of Santa Fe campus, offers weeklong workshops with internationally known artists such as Ron Cooper, Yaneer Bar-Yam, and Marcos Novak.

Many of the world's outstanding photographers, including Nevada Weir, David Alan Harvey, Keith Carter, and Joyce Tennison, lead weeklong photography and digital imaging workshops at the **Santa Fe Workshops**, Mt. Carmel Rd. (☎ **505-983-1400;** Internet: www. santafeworkshops.com). **Southwest Literary Center** at **Recursos de Santa Fe**, 826 Camino del Monte Rey (☎ **505-988-5992**), offers writing workshops, led by such heavyweights as Grace Paley, Robert Stone, Mickey Pearlman, and Phillip Lopate. On Friday nights, you can take free salsa dancing lessons at **Club Alegría,** Agua Fria Road, two blocks south of Siler Road (☎ **505-471-2324**), where band leader Father Frank Pretto (the "salsa priest") has been enticing local hips to swivel for years. For a class in regional cooking, try the **Santa Fe School of Cooking** on the upper level of the Plaza Mercado, 116 W. San Francisco St. (☎ **505-983-4511;** Internet: www.santafeschoolofcooking.com).

✔ **Ride the Old Santa Fe.** Despite its name, the main route of the historic Atchison, Topeka & Santa Fe Railroad bypassed Santa Fe to the south, but an 18-mile spur was run from the main line to Santa Fe in 1880, and you can ride it on the **Santa Fe Southern Railway,** 410 S. Guadalupe St. (☎ **888-929-8600** or 505-989-8600; Internet: www.sfsr.com). The tiny railway uses restored coaches to bring passengers on scenic excursions along the rim of the Galisteo basin to the small town of Lamy. They offer different theme rides, including the High Desert Highball Train, a booze-drenched sunset ride which runs on Friday nights through the summer. Tickets range from $5 for children to $21 for adults; $25 to $65 for Friday and Saturday evening rides (April through October).

✔ **Get yourself kneaded.** You won't have a problem finding a massage in Santa Fe, because there are probably more therapists per square inch here than any other place on the planet. The **Avanyu Spa at La Posada de Santa Fe Resort & Spa** and the **Vista Clara Ranch Resort and Spa** have day spas (see "Staying in Style," earlier in this chapter). **Ten Thousand Waves Japanese Health Spa** (☎ **505-982-9304**) has Japanese-style outdoor hot tubs. This spa is located on the way to the Ski Area on Hyde Park Road, a 10-minute drive from the Plaza.

Keeping active

Ah, sweet Santa Fe. Where else can you spend your day skiing or hiking some of the most awesome terrain in the West, eat at a five-star restaurant, and finish the night with world-class opera? Best of all, because this is the high desert, temperatures vary with the elevation, making it a year-round play land.

Ballooning

Santa Fe itself isn't cut out for ballooning — too many hills and trees to crash into. But you can book a trip here and then cruise to Albuquerque or Taos for the actual event. **Santa Fe Detours,** 54½ East San Francisco St. (☎ **800-338-6877** or 505-983-6565), arranges early morning flights to meet your schedule at a cost of about $145 per person. (They also operate a summer tour desk at 107 Washington Ave.)

Biking

The popularity of mountain biking has exploded here, particularly in the spring, summer, and fall; the high desert terrain is rugged and challenging, but mountain bikers of all levels can find exhilarating rides. The tourist information center in the **Sweeney Convention Center** (see "Finding information after you arrive," earlier in this chapter) can supply you with bike maps.

I recommend the following trails: The Windsor Trail System allows bikers to travel from 4 to 17 miles and more through the mountains above Santa Fe. The trails are moderate to strenuous, and you'll want to allow a half-day or more to traverse them. The easiest access is from the Borrego Trail: Take Hyde Park Road/N.M. 475 northeast of Santa Fe. Drive 8³⁄₁₀ miles to the trailhead. Look for a small parking area on the left. The railroad tracks south of Santa Fe provide wide-open biking on beginner-to-intermediate technical trails. To reach them, head south of town on St. Francis Drive, turn right on Saw Mill Road, and right again on Rodeo Road, which you follow to the railroad tracks. The trails head south from there.

Santa Fe Mountain Sports, 606 Cerrillos Rd. (☎ **505-988-3337**), rents bikes in spring, summer, and fall, as does **Sun Mountain Bike Company,** 107 Washington Ave. and 905 St. Francis Dr. (☎ **505-820-2902**), which rents year-round, but call first. Prices run between $25 and $35 for a full day. Both shops supply accessories such as helmets, water, maps, and trail information.

Sun Mountain Bike Company also runs bike tours from April to October at some of the most spectacular spots in Northern New Mexico. Trips range from the "Beginner Breeze" to "Extreme Downhill," with prices from $60 to $109. All tours include bikes, transportation, and a snack. Located in the village of Cerrillos, south of Santa Fe, **Mountain Bike Adventures** (☎ **505-474-0074;** Internet: www.bikefun.com) offers a variety of day and multi-day trips through old mining towns to an ancient turquoise mine, Indian ruins, and high desert terrain. Their trips range from $50 to $700.

Bird-watching

If your hunger for bird life extends beyond the pigeons on the Plaza, you're in luck. Not far from there, at 1800 Upper Canyon Rd. (at the east end of Canyon Road), is the **Randall Davey Audubon Center** (☎ **505-983-4609**), a great place to hike and see birds (120 species) and other animals. Named for the late Santa Fe artist who willed his home to the National Audubon Society, this wildlife refuge occupies 135 acres at the mouth of Santa Fe canyon. Trails winding through a nature sanctuary are open to day hikers, but not to pets. On-site is a nature store. The center is open daily from 10 a.m. to 4 p.m. Trail admission is $1.

Golfing

You duffers won't exactly find tons of courses in Santa Fe, but what's here is, well, decent, and very scenic. The 18-hole course at **Santa Fe Country Club,** on Airport Road (☎ **505-471-2626**), is an older style course with trees and small greens. The often-praised 18-hole **Cochiti Lake Golf Course,** 5200 Cochiti Hwy., Cochiti Lake, about 35 miles southwest of Santa Fe via I-25 and N.M. 16 and 22 (☎ **505-465-2239**), is a short, tight course with spectacular views. And Santa Fe's newest 18-hole addition, **Marty Sanchez Links de Santa Fe,** 205 Caja del Rio (☎ **505-955-4400**), is a straightforward course (no big surprises) with contours that follow the original landscape of rolling hills west of town. Both the Santa Fe Country Club and the Marty Sanchez offer driving ranges as well. Greens fees in the area range from $25 to $55.

Hiking

With some 1,000 miles of National Forest trails in the area, everyone from mild meanderers to hard-core adventurers can find satisfaction here. If you're in the center of town and want a scenic stroll, head to **Santa Fe River Park.** It runs east–west along Alameda Street, following the trickle of the mighty Santa Fe River. Parts of it are shady and have green grass and picnic tables. The park extends over 4 miles from St. Francis Drive to Camino Cabra. Within town, locals like to head up the fairly steep **Atalaya Mountain Trail,** a 6-mile jaunt that takes about three to four hours and offers great views of the city. The trailhead is at St. Johns College. En route to the Santa Fe Ski Area is the scenic **Aspen Vista Trail,** with broad views and large stands of aspen trees. Leaving from the Santa Fe Ski Area parking lot is the **Windsor Trail,** which takes you on a full-day or multi-day hike into the 223,000-acre Pecos Wilderness.

Although we're not talking Denali here, the weather and terrain in Northern New Mexico can prove dangerous. Always be prepared. Because this is high desert, it's easy to get dehydrated, so drink water often, whether you're thirsty or not. Carry two to four quarts for a day hike. You also want to bring a jacket any time of year. Spring and fall can surprise you with snow showers, and summer can hammer you with hail.

Horseback riding

Looking for a little giddyup in your trip? Santa Fe has a few options that are worth shining your spurs. You can arrange trips ranging in length from a few hours to overnight through **Santa Fe Detours,** 54½ East San Francisco St. (☎ **800-338-6877** or 505-983-6565), with a summer tour desk at 107 Washington Ave. Trips range from $45 for 1 hour to $275 for overnight. **Broken Saddle Riding Company** (☎ **505-424-7774**), in Cerrillos on the Turquoise Trail, offers riding through the spectacular Devil's Canyon in the Cerrillos Hills southeast of Santa Fe at prices ranging from $45 for one-and-a-half hours to $70 for three hours.

Skiing and snowboarding

It's not Taos or Tahoe, but **Santa Fe Ski Area** usually has snow in winter and plenty of terrain to explore. What's best about this area is that the slopes can quench the shushing thirst of any level of skier; the down side is that the runs are relatively short. Lots of locals ski here, particularly on weekends; if you can, go on weekdays. Five lifts, including two triple chairs, a quad chair, and two double chairs serve 43 runs. The ski area is open daily from 9 a.m. to 4 p.m.; the season often runs from Thanksgiving to early April, depending on snow conditions. Rates for all lifts are $42 for adults, $36 for teens (age 13–20), $30 for children and seniors, free for kids less than 46 inches tall (in their ski boots), and free for seniors age 72 and older. For more information, contact **Ski Santa Fe,** 2209 Brothers Road, Suite 220 (☎ 505-982-4429). For 24-hour reports on snow conditions, call ☎ **505-983-9155.** Ski packages are available through **Santa Fe Central Reservations** (☎ **800-776-7669** outside New Mexico or 505-983-8200 within New Mexico). Santa Fe Ski Area is located about 16 miles northeast of Santa Fe via Hyde Park (Ski Basin) Road.

Tennis

Santa Fe has 44 public tennis courts. The **City Recreation Department** (☎ **505-955-2100**) can help you locate indoor, outdoor, and lighted public courts.

Seeing Santa Fe by guided tour

If you didn't bring your own burro to get around on, or you just feel like getting an expert's insight into Santa Fe, you can find a wide variety of options for sightseeing tours of the City Different and points beyond.

General tours

Santa Fe Detours (☎ **800-338-6877** or 505-983-6565; Internet: www.sfdetours.com) is Santa Fe's most extensive tour-booking agency and can accommodate almost every traveler's taste, from bus and rail tours to river rafting, backpacking, and cross-country skiing. Don Dietz of **Pathways Customized Tours** (☎ **505-982-5382;** Internet: www.santafepathways.com) offers several planned tours, including a downtown Santa Fe walking tour, a full city tour, a trip to the cliff dwellings and native pueblos, a "Taos adventure," and a trip to Georgia O'Keeffe country. Don has extensive knowledge of the area's culture, history, geology, and flora and fauna. Pathways' tours range from $50 to $200 per couple.

Bus, car, and tram tours

For an open-air tour of the city, contact **LorettoLine** (☎ **505-983-3701** at the Hotel Loretto). Tours last one-and-a-quarter hours and are offered daily from April to October. Tours depart at 10 a.m., noon, and 2 p.m.

Tickets are $9 for adults, $4 for children. **Fiesta City Tours** (☎ 505-983-1570) depart daily from the corner of Lincoln and Palace Avenues at 11 a.m., 1 p.m., and 3 p.m. The one-hour, fifteen-minute sightseeing tour of the historic district costs $7 for adults and $4 for children under 12. You buy your tickets from the driver.

Walking tours

One of the best ways to get a feel for Santa Fe's history and culture is on foot, and several walking tours are available. **Aboot About/Santa Fe Walks** (☎ 505-988-2774) leave daily from the lobby of the Eldorado Hotel at 9:30 a.m. and 1:30 p.m., and from the Hotel St. Francis at 9:45 a.m. and 1:45 p.m. The tours visit every significant historic sight and cost $10 for adults (kids under age 16 are free). No reservations are necessary. The company also offers the very popular **Aspook About** (☎ 505-988-2774) walking tour of Santa Fe's eerie past, which costs $10 and starts at 5:30 p.m. at the Eldorado Hotel lobby on Tuesday and Friday, and at 5:30 p.m. at La Posada Hotel on Monday and Saturday. (See "Staying in Style," earlier in this chapter, for the hotel locations.)

Archaeological tours

You can arrange customized private tours to pueblos, ruins, and cliff dwellings through **Rojo Tours & Services** (☎ 505-474-8333; Internet: www.rojotours.com). **Recursos de Santa Fe/Royal Road Tours** (☎ 505-982-9301) specializes in tours highlighting the archaeology, art, literature, spirituality, architecture, environment, food, and history of the Southwest and offers custom-designed itineraries to meet the interests of any group.

Native American tours

Navajo anthropologist, artist, and curator **Rain Parrish** (☎ 505-984-8236) offers custom guide services focusing on cultural anthropology, Native American arts, and the history of the Native Americans of the Southwest, including visits to local pueblo villages. Prices average approximately $130 per couple.

Soar like a buzzard

By far, the best way to get a sense of the surrounding high desert landscapes is to see them from the air, which you can arrange through **Southwest Safaris** (☎ 800-842-4246 or 505-988-4246; Internet: www.southwestsafaris.com). This outstanding aerial tour company specializes in educational scenic flights over Acoma Pueblo, Taos, and the Abiquiu Valley, as well as full-day air/land excursions to the Grand Canyon, Monument Valley, and other destinations. Prices range from $75 to $599, and lunch is included in the day trips. Tours depart from the Santa Fe Airport.

Following one-, two-, and three-day itineraries

Many of Santa Fe's greatest hits are conveniently located in the downtown area (most likely within walking distance of your hotel), and you can easily spend several days exploring the city without venturing beyond its limits. Because most of the city's top attractions have a historical and/or cultural bent, I include several museums in the itineraries that follow. But you don't have to see everything to appreciate Santa Fe — you may be just as happy wandering the streets of downtown as exploring a museum. For details on the attractions and restaurants mentioned here, refer to the relevant sections earlier in this chapter.

One-day itinerary

If you have only one day to spend in Santa Fe, head straight to **the Plaza** and join the lively mix of locals for an early breakfast at the **Plaza Café.** Once properly fortified, stroll over to the **Palace of the Governors.** After an hour or two of wandering through the museum, make your way over to the **Georgia O'Keeffe Museum.** Then, if taking in all those paintings of flowers and skulls revives your appetite, head to **The Shed** restaurant for a classic Northern New Mexican lunch. After feasting on enchiladas, make for the nearby **St. Francis Cathedral,** and then continue onwards to **Canyon Road.** Depending on your interest in (or tolerance for) fine art, you can either spend the entire afternoon gallery hopping on Canyon Road, or just spend an hour or so wandering up and down it. If you take your time on Canyon Road, your afternoon can easily end here with an early dinner at **Geronimo** restaurant, followed by a raucous evening of margarita-drinking and dancing to live music at the **El Farol** bar and restaurant next door (where you can also have dinner). If you don't last long on Canyon Road and feel like taking in another attraction, head up to the **Museum of International Folk Art** on Camino Lejo (it's too far to walk, however), and then come back to Canyon Road for dinner and dancing. If you require a coffee break, stop by the very popular **Downtown Subscription** (☎ 505-983-3085) at the corner of Garcia Street and Acequia Madre.

Two-day itinerary

On day one, follow the one-day itinerary, but maybe save the **Georgia O'Keeffe Museum** for after lunch, and pencil in the **Museum of International Folk Art** for the morning of day two.

On day two, after breakfast, head up to the **Museum of International Folk Art.** Follow this stop with a trip to the **Museum of Indian Arts and Crafts** and the **Wheelwright Museum of the American Indian** (both at the same location). Return to downtown for a lunch splurge at the **Santacafé** restaurant, before diving into an afternoon of downtown shopping combined with visits to the **Museum of Fine Arts** and the **Loretto Chapel Museum.** In the warmer months, you can enjoy a *fabuloso* sunset vista (and maybe a cocktail or two) from atop the bell tower of the historic **La Fonda** hotel. Eat dinner at the **Coyote Café** or its **Rooftop Cantina,** and if you're still alive and kickin', head over to the **Cowgirl Hall of Fame** bar and restaurant or the **Paramount** nightclub for some live music and/or dancing, or maybe check out the piano bars at **Vanessie's** or the **Palace.**

Three-day itinerary

For the first two days, follow the two-day itinerary. Start your third day with breakfast at **Café Pasqual's,** and if it's a weekend, drive out to the **Pueblo of Tesuque Flea Market** near the **Santa Fe Opera,** where you can easily spend an entire morning wandering through the endless aisles of vendors. You might try a *Frito pie* (made with Fritos, chiles, cheese, lettuce, tomatoes, onions, and sour cream) at the flea market for lunch, or head to one of the excellent restaurants in town. (If the flea market is closed, head down Cerrillos Road to **Jackalope,** which offers almost as much opportunity for shopping.) After lunch, visit **SITE Santa Fe,** spend the rest of the afternoon shopping, or go for a drive up Hyde Park Road toward the ski basin and stroll along the spectacular **Aspen Vista** trail. On your way back down to town, stop by **Ten Thousand Waves Japanese Health Spa** for a sunset soak in one of their relaxing outdoor hot tubs. Enjoy dinner at one of the many restaurants listed in the "Dining Out" section of this chapter, and maybe follow it with a drink at the **Dragon Room** bar. If you're up for a more lively evening's entertainment, try catching a performance by the **María Benítez Teatro Flamenco** troupe, or, if it's Friday night, head to **Club Alegría** for free salsa dancing lessons to the infectious Latin beats of Pretto y Parranda.

Shopping 'til You Drop

Santa Fe is not only a shopping mecca but also quite likely the artsy-craftsy-est enclave on the planet. Although the town at the end of the Santa Fe Trail has long been a marketplace, these days it's better known as an important spot for buying and selling art than it is known for trading buffalo hides for blankets. Art galleries (more than 150 of them) and boutiques selling an amazing array of items from all over the world dominate the Santa Fe shopping scene. However, if you're not in the market for art and/or exotic home decor, do not despair — an outlet mall with designer stores and rock bottom prices is on the town's Southside. Business hours tend to vary quite a bit among establishments, but most are open at least Monday through Friday from 10 a.m. to 5 p.m., usually with similar hours on Saturday. Many are also open on Sunday afternoon during the summer. Winter hours tend to be more limited.

Best shopping areas

Most of Santa Fe's retailing happens in the downtown area and along Cerrillos Road on the town's Southside. As a rule, you find sophisticated and expensive boutiques downtown, and strip malls with chain stores on the Southside. So, if you need to get your oil changed or buy some sundries, think Cerrillos Road, but if you're in the market for a six-figure painting by a Taos Master, think downtown. Got it?

Downtown

You find a mind-boggling variety of Southwestern and international goods in the downtown area, which for shopping purposes also includes Canyon Road and the Guadalupe District. You can easily spend hours just window-shopping, let alone actually entering the multitude of galleries and fine boutiques. The **Sanbusco Market Center,** 500 Montezuma St. (☎ **505-989-9390**), is a great place for shopping, as is the neighborhood around it. The atmospheric old **Sena Plaza,** 125 E. Palace Ave., also has a number of fine boutiques and is the perfect place to take a break between credit card cha-chings.

Southside

Santa Fe's unsightly zone of refreshingly anti-chic sprawl, Cerrillos Road is home to megachains such as Wal-Mart, Home Depot, and Target, as well as a flotsam and jetsam of car washes, motels, and fast-food joints. The **Villa Linda Mall,** 4250 Cerrillos Rd. at Airport Rd. (☎ **505-473-4253**), includes Sears, Dillard's, Victoria's Secret, and J.C. Penney among its many tenants. **Santa Fe Premium Outlets,** 8380 Cerrillos Rd., just before it hits I-25 (☎ **505-474-4000**), is a shopaholic's fantasy destination, with Donna Karan, Coach, and Dansk outlets, as well as a Brooks Brothers Factory Store.

What to look for and where to find it

Art rules here, and it sure ain't free. Santa Fe attracts way serious art collectors (mostly ones looking for Southwestern pieces), whose interest contributes to making the sticker prices next to all those purple buffalo paintings shocking. Likewise, Santa Fe has no shortage of multimillionaires with third and fourth homes here, and legions of decorators and shops exist to serve their home-improvement needs. This is just to warn you that more often than not, Santa Fe is an expensive place to shop.

Antiques, crafts, furniture, ceramics, and rugs

A Santa Fe shopping spree would be incomplete without a visit to **Jackalope,** 2820 Cerrillos Rd. (☎ **505-471-8539**), a quirky Southwestern bazaar spread over 7 acres. *Kid alert:* Junior will love Jackalope's petting zoo and prairie dog village. The sprawling **Seret & Sons Rugs, Furnishings, and Architectural Pieces,** 149 E. Alameda St. and 232 Galisteo St. (☎ **505-988-9151**), has an amazing array of colorful *kilims* (flat, handwoven rugs) and Persian and Turkish rugs, as well as antique doors and furnishings.

The **El Paso Import Company,** 418 Sandoval St. (☎ **505-982-5698**), is packed with colorful, weathered colonial and ranchero furniture from

Footloose and fancy flea

The **Pueblo of Tesuque Flea Market,** U.S. 84/285 (about 8 miles north of Santa Fe), is a world-class flea market that attracts in-the-know bargain hunters from across the globe. More than 500 vendors sell everything from used cowboy boots (which lure aficionados all the way from Paris) to Southwestern clothing and jewelry, rare books, antique furniture, and power tools. The flea market sprawls over a spectacular spit of land alongside the Santa Fe Opera, with expansive vistas of Northern New Mexico. Be sure to check out the **Joelle of Santa Fe** booth (rows C and D, spaces 50–55), where you can pick up Afghan rugs and exotic antiques for a fraction of what you would pay for the same quality items at downtown boutiques. The flea market is open from March to late November, on Friday, Saturday, and Sunday.

Mexico. If you look for cooking, serving, and decorating pieces, the **Nambe Outlet,** 924 Paseo de Peralta at Canyon Rd. (☎ 800-443-0339), has items fashioned from a beautiful sand-cast and handcrafted alloy. They also have a store at 104 W. San Francisco St. (☎ 505-988-3574). **Joshua Baer & Company,** 116½ E. Palace Ave. (☎ 505-988-8944) is a great place to find 19th-century Navajo blankets, pottery, jewelry, and primitive art from around the world.

You can spend hours in **Ortega's on the Plaza,** 101 W. San Francisco St. (☎ 505-988-1866), where you find turquoise and silver jewelry, beadwork, rugs, and pottery. For ceramics, check out **Artesanos Imports Company,** 222 Galisteo St. (☎ 505-983-1743), which has a nice selection of Talavera tile and pottery, as well as light fixtures and other home accessories. **Packards,** 61 Old Santa Fe Trail (☎ 505-983-9241), is the classic old store on the Plaza for Native American arts and crafts.

Art galleries

Santa Fe claims to be the third largest art market in the United States, after New York and Los Angeles, and the City Different is crawling with artists working in every medium imaginable, many of them drawn to the famous high desert light of Northern New Mexico. As you wander through the local galleries, you find everything from cutting-edge contemporary art to the finely painted western landscapes of 19th-century masters. If you're a serious collector, try to be in town for the **Spanish Market** in July, or the **Indian Market** in August, which attract jet-setting aficionados from all over the world. It takes months to peruse every gallery in town, but here are some of the most interesting ones, grouped together by location:

> ✔ **Canyon Road and nearby.** Begin your gallery tour at the **Gerald Peters Gallery,** 1011 Paseo de Peralta (☎ 505-954-5700), a two-story pueblo-style building showing museum-quality works by

artists such as Georgia O'Keeffe, Dale Chihuly, Jim Dine, and the founders of the Santa Fe and Taos artist colonies. Next door, you find the **Nedra Matteucci Galleries,** 1075 Paseo de Peralta (☎ 505-982-4631), which specialize in 19th- and 20th-century American art, including works by early Taos and Santa Fe painters. Around the corner at the **Photo-Eye Gallery,** 370 Garcia St., a block from Canyon Road (☎ 505-988-5152), you find contemporary photography by emerging artists and internationally known photographers such as Jock Sturges. As you make your way up Canyon Road, check out the **Munson Gallery,** 225 Canyon Rd. (☎ 505-983-1657), and the **Karan Ruhlen Gallery,** 225 Canyon Rd. (☎ 505-820-0807), both representing contemporary artists. The **Morning Star Gallery,** 513 Canyon Rd. (☎ 505-982-8187), is the world's largest gallery dealing exclusively in museum-quality Native American antiques. The **Zaplin-Lampert Gallery,** 651 Canyon Rd. (☎ 505-982-6100), specializes in the work of the early artists of Santa Fe, Taos, and the American West. **Helix Fine Art,** 670 Canyon Rd. (☎ 505-988-2888), is easily the hippest gallery on Canyon Road and shows cutting-edge art by artists such as Richard Campiglio. The **Turner-Carroll Gallery,** 725 Canyon Rd. (☎ 505-986-9800), exhibits the work of inventive painters such as Alexandra Eldridge.

✔ **Downtown.** As you explore the downtown area, check out **LewAllen Contemporary,** 129 W. Palace Ave. (☎ 505-988-8997), an expansive gallery showing contemporary work by international and national artists such as Ramona Sakiestewa. Housed within the Historic Spiegelberg House, a refurbished Victorian adobe, the **Peyton-Wright Gallery,** 237 E. Palace Ave. (☎ 505-989-9888), shows African, contemporary, Spanish Colonial, Russian, Native American, and Pre-Colombian art and antiquities. The **Andrew Smith Gallery,** 203 W. San Francisco St. (☎ 505-984-1234), displays photography by Annie Lebowitz, Edward Curtis, Henri Cartier-Bresson, Ansel Adams, and too many other famous names to mention. The **Davis Mather Folk Art Gallery,** 141 Lincoln Ave. (☎ 505-983-1660), is the place to find folk art carvings. **Owings Dewey Fine Art,** 76 E. San Francisco St. (☎ 505-982-6244), exhibits 19th- and 20th-century American painting and sculpture, including works by Georgia O'Keeffe and Fremont Ellis.

✔ **Points beyond.** Serious collectors make the 25-minute drive to the sleepy village of Galisteo to visit **Linda Durham Contemporary Art,** 12 La Vega (☎ 505-466-6600), one of the most exciting galleries in the Santa Fe area, showing the abstract work of painters Charles Thomas O'Neil, Robert Kelly, and others. The **Shidoni Foundry, Gallery, and Sculpture Gardens,** 5 miles north of Santa Fe on Bishop's Lodge Road in Tesuque (☎ 505-988-8001), is a mecca for sculptors and sculpture enthusiasts. Visitors can tour two galleries, a sprawling sculpture garden, and the foundry to view casting processes.

Art speak

For the hip and happening word on the Santa Fe arts scene, pick up a copy of *THE Magazine*, a free monthly tabloid distributed in street boxes, galleries, and restaurants around town. Likewise, check out the weekly *Santa Fe Reporter* (also free) or the Friday *Pasatiempo* entertainment section of the *Santa Fe New Mexican*. In the galleries, you may want to pick up a free copy of *The Collector's Guide to Santa Fe, Taos, and Albuquerque*, a useful catalogue of local art dealers.

Books

Santa Feans are big readers, and several excellent locally-owned bookstores await visitors. One of the most interesting is **Allá**, upstairs at 102 W. San Francisco St. (☎ 505-988-5416), which specializes in hard-to-find Spanish and Native American books and music. The **Collected Works Bookstore** nearby, 208-B W. San Francisco St. (☎ 505-988-4226), has a carefully chosen selection of fiction and non-fiction books on a wide selection of topics. **Garcia Street Books,** 376 Garcia St. (☎ 505-986-0151), also has a great selection and is complemented by **Photo-Eye Books & Prints** next door (☎ 505-988-5152), which carries high-end photography books. Head to **Nicholas Potter, Bookseller,** 211 E. Palace Ave. (☎ 505-983-5434), for rare and used hardcover books. Last but not least is **Borders Books and Music** at 500 Montezuma Ave. (☎ 505-984-4707), part of the national chain and always packed with browsers.

Clothing, belts, hats, shoes, and jewelry

The clothing selection for men is weak in Santa Fe, but women have some interesting options to choose from. **Spirit Clothing,** 109 W. San Francisco St. (☎ 505-982-2677), specializes in French and Italian imports. **Judy's Unique Apparel,** 714 Canyon Rd. (☎ 505-988-5746), offers eclectic separates made locally or imported from around the globe. **Michael Robinson Collections,** 708 Canyon Rd. (☎ 505-989-7771), carries beautifully designed velvet shearlings in a variety of colors. **Origins,** 135 W. San Francisco St. (☎ 505-988-2323), is packed with wearable art, folk art, and the work of local designers. **Overland Sheepskin Company,** 217 Galisteo St. (☎ 505-983-4727), draws you in the door with a rich smell of leather and may hold you there until you purchase a coat, blazer, hat, or other finely made leather item. **Caballo,** 727 Canyon Rd. (☎ 505-984-0971), carries custom-made belts and handcrafted silver belt buckles made by designer Wendy Krag. **Tresa Vorenberg Goldsmiths,** 656 Canyon Rd. (☎ 505-988-7215), **Luna Felix Goldsmith,** 116 W. San Francisco St., (☎ 505-989-7679), and **Dell Fox Jewelry,** 500 Montezuma St., (☎ 505-986-0685), are all superb jewelry shops worth stopping by. Hat lovers appreciate the **Montecristi Custom**

Hat Works, 322 McKenzie St. (☎ 505-983-9598). **Wild Things,** 316 Garfield St. (☎ 505-983-4908), is a fun place to shop for vintage clothing and is a favorite haunt of visiting movie stars such as Patricia Arquette.

Food

A great spot to find fresh goat cheese, cider, salsa, baked goods, and other locally made treats (as well as fresh produce) is the **Farmer's Market** in the rail yard adjacent to Sanbusco Market Center, 500 Montezuma St. (☎ 505-983-4098). The market is open every Saturday and Tuesday from 7 a.m. to noon from late April to mid-November. **The Chile Shop,** 109 E. Water St. (☎ 505-983-6080), and the **Coyote Café General Store,** 132 W. Water St. (☎ 505-982-2454), are two well-stocked chile emporiums, selling hot sauces, salsas, and cookbooks. Sweet-tooths find relief at **Señor Murphy Candy Maker,** 100 E. San Francisco St. at La Fonda hotel (☎ 505-982-0461), where everything is made with local ingredients — try the chile piñon-nut brittle.

Living It Up After Dark

The City Different is better known for its world-famous classical music scene than its rather sleepy nightlife, but you don't have to spend every night at the opera. If your taste runs more toward tequila than chardonnay, some fun little hot spots await where you can let the good times roll.

Consult the *Pasatiempo* section, published in the *Santa Fe New Mexican* every Friday, for arts events and club listings. Also check out the listings in the *Santa Fe Reporter,* a free alternative weekly that comes out on Wednesdays. Santa Fe is its most action-packed in summer.

Nightlife

Most major musical acts bypass Santa Fe for Albuquerque (or skip New Mexico altogether), except during summer, when you can catch big-name performers at the open-air **Paolo Soleri Outdoor Amphitheater** at the Santa Fe Indian School, 1501 Cerrillos Rd. (☎ 505-989-6318). For tickets or event information, call **TicketMaster** at ☎ 505-883-7800. A fantastic place to see a show, this intimate, sunken amphitheater has excellent sightlines.

Throughout the rest of the year, a steady stream of touring indie rock bands and world music artists perform at **The Paramount,** 331 Sandoval St. (☎ 505-982-8999), a stylish space with a large dance floor and a long bar. The **Sweeney Convention Center,** 201 W. Marcy St. (☎ 800-777-2489 or 505-955-6200), also presents sporadic musical performances.

Bars

Santa Fe's limited bar scene is anchored by several old standards, and being a tourist town, you also find bars in many of the hotels. Bars close at 2 a.m. (last call's usually at 1:30 a.m.), and if you have to pay a cover, it's usually not more than $5. The most popular bars are in the downtown area.

The classic watering hole for Santa Fe face time is the **Dragon Room,** 406 Old Santa Fe Trail (☎ **505-983-7712**), which often has live *nuevo* flamenco music. Santa Fe's only downtown dive is **Evangelo's,** 200 W. San Francisco St. (☎ **505-982-9014**), a smoky, Polynesian-themed joint with pool tables in the basement. **Tiny's Lounge,** southeast corner of Cerrillos Road and St. Francis Drive (☎ **505-983-9817**), is a fabulously kitschy watering hole with red leatherette booths. The **Bar B** at the Paramount nightclub, 331 Sandoval St. (☎ **505-982-8999**), strives to create the hippest scene in Santa Fe, with DJs spinning trendy tunes for the Generation X crowd. For just an all-around pleasant place to enjoy a drink, head to the **Artist's Pub** at the Hotel St. Francis, 210 Don Gaspar Ave. (☎ **505-983-5700**).

Blues, rock, reggae, Latin, and country and western

For live music in Santa Fe, all roads seem to lead to **El Farol,** 808 Canyon Rd. (☎ **505-983-9912**), a rustic, western hacienda-style bar that's always packed with colorful characters shaking a leg to blues and rock bands. **The Catamount,** 125 Water St. (☎ **505-988-7222**), is a hopping bar/restaurant with blues, rock, and reggae acts, along with a popular upstairs pool hall. The **Cowgirl Hall of Fame,** 319 Guadalupe St. (☎ **505-982-2565**), is a lively bar restaurant (a sort of El Farol junior), which showcases local musical talent. **Rodeo Nites,** 2911 Cerrillos Rd. (☎ **505-473-4138**), draws the two-stepping country and western crowd. **Club Alegría,** Agua Fria Road, two blocks south of Siler Road (☎ **505-471-2324**), is the place to catch the hot Latin music of the very popular Pretto y Parranda on Friday nights.

Piano bars

If listening to a crooner tinkle the ivories tickles your fancy, try **Vanessie of Santa Fe,** 434 W. San Francisco St. (☎ **505-982-9966**), Santa Fe's most popular piano bar, where Doug Montgomery (also known as the "silver fox") has a loyal following. Also, stop by the wonderful old saloon-style piano bar at **The Palace Restaurant & Saloon,** 142 W. Palace Ave. (☎ **505-982-9893**), or the **Mañana Restaurant and Bar,** Alameda and Don Gaspar Avenue(☎ **505-982-4333**).

The Arts

There are no fewer than 24 performing arts groups in Santa Fe — not bad for a city of 70,000. Most of them perform year-round, but come summer, the arts blossom in Santa Fe, and many visitors come to town specifically for opera performances and the Santa Fe Chamber Music Festival.

Olde English at high altitude

Among Santa Fe's most fun summer arts treats are the outdoor performances of **Shakespeare in Santa Fe**, whose box office is at 355 E. Palace Ave. (☎ 505-982-2910). Every Friday, Saturday, and Sunday during July and August, the group presents Shakespeare in the Park — fun performances by talented actors in the library courtyard of St. John's College located southeast of downtown, off Camino del Monte Sol. Bring a picnic, a blanket (a must, as well as a warm hat), and a hearty appreciation for El Bard.

An exciting new addition to the Santa Fe arts scene is the recently opened **Lensic Performing Arts Center,** 211 W. San Francisco St. (☎ 505-988-7050). Housed in a wonderfully atmospheric Arabian Nights–themed former movie palace (opened in 1931), the old theater received a multi-million dollar facelift from 2000 to 2001, reinventing it as a state-of-the-art performance facility. It hosts most of the city's top arts performances.

Cinema

Lots of film lovers live in Santa Fe, and two outstanding cinematheques are **Plan B,** 1050 Old Pecos Trail (☎ 505-982-1338), and **The Screen,** 1600 St. Michael's Dr. at the College of Santa Fe (☎ 505-473-6494). Both show an amazing variety of classic and cutting-edge cinema from around the world.

Classical music

One of Santa Fe's crown jewels (some would say *the* crown jewel) is the **Santa Fe Opera,** 7 miles north of the city off U.S. 84/285 (☎ 800-280-4654 or 505-986-5900 for tickets; Internet: www.santafeopera.org). The open-air opera is noted for its world-class performances of classics, little-known works by European composers, and American premieres of 20th-century works. Many rank it second only to the Metropolitan Opera of New York as the finest opera company in the United States. The eight-week, 40-performance opera season runs from late June to late August. Tickets range from $20 to $128 (opening night gala tickets $50–$200). Almost as impressive is the equally outstanding **Santa Fe Chamber Music Festival,** 239 Johnson St. (☎ 505-983-2075 or ☎ 505-982-1890 for the box office June through August; Internet: www.santafechambermusic.org). Some of the biggest names in classical music come to Santa Fe each summer for this festival's six-week season, which features chamber-music masterpieces, new music by a composer in residence, and jazz. Tickets range from $15 to $40. The **Santa Fe Symphony Orchestra and Chorus** (☎ 800-480-1319 or 505-983-1414) is a 60-piece symphony orchestra performing classical and popular works at the Lensic Performing Arts Center, 211 West San Francisco St. Tickets go for between $10 and $40.

Theater and dance

Thanks to **Santa Fe Stages,** 100 N. Guadalupe St. (☎ **505-982-6683;** Internet: www.santafestages.org), Santa Fe is blessed with year-round performances by international theater and dance troupes. To check out local thespian talent, head for the **Santa Fe Playhouse,** 142 E. de Vargas St. (☎ **505-988-4262**), where the oldest extant theater group in New Mexico performs in a historic adobe theater. If you like flamenco, you won't want to miss the **María Benítez Teatro Flamenco,** Institute for Spanish Arts, P.O. Box 8418 (☎ **800-905-3315** or 505-982-1237 for the box office June 16–Sept 3). Trained in Spain, María Benitez is an enthralling performer. The Benitez Company's "Estampa Flamenca" summer series is performed nightly — except Tuesday from late June to early September — in the **María Benitez Theater** at the Radisson Hotel, 750 N. St. Francis Dr. (☎ **505-992-5800**).

Quick Concierge: Santa Fe

AAA

Find the local office at 1644 St. Michael's Dr. (☎ 505-471-6620).

American Express

Santa Fe does not have a branch of American Express.

Area Code

The area code for Santa Fe is **505,** but may change. For updates, contact the New Mexico Department of Tourism (☎ 800-733-6396; Internet: www.newmexico.org).

ATMs

You find ATMs (also known as *cash pueblos*) all over town, at supermarkets, banks, and drive throughs, including several branches of Bank of America.

Credit Cards

For lost or stolen cards, contact the following: Visa (☎ 800-847-2911), MasterCard (☎ 800-307-7309), American Express (☎ 800-668-2639), or Discover (☎ 800-347-2683).

Doctors

You should first contact your insurance provider for recommended local physicians.

You can also try the Lovelace clinic, 440 St. Michael's Dr. (☎ 505-995-2400).

Emergencies

For police, fire, or ambulance, dial ☎ **911.**

Hospitals

The major facility is St. Vincent's Hospital, 455 St. Michael's Dr. (☎ 505-820-5250).

Information

The Santa Fe Convention and Visitors Bureau is at 201 W. Marcy St. (☎ 800-777-2489 or 505-955-6200; Internet: www.santafe.org or www.visitsantafe.com).

Internet Access & Cyber Cafes

Enjoy an espresso with your e-mail at Aztec Café, 317 Aztec St. (☎ 505-983-9464). Retrieve your e-mail at Kinko's, 301 N. Guadalupe (☎ 505-473-7303), for 20¢ a minute or $12 an hour.

Liquor Laws

The legal drinking age is 21 in New Mexico. Alcohol is sold every day, although many liquor establishments are closed on Sundays.

Maps

You can pick up a free copy of the *Santa Fe Official Visitor's Guide,* which includes a map of downtown, at the Santa Fe Convention and Visitors Bureau (see "Information," earlier in this listing). For topographic maps of New Mexico, head to Travel Bug, 328 S. Guadalupe (☎ 505-992-0418; Internet: www.mapsofnewmexico.com), where you find one of the best selections of U.S. Geological Survey maps in the state.

Newspapers & Magazines

The *Santa Fe New Mexican* (the oldest newspaper in the West) and the *Albuquerque Journal North* are the local dailies, with the *New Mexican's* Friday *Pasatiempo* section offering the most comprehensive entertainment listings and extensive arts coverage. The *Santa Fe Reporter* is a free alternative weekly that comes out every Wednesday. *THE Magazine* is a free monthly tabloid covering the local and national arts scene. The glossy *Santa Fean* magazine is a monthly covering the City Different and points beyond. *New Mexico* magazine is another monthly glossy — the title says it all.

Pharmacies

You can find a 24-hour pharmacy at Walgreens, 1096 S. St. Francis Dr. (☎ 505-982-9811).

Police

Call ☎ **911** for emergencies. For non-emergencies call ☎ 505-473-5080.

Post Office

The Main Post Office is at 120 S. Federal Place (☎ 505-988-6351), two blocks north and one block west of the Plaza. Window services are open from 7:30 a.m. to 5:45 p.m. The zip code for central Santa Fe is 87501.

Restrooms

Public restrooms are available in the Sweeney Convention Center, 201 W. Marcy St. (☎ 800-777-2489 or 505-955-6200). You can also find restrooms in museums and businesses around town.

Road Conditions

For a road report, call ☎ 800-432-4269.

Safety

Although the downtown area is relatively safe, Santa Fe has nevertheless been experiencing an increasing number of thefts and reports of rape. Guard your valuables when walking the streets of Santa Fe, especially during the summer tourist months when purse-snatching usually increases.

Smoking

Most public buildings and restaurants are non-smoking, but Santa Fe bars are usually on the smoky side, despite all the health nuts in town.

Taxes

Establishments add a tax of 11.44% to all lodging bills.

Taxis

Capital City Cab is the only game in town (☎ 505-438-0000).

Time Zone

Mountain standard time.

Transit Information

Santa Fe Trails (☎ 505-955-2001) offers local bus service.

Weather

For weather forecasts, call ☎ 505-988-5151. To get a local weather forecast on the Internet, log on to www.accuweather.com and use the Santa Fe zip code, 87501.

Chapter 14

Side Trips from Santa Fe

• •

In This Chapter

▶ The ancient and modern: The northern pueblos

▶ Cliff dwellings and *the* bomb: Bandelier and Los Alamos

▶ Bring your convertible: The High Road to Taos

▶ Georgia on my mind: O'Keeffe country and Ojo Caliente

• •

Don your shades and your holiest jeans; it's time to hit the road in search of pueblos, black holes, sacred shrines, and everything in between. Within hours of Santa Fe, you find more exotic sights than most countries can boast, from pueblos to ancient ruins to Hispanic villages to hot springs. Or you may find yourself just cruising the blue highways chasing down a blazing sunset — they don't call this the Land of Enchantment for nothing.

Day Trip 1: Touring the Northern Pueblos

If you enjoy tripping across centuries within a single moment, you should definitely tour some of Northern New Mexico's pueblos. The very best pueblos to visit are Acoma (see Chapter 19) and Taos Pueblo (see Chapter 15), but some of the others offer a good glimpse of the melding of ancient and contemporary life.

This first trip is a great one to take if you want to see something rich and interesting but don't feel like doing a lot of driving. Because six of the eight northern pueblos are within 30 miles of Santa Fe, you can visit several of them and still make a leisurely day of it. Touring the pueblos is also a good way to make your way to or from Taos, putting you on the "Low Road" rather than the "High Road," which I detail in "Day Trip 3," later in this chapter. This itinerary takes you to pueblos that really give you a sense of the ancient lifestyle: **San Ildefonso,** with its broad plaza; **Santa Clara** and the **Puye Cliff Dwellings;** and **San Juan** and its arts cooperative. This trip also visits the village of **Española,** a great place to eat New Mexican food.

Courting Lady Luck

For those of you who like to test your luck against fate's churning wheel, plenty of places await you in Northern New Mexico. Though you don't encounter the finely-tuned operations of Las Vegas here, you find all the casino games you're accustomed to. I recommend **Camel Rock Casino** (☎ **505-984-8414**), located about 9 miles north of Santa Fe on U.S. 84/285, because it's fairly close to Santa Fe and has a broad and open feel inside. The casino is open Sunday to Thursday from 8 a.m. to 4 a.m., and Friday and Saturday 24 hours. A snack bar is on the premises.

Before visiting the pueblos, be sure to read the **rules of etiquette** outlined in Chapter 21.

Getting there

To reach the pueblos, drive north of Santa Fe on U.S. 84/285 for 15 miles. At the village of Pojoaque, take the exit for N.M. 502, the road to Los Alamos. Follow this road for 6 miles and turn north into San Ildefonso Pueblo. After touring the pueblo, continue west on N.M. 502 for 2 miles to the exit for N.M. 30. Follow N.M. 30 north for 4 miles to Indian Road 601. Take this road for 7 miles to the Puye Cliff Dwellings. Backtrack to N.M. 30 and drive 3 miles north to Santa Clara Pueblo. After touring Santa Clara, return to N.M. 30, and follow it north a mile to Española, a good place to stop for lunch. In Española, get onto N.M. 68 and follow it north through town and for 4 more miles to N.M. 74, where you turn west and drive 1 mile to San Juan Pueblo, your last stop.

Seeing the sights

En route north, about 9 miles from Santa Fe, you pass through lands belonging to **Tesuque** (Te-*soo*-keh) **Pueblo.** Here, farm fields line the sides of the highway, where some of the 400 pueblo dwellers cultivate crops. About 6 miles farther north you pass through **Pojoaque** (po-*wah*-key) village. Though Pojoaque Pueblo doesn't have a traditional village to visit, you do find the Poeh Center, a museum and crafts store operated by the pueblo, and a casino.

Turn left on N.M. 502 at Pojoaque, and drive about 6 miles to the turnoff to **San Ildefonso Pueblo** (☎ **505-455-3549**). Called *Po who ge* (Po-*ho*-gay) in its own Tewa language, the name means "place where the water cuts down through," a reference to the fact that the Rio Grande cuts through the land on this pueblo. Set along the river bottom, the pueblo's real draw (bringing some 20,000 visitors each year) is the broad, dusty plaza, with a *kiva* (a circular, underground

Side Trips from Santa Fe

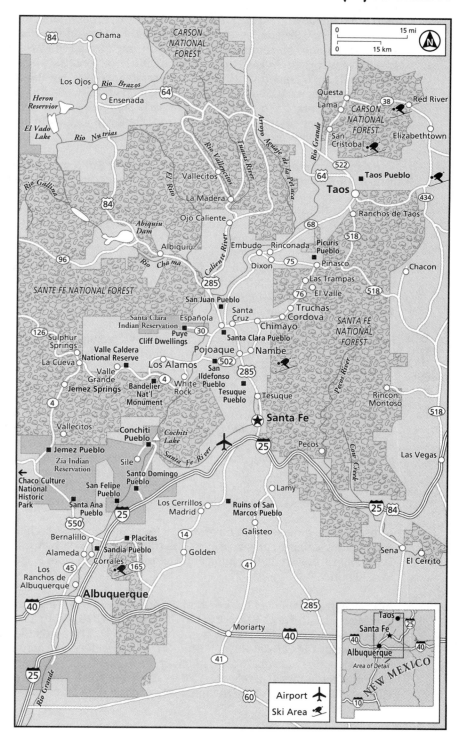

ceremonial chamber) on one side, ancient dwellings on the other, and a church at the far end. The pueblo is also nationally famous for its matte-finish black-on-black pottery, developed by tribeswoman María Martinez in the 1920s. A few shops surround the plaza, and the **San Ildefonso Pueblo Museum** (open Monday through from Friday 8 a.m. to 4 p.m.) is tucked away in the governor's office beyond the plaza. I especially recommend visiting during ceremonial days. **San Ildefonso Feast Day** is January 23 and features the buffalo and Comanche dances in alternate years. **Corn dances,** held in early September, commemorate a basic element in pueblo life, the importance of fertility in all creatures (humans as well as animals) and plants.

The admission charge to the pueblo is $3. You pay $10 to use a still camera during your visit, $20 to use a video camera, and $25 to sketch what you see. The pueblo is open to the public weekdays from 8 a.m. to 5 p.m. in the summer (call for weekend hours), and Monday to Friday from 8 a.m. to 4:30 p.m. in winter. It's closed to the public for major holidays and tribal events.

From San Ildefonso, continue west on N.M. 502 for 2 miles to the exit for N.M. 30, which you follow north for 4 miles to Indian Road 601, with signs pointing west to the **Puye Cliff Dwellings** (☎ 505-753-7326). Travel this paved road for 7 miles to the ruins.

In 2000, a forest fire devastated the Puye ruins, forcing the tribe to close them for repairs. They're scheduled to reopen in 2002, but you definitely want to call before venturing out.

These ruins are so well preserved that you swear you can hear ancient life clamoring around you. You first encounter dwellings built around 1450. Above on a 200-foot *tuff* (gray, crumbly volcanic rock) cliff face are dwellings dating from 1200. By 1540, this dwelling's population was at its height and Puye was the center for a number of villages on the Pajarito Plateau. Today, you get to climb up sturdy ladders and wander through the remaining walls of bedrooms and kitchens. *Petroglyphs* (paintings on rock) are evident on many of the rocky cliff walls.

At press time, admission to Puye was $6 for adults and $5 for children and seniors; call for current prices. The ruins are open daily April to September from 8 a.m. to 8 p.m., and October to March from 8 a.m. to 4:30 p.m.

After leaving Puye, head back to N.M. 30 and drive north a few miles, turning east into **Santa Clara Pueblo** (☎ 505-753-7326). With a population of about 1,600, this pueblo is one of the largest. The Santa Clarans once lived at the cliffs at Puye. In the 13th century, they migrated down to this riverside village. Though much of the contemporary village consists of tract homes (there's not a lot to see here), the heart of the old village still survives. Follow the main route to the old village, where you come to the visitor center, also known as the neighborhood center. There you can get directions to small shops that sell the distinctive black incised Santa Clara pottery and other crafts. You should also stop at the church to see the cemetery. Corn and harvest dances occur on **Santa Clara Feast Day,** August 12.

Admission is free. The charge for still cameras is $5, if allowed at all (depending on the Pueblo's activities for the day); call for information about using movie cameras and sketching. The pueblo is open daily during daylight hours; visitor center hours are Monday to Friday from 8 a.m. to 4:30 p.m.

One mile north you come to the town of **Española,** one of my favorite places to eat New Mexican food. This community of 7,000 residents is cruising central in New Mexico. At times (on weekend nights in particular), the main street can become so choked with cars that your travel time through town can double. What's great about being caught in such a rumble of cars is the quality of them. This is the home of the low-rider, a celebration of the automobile as an art form (see the sidebar "Lowriders: Car art").

If you'd like to explore Española further, check out the **Santa Cruz Church** (east of town on N.M. 76). Built in 1733, it houses many fine examples of Spanish colonial religious art.

In Española, get onto N.M. 68 and continue north. Drive about 4 miles, turn west onto N.M. 74, and drive a short distance to **San Juan Pueblo** (☎ **505-852-4400**), one of the best places in the state to glimpse the history of the Spanish Conquest in New Mexico. With a population of 1,950, the pueblo sits across the Rio Grande from the 1598 site of San Gabriel, the first Spanish settlement east of the Mississippi River and the first capital of New Spain. This was the first pueblo to undergo Spanish colonization. A generous people, the San Juans provided food and shelter for Spanish explorer Juan de Oñate and his troops, and years later found themselves enslaved by their guests. In reaction to barbarous treatment, a San Juan Pueblo Indian named Po'Pay became a leader in the Great Pueblo Revolt of 1680, which led to freedom from Spanish rule for 12 years.

The annual **San Juan Fiesta** is held June 23 and 24 and features buffalo and Comanche dances. Another annual ceremony is the **turtle dance** on December 26. The **matachine dance,** performed here Christmas day, vividly depicts the subjugation of the Native Americans by the Catholic Spaniards.

Admission to San Juan Pueblo is free. Photography or sketching may be allowed with prior permission from the pueblo's governor's office. The pueblo is open every day during daylight hours.

Lowriders: Car art

While visiting Española, don't drop your jaw if you see the front of a car raise up off the ground and then sink down again, or if you witness another that appears to be scraping its underbelly on the pavement. These novelties are part of a whole car culture that thrives in northern New Mexico. Traditionally, the owners use late-model cars, which they soup up with such novelties as elaborate chrome, metal chain steering wheels, even portraits of Our Lady of Guadalupe painted on the hood. If you're interested in seeing the "Custom Car and Truck Show" put on by local car clubs (and often co-sponsored by local casinos), call the **Española Chamber of Commerce** (☎ **505-753-2831**) for a schedule.

The **Oke Oweenge Arts and Crafts Cooperative** (☎ **505-852-2372**), a craft shop in the pueblo, specializes in local wares. This is a fine place to seek out San Juan's distinctive red pottery, a lustrous ceramic incised with traditional geometric symbols. The shop is open Monday to Saturday from 9 a.m. to 5 p.m., but may be closed on San Juan Feast Day, June 24.

Unless you plan to continue north to Taos, this is your turn-around point. You may want to end your day with a soak at **Ojo Caliente** (see Day Trip 2 in this chapter for details).

Taking a tour

Pathways Customized Tours (☎ **505-982-5382**; Internet: www.santafe pathways.com) offers a trip to the cliff dwellings and native pueblos of Northern New Mexico, where you can learn about history, culture, and current economic conditions and see a demonstration of how pottery is made. The trip costs $35 per hour per couple. Another Santa Fe tour operator, **Rain Parrish** (☎ **505-984-8236**), offers anthropological tours of the area. Prices average approximately $130 per couple. Some of these tours are true adventures to insider locations that aren't generally open to public tours.

Dining on the road

Española is chile central in northern New Mexico. My very favorite spot to get an enchilada is **El Paragua** ($$–$$$; ☎ **505-753-3211**), 603 Santa Cruz Rd., off the main drag; turn east at Long John Silver. With its golden ceramic Saltillo tiles, this place quickly transports you to Mexico, though the food is pure *New* Mexican, with one of the best enchiladas in the state. Next door, owned by the same biz, is my favorite spot to stop after a day of kayaking on the Rio Grande near

Taos. **El Parasol** ($) is a taco stand with the world's best chicken tacos and outdoor picnic tables. Both restaurants are open daily from 11 a.m. to 9:30 p.m. in summer, and from 11 a.m. to 8:30 p.m. in winter.

Day Trip 2: Bandelier National Monument and Los Alamos

On this trip, you encounter the ruins of an ancient civilization and the birthplace of the atomic bomb — just a short distance away from each other atop the spectacular 7,300-foot Pajarito Plateau. This is one of New Mexico's most beautiful spots, so it's no surprise that pueblo tribes have lived in the area for well over 1,000 years (you can see the evidence at **Bandelier National Monument**). But it's hard to imagine a more out-of-place haunt for the top secret **Manhattan Project,** which was set up here in the early 1940s on the idyllic sight of an exclusive ranch school for boys. Nevertheless, this is where Fat Man and Little Boy (nicknames for the first two atomic bombs) were born, which changed the course of world history forever.

In May 2000, the tragic Cerro Grande fire destroyed over 48,000 acres of the area, and more than 400 Los Alamos residents lost their homes. This was the largest recorded fire in the history of New Mexico, and as you drive into **Los Alamos,** you notice an eerie mountainside of blackened tree trunks towering above the town.

Getting there

Los Alamos is located about 35 miles west of Santa Fe; the drive takes about 50 minutes. From Santa Fe, take U.S. 84/285 north approximately 16 miles to the Pojoaque junction, and then turn west on N.M. 502. Bandelier National Monument is about 15 miles south of Los Alamos along N.M. 4.

Seeing the sights

The sprawl of fenced-off, high-tech laboratories, parks, strip malls, and suburban dwellings that makes up **Los Alamos** (pop. 18,000) is also known as *The Hill.* Another nickname is the *Secret City,* because much of the area is occupied by the security-sensitive **Los Alamos National Laboratory (LANL),** which employs more than 10,000 people and has 32 technical areas occupying 43 square miles of land. One of the world's foremost scientific institutions, LANL is best known for the Manhattan Project (directed by J. Robert Oppenheimer), and defense research is still the primary focus of the lab. LANL is not open to visitors, but for information about Los Alamos's public-friendly attractions, stop by the **Visitor Center** operated by the local Chamber of Commerce, 109 Central

Park Sq. (☎ **505-662-8105**), open Monday to Friday from 9 a.m. to 5 p.m., Saturday from 9 a.m. to 4 p.m., and Sunday from 10 a.m. to 3 p.m.

Not surprisingly, the top sights in Los Alamos have an atomic theme, the most important of which is the **Bradbury Science Museum** at the corner of 15th Street and Central Avenue (☎ **505-667-4444**). The museum is run by LANL and offers more than 40 high-tech, interactive exhibits in five galleries. The exhibits explain some of LANL's defense, technology, and basic research projects, as well as the history of the Manhattan Project. A 20-minute film about the race to build the atomic bomb is shown throughout the day. The museum's hours are Tuesday to Friday from 9 a.m. to 5 p.m. and Saturday to Monday from 1 to 5 p.m. Admission is free. The rustic and welcoming **Los Alamos Historical Museum,** 1921 Juniper St. (☎ **505-662-4493**), is housed in a log-and-stone building next to the **Fuller Lodge** (an impressive John Gaw Meem–designed building from 1928) and is well worth a visit. The museum displays everything from Native American artifacts to wartime memorabilia from the Manhattan Project. The museum is open in summer Monday to Saturday from 9:30 a.m. to 4:30 p.m. and Sunday from 11 a.m. to 5 p.m.; and in winter Monday to Saturday from 10 a.m. to 4 p.m. and Sunday 1 to 4 p.m. Admission is free.

When all things geek start to overwhelm you, take N.M. 4 15 miles south to rural **Bandelier National Monument** (☎ **505-672-3861,** ext 517). Operated by the National Park Service, the area contains extensive ruins of the cliff-dwelling ancestral Puebloan (Anasazi) culture, amid 46 square miles of canyon-and-mesa wilderness. You find a visitor's center, a small museum displaying artifacts found in the area, cliff dwellings, and plenty of great hiking trails. You can follow a pretty trail along Frijoles Creek to the principal ruins of the Puebloan ancestors who lived here between 1100 and 1550. The highlight is climbing a series of ponderosa pine ladders 140 feet up to visit a rock alcove with a sunken kiva. Elsewhere in the monument area, 70 miles of maintained trails lead to more ruins, waterfalls, and wildlife habitats. The 2000 Cerro Grande fire began here as a controlled 300-acre burn. Because the blaze incinerated parts of this area when it spread out of control, periodic closings take place to allow the land to recover. The monument is open daily during daylight hours, except on New Year's Day and Christmas Day. Admission is $10 per vehicle.

First church of high technology

For an offbeat attraction, check out **The Black Hole,** 4015 Arkansas (☎ **505-662-5053**), a techie's fantasyworld run by the outspoken Edward Grothus. He has amassed an enormous collection of Los Alamos lab debris — from Geiger counters to missile casings — that now spills from a former grocery store out onto the parking lot.

The **White Rock Overlook,** in the little town of White Rock (about 10 miles southeast of Los Alamos on N.M. 4), offers extraordinary vistas of the Rio Grande valley in the direction of Santa Fe. The view is well worth a stop on the way between Bandelier National Monument and Los Alamos. When you reach White Rock, follow the signs from N.M. 4.

If you wind your way 15 miles up into the Jemez Mountains west of Bandelier National Monument on N.M. 4, you arrive at the newly designated **Valle Caldera National Reserve** (☎ 505-829-3535). This expansive caldera is one of the largest in the world and was a privately owned ranch until its recent acquisition by the U.S. government. The dramatic, meadowed bowl was created when the underground magma chambers of a gigantic volcano collapsed.

Taking a tour

Georgia Strickfaden's **Buffalo Tours** (☎ 505-662-3965) depart daily at 1 p.m. from the **Ottowi Station Bookstore and Science Museum Gift Shop,** 1350 Central Ave. (☎ 505-662-9589), next door to the Bradbury Science Museum. Strickfaden's 1½-hour tour of Los Alamos includes an informative drive through LANL and a stop at the White Rock Overlook; it costs $10 for adults. From November to March the tours are offered only by request, so call ahead.

Staying in style

The **Best Western Hilltop House Hotel** ($$), 400 Trinity at Central Avenue (☎ 800-462-0936 or 505-662-2441), is a standard hotel with a pool and central location near the museums. For more intimacy, try **Renata's Orange Street Bed and Breakfast** ($–$$), 3496 Orange St., off of Diamond Road (☎ 800-662-3180 or 505-662-2651). The friendly inn sits atop a finger mesa, and most of the rooms have views of a forested canyon.

Dining on the road

Unlike Santa Fe, Los Alamos isn't known for fine cuisine, but you can grab a bite at a few good places. **Tony's Pizzeria** ($–$$), 723 Central Ave. (☎ 505-662-7799), serves pizzas, sandwiches, and pasta dishes. It's open Monday through Saturday for lunch and dinner. The more upscale **Blue Window Bistro** ($$$–$$$$), 813 Central Ave. (☎ 505-662-6305), is a bright, colorful restaurant offering French and New Mexican flavors along with a decent wine list. It's open Monday through Saturday for lunch and dinner, and Saturday for breakfast as well.

Day Trip 3: The High Road to Taos

One of New Mexico's classic drives, the **High Road** from Pojoaque to Ranchos De Taos (also known as the King's Road) is a windy, scenic route ideally enjoyed in a vintage convertible on a sunny fall day, but you'll love it just as much in your rental car. En route, you find picturesque Hispanic villages, including **Chimayo, Cordova,** and **Truchas,** where life has changed little for well over a century. You also discover gorgeous vistas of densely wooded mountains, as well as dramatic, windswept rock formations that continually change in appearance as the high desert light plays across them throughout the day.

If you've already taken the High Road to Taos, you may enjoy driving the Low Road north of Santa Fe to visit some of the pueblos. See Day Trip 1, at the beginning of this chapter, for details on this route.

Getting there

To drive the High Road to Taos, you want to do the following:

1. Head about 16 miles north on N.M. 84/285, and turn right on N.M. 503 toward Nambe, just after you pass through Pojoaque.

2. Continue on N.M. 503 approximately 16 miles past the Pojoaque junction to Chimayo at the junction of N.M. 520 and N.M. 76.

3. From Chimayo, drive north on N.M. 76 past Cordova and Truchas to Peñasco, and then head a few miles east on N.M. 75 towards Mora until you reach N.M. 518.

4. Follow N.M. 518 north the rest of the way to Ranchos de Taos. To reach Dixon and Embudo, head west on N.M. 75.

Seeing the sights

Your first stop is the historic weaving village of **Chimayo,** about a 32-mile drive north of Santa Fe. Visitors come from all over the world to visit the cute, much photographed **El Santuario de Nuestro Señor de Esquipulas** (the Shrine of Our Lord of Esquipulas), better known as "El Santuario de Chimayo." A National Historic landmark (built in 1814–16), the tiny church is believed to have miraculous healing powers, and as many as 30,000 people join a Good Friday pilgrimage to visit the shrine each year. In the days leading up to the holiday, it's not uncommon to see cross-bearing pilgrims trudging along the state highways from as far away as Albuquerque. In an anteroom beside the altar, you usually find someone scooping loose dirt, believed to have miraculous healing powers, from a hole in the floor. You also find a beautifully painted altar screen and side panels in the highly atmospheric church itself. In the nearby gift shops, you can buy religious articles such as the tiny charms known as *milagros,* and cool little gearshift knobs with images of the Virgen de Guadalupe. In the surrounding village of Chimayo, generations of weavers have been crafting textiles since the early 1800s. Stop by **Ortega's Weaving Shop** and **Galeria Ortega,** at the corner of N.M. 520 and N.M. 76, and **Trujillo Weavings** on N.M. 76.

Continuing about 7 miles east on N.M. 76 past Chimayo, you come upon a sharp right turn to the tiny village of **Cordova,** which is as famous for its wood carvings as Chimayo is for its weavings. The **Castillo Gallery,** about a mile into the village, exhibits contemporary woodcarvings by local artists.

After winding your way 4 miles east of Cordova on N.M. 76, you enter the picturesque hilltop town of **Truchas,** at 8,000 feet, which was featured in Robert Redford's 1988 movie *The Milagro Beanfield War.* The scenery here is spectacular — 13,101-foot Truchas Peak towers over the town, while the Rio Grande valley sweeps beyond.

Continuing 6 miles east of Truchas on N.M. 76, you pass through the little town of **Las Trampas.** Many consider its **San José Church** to be one of the most beautiful Spanish colonial churches in New Mexico.

Just outside the little town of **Peñasco,** about 24 miles from Chimayo near the intersection of N.M. 75 and N.M. 76, you find the **Picuris (San Lorenzo) Pueblo** (☎ 505-587-2519). The Picuris have never made a treaty with any foreign country, including the United States, and the pueblo's 375 citizens, native Tiwa speakers, consider their 15,000 mountain acres a sovereign nation. Some of the pueblo's historic kivas and storerooms are open to visitors, and weaving, beadwork, and pottery are on display at the **Picuris Pueblo Museum and Visitor's Center,** open daily from 9 a.m. to 6 p.m. Self-guided tours through ruins begin at the museum and cost $1.75; the fee to tour the museum and take photographs is $5.

Taos is about 24 miles north of Peñasco via N.M. 518, but you can loop back to Santa Fe by taking N.M. 75 west from Picuris Pueblo to N.M. 68, and then heading south. **Dixon,** a pleasant little apple-growing arts town approximately 12 miles west of Picuris, and the village of **Embudo,** a mile farther on N.M. 68 at the Rio Grande, are both home to a number of artists and craftspeople.

Staying in style

A handful of inns exist in and around Chimayo. **Casa Escondida** ($$–$$$), just off N.M. 76 at mile marker 100 (☎ 800-643-7201 or 505-351-4805), is a sweet retreat and makes a good base for explorations of the area. **Rancho Manzana** ($$), 26 Camino de misión (☎ 888-505-2227 or 505-351-2227; Internet: www.taoswebb.com/manzana), offers well-appointed lodgings in an elegantly restored historic building on the old Plaza del Cerro in Chimayo. A lovely lavender garden exists in back.

Dining on the road

You may want to consider planning your excursion around a long lunch at the **Rancho de Chimayo** restaurant ($$–$$$), just up the road from the Santuario on N.M. 76 (☎ **505-351-4444**). This is a northern New Mexico classic, with native New Mexican food (prepared from generations-old family recipes) served in warm, rustic rooms with high ceilings and wooden floors, or in a terraced garden during the warmer months. The restaurant is open daily for lunch and dinner, with breakfast on weekends only. Alternatively, you can try the popular taco and burrito stand, **Leona's de Chimayo** ($), next to the Santuario de Chimayo (☎ **505-351-4569**), which is open Wednesday to Monday from 9 a.m. to 5 p.m.

Day Trip 4: Georgia O'Keeffe Country and Ojo Caliente

Many visitors to New Mexico arrive with visions of the state influenced by the works of the late painter Georgia O'Keeffe. If you admire her work, it's worth taking the drive up to Abiquiu to tour her former home and take in some of the stunning landscapes that influenced her artistic vision. You can also have a soak in the ancient hot springs at Ojo Caliente, which the early Spanish explorer Cabeza de Vaca thought were the legendary fountains of youth.

Getting there

To reach the tiny town of Abiquiu from Santa Fe, take U.S. 84/285 north to Española (25 miles). Once in Española, bear left to stay on U.S. 84/285. Routes 84 and 285 split, and you find Abiquiu about 22 miles north on U.S. 84.

To reach Ojo Caliente (about 55 miles north of Santa Fe), take U.S. 84/285 north to Española (25 miles). Once in Española, bear left to stay on U.S 84/285, and continue north on highway 285 after it splits to the right from U.S. 84.

Seeing the sights

After you reach the little village of **Abiquiu,** the main attraction is the former home of **Georgia O'Keeffe** (1887–1986). You can tour her home only by appointment (see the next section, "Taking a tour"), and you need to make reservations several months in advance to do so. The guided tour takes you through the old adobe house and studio where she created some of her most memorable works.

If you bathe your bod in the geothermal waters at **Ojo Caliente Mineral Springs** in the town of Ojo Caliente (☎ **800-222-9162**), you share an experience that Native Americans, Spanish explorers, New Agers, and local bikers have all enjoyed as well. The springs in the rustic, Victorian-style resort tend to be on the grungy side, but just remember that Ojo Caliente is the only place in the U.S. where you can find five different types of hot springs: arsenic, iron, lithia, soda, and salt.

You can obtain more information on the area from the **Española Valley Chamber of Commerce,** 417 Big Rock Center, Española (☎ **505-753-2831**).

Taking a tour

You need to call several months in advance to book tours of Georgia O'Keeffe's home and studio, which are led by the **Georgia O'Keeffe Foundation** (☎ **505-685-4539;** Fax: 505-685-4551). They conduct tours from mid-April through late November, at 9:30 a.m., 11 a.m., 2 p.m., and 3:30 p.m. on Tuesdays, Thursdays, and Fridays. Tours last approximately one hour and are limited to 12 people. A fee of $22 per person is due one month before the tour date, and no refunds are given. Visitors are not permitted to take pictures. Tours start at the Abiquiu Inn on U.S. 84.

Staying in style

The **Abiquiu Inn** ($), on U.S. 84 just south of Abiquiu (☎ **800-447-5621** or 505-685-4378), is a pleasant, Southwestern inn with several *casitas* (little houses) and a nice little restaurant. The very upscale **Ranchos de San Juan** ($$$$), on U.S. 285 just south of Ojo Caliente (☎ **505-753-6818**), is an exclusive retreat with beautifully built casitas, a gourmet restaurant, and an extraordinary chapel carved out of a small sandstone butte. The resort is popular with Europeans and celebrities; Gene Hackman, Shirley McClaine, Val Kilmer, and Neil Diamond have all stayed here.

Dining on the road

Two restaurants worth trying are those at the **Abiquiu Inn** ($$–$$$) (☎ **800-447-5621**), which is open daily for breakfast, lunch, and dinner, and at **Ranchos de San Juan** ($$$$; ☎ **505-753-6818**), which is open for dinner only, Tuesday through Saturday. If you just want something basic, such as a deli sandwich or a *Frito pie* (made with Fritos, chiles, cheese, lettuce, tomatoes, onions, and sour cream), head to **Bode's** ($) on U.S. 84 in Abiquiu (☎ **505-685-4422**), a wonderful old general store, which is open daily for breakfast and lunch.

Chapter 15

Taos

. . . .

In This Chapter

▶ Finding your way to and around Taos

▶ Locating a bunk

▶ Chowing down

▶ Exploring the sights on your own or with a guide

▶ Getting outdoors

▶ Shopping for arts, crafts, and funky Taos stuff

▶ Discovering the primo after-dark diversions

. . . .

*N*ew Mexico's favorite arts town, Taos is like one of those kids who is always in trouble with his parents but is so wild and creative that everybody loves him. The town of 5,000 residents combines 1960s hippiedom (thanks to communes that set up in the hills back then) with the ancient culture of Taos Pueblo (some people still live without electricity and running water as their ancestors did 1,000 years ago). In this odd place, many people hear a mysterious, untraceable humming noise known as the Taos hum, while others completely eschew materialism and live off the grid in half underground houses called *earthships*. Taos boasts some of the best restaurants in the state; a hot and funky arts scene, with many artists selling works from their own art studios; and incredible outdoors action, including a world-class ski area.

For locations of the accommodations, restaurants, and attractions mentioned in this chapter, see the corresponding maps of central Taos or the Greater Taos map, all in this chapter.

Getting There

Chapter 6 gives you the skinny on airlines that fly into Albuquerque and Santa Fe, points from which most people rent cars and head north to Taos. Other people take a bus into town. If you can't hack the couple hours on the road, an air shuttle now services Taos. In any case, you probably want a rental car to get around this town where some major miles stretch between sights.

Greater Taos

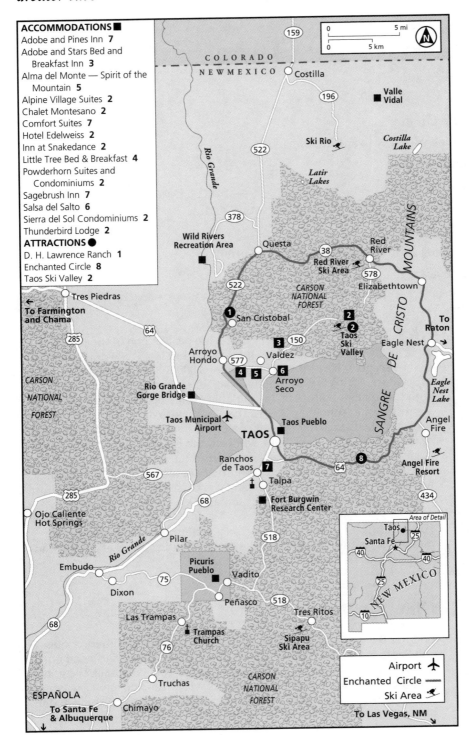

ACCOMMODATIONS ■
Adobe and Pines Inn **7**
Adobe and Stars Bed and
  Breakfast Inn **3**
Alma del Monte — Spirit of the
  Mountain **5**
Alpine Village Suites **2**
Chalet Montesano **2**
Comfort Suites **7**
Hotel Edelweiss **2**
Inn at Snakedance **2**
Little Tree Bed & Breakfast **4**
Powderhorn Suites and
  Condominiums **2**
Sagebrush Inn **7**
Salsa del Salto **6**
Sierra del Sol Condominiums **2**
Thunderbird Lodge **2**
ATTRACTIONS ●
D. H. Lawrence Ranch **1**
Enchanted Circle **8**
Taos Ski Valley **2**

Flying in

The **Taos Municipal Airport** (☎ 505-758-4995) is about 8 miles northwest of town on U.S. 64. **Rio Grande Air** (☎ 877-I-FLY-RGA or 505-737-9790; Internet: www.iflyrga.com) has recently initiated passenger service between Albuquerque and Taos. The airline offers two flights daily for $79 one-way and $150 round-trip. Another option is to fly into Albuquerque International Airport or Santa Fe Municipal Airport (which has fewer flight options), rent a car, and drive up to Taos from there (see Chapters 11 and 13, respectively, for airport information). The drive takes approximately 2½ hours. Following is the lowdown on traveling by car or shuttle from the Taos, Albuquerque, or Santa Fe airports:

- ✔ **Renting a car.** You need a car in Taos, so you may want to rent one at the airports in Albuquerque or Santa Fe and drive up (see Chapters 11 and 13, respectively, for rental-car info). If you fly into Taos, you can rent a car at the airport from **Dollar Rent a Car** (☎ 800-369-4226 or 505-737-0505).

- ✔ **Hopping a shuttle. Faust's Transportation, Inc.** (☎ 505-758-3410) offers daily bus service from Albuquerque and Santa Fe to Taos as well as taxi service from Taos town to Taos Ski Valley. **Twin Hearts Express & Transportation** (☎ 800-654-9456 or 505-751-1201) also runs a shuttle service from Albuquerque and Santa Fe to Taos. **Greyhound/Trailways** and **TNM&O Coaches** run buses from Albuquerque and Santa Fe to Taos, though the money you save may not be worth the time you spend (see "Riding in" below for details).

Driving in

Most visitors arrive in Taos via either N.M. 68 or U.S. 64. Northbound travelers should exit I-25 at Santa Fe, follow U.S. 285 as far as San Juan Pueblo, and then continue on the divided highway when it becomes N.M. 68. Taos is about 79 miles from the I-25 junction. Southbound travelers from Denver, Colorado on I-25 should exit about 6 miles south of Raton at U.S. 64 and then follow it about 95 miles to Taos. Another major route is U.S. 64 from the west (214 miles from Farmington, New Mexico).

Riding in

Greyhound/Trailways (☎ 800-231-2222 for schedules, fares, and information; Internet: www.greyhound.com or www.trailways.com) and **TNM&O Coaches** (☎ 800-231-2222) offer daily bus service from Albuquerque and Santa Fe to the Taos Bus Center, Paseo del Pueblo Sur, at the Chevron station (☎ 505-758-1144), which is not far from the Plaza.

Orienting Yourself

Taos is not a large place, so despite its many narrow and winding streets, finding your way around is not too difficult. This section gives you the lowdown on the main geographical areas and directs you to a few more places to seek help.

Discovering the neighborhoods

Taos has three geographic areas stacked from south to north along U.S. 68.

The Plaza

In some amazing feat of retention, Taos has managed to keep its historic plaza as its center of activity (unlike many towns throughout the country that have been mall-ed). In the vicinity of the Plaza you find some of the best **museums, restaurants, art galleries,** and **accommodations.** The Plaza is a short block west of Taos's major intersection — where U.S. 64 (Kit Carson Road) from the east joins N.M. 68, Paseo del Pueblo Sur.

Ranchos de Taos

About 5 miles south of the Plaza, this poetic community has its own plaza and center of life. Ranchos de Taos is best known for the Saint Francis de Asis Church, which has been captured on canvas by Georgia O'Keeffe and photographed by Ansel Adams. Technically, though, Ranchos de Taos stretches beyond its darling little plaza, with its excellent shops and nearby restaurants, north on U.S. 68 to encompass a strip-malled stretch of highway where you can get all of your needs met from salt and fat to motor oil and car washing.

North Taos

This is the launch pad for some of Northern New Mexico's greatest adventures, including an exploration of the **Rio Grande Gorge, Taos Pueblo,** and the **Millicent Rogers Museum.** A few fine bed and breakfasts have opened up near the village of **Arroyo Seco,** which itself is a good place to buy coffee and funky gifts. And, of course, I can't forget the world-renowned **Taos Ski Valley,** where my friend Tim says you learn to do "controlled falling" (you also find some easy runs too).

Finding information after you arrive

The **Taos County Chamber of Commerce,** 1139 Paseo del Pueblo Sur, at the junction of N.M. 68 and N.M. 585 in Taos (☎ **800-732-TAOS** or 505-758-3873; Internet: www.taoschamber.com), is open year-round, daily from 9 a.m. to 5 p.m., but closed on major holidays. This is a good place to pick up a detailed map of the area. **Carson National Forest** also has an information center in the same building.

Getting Around

Though the core of Taos is small and everything is within walking distance of some good inns, the very nature of the town screams out for private wheels, so I recommend that you rent a car. If you just can't bring yourself to put the pedal to the metal, a city bus system offers limited service.

Exploring by car

Most people drive into Taos from Santa Fe and Albuquerque. After you fasten your seatbelt (a law in this state), you find getting around Taos less daunting than it appears. Though plenty of drunken side streets stumble this direction and that, sometimes going nowhere, you likely won't spend a lot of time on them. Most everything in town happens off the main drag, called Paseo del Pueblo Norte (North Town Way) — north of the Plaza — and Paseo del Pueblo Sur (South Town Way) — south of the Plaza. This is also U.S. 68. Other main streets that you may travel are U.S. 64, which cuts east–west through town, and N.M. 150, the road to Taos Ski Valley.

 If you drive in Taos, you definitely want to avoid the downtown **bottleneck** in the morning between 8 and 9 a.m. and especially in the evening between 4 and 5:30 p.m. Backups happen on the main drag at the intersection of U.S. 64 and Paseo del Pueblo Norte. Instead, route around the Plaza to the west on Camino de la Placita.

Taos roads are barely wide enough to drive a car on, much less *park* one, so spaces are definitely limited. You can find a good **parking** lot one block north of the Plaza, and many metered spaces on Kit Carson Road (U.S. 64).

 If you're one of those renegade travelers who likes to get off the beaten track, you can find plenty of **forest service roads** that lead to hidden peaks and lakes, but beware out there. What at first may resemble the Mother Road may end up like a squirrel's path along a precipice. Don't head out without a four-wheel-drive vehicle and plenty of provisions.

Riding the bus

You may laugh at the name of Taos's public bus system, the **Chile Line** (☎ **505-751-4459**), but it's really a decent system for a town of this size. It operates Monday to Friday from 7 a.m. to 9 p.m. in summer (until 7 p.m. in winter), with more limited service on Saturday and

Sunday. Two simultaneous routes run on the half hour southbound from Taos Pueblo and northbound from the Ranchos de Taos Post Office. Each route makes stops at the casino and various hotels in town. Bus fares are 50¢ one-way, $1 round-trip, and $5 for a seven-day pass (which you can purchase from the driver). During ski season, a bus runs to and from Taos Ski Valley every hour and a half from 7 a.m. to 8:30 p.m. The ride costs $5 round-trip and picks up all along the way.

Calling a taxi

Faust's Transportation, Inc. (☎ 505-758-3410) offers town taxi service daily from 7 a.m. to 8 p.m., with fares of about $7 anywhere within the city limits for up to two people.

Moving those feet

Even a person completely lacking imagination would find plenty to do within **walking** distance of the Plaza. But you'll likely want a car to see some of the outlying attractions such as the Rio Grande Gorge Bridge and Ranchos de Taos. If you're fit, a good way to get around is by **bicycle.** (Lowlanders beware: At an elevation of about 7,000 feet, this town lacks oxygen.) See "Keeping active," later in this chapter, to find out where to rent bikes.

Staying in Style

A tiny town with a big tourist market, Taos has literally thousands of rooms to rent. Many new properties have recently opened, turning this into a buyer's market. In the slower seasons (January to February, April to May, and October to November), you may even want to try bargaining your room rate down, because competition for travelers is steep. During peak seasons (summer and ski season), visitors without reservations may have difficulty finding a vacant room. **Taos Central Reservations** (☎ 800-821-2437 or 505-758-9767) may be able to help. Other good resources are the **Taos Valley Resort Association** (☎ 800-776-1111 or 505-776-2233; Internet: www.visitnewmexico.com) and the **Taos Association of Bed and Breakfast Inns** (☎ 800-939-2215 or 505-758-4246; Internet: www.taos-bandb-inns.com). Except at a few places where I've noted differently, all parking is free.

A tax of approximately 11% is added to every hotel bill.

Most accommodations at Taos Ski Valley won't win awards for solid, soundproof construction. If you prefer quieter places, don't plan to lodge here. If you do stay here, you have at least one factor in your favor: After a day on the steeps at Taos, most of your neighbors will go to bed early.

Central Taos Accommodations

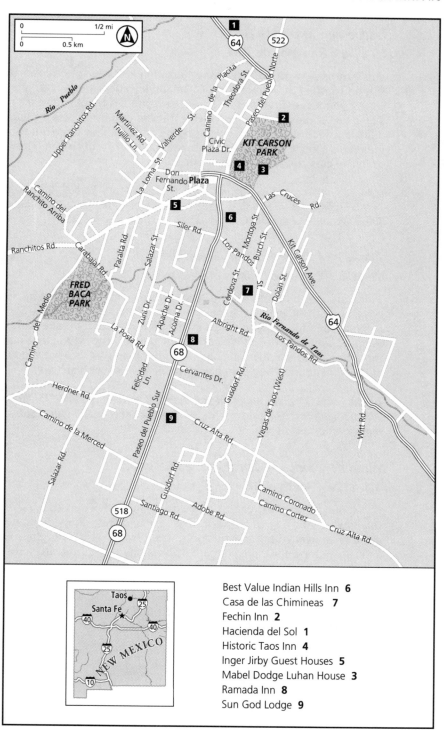

Best Value Indian Hills Inn **6**
Casa de las Chimineas **7**
Fechin Inn **2**
Hacienda del Sol **1**
Historic Taos Inn **4**
Inger Jirby Guest Houses **5**
Mabel Dodge Luhan House **3**
Ramada Inn **8**
Sun God Lodge **9**

The top hotels and B&Bs

Adobe and Pines Inn
$$–$$$$ Ranchos de Taos

You can have a romantic escape here in a 150-year-old adobe about a ½ mile south of St. Francis Plaza. The inn is set around a courtyard with a long *portal* (covered porches) and surrounded by pine and fruit trees. The guest rooms all have private entrances and fireplaces and are each uniquely decorated in rich colors. Some of them have large hot tubs. The innkeepers serve a full gourmet breakfast in front of the fire (in winter) or in the glassed-in breakfast room.

N.M. 68 (within a half mile south of St. Francis Plaza). ☎ *800-723-8267 or 505-751-0947. Fax: 505-758-8423. E-mail:* adobepines@newmex.com. *Rack rates: $95–$185 double. Rates include breakfast. AE, DC, DISC, MC, V.*

Adobe and Stars Bed and Breakfast Inn
$$–$$$$ En route to Taos Ski Valley

This inn helps make up for the lack of whimsy in today's tough and over-paved world. Sitting on the mesa between Taos town and Taos Ski Valley (a great location for you skiers), this B&B is a sunny place with lots of magical touches, the most important being large windows facing the mountains and comfortable beds. The full breakfast is always good, and in the afternoons, they serve New Mexico wines with snacks.

At the corner of State Hwy. 150 and Valdez Rim Road. ☎ *800-211-7076 or 505-776-2776. Internet:* www.taosadobe.com. *Rack rates: $95–$180 double. Rates include breakfast. AE, MC, V.*

Alma del Monte — Spirit of the Mountain
$$$–$$$$ North of Taos

If you have a luxury lover lurking within you, full of sensual desires, this inn may be your key to satiation. The new hacienda-shaped, pueblo-style adobe has everything a body could want, from hot tubs in the rooms to rich designer bedding to decadent breakfasts, such as stuffed French toast served on china.

372 Hondo Seco Rd. ☎ *800-273-7203 or 505-776-2721. Fax: 505-776-8888. Internet:* www.almaspirit.com. *Rack rates: $150–$250 double, depending on seasons and holidays. Rates include full breakfast and afternoon refreshments. AE, MC, V.*

Alpine Village Suites
$–$$$$ Taos Ski Valley

This inn at the center of the Taos Ski Valley, just steps from the lift, has a dual personality. Part of it sits above a ski shop and is less formal, each room with a climb-in sleeping loft (acrophobics beware). The other is this section's snobbier cousin, quite new, with handcrafted Mexican furniture and inventive tile. Both share a hot tub, which has the most primo view in the valley, and a restaurant/bar that rocks after the lifts close down.

100 Thunderbird Rd. ☎ *800-576-2666 or 505-776-8540. Fax: 505-776-8542. Internet:* www.alpine-suites.com. *Valet parking $10 per night. Rack rates: Summer $65–$120 double (includes continental breakfast); ski season $70–$265 double. AE, DISC, MC, V.*

Best Value Indian Hills Inn

$–$$ Downtown

Taos has a few functional hotels like this one where the bedding may not be designer, but you still can get a good night's rest — and have some fun. Just two blocks from the Plaza, the hotel has clean, comfortable rooms surrounding a broad lawn studded with towering blue spruce trees, picnic tables, barbecue grills, and a pool.

233 Paseo del Pueblo Sur (2 blocks south of the Plaza). ☎ *800-444-2346 or 505-758-4293. Internet:* www.taosnet.com/indianhillsinn. *Rack rates: $49–$99 double. Rates include continental breakast. AE, DC, DISC, MC, V. Small pets welcome with prior arrangement.*

Casa de las Chimineas (Bed & Breakast)

$$$–$$$$ Downtown

This inn is your one-way ticket to nirvana, where treatments at the adjacent spa complete the ascension. All rooms are impeccable, as is the service. Each unit contains original works of art, elegant bedding, and a *kiva fireplace* (a traditional rounded fireplace). Breakfasts are pure gourmet, and evenings bring hearty hors d'oeuvres. Smoking is not permitted.

405 Cordoba Lane (at Los Pandos Rd.). ☎ *877-758-4777 or 505-758-4777. Fax: 505-758-3976. Internet:* www.taoswebb.com/visittaos.com. *Rack rates: $150–$325 double. Rates include breakfast and evening hors d'oeuvres. AE, DC, DISC, MC, V.*

Chalet Montesano

$$$$ Taos Ski Valley

Innkeepers and avid skiers Victor and Karin Frohlich have been in the Taos Ski Valley since the 1960s, and getting their insider's knowledge of the local slopes is one of the benefits of staying at their cozy, Bavarian-style lodge. Ski memorabilia, attractive wooden furniture, and comfy beds decorate the guest rooms. Most importantly, the chalet has an airy spa with a stunning lap pool, weight machines, a hot tub, and a sauna.

3 Pattison Loop (follow TwiningRoad from the upper level of the ski area parking lot, and turn right on Pattison Loop). ☎ **800-723-9104** *or 505-776-8226. Fax: 505-776-8760. Internet:* www.chaletmontesano.com. *Rack rates: $183–$201 double. AE, DISC, MC, V.*

Comfort Suites
$–$$$ Ranchos de Taos

Predictable as fast food, this inn does its job well, especially for families. Each room has a small living/dining area, with a sleeper/sofa, microwave, mini-refrigerator, and coffeemaker, and a bedroom with handcrafted wood furniture and a comfortable king and queen bed. If you have kids, you may want a ground floor, poolside room. Though not landscaped, the pool is warm and roomy and accompanied by a hot tub.

1500 Paseo del Pueblo Sur. ☎ **888-751-1555** *or 505-751-1555. Internet:* www.taoshotels.com/comfortsuites/. *Rack rates: $59–$149 double. Rates include continental breakfast. AE, DC, DISC, MC, V.*

Fechin Inn
$$–$$$ Downtown

Although it doesn't replicate the house built next door by Russian artist Nicolai Fechin (see the Fechin Institute in "Discovering the top attractions," later in this chapter), this newer hotel (built in 1996) provides enough carved wood and shiny marble to transport you at least halfway to the Kremlin. The spacious rooms have a Southwestern decor with nice touches such as hickory furniture and flagstone-topped tables, and they include guest robes, hair dryers, and mini-refrigerators. A health club, hot tub, and laundromat are on-site.

227 Paseo del Pueblo Norte (two blocks north of the Plaza). ☎ **800-811-2933** *or 505-751-1000. Fax: 505-751-7338. Internet:* www.fechin-inn.com. *Rack rates: $109–$179 double, depending on the season. AE, DC, DISC, MC, V. Small dogs are welcome.*

Hacienda del Sol (Bed & Breakfast)
$$–$$$$ North of Downtown

This pleasant bed-and-breakfast with spectacular views of Taos Mountain was once owned by celebrated arts patron Mabel Dodge Luhan and is the site where local author Frank Waters wrote *The People of the Valley.* The 190-year-old main house contains some of the inn's comfortable, well-decorated guest rooms, as well as a spacious dining area where breakfast is served. Most of the guest rooms have fireplaces, three have hot tubs, and three have private steam rooms. An outdoor hot tub overlooks a grand expanse of land owned by the Taos Pueblo.

109 Mabel Dodge Lane. ☎ ***505-758-0287***. *Fax: 505-758-5895. Internet:* www.taos haciendadelsol.com. *Rack rates: $85–$190 double; rates include full breakfast. MC, V.*

Historic Taos Inn

$–$$$$ Downtown

If you're into funky, historic charm, this is the place to stay: smack in the middle of town, and listed on both the State and National Registers of Historic Places. The airy lobby doubles as the Adobe Bar, a local hot spot for drinking margaritas. The guest rooms are quirky but comfortable, decorated with Taos-style furniture and Spanish colonial art, and many have fireplaces. The Doc Martin's restaurant is popular for dinner (see "Dining Out," later in this chapter).

125 Paseo del Pueblo Norte. ☎ ***800-TAOS-INN*** *or 505-758-2233. Fax: 505-758-5776. Internet:* www.taosinn.com. *Rack rates: $60–$225 double. AE, DISC, MC, V.*

Hotel Edelweiss

$$–$$$ Taos Ski Valley

No getting lost between lift and lodge here: Two of this inn's rooms allow you to ski practically into bed. All the rooms are medium-size and functional, with comfortable beds. Your best bets are the rooms on the second and third floors, which are the most quiet. You can look forward to a full, complimentary breakfast, as well as to healthy lunches served in the sunny cafe. For dinner, guests dine at the nearby **Hotel St. Bernard** (☎ **505-776-2251**) — some of the best food at any ski area anywhere. The hotel's kids' club includes dinner and activities.

106 Sutton Place (at the Guard House turn right; the hotel is on the right). ☎ ***800-I-LUV-SKI*** *or 505-776-2301. Fax 505-776-2533. Internet:* www.taosnet.com/ edelweiss. *Free valet parking. Rack rates: $118–$160 double. Rates include breakfast. MC, V.*

Inn at Snakedance

$$–$$$$ Taos Ski Valley

With a prime location just steps from the lift, this inn offers all the luxuries of a full-service hotel. Here you find comfortable, tastefully furnished guest rooms, many with fireplaces and/or views, as well as a small health club with hot tub, sauna, exercise equipment, and massage facilities. Other amenities include a sundeck, in-house ski storage and boot dryers, and a convenience store. The Hondo Restaurant and Bar offers dining and entertainment daily during the ski season. This is a great place for families.

110 Sutton Place. ☎ ***800-322-9815*** *or 505-776-2277. Fax: 505-776-1410. Internet:* www.innsnakedance.com. *Rack rates: $75–$270 double. AE, MC, V.*

Little Tree Bed & Breakfast
$$–$$$ **North of Taos**

Located on a quiet mesa north of Taos, this inn built of raw adobes promises a rich northern New Mexico experience. The charming and cozy rooms surround a courtyard garden, centered around the namesake little tree. Innkeepers treat guests to refreshments in the afternoons, as well as a gourmet breakfast in the morning.

On the Hondo Seco Road. ☎ *505-776-8467. Internet:* www.littletree bandb.com. *Rack rates: $95–$145 double. Rates include breakfast and afternoon snack. AE, DISC, MC, V.*

Powderhorn Suites and Condominiums
$$–$$$ **Taos Ski Valley**

"New" and "moderately priced" are the words that best define the rooms at this inn, just a two-minute walk from the lift. You find consistency here and a greater variety of types of rooms than at the Inn at Snakedance (which offers higher quality, however). All rooms are fairly spacious with spotless bathrooms and comfortable beds. Each also has a microwave, coffeemaker, and mini-refrigerator. Some rooms have stoves, balconies, and fireplaces. If you're elderly or out of shape, request a room on the lower floors, because they don't have an elevator. Smoking is not allowed.

5 Ernie Blake Rd. (in the center of Taos Ski Valley Village, 100 yards up Ernie BlakeRoad). ☎ *800-776-2346 or 505-776-2341. Fax: 505-776-2341, ext. 103. Internet:* www.http://taoswebb.com/powderhorn. *Rack rates: Ski season $99–$155 double, $125–$200 suite, $195–$385 condo (sleeps up to six); summer $69–$129 all accommodation types. MC, V.*

Salsa del Salto
$$–$$$ **Arroyo Seco (north of Taos)**

Not content to sit on your duff during your holiday? Well, this inn gives you so much to do that you may need a vacation from your vacation. With a pool, hot tub, tennis courts, and two world-class athletes as innkeepers, you can definitely stay busy. And you probably won't gain a pound from the gourmet breakfasts served here either. Situated between Taos town and the Taos Ski Valley, the inn has comfortable rooms, each with a view.

543 Hwy. 150. ☎ *800-530-3097 or 505-776-2422. Fax: 505-776-5734. Internet:* www.bandbtaos.com. *Rack rates: $85–$160 double. Extra person $20. Rates include breakfast. AE, MC, V.*

Sierra del Sol Condominiums
$$–$$$ **Taos Ski Valley**

My own scrambled eggs for breakfast and my own tuna sandwich for lunch: Those are my biggest reasons for choosing a condo over a hotel room. If you like to make your own food and enjoy the privacy of a large family space, this is your spot. Just a two-minute walk from the lift, these smartly built condos come in a few sizes. Most have fireplaces, full kitchens, and porches that look out on the ski runs. Hot tubs and saunas keep your spent muscles happy.

13 Thunderbird Rd. (follow N.M. 150 from Taos through the Taos Ski Valley parking lot and turn right on Thunderbird Road) ☎ *800-523-3954 or 505-776-2981. Fax: 505-776-2347. Internet:* www.taoswebb.com/sierradelsol. *Rack rates: Summer $70–$80 studio, $130–$190 two-bedroom condo; winter $125–$135 studio, $295–$385 two-bedroom condo. AE, DISC, MC, V.*

Sun God Lodge

$–$$$ **South of the Plaza**

You want New Mexico flavor but don't want to max out your credit cards? This is the best moderately-priced hotel in town. A five-minute drive from the Plaza, it has three distinct parts — some older than others, but all in good shape — spread across 1½ acres of landscaped grounds. All have *Talavera* (painted ceramic) tile sinks, Taos-style furniture, and new carpeting. Some rooms have kitchenettes. The hot tub sits in a parking lot but is no less warm for it.

919 Paseo del Pueblo Sur (1½ miles from the Plaza, across from Wal-Mart). ☎ *800-821-2437 or 505-758-3162. Fax: 505-758-1716. Internet:* www.sungodlodge.com. *Rack rates: $50–$169 double. AE, MC, DISC, V. Pets allowed with $10 per-day fee.*

Thunderbird Lodge

$$–$$$ **Taos Ski Valley**

If guest loyalty is the measure for quality, this is the best of the best — some of their guests have been returning for more than 30 years! This, despite the fact that the rooms are small and noise tends to travel. The reason for the loyalty? Great service and some of the best food in the region. Another big draw is the Thunderbird Bar, with booths, a grand piano, and fireplace, where live entertainment plays during the evenings through the winter.

3 Thunderbird Rd. (100 yards from the main lift). ☎ *800-776-2279 or 505-776-2280. Fax: 505-776-2238. Internet:* www.thunderbird-taos.com. *Free valet parking. Rack rates: Beginning at $105 per person. Rate includes breakfast and dinner. AE, MC, V.*

The runner-up hotels and B&Bs

Inger Jirby Guest Houses

$$$–$$$$ **Downtown**   If you like to rub elbows with artists, get one of these casitas (little houses) created by artist Inger Jirby from a 400-year-old adobe. *207 Ledoux St.* ☎ *505-758-7333. Internet:* www.jirby.com.

Mabel Dodge Luhan House

$$–$$$ **Downtown**   The former home of arts patron Mabel Dodge Luhan (1879–1962), this inn has guest rooms that aren't as nice as some of the other B&Bs in town, but the place oozes with atmosphere. *240 Morada Lane.* ☎ *800-84-MABEL or 505-751-9686. Internet:* www.mabeldodge luhan.com.

Ramada Inn

$$ **Downtown**   Don't like surprises? This recently remodeled adobe-style hotel, a ten-minute walk from the Plaza, gives you what you expect from a chain — predictability. *615 Paseo del Pueblo Sur.* ☎ *800-659-TAOS or 505-758-2900. Internet:* www.ramada.com.

Sagebrush Inn

$–$$$ **Ranchos de Taos**   Sagebrush, coyotes, and Georgia O'Keeffe — this very Taos inn has a variety of types of rooms, some where O'Keeffe hung out for ten months. *1508 Paseo del Pueblo Sur.* ☎ *800-428-3626 or 505-758-2254. Internet:* www.taosweb.com/taoshotels/sagebrushinn.

Dining Out

Taos dining can be summed up with one word: amazing. Surprisingly, for a town of about 5,000 residents, the place has some of the best food in the Southwest. Informality reigns; at a number of restaurants you can dine on world-class food while wearing jeans or even ski pants. Nowhere are a jacket and tie mandatory. This informality doesn't extend to reservations, however; especially during the peak season, it is important to make them well in advance.

Although the food is sophisticated here, the city isn't: Most places shut down seriously early. Do your feasting before 8:30 p.m. because kitchens generally close by 9 p.m.

It's tough to tell whether restaurants will be closed on Sunday or Monday in this town, so call ahead. Also, be aware that when snow dumps on the mountain (skiers delight!), some establishments shut down early or don't open at all.

The top restaurants

The Apple Tree

$$–$$$$ **Downtown**   SOUTHWESTERN/AMERICAN

Original food and art make this a popular spot for locals and tourists. The walls of its four adobe rooms show off paintings by Taos Masters, while in the courtyard outside you can dine under (you guessed it) an

Central Taos Restaurants

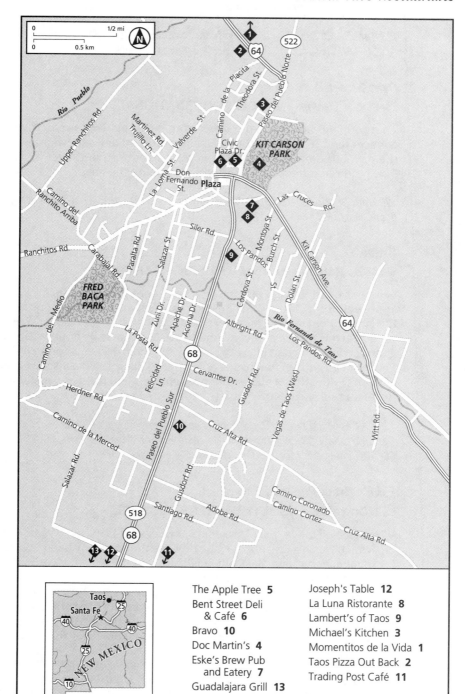

The Apple Tree **5**
Bent Street Deli & Café **6**
Bravo **10**
Doc Martin's **4**
Eske's Brew Pub and Eatery **7**
Guadalajara Grill **13**

Joseph's Table **12**
La Luna Ristorante **8**
Lambert's of Taos **9**
Michael's Kitchen **3**
Momentitos de la Vida **1**
Taos Pizza Out Back **2**
Trading Post Café **11**

apple tree. Try the Apple Tree salad and the mango chicken enchiladas. The wine list is award-winning, and desserts are prepared in-house.

123 Bent St. ☎ *505-758-1900. Reservations recommended. Main courses: $9–$22. AE, CB, DC, DISC, MC, V. Open: Daily 5–9 p.m.*

Bent Street Deli & Café

$$–$$$$ **Downtown** **DELI/INTERNATIONAL**

This hopping cafe across the street from the Apple Tree serves inventive comfort food. They serve breakfast burritos and deli sandwiches during the day, but dinner gets a little more upscale: You find dishes such as beef tenderloin medallions and roja shrimp on the menu.

120 Bent St. ☎ *505-758-5787. Main courses: $10–$18.95. MC, V. Open: Mon–Sat 8 a.m.–9 p.m.*

Bravo

$–$$$$ **Ranchos de Taos** **AMERICAN BISTRO**

Left your heart in San Francisco? Or your core in the Big Apple? With its atmosphere and flavors, this bustling cafe just may transport you back to the land of concrete, skyscrapers, and refined tastes. As well as a restaurant, Bravo is a specialty wine and beer shop, package liquor store, and gourmet deli — a great place to stock your picnic basket. Informality rules here; though with a French chef doing the cooking, the dishes have plenty of chic. Try the Bravo pizza with three cheeses and roasted vegetables or the elaborate salad bar complete with pasta and bean concoctions.

1353-A Paseo del Pueblo Sur (2½ miles south of downtown and 1 block south of the Cañon bypass). ☎ *505-758-8100. No reservations. Main courses: $5–$10 lunch; $6–$18 dinner. AE, MC, V. Open: Mon–Sat 11 a.m.–8:45 p.m.*

Eske's Brew Pub and Eatery

$$ **Downtown** **SOUTHWESTERN PUB FARE**

When I asked Steve "Eske" Eskeback, owner of this excellent microbrewery, which was his favorite beer, he replied "the one in my hand." So much for recommendations. Basically he likes all the beers, which are his own recipes, and I have to say that I do too. As for the food, it's imaginative, with big enough portions to appeal to the likes of ski patrollers and mountain guides who frequent the place. Wanda's green chile turkey stew gets your blood circulating, and The Fatty, an eclectic burrito with mashed potatoes and feta cheese, will probably put you down for the night.

106 Des Georges Lane (½ block southeast of the Plaza). ☎ *505-758-1517. Reservations not accepted. Main courses: $6.50–$11. MC, V. Open: Mar–Sept and during spring and winter breaks daily lunch and dinner; the rest of winter Fri–Sun lunch and dinner.*

Guadalajara Grill

$$ South of Downtown   MEXICAN

Viva Zapata! That's what I feel like shouting whenever I eat at this restaurant run by a bunch of Guadalajaran brothers. Though the place is attached to a car wash, don't be deceived; the food here is excellent. It's Mexican rather than *New* Mexican, a refreshing treat. I recommend the tacos, particularly pork or chicken, served in soft homemade corn tortillas, with the meat artfully seasoned and grilled. Beer and wine are available.

1384 Paseo del Pueblo Sur (2 miles south of the Plaza, across from Ace Hardware Store). ☎ *505-751-0063. Reservations not accepted. Main courses: $4.75–$12.95. MC, V. Open: Daily lunch and dinner.*

Joseph's Table

$$$$ Ranchos de Taos   CONTINENTAL

Many consider this memorable restaurant the best in New Mexico. The very essence of Taos funky chic, Joseph's Table has rough wooden floors, fresco-covered walls, and diner-style chairs whimsically covered with slipcovers. Start with the risotto cake with Parma prosciutto and Portobello mushroom syrup, move on to the mixed greens with dried cherries and goat cheese in warm bacon vinaigrette, and follow with the American steak au poivre: a pan seared, peppercorn crusted filet of beef tenderloin served on smashed potatoes with Madeira mushroom sauce. The wine list is a small and eclectic selection of superb bottles.

4167 Hwy. 68. ☎ *505-751-4512. Reservations recommended. Main courses: $16–$30. AE, DC, DISC, MC, V. Open: Wed–Sun 5–11 p.m.*

La Luna Ristorante

$$–$$$$ Downtown   ITALIAN

This restaurant does its best to make you feel like you're in a cafe in Italy, and it largely succeeds. The pizzas are great, but you may also want to try the pasta with spicy Italian sausage and tomato sauce for an entree. Beer and wine are available by the glass or bottle.

223 Paseo del Pueblo Sur. ☎ *505-751-0023. Reservations recommended. Main courses: $7–$19. AE, DISC, MC, V. Open: Daily 5–10 p.m.*

Michael's Kitchen

$–$$$ Downtown   AMERICAN/NEW MEXICAN

Some days I think heaven is breakfast served all day long — a continuous flow of pancakes, fried eggs, and hash browns, with a waffle for bedtime. If you have a similar hankering for a syrupy/fried heaven, head to Michael's, where they actually do serve all those great treats day in and day out. Kids enjoy the relaxed atmosphere and their own menu. My friend Michael says the donuts here are some of the best on Earth.

304 C Paseo del Pueblo Norte (3 blocks north of the Plaza). ☎ **505-758-4178.**
Reservations not accepted. Main courses: $3–$7.95 breakfast; $4–$9.50 lunch;
$6–$13.95 dinner. AE, DISC, MC, V. Open: Daily 7 a.m.–8:30 p.m. (except major
holidays).

Momentitos de la Vida

$$$$ Arroyo Seco   NEW AMERICAN

"Little moments of life" — that's how this restaurant's moniker translates —
is an apt name for a place that pays *serious* attention to detail. This trendy
new restaurant outside the village of Arroyo Seco calls on a broad range of
identities to fill its plates, from New Orleans to Morocco to Egypt. You may
try grilled prawns, habañero chili peppers, or lobster risotto. In warm
months you can enjoy your meal on the patio surrounded by a plum
orchard. A jazz band plays fireside Thursday to Sunday.

N.M. 150 (4 miles north of the intersection of N.M. 150 and N.M. 522). ☎ **505-**
776-3333. *Reservations recommended on weekends. Bar menu items: $10 and under.*
Main courses: $18–$34. AE, MC, V. Open: Tues–Sun dinner; bar 5 p.m.–closing.

Taos Pizza Out Back

$$ North of Downtown   PASTA/GOURMET PIZZA

Grab your appetite, don your love beads, and head to this hippieish cafe
for the best pizza in town. This raucous place has funky decor (an old
gas pump topped with a lampshade in the dining room) and an eager wait
staff. What to order? I have one big recommendation: pizza. Sure the
spicy Greek pasta and Greek salads are good, but the pizzas are incredi-
ble. All come with a delicious thin crust (no sogginess here) that's folded
over on the edges and sprinkled with sesame seeds. Kids enjoy the funky
decor and, of course, the pizza. Check out the small selection of wines
and large selection of microbrews.

712 Paseo del Pueblo Norte (just north of Allsup's). ☎ **505-758-3112.** *Reservations*
recommended on holidays. Main courses: $11.95–$23.95 pizzas; $6.75–$10.95 pastas
and calzones. AE, DISC, MC, V. Open: Daily lunch and dinner.

Trading Post Café

$–$$$$ Ranchos de Taos   NORTHERN ITALIAN/INTERNATIONAL

This bustling place comes in a close second to Joseph's Table as Taos's
funkiest dining establishment, with a cluster of art-filled rooms branch-
ing from a long bar that encloses an exhibition-style kitchen. Start with
the Caesar salad, and then move on to one of the signature pasta dishes,
or try one of the excellent daily specials. The tarts are the best choice
for dessert.

Margaritaville

If you like the notion of sipping a margarita on a New Mexican plaza, head to **Ogelvie's Bar & Grill** ($$–$$$), 1301 East Plaza, on the east side of the Plaza (☎ 505-758-8866). Though I don't recommend it for a fabulous dinner, the restaurant offers good frosty concoctions as well as chips and salsa and other appetizers served indoors in winter and on a balcony overlooking the Plaza during summer. Open daily from 11 a.m. to 9 or 9:30 p.m.

4179 Paseo del Pueblo Sur. ☎ *505-758-5089. Reservations recommended. Main courses: $6–$28. CB, DC, DISC, MC, V. Open: Tues–Sat 11:30 a.m.–9:30 p.m.*

The runner-up restaurants

Doc Martin's

$$–$$$ **Downtown** You won't likely find the urban-warrior "Doc Marten" boots here, but you do find good eclectic cuisine in a rich atmosphere full of Taos history. *In the Historic Taos Inn, 125 Paseo del Pueblo Norte (1 block northeast of the Plaza).* ☎ *505-758-1977. Internet:* www.taosinn.com.

Lambert's of Taos

$$$–$$$$ **Downtown** This is a good spot for someone like my mother, who likes traditional continental food, versus the more nouveau cuisine that I like. Lambert's is best known for fresh fish. *309 Paseo del Pueblo Sur (3 blocks south of the Plaza).* ☎ *505-758-1009.*

Exploring Taos

Taos's biggest draw is the variety of activities available within a relatively small region. This allows you to mix indoor and outdoor activities within a day, so you don't end up with either a sunburn or that museum gray cast that can overtake indoor dwellers. Check out "Following one-, two-, and three-day itineraries," later in this chapter, for ideas on how to mix and match your indoor/outdoor schedule. Be aware that winter can be cold in Taos, generally too cold (and snowy) to ride a mountain bike, but with proper clothing, you should be warm enough to hike in the lowlands (such as the Gorge). Summers are comfortable for just about any outdoor activity.

Central Taos Attractions

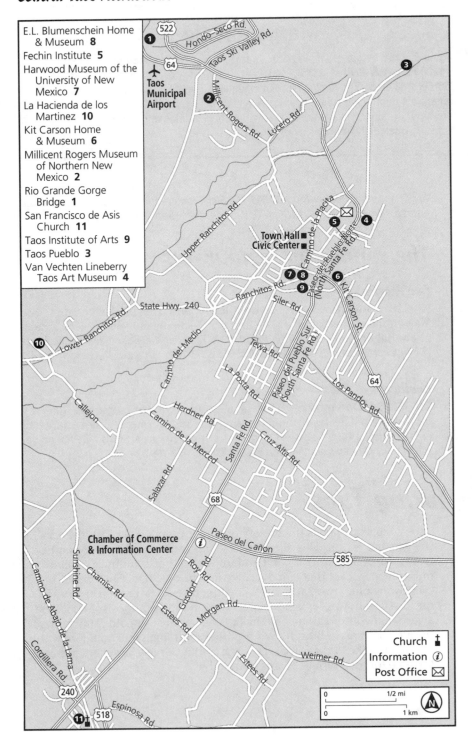

E.L. Blumenschein Home & Museum **8**
Fechin Institute **5**
Harwood Museum of the University of New Mexico **7**
La Hacienda de los Martinez **10**
Kit Carson Home & Museum **6**
Millicent Rogers Museum of Northern New Mexico **2**
Rio Grande Gorge Bridge **1**
San Francisco de Asis Church **11**
Taos Institute of Arts **9**
Taos Pueblo **3**
Van Vechten Lineberry Taos Art Museum **4**

Hondo-Seco Rd.
522
Taos Ski Valley Rd.
64
Taos Municipal Airport
Millicent-Rogers Rd.
Lucero Rd.
Upper Ranchitos Rd.
Camino de la Placita
Town Hall
Civic Center
Paseo del Pueblo Norte (North Santa Fe Rd.)
Kit Carson St.
Ranchitos Rd.
Siler Rd.
State Hwy. 240
Lower Ranchitos Rd.
Camino del Medio
Tewa Rd.
La Posta Rd.
Paseo del Pueblo Sur (South Santa Fe Rd.)
Los Pandos Rd.
64
Callejon
Herdner Rd.
Camino de la Merced
Santa Fe Rd.
Cruz Alta Rd.
Salazar Rd.
68
Chamber of Commerce & Information Center
Paseo del Cañon
585
Sunshine Rd.
Chamisa Rd.
Roy Rd.
Gusdorf Rd.
Morgan Rd.
Camino de Abajo de la Lama
Cordillera Rd.
Estes Rd.
Estes Rd.
Weimer Rd.
240
Espinosa Rd.
518

Church ✝
Information ⓘ
Post Office ✉

0   1/2 mi
0   1 km
N

The Taos Society of Artists

One of the most influential American schools of art, the Taos Society of Artists, was formed in 1914 by Bert Phillips and Ernest Blumenschein, two painters from back East who attracted others — including Oscar Berninghaus, Herbert Dunton, Victor Higgins, and Walter Ufer — to join them in sharing the magical spell of the high desert light. While in Taos, visits to the E.L. Blumenschein Home & Museum (see the "Taos historic museums" box in this chapter) and the Harwood Museum of the University of New Mexico (see the listing below), offer windows into the worlds of these artists.

Discovering the top attractions

Fechin Institute
Downtown

If you ever fantasize about what it would be like to live in a true artist's home, full of eccentricities and beauty, let your imagination bed down at this museum, home of Russian artist Nicolai Fechin (*feh*-shin). The 20th-century Renaissance man made this house his own personal artwork, using his masterful painting, drawing, and sculpting skills while living here from 1927 until 1933. (Fechin died in 1955.) Plan to spend about 45 minutes.

227 Paseo del Pueblo Norte (3 blocks north of the Plaza). ☎ **505-758-1710.** *Admission: $4. Open: Wed–Sun 10 a.m.–2 p.m.*

Harwood Museum of the University of New Mexico
Downtown

This beautifully restored museum is the place to view paintings, drawings, prints, sculpture, and photographs by Taos-area artists from 1800 to the present. The walls are hung with the works of such greats as Ernest Blumenschein, Victor Higgins, Andrew Dasburg, Agnes Martin, and Larry Bell. You find an excellent collection of Spanish colonial art on view upstairs. The museum schedules several exhibitions a year. Allow one hour.

238 Ledoux St. (3 blocks west of the Plaza). ☎ **505-758-9826.** *Admission $5. Open: Tues–Sat 10 a.m.–5 p.m., Sun noon to 5 p.m.*

Millicent Rogers Museum of Northern New Mexico
Northwest of Downtown

This place wins my "finest stuff" award. It has an incredible collection of Native American, Hispanic, and Anglo arts and crafts started in the 1940s by a wealthy Taos émigré. Plan at least an hour to gawk at the jewelry, pottery, textiles, kachina dolls, paintings, furniture, and tin work. If these items whet your appetite to acquire, check out the gift shop.

1504 Millicent Rogers Rd. (4 miles north of Taos Plaza). ☎ *505-758-2462. Admission: $6 adults (New Mexico residents $4), $5 students and seniors, $12 family rate, $1 children age 6–16. Open: Daily 10 a.m.–5 p.m. Closed: Mondays Nov–Mar, Easter, San Geronimo Day (Sept 30), Thanksgiving, Christmas Day, and New Year's Day.*

Rio Grande Gorge Bridge
Northwest of Downtown

Few thrills are free these days, so be sure to take advantage of this one: Stand on this bridge — one of America's highest — 650 feet above the Southwest's greatest river, and feel it sway under your feet. Then look down — instant vertigo. Further the thrill by remembering the wedding scene in that sweet little Oliver Stone flick *Natural Born Killers,* which was filmed here. Yikes!

U.S. 64, 10 miles west of Taos.

San Francisco de Asis Church
Ranchos de Taos

Sitting at the edge of my favorite New Mexico Plaza in Ranchos de Taos is this sculpture of a church with unimaginably thick walls and, from the front, no apparent entryway. Photographer Ansel Adams focused on this aspect when he shot the place, as did Georgia O'Keeffe when she painted it. The east side actually has a door where visitors and worshippers can enter to see lovely *vigas* (ceilings beams) and murals.

Across the driveway, the church office displays a "mystery painting," *The Shadow of the Cross* (1896), by Henri Ault. Under ordinary light it portrays a barefoot Christ at the Sea of Galilee; in darkness, however, the portrait becomes luminescent, and the perfect shadow of a cross forms over the left shoulder of Jesus's silhouette. The artist reportedly was as shocked as everyone else to see this. The reason for the illusion remains a mystery.

St. Francis Plaza #60. ☎ *505-758-2754. Admission: Donations appreciated, $2 minimum. Open: Mon–Sat 9 a.m.–4 p.m. Visitors may attend Mass daily at 5:30 p.m.; Sat at 6 p.m. every fourth week (Mass rotates from this church to the three mission chapels); and Sun at 7 (Spanish and English), 9, and 11:30 a.m. Closed to the public the first two weeks in June, when repairs are done; however, services still take place during this time.*

Taos historic museums

Operated as museums, three historic homes, **La Hacienda de los Martinez,** the **Kit Carson Home & Museum,** and the **E.L. Blumenschein Home & Museum,** offer a taste of Taos-style living over the past 200 years. The hours for all three are April through October daily from 9 a.m. to 5 p.m.; call for winter hours. Admission fees are $5 for adults, $3 for seniors and children. You can also buy a special $10 pass that is good for visiting all three properties. You can look them up on the Internet at www.taosmuseums.org. Allow about one hour for each museum.

An atmospheric, rambling, adobe _hacienda_ (great house), **La Hacienda de los Martinez,** Lower RanchitosRoad, Hwy. 240 (☎ **505-758-0505**), is the former home of merchant/trader Don Antonio Severino Martinez and was built in 1804. Twenty-one rooms, including bedrooms, servants' quarters, a granary, a kitchen, and a shrine, surround two interior courtyards. In summer, the hacienda is a living museum with weavers, blacksmiths, and wood carvers.

The **Kit Carson Home & Museum,** East Kit CarsonRoad, located a short block east of the Plaza intersection (☎ **505-758-0505**), occupies the large adobe dwelling of the legendary Christopher "Kit" Carson (1809–1868). The mountain man, Indian agent, and scout was an important figure in Taos history. Part of the museum recreates his original home, while other exhibits showcase artifacts from the Native American and Hispanic cultures of northern New Mexico.

The **E.L. Blumenschein Home & Museum,** 222 Ledoux St. (☎ **505-758-0505**), is the former home of one of the founders of the famous Taos Society of Artists (set up in 1915). As you wander through the adobe home, you can check out period furnishings and a terrific collection of works by some of Taos's early 20th-century artists.

Taos Pueblo
North of Downtown

One of New Mexico's must-see destinations, the Taos Pueblo is home to about 200 residents who still live much as their ancestors did more than 1,000 years ago, mostly in a pair of impressive adobe buildings with rooms stacked on top of each other. The structures look much as they did when first encountered by Spanish explorers in 1540. Although much of Taos Pueblo remains off limits (including its kivas and other ceremonial areas), several of the residents have shops with jewelry and crafts on display that you can visit, and the San Geronimo Chapel is open to visitors. Remember that you're wandering through someone's home here, so ask permission before taking anyone's picture.

Three miles from the Plaza (head north on Paseo del Pueblo Norte past Kachina Lodge; bear right and follow the signs). ☎ **505-758-1028.**

Admission cost, as well as camera and video fees, are subject to change on a yearly basis; you can obtain detailed information at the number given. Open: Daily 8 a.m.–4:30 p.m., but call ahead because periodic closures, including 45 consecutive days in late winter or early spring, often occur.

Van Vechten Lineberry Taos Art Museum
Downtown

In some ways, Taos has changed little in the past century. Sure, the luxury SUVs and art galleries weren't around back then, but the narrow streets and the mud homes were. However, don't take my word for it; head to this museum on the north end of town and see works by the Taos Society of Artists, established in 1915. They captured panoramas as well as the personalities of the Native American and Hispanic villagers. The 20,000-square-foot state-of-the-art gallery also displays lovely paintings by Duane Van Vechten; her husband built the place as a memorial to her.

501 Paseo del Pueblo Norte (1 mile north of the Plaza). ☎ *505-758-2690. Admission: $6 adults, $3 children age 6–16, free for children under age 6. Open: Wed–Sun 10 a.m.–5 p.m.*

Finding more cool things to see and do

From reverence to rebellion to escape, Taos has long been the place to make a statement. Here are a few ways that you can do so:

- **Make a pilgrimage.** A trip to the **D. H. Lawrence Ranch** (☎ 505-776-2245), north of Taos near the village of San Cristobal, leads you into odd realms of devotion for the controversial early 20th-century author who lived and wrote in the area between 1922 and 1925. To reach the site, head north from Taos about 15 miles on N.M. 522, and then another 6 miles east into the forested Sangre de Cristo Range via a well-marked dirt road. The views getting there and upon arrival are spectacular. The ranch is open from 8 a.m. to 5 p.m. and is free.

- **Stretch out on the grass or wander among tombstones.** If you've had enough of Taos's literati and oddball artists and want to do something American like throwing a football, head to Kit Carson Park in the center of town just north of the Plaza on the east side of Paseo del Pueblo Norte. The park's also a good spot to satiate the morbid among you who like to walk among the dead: Established in 1847, the park's cemetery contains the graves of Kit Carson, his wife, Governor Charles Bent, and many other noted historical figures and artists. Their lives are described briefly on plaques.

- **Get artsy.** Looking for your own little arts adventure? Check out the weeklong classes in such media as writing, sculpture, painting, jewelry making, photography, clay working, and textiles available at the **Taos Institute of Arts,** 108-B Civic Plaza Dr. (☎ **800-822-7183** or 505-758-2793; Internet: www.tiataos.com). Call in advance to reserve space.

✔ **Drive the Enchanted Circle.** Longing for a little road tripping? Few places offer more white-stripe adventure than the 90-mile loop around northern New Mexico's Enchanted Circle. The road leads through old Hispanic villages such as Arroyo Hondo, into a pass the Plains Indians once used, to the Wild-West mining town of Red River, along the base of some of New Mexico's tallest peaks , to the resort village of Angel Fire, and back to Taos along the meandering Rio Fernando de Taos. Although you can drive the entire loop in two hours from Taos, most folks prefer to take a full day, and some take several days. If you get hungry along the way, stop for lunch at **Main Street Deli** ($), 316 E. Main St. in Red River (☎ **505-754-3400**), where you find tasty home-baked muffins and sub sandwiches.

To drive the loop, travel north on N.M. 522 10 miles to Arroyo Hondo. Then drive another 13 miles to Questa. Turn right on N.M. 38, traveling 12 miles to Red River. Stay on N.M. 38 and drive 16 miles to Eagle Nest. From there you come to U.S. 64, which travels west for 12 miles to Angel Fire. The final leg is a lovely 21-mile jaunt on U.S. 64 back to Taos.

Keeping active

The 2,200-square-mile Taos county can take you way high (up New Mexico's highest mountain, 13,161-foot Wheeler Peak) or way low (down the 650-foot-deep chasm of the Rio Grande Gorge). So lace up, buckle on, or don your gear however you need to, and hold on for a wild ride.

Ballooning

Possibly the very best way to see the Rio Grande Gorge is by floating quietly above it in a hot-air balloon. **Paradise Hot Air Balloon Adventure** (☎ 505-751-6098) can make it happen for you. Trips run about $195 per person for about one hour 15 minutes. The **Taos Mountain Balloon Rally** (☎ 800-732-8267) happens each year in late October.

Biking

Whether you're looking to simply cruise around town or wanting to gnash your way along some gnarly single track, you're in luck in Taos: It's a great place to bike. Possibly the most scenic trail in the area, and certainly the easiest, is the **Taos Box Canyon West Rim Trail** near the village of Pilar. The most notable route in the region is the strenuous 20-mile one-way **South Boundary Trail,** which runs from the Angel Fire area back toward Taos, a trip for which you want to hire **Native Sons**

Adventures (☎ 800-753-7559 or 505-758-9342) as your guide. Inquire at the U.S. Forest Service office, 208 Cruz Alta Rd. (☎ **505-758-6200**), for excellent materials that map out these and other trails in the area. Bicycle rentals are available from the **Gearing Up Bicycle Shop,** 129 Paseo del Pueblo Sur (☎ **505-751-0365**), and **Native Sons Adventures,** 1033-A Paseo del Pueblo Sur (☎ **800-753-7559** or 505-758-9342). Annual touring events include Red River's **Enchanted Circle Century Bike Tour** (☎ **505-754-2366**) on the weekend following Labor Day.

Cross-country skiing

If you're one of those kick-and-glide types or you like to do a *tele* turn or two, you find plenty of fun at **Enchanted Forest Cross-Country Ski Area** (☎ **505-754-2374**). It has more than 16 miles of groomed trails (in addition to over 6 miles of trails strictly for snowshoers) in 400 acres of forestlands atop Bobcat Pass. Full-day trail passes, good from 9 a.m. to 4:30 p.m., are $12 for adults, $7 for children, and free for seniors age 70 and over and children age 6 and under. You can arrange equipment rentals and lessons at **Miller's Crossing** ski shop on Main Street in Red River (☎ **505-754-2374**).

Fishing

Anglers will be happy to know that they can fish many of New Mexico's waters year-round. The lowlands provide good winter fishing, while the highlands are best in summer. Overall, the best fishing is in the spring (after run-off) and fall. Locals head to the **Rio Grande** and to many other mountain streams such as the **Rio Hondo, Rio Pueblo** (near Tres Ritos), **Rio Fernando** (in Taos Canyon), **Pot Creek,** and **Rio Chiquito.** Rainbow, cutthroat, and German brown trout, as well as *kokanee* (a freshwater salmon), are commonly stocked and caught. Licenses are required and are sold, along with tackle, at several Taos sporting-goods shops. **Taylor Streit Flyfishing Service** in Taos (☎ **505-751-1312;** Internet: www.streitflyfishing.com) can guide you.

Golfing

Duffers can find some happiness in the Taos area, particularly at the 18-hole course at the **Taos Country Club,** 54 Golf Course Dr., 6 miles south of the Plaza (☎ **888-TAOS-GOLF** or 505-758-7300). Rated the fourth best in the state by *Golf Digest,* the course has open fairways and no hidden greens. The club also features a driving range, practice putting, chipping green, and instruction by PGA professionals. Greens fees start at $36. The course is open year-round except when snow covers the ground. The par-72, 18-hole course at the **Angel Fire Resort Golf Course** (☎ **800-633-7463** or 505-377-3055) sits within stands of ponderosa pine, spruce, and aspen. At 8,500 feet, Angel Fire is one of the highest regulation golf courses in the world. You also find a driving range and putting green here. Fees range from $40 to $50.

Hiking

Hundreds of miles of hiking trails cross Taos County's mountain and high-mesa country. They're especially well traveled in the summer and fall, although nights turn chilly and mountain weather may be fickle by September. You can get free materials and advice on all **Carson National Forest** trails and recreation areas at the **Forest Service Building,** 208 Cruz Alta Rd. (☎ **505-758-6200**), open Monday to Friday from 8 a.m. to 4:30 p.m. Two wilderness areas close to Taos offer outstanding hiking possibilities. The 19,663-acre **Wheeler Peak Wilderness** is a wonderland of alpine tundra, encompassing New Mexico's highest peak (13,161 feet). A favorite (though rigorous) hike to **Wheeler Peak's** summit (15 miles round-trip with a 3,700-foot elevation gain) makes for a long but fun day. The trailhead is at Taos Ski Valley. For year-round hiking, head to the **Wild Rivers Recreation Area,** near Questa. My favorite hike there is the **Cebolla Mesa** hike, which takes you down into the Rio Grande Gorge. Other hikes in this area head down into the Gorge as well.

 Unless you want a literal brain fry, head out early during the months of July through September. Thunderstorms that roll in by early afternoon can prove treacherous. You want to be off the peaks by the time the lightning strikes.

Horseback riding

If you have fantasies of riding the West, few places are more romantic than Taos, with its sage meadows and pine-covered mountains. **Taos Indian Horse Ranch,** off Ski Valley Road, just before Arroyo Seco (☎ **505-758-3212**), can saddle up a pony and take you into the mountains on Taos Pueblo land, from 6,800 feet up to 9,000 feet (they promise no cliffs). Open by appointment; call ahead for reservations and prices.

Ice skating

If a latent Michelle Kwan or Brian Boitano dwells in you, try your blades at **Taos Youth Family Center** (☎ **505-758-4160**). Located in Kit Carson Park, the rink is open daily from early November through mid-March. Call for hours. Skate rentals are available for adults and children. Admission is $3.

Llama trekking

I'll take any excuse to let someone else carry my load. That's why llama trekking is such a treat. These docile beasts carry your stuff on a variety of hikes on Forest Service trails, from day-hikes (year-round) to extended wilderness adventures (warm months only). Prices start at about $60 to $75 per person (with discounts for children) and include a gourmet lunch. Call either **El Paseo Llama Expeditions** (☎ **800-455-2627** or 505-758-3111; Internet: www.elpaseollama.com) or **Wild Earth Llama Adventures** (☎ **800-758-LAMA** (5262) or 505-586-0174; Internet: www.llamaadventures.com).

River rafting

Have all of those beer commercials with bold athletes blasting through white water whetted your appetite for some high adrenaline? Then Taos is your destination. Half- or full-day white-water rafting trips down the Rio Grande and Rio Chama originate here and can be booked through a variety of outfitters. The wild **Taos Box Canyon,** a steep-sided canyon south of the Wild Rivers Recreation Area, offers 17 miles of class IV rapids (on a scale from I, which is flat water, to VI, which is unrunnable by most watercrafts) — one of the most exciting one-day white-water tours in the West. May and June, when the water rises, is a good time to go. Experience is not required, but you must wear a life jacket (which is provided) and be willing to get wet.

Most of the companies listed run the Taos Box Canyon ($90 to $104) and **Pilar Racecourse** ($45 for half-day; $85 to $104 for full day, with discounts for children) on a daily basis. I highly recommend **Los Rios River Runners** (☎ 800-544-1181 or 505-776-8854). Other safe bets are **Native Sons Adventures,** 1033-A Paseo del Pueblo Sur (☎ 800-753-7559 or 505-758-9342; Internet: www.newmex.com/nsa), and **Far Flung Adventures** in El Prado (☎ 800-359-2627 or 505-758-2628).

Skiing and snowboarding

Three alpine resorts are within an hour's drive of Taos; all offer complete facilities, including equipment rentals. Although exact opening and closing dates vary according to snow conditions, the season usually begins around Thanksgiving and continues into late March or early April, and lifts generally run daily from 9 a.m. to 4 p.m.

Don't take my word for how great the skiing is at **Taos Ski Valley** (☎ 505-776-2291; Internet: www.skitaos.org). I'm way too biased about this place, my favorite ski resort anywhere. Instead, ask the *London Times* who called the valley "without any argument the best ski resort in the world." Founded in 1955 by a Swiss-German immigrant, Ernie Blake, Taos Ski Valley has an intimate, Alps-like ambiance and a *lot* of verticality. Some people are daunted by the slopes, which are best enjoyed by more experienced skiers. But if that's not you, take heart: Taos has one of the best ski schools in the world so they can likely get you comfortable on the mountain within days. An added bonus for beginners is the fact that at this writing, snowboards aren't allowed on the mountain, so you don't have to watch your back as seriously as you do at other resorts. Another bonus here is the internationally renowned light, dry powder that can accumulate (as much as 312 inches annually). The mountain, with 2,612 vertical feet, has 72 trails (24% beginner, 25% intermediate, 51% advanced). The area has four quad, one triple, and five double chairs, and two surface tows. Full-day lift tickets average $47 for adults, $38 for teens (13- to 17-year-olds), $29 for children age 12 or younger, $27 seniors age 65 to 69, and free for seniors over 70. An 18,000-square-foot children's center makes this an excellent resort for skiing families.

Free tacos — I mean, Free Taos!

No, the *Free Taos* bumper stickers you see aren't the workings of some kind of separatist militia. Actually they're the work of some bold snowboarders who want to surf the runs at Taos, one of the few resorts in the United States that bans them. The resort has stood steadfast in its refusal to allow them on the mountain, but its position is softening: Apparently the revenues these "shredders" could bring outweigh the danger and inconvenience of having them on this ultra-steep and traditional mountain. In recent years, an organization called **Free the Snow** (Internet: www.freethesnow.com) has formed to promote the cause, with sponsors such as Burton Snowboards and Nike ACG joining in to liberate not only Taos, but also other ski areas. The Free Taos bumper stickers have become so popular that comic offshoots have arisen, the most notable one using the same black-and-white lettering proclaiming *Free Tacos*.

If you like your skiing with a twang, head to **Red River Ski Area** (☎ **505-754-2223** for information, 800-331-7669 for reservations; Internet: http://redriverskiarea.com/), where most of the clientele is from Texas and the South. One of the bonuses of this ski area is that lodgers can walk out of their doors and be on the slopes. Two other bonuses: Most of its 57 trails are geared toward the intermediate skier, though beginners and experts also have some trails; and lastly, good snow is guaranteed early and late in the year due to ubiquitous snowmaking. Servicing a 1,600-foot vertical drop are four double chairs, two triple chairs, and a surface tow. The cost of a lift ticket averages $44 for adults for a full-day, $39 for teens ages 13 to 17, $30 for children ages 7 to 12, and free for children age 6 and under and seniors age 65 and over.

If you don't feel like braving the steeps of Taos, check out nearby **Angel Fire Resort** (☎ **800-633-7463** or 505-377-6401; Internet: www.angelfire resort.com). This resort is more like Vail, equipped with 2,077 vertical feet serviced by two high-speed quads, three double lifts, and one surface lift. It has 66 trails heavily oriented to beginner and intermediate skiers and snowboarders, with a few runs for more advanced skiers and snowboarders. Cross-country skiing, snowshoeing, and snowbiking are also available. All-day lift tickets cost $44 for adults, $36 for teens (13 to 17 years old), and $28 for children (7 to 12 years old). Kids age 6 and under and seniors age 65 and over ski free.

Spas

Taos doesn't have the spa scene that Tucson and Phoenix do, but you can get pampered at **Mountain Massage & Spa Treatments,** 405 Cordoba Rd. (☎ **505-758-9156**). Though a small place, it has large treatments. If you'd like a pampered lodging experience, you're in luck because Mountain Massage is located at Casa de las Chimineas, a luxury bed and breakfast.

Tennis

Though Taos isn't exactly a tennis destination, you can find a few courts here. **Quail Ridge Inn** on Ski Valley Road (☎ **800-624-4448** or 505-776-2211) is a tennis resort with six outdoor and two indoor tennis courts, available to guests staying in the accompanying condos. The **Taos Spa and Tennis Club,** 111 Dona Ana Dr. (☎ **505-758-1980**), has five courts and the fee is $12 for a full day. In addition, four free public courts are in Taos, two at **Kit Carson Park,** on Paseo del Pueblo Norte, and two at **Fred Baca Memorial Park,** on Camino del Medio south of Ranchitos Road.

Seeing Taos by guided tour

With so much history, Taos calls for someone to tell it to you (as opposed to driving around with your face in a guide book). So I say sit back and enjoy the stories presented by some of the town's excellent guides.

General tours

Enchantment Dreams Walking Tours (☎ **505-776-2562**) offers van tours year-round to major sites throughout Taos, including Taos Pueblo, Ranchos de Taos, and La Hacienda de los Martinez. The tour takes about two to two and a half hours and costs $25 for adults and $10 for teens 12 to 16; kids under 12 are free.

Walking tours

You may as well enjoy the sun while you're in Taos and hit the sidewalks with one of the local walking tours. Doing so gives you a dose of history and your daily exercise. **Taos Historic Walking Tours** (☎ **505-758-4020**) offers tours leaving from the Mabel Dodge Luhan House (240 Morada Ln.) at 10 a.m. daily (May through September). Tours cost $10 and take one and a half to two hours.

If you're like me and can never really get enough drama in life, check out **Enchantment Dreams Walking Tours** (☎ **505-776-2562**). Roberta Courtney Meyers, a theater artist and composer, tours you through Taos's history while performing a number of characters such as Georgia O'Keeffe and Kit Carson. The tour takes about two hours and costs $20 for adults and $10 for teens 12 to 16; kids under 12 are free.

Following one-, two-, and three-day itineraries

One of Taos's biggest assets is its small size. You can spend a whole day sightseeing and never get in a car, if that pleases you. (I include such a day in the two-day itinerary later in this chapter, but beware that this day does include lots of walking.) For details on all the sights and restaurants mentioned in these itineraries, see the relevant sections of this chapter.

Two activities deserve priority status in your plans, but both are seasonal, so I didn't include them in the itineraries. If you're a skier and you visit in winter, you definitely want to head up to **Taos Ski Valley** for a day. And if it's spring or early summer and you like the outdoors, you definitely want to plan a raft trip down the notorious **Taos Box Canyon** or on the **Pilar Racecourse.**

One-day itinerary

Begin your day at **Taos Pueblo,** where you should spend about two hours. While on that end of town, stop in at the **Millicent Rogers Museum** for an hour of browsing through the incredible handiwork displayed there. Next, head out to the **Rio Grande Gorge Bridge** for a half hour of outdoor sightseeing. By now you may be famished, so head back to town for lunch at one of the many great restaurants. Then head south to Ranchos de Taos to see the **San Francisco de Asis Church** and to shop on the **Plaza** there. You can cover both places in about an hour, even if you're not a power shopper. If you still have some steam, head out to **La Hacienda de los Martinez,** where you can spend an hour pretending you live in the 19th century. By now you're probably ready to head back to your inn and rest, but if you like to shop, there may be an hour left to do so in the Plaza area. If you're one of those who likes to have fun at night, head out to the **Sagebrush Inn** for some true country-and-western music and dancing.

Two-day itinerary

On the first day, follow the schedule for the one-day itinerary. On the second day, explore the rest of the Taos historic museums. Start at the **Kit Carson Home & Museum,** just off the Plaza, where you can spend about one hour. From there you may want to do some shopping and gallery hopping in the Plaza area en route to the **E.L. Blumenschein Home & Museum,** where you can spend about an hour exploring the architecture and art. Right next door, stop in at the **Harwood Museum of the University of New Mexico.** By now, you may need a lunch break. In the afternoon, if you're an outdoors person, you may want to contact one of the companies that rents bicycles and spend part of the day cycling in the area. Otherwise, head to the **Fechin Institute,** where you can spend an hour basking in delicious Russian art ambiance. From there, continue north to the **Van Vechten Lineberry Taos Art Museum,** which requires about an hour to visit. At cocktail hour, head to the **Adobe Bar** at the Historic Taos Inn for a little local flavor. Later, head out to **Momentitos de la Vida** to hear some jazz (but call first, because some nights this restaurant features other types of music — even disco).

Three-day itinerary

For the first two days, follow the two-day itinerary. On your third day, either bike along the **Rio Grande Gorge,** hike down into the Gorge, or drive the **Enchanted Circle** through Red River, Eagle Nest, and Angel Fire. You can have lunch along the way and arrive back in Taos in time for some shopping and a good dinner. If you want to explore Taos's limited bar scene, head to **Alley Cantina,** where you can play a game of shuffleboard or pool.

Shopping 'til You Drop

Aside from a plethora of touristy knick-knack shops, the Taos shopping scene is dominated by arts and crafts, ranging from fine art to locally crafted drums.

Best shopping areas

One of the best places to shop is on the **St. Francis Plaza** in Ranchos de Taos, just a few miles south of the Plaza, where you find an appealing assortment of boutiques. Otherwise, most of the local retail is clustered in the downtown area, with touristy shops ringing the **Plaza** and tony establishments lining historic **Bent Street.**

What to look for and where to find it

You can find plenty of art and/or local crafts in Taos. Here are my recommendations for what to buy and where to go.

Art

Because Taos is an art colony, the presence of a large number of galleries (about 50) comes as no surprise. Most places are within walking distance of the Plaza and are generally open daily from 9 a.m. to 5 p.m.; some are closed on Sundays.

One of the best-known contemporary Taos artists is R. C. Gorman, and you may recognize his much-reproduced, pastel-hued depictions of Navajo women when you see his work at his **Navajo Gallery,** 210 Ledoux St. (☎ **505-758-3250**). Nearby, you can visit the **Inger Jirby Gallery,** a 400-year-old adobe at 207 Ledoux St. (☎ **505-758-7333**), which shows the fine paintings of internationally known artist Inger Jirby.

Other galleries worth paying a visit are the **New Directions Gallery,** 107B North Plaza (☎ **800-658-6903** or 505-758-2771), which is the place to find contemporary work by local names such as Larry Bell and Tom Noble. The **Act I Gallery,** 226D Paseo del Pueblo Norte (☎ **800-666-2933** or 505-758-7831), exhibits a broad range of works in a variety of media. The **Fenix Gallery,** 228B Paseo del Pueblo Norte (☎ **505-758-9120**), displays mostly contemporary work by many of the better-known Taos artists. **Lumina of New Mexico,** 239 Morada Rd. (☎ **505-758-7282**), is housed in the historic Victor Higgins home (next to the Mabel Dodge Luhan estate) and shows a tasteful variety of painting, sculpture, and photography.

Books

Taos has several fine bookshops to browse your way through, including the **Brodsky Bookshop,** 226 Paseo del Pueblo Norte (☎ **888-223-8730** or 505-758-9468); the **Moby Dickens Bookshop,** 124A Bent St. (☎ **888-442-9980** or 505-758-3050); and the **Taos Book Shop,** 122D Kit Carson Rd. (☎ **505-758-3733**).

Clothing

Taos isn't exactly full of Madison Avenue boutiques, but the **Overland Sheepskin Company** on N.M. 522, a few miles north of town (☎ **505-758-8822**), is worth a pit stop to feel the local leather. You find clothing crafted from a variety of leathers, from sheepskin to buffalo hide. The **Mariposa Boutique,** 120-F Bent St. (☎ **505-758-9028**), is the place to pick up Mexican-style dresses and colorful broomstick skirts for that romantic, Stevie Nicks vibe.

Crafts, pottery, and tiles

A good place to find a cross-section of work by local artisans is at the **Taos Artisans Cooperative Gallery,** 107A Bent St. (☎ **505-758-1558**). The gallery is owned by several local artists and sells jewelry, wearables, clay work, glass, leather work, and garden sculpture. **Taos Blue,** 101A Bent St. (☎ **505-758-3561**), carries contemporary and Native American handicrafts and specializes in fiber and clay. If you like ceramics, you may enjoy a visit to **Stephen Kilborn Pottery,** 136A Paseo del Pueblo Norte (☎ **800-758-0136** or 505-758-5760), where you can watch the talented potter at work. The **Vargas Tile Co.,** on the southside of town on N.M. 68 (☎ **505-758-5986**), has an interesting collection of hand-painted Mexican tiles and ceramic pieces for the home. The **Clay & Fiber Gallery,** 201 Paseo del Pueblo Sur (☎ **505-758-8093**), shows ceramics, fiber arts, and jewelry created by some 150 artists from around the country. For woven items, head to **Twining Weavers and Contemporary Crafts,** 133 Kit Carson Rd. (☎ **505-758-9000**), which offers a mix of hand-woven wool rugs and pillow covers by artist/owner Sally Bachman. **Weaving Southwest,** 216B Paseo del Pueblo Norte (☎ **505-758-0433**), shows contemporary tapestries, rugs, and blankets.

Drums and moccasins

If you fly home on the plane sporting a pair of moccasins and beating a handmade drum, you probably wouldn't be the first Taos visitor to do so. **Southwest Moccasin & Drum,** 803 Paseo del Pueblo Norte (☎ **800-447-3630** or 505-758-9332), carries a wide selection of drums in various shapes and sizes, which have been handmade by master drum makers from Taos Pueblo. The emporium also has an enormous selection of moccasins (the country's second-largest). The **Taos Drum Company,** 5 miles south of Taos Plaza, just off N.M. 68 (☎ **505-758-3796**), has the largest selection of Native American log and hand drums in the world.

Furniture

Taos is well known for its handcrafted wooden furniture. **Greg Flores Furniture of Taos,** 120 Bent St. (☎ **800-880-1090** or 505-758-8010), sells the well-crafted Southwestern furniture of Greg Flores, a Taos native. **Los Ancestros,** 109-A Kit Carson Rd. (☎ **505-737-5053**), sells very reasonably priced handcrafted furniture, including *trasteros* (armoires) and kitchen tables. **The Taos Company,** 124K John Dunn Plaza, Bent St. (☎ **800-548-1141** or 505-758-1141), specializes in antique Southwestern furniture.

Jewelry

If you're looking for turquoise jewelry, head for **El Rincòn,** 114 Kit Carson Rd. (☎ **505-758-9188**), which has the atmosphere of a trading post with a small museum of Native American and Western artifacts in back. The **Leo Weaver Jewelry Gallery,** 62 St. Francis Plaza in Ranchos de Taos (☎ **505-751-1003**), carries the work of dozens of local gold and silversmiths. For a departure from the traditional, stop by **Artwares Contemporary Jewelry,** 129 N. Plaza (☎ **800-527-8850** or 505-758-8850), where you find an interesting selection of contemporary jewelry.

Living It Up After Dark

Despite its status as a small, sleepy town, Taos has a number of fine watering holes catering to the fiery needs of its residents. (After all, artists are known for raising hell on occasion.) The town also has some interesting film, music, and literary programs to offer visitors.

Events are often scheduled by the **Taos Art Association** (TAA), 133 Paseo del Pueblo Norte (☎ **505-758-2052**), at the **Taos Community Auditorium** (☎ **505-758-4677**). The association brings in local, regional, and national performers in theater, dance, and music, and it also offers a weekly film series.

You can find information on current events in the *Taos News,* published every Thursday, and through the **Taos County Chamber of Commerce** (☎ **800-732-TAOS** or 505-758-3873; Internet: www.taoschamber.com), which publishes semiannual listings of "Taos County Events" in addition to its listings in the annual *Taos Vacation Guide.* Cover charges are usually minimal.

Bars and live music

The **Adobe Bar,** in the Historic Taos Inn at 125 Paseo del Pueblo Norte (☎ **505-758-2233**), is a popular meeting place for margarita swilling, and it showcases a variety of music by local performers. The **Alley Cantina,** 121 Teresina Lane (☎ **505-758-2121**), is another place to head for live music (you also find plenty of local pool sharks) and is one of the more popular late-night spots in Taos. **Eske's Brew Pub,** 106 Des Georges Lane (☎ **505-758-1517**), has enough ale on tap to satisfy even the most parched of tongues. The classic Old West–style bar at the **Sagebrush Inn,** Paseo del Pueblo Sur (☎ **505-758-2254**), is the place to find country and western two-steppers making their way round the wooden dance-floor.

The arts

Taos has two major performance halls, featuring classical music and ballet: the **Civic Plaza and Convention Center,** 121 Civic Plaza Dr. (☎ **505-758-4160**) and the **Taos Community Auditorium** at Kit Carson Memorial State Park (☎ **505-758-4677**).

Sponsored by the Taos Art Association, the **Taos School of Music** (☎ **505-776-2388**) presents chamber music performances in summer at the Hotel St. Bernard at the base of the chairlifts in Taos Ski Valley. Tickets cost $15 for adults, $12 for children under age 16. An eight-week **Chamber Music Festival,** in association with the school, also offers concerts at the Taos Community Auditorium as well as the Hotel St. Bernard.

Quick Concierge: Taos

AAA

AAA does not have an office in Taos.

American Express

Taos does not have a branch of American Express.

Area Code

The area code for Taos is **505**. Although some area codes in the state may change in 2002, Taos will most likely retain this one. For updates, contact the New Mexico Department of Tourism (☎ 800-733-6396; Internet: www.newmexico.org).

ATMs

You can find ATMs (also known as *cash pueblos*) all over town, at supermarkets, banks, and drive throughs.

Credit Cards

For lost or stolen cards, contact the following: Visa (☎ 800-847-2911), MasterCard (☎ 800-307-7309), American Express (☎ 800-668-2639), or Discover (☎ 800-347-2683).

Doctors

You should first contact your insurance provider for recommended local physicians. You can also try the Taos Medical Group, 1399 Weimer Rd., Suite 200 (☎ 505-758-2224).

Emergencies

Call ☎ **911** for ambulance, fire, and police.

Hospitals

If you need to go to an emergency room, head to Holy Cross Hospital, 1397 Weimer Rd. (☎ 505-758-8883).

Information

Contact the Taos County Chamber of Commerce, 1139 Paseo del Pueblo Sur (☎ 800-732-TAOS or 505-758-3873; Internet: www.taoschamber.com).

Internet Access & Cyber Cafes

You can retrieve your e-mail at JJ's Bagels, 710 Paseo del Pueblo Sur (☎ 505-758-0045). They charge 10¢ per minute.

Liquor Laws

The legal drinking age is 21 in New Mexico. Bars may remain open until 2 a.m. Monday to Saturday and until midnight on Sunday. Licensed supermarkets and liquor stores sell wine, beer, and spirits daily until midnight, but package sales are not allowed on election days until after 7 p.m. and on Sundays until after noon.

Maps

To find your way around town, pick up a free copy of the Taos map from the Chamber of Commerce at Taos Visitor Center, 1139 Paseo del Pueblo Sur (☎ 505-758-3873).

Newspapers & Magazines

The Taos News is published every Thursday. *Taos Magazine* is also a good source of local information.

Pharmacies

You can find pharmacies at Furr's Supermarket, 1100 Paseo del Pueblo Sur (☎ 505-758-1203), and at Wal-Mart, 926 Paseo de Pueblo Sur (☎ 505-758-2743).

Police

In case of emergency, dial ☎ **911**. Direct all other inquiries to Taos Police, Civic Plaza Drive (☎ 505-758-2216).

Post Offices

The main Post Office is at 318 Paseo del Pueblo Norte (☎ 505-758-2081), a few blocks north of the Plaza traffic light. The hours are Monday to Friday from 8:30 a.m. to 5 p.m. The zip code for Taos is 87571.

Restrooms

At press time, public restrooms for the Plaza area were in the planning stages. Visitors may use facilities at the Taos County Chamber of Commerce, 1139 Paseo del Pueblo Sur.

Road Conditions

Call ☎ 800-432-4269 for local road conditions.

Safety

Although Taos has a quaint feel, it is not a safe place to wander around at night. You are fairly safe around the Plaza area, but avoid walking elsewhere in the city after dark, especially if you're alone.

Smoking

Taos doesn't have quite as many non-smokers as does Santa Fe, so many restaurants still have smoking sections. However, some don't, and many of the smaller inns restrict smoking as well.

Taxes

Gross receipts tax for Taos town is 6.875%, and for Taos County it's 6.3125%. An additional local bed tax exists of 4.5% in Taos town and 5% in Taos County.

Taxis

Faust's Transportation, Inc. (☎ 505-758-3410) provides taxi service in town.

Time Zone

Mountain standard time.

Weather Updates

There is no local phone number to check on the weather. To get a local weather forecast on the Internet, log on to www.accuweather.com, and use the Taos zip code, 87571.

Part IV

Discovering the Outback: New Mexico's Regions

TRUTH OR CONSEQUENCES, NM~7mi
JUDGE OR BE JUDGED, NM~25 mi
SPEAK OR LOOK DUMB, NM~100 mi
SING OR SHUT UP, NM~48 mi

In this part . . .

Buckle up, cuz here comes a rootin' tootin' road trip around New Mexico. This section covers four regions: The Southeast, with its sand dunes and caves; the Southwest, with its ghost towns and vast wilderness areas; the Northeast, where Native American ghosts still wander among ancient ruins; and the Northwest, where outlaws and volcanoes have left their marks.

Chapter 16

Southeastern New Mexico

. . . .

In This Chapter

▶ Following in the footsteps of Billy the Kid

▶ Spending some time on the moon

▶ Going underground and out of this world

. . . .

*I*f you're under the mistaken impression that adobe and art are all that New Mexico's about, an exploration of the southeast quadrant introduces you to the state's many other offerings. Here you find an astonishing array of singular landscapes and unusual attractions, from the rolling gypsum sand dunes of White Sands National Monument and the underground natural cathedrals of Carlsbad Caverns National Park, to the International UFO Museum and Research Center in Roswell, the ski slopes in the mountain resort town of Ruidoso, and the Wild-West haunts of Billy the Kid.

Most of the attractions in the area are just too far to visit during day trips from Albuquerque or Santa Fe (unless you enjoy spending about 10 hours in a car). Your best bet is to set up your base of operations in Alamogordo, Carlsbad, Ruidoso, or, if you visit White Sands only, Las Cruces (see Chapter 17). You can easily spend two or three days exploring just one or two attractions in this area, but if you really want to get to know the region, plan to stay at least five days. For the most part, you won't find the kind of high-end lodgings and restaurants you get up north, but what you lose in pampering, you gain in the sweeping, soul-enriching landscapes of the southern part of the state. As an added bonus, it's generally cheaper in these parts.

You need a car to get around this region, and keep an eye on the gas tank during the looooong drives, especially if you come down from Albuquerque or Santa Fe. Roadside services can be few and far between, so be extra cautious about checking your vehicle's fluids and tires, and don't forget to bring along plenty of drinking water, because you can easily become dehydrated in the desert heat.

Southeastern New Mexico

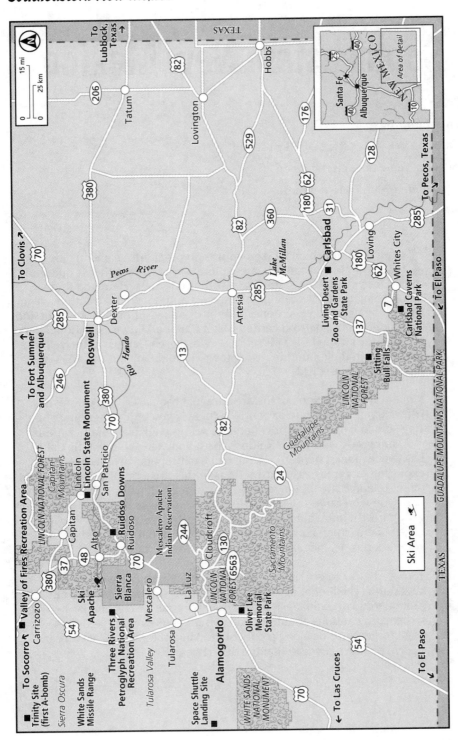

What's Where? Southeastern New Mexico and Its Major Attractions

This chapter is divided into three regions, each with its own set of highlights.

Ruidoso and the Lincoln Loop

With a high-altitude resort town (Ruidoso) and a Wild-West village (Lincoln), this land thrills active adventurers, young and old. Here you find the following:

- **Hubbard Museum of the American West.** All things horsy, great and small, greet you at this Ruidoso sight.

- **Lincoln State Monument.** In the 19th-century village of Lincoln, Billy the Kid made a name for himself and shot his way out of jail.

- **Mescalero Indian Reservation.** Covering 719 miles of prime forested mountain land, this reservation is most known for its swanky and poetically named resort, **Inn of the Mountain Gods.**

- **Smokey the Bear Historical Park.** Meet the legend of the bear who taught us that only we can prevent forest fires.

- **Three Rivers Petroglyph National Recreation Area.** More than 20,000 images adorn the rocks of this park set against the bold backdrop of the White Mountains.

- **Valley of Fires Recreation Area.** Meander through one of the nation's youngest lava fields.

White Sands National Monument, Alamogordo, and the Tularosa Valley

The grand basin that makes up the Tularosa Valley offers sand and space among its main attractions, which include the following:

- **New Mexico Museum of Space History.** With its International Space Hall of Fame and IMAX Dome Theater, this five-story center satisfies your other worldly desires.

- **The Tularosa Valley.** In addition to space and sand, some enjoyable hikes await you here.

- **White Sands National Monument.** The world's largest gypsum dune field offers the cheapest way to visit the moon.

Carlsbad Caverns National Park and the Pecos River Valley

You don't have to be an avid *spelunker* (cave explorer) or bat-lover to enjoy the extraordinary natural wonders of this desert region. In this area you can acquaint yourself with:

- ✔ **Carlsbad Caverns National Park.** Here, the combo of bats and giant stalactites (and stalagmites) creates the perfect setting for pretending you're in a 1950s sci-fi flick.

- ✔ **International UFO Museum.** This place presents just enough "proof" to *almost* convince you that aliens actually landed in Roswell in 1947.

- ✔ **Living Desert Zoo and Gardens State Park.** More than 50 species of desert mammals, birds, and reptiles live happily on 1,200 acres here.

Discovering the Wild West: Ruidoso and the Lincoln Loop

Don your ten-gallon hat and slip into your Texas accent — you're headed into Wild-West country. A trip through this part of the state takes you to **Ruidoso** (pronounced ree-uh-*do*-so), a resort town 6,900 feet high in the Sacramento Mountains frequented by southern folks who talk with a heck of a twang. Ruidoso is most known for Ski Apache, its ski area. Out on the plains north of Ruidoso is the Wild-West town of **Lincoln,** where you can trace the footsteps of the notorious punk outlaw **Billy the Kid.**

The town of Ruidoso draws big crowds in summer and during winter holidays. Ruidoso is fine for some, but I find the place a bit overwhelming and prefer to spend my time in the quieter parts of the region, hiking in the **Sacramento Mountains** and lounging at one of Lincoln's bed-and-breakfasts. Whichever your preference, you want to devote at least two days to exploring the area. A good way to apportion your time is to drive the fun **Lincoln Loop,** which I describe later in this section; doing so takes one to two days.

Getting there

From Albuquerque, take I-25 south 87 miles to San Antonio; turn east on U.S. 380 and travel 74 miles past Carrizozo; then go south on N.M. 37/48 approximately 25 miles to Riodoso. From Alamogordo, drive north on U.S. 54 to Tularosa; then take U.S. 70 northeast for one hour to Ruidoso.

There is no commercial service to the area's one airport, Sierra Blanca Regional Airport. **Greyhound/Trailways** (☎ **800-231-2222;** Internet: www.greyhound.com or www.trailways.com) services the area with buses daily.

Staying in style

Unfortunately, Ruidoso is not known for its quality accommodations. The truth is, the place gets so much business during peak seasons that the innkeepers don't have to try very hard. If you're looking for a budget stay in Ruidoso, a **Motel 6** (☎ **800-466-8356**) on the outskirts of town has clean, reliable rooms.

Best Western Swiss Chalet Inn
$–$$ Ruidoso

Don your lederhosen and sing a yodel and you'll fit in well at this blue-and-white chalet-style motel set among the pines on the north end of town. Though you may hear others yodeling (or talking) through the thin walls, the place quiets down at night. Rooms are spacious with comfortably firm beds and very clean bathrooms. A restaurant, indoor swimming pool, and hot tub round out the experience.

1451 Mechem Dr. (4½ miles north of Main Street). ☎ 800-477-9477 or 505-258-3333. Fax: 505-258-5325. Internet: www.ruidoso.net/swisschalet. *Rack rates: $64–$114 double. AE, DC, MC, V. Small pets are welcome.*

Casa de Patrón Bed and Breakfast
$$ Lincoln

If you've ever fancied yourself an outlaw hiding out in a small Southwestern town, slip on your chaps and head to this inn within the Wild-West town of Lincoln. The main building, an adobe, was built around 1860 and housed Juan Patrón's old store (now on the National Register of Historic Places). In addition, Billy the Kid used part of the house as a hideout at some point during his time in the Lincoln area. Today, the place is full of portraits and photographs of the notorious punk. Rooms in the main house are quite cozy, while those in the Old Trail House are more luxurious, with fireplaces and mini-refrigerators. Families enjoy nearby *casitas* (little houses) with kitchens.

On U.S. 380 (in the center of Lincoln). ☎ 800-524-5202 or 505-653-4676. Fax: 505-653-4671. Internet: www.casapatron.com. *Rack rates: $87–$117 double. Rates include breakfast. MC, V.*

Ellis Store Country Inn

$$–$$$ Lincoln

Another haunt of Billy the Kid (who stayed here a few weeks under house arrest), this 1850s inn offers a real back-to-the-past stay with modern amenities. The rooms in the main house have wood-burning fireplaces or stoves, antique furnishings, and handmade quilts. The separate Mill House isn't quite as cozy, but provides plenty of Old West ambiance. Two new suites are a good option for families. Breakfasts here are pure gourmet.

U.S. 380 (in the center of Lincoln). ☎ *800-653-6460 or 505-653-4609. Internet:* www. ellisstore.com. *Rack rates: $79–$139 double. Rates include breakfast. AE, DC, DISC, MC, V. Pets are not permitted inside, but kennels are available.*

Inn of the Mountain Gods

$$–$$$ Ruidoso

Set on a grassy slope above a mountain lake on the Mescalero Apache Reservation, this resort must be a suburb of heaven. Though the rooms aren't *luxurious* (as the inn proclaims), they are spacious and have views out across the lake. The property includes an 18-hole golf course. The resort has a dining room, lounge, piano bar, and casino. You also find a pool, hot tub, and sauna, as well as plenty of activities.

Carrizo Canyon Rd. (3½ miles from downtown Ruidoso, in Mescalero) ☎ *800-545-9011 or 505-257-5141. Fax: 505-257-6173. Internet:* www.innofthemountain gods.com. *May–Labor Day $135 double; Labor Day–Oct $110 double; Nov–Apr $95 double. Golf, tennis, and ski packages available. AE, DC, DISC, MC, V.*

Shadow Mountain Lodge

$–$$ Ruidoso

Located in the "Upper Canyon," this is one of Ruidoso's nicer and more reliable accommodations. Advertising "luxury lodging for couples," the lodge is a good spot for a romantic getaway, and the owners hold to that notion by not encouraging guests to bring children. Each room has a comfortable king-size bed, kitchenette, and a fireplace. The grounds are attractive, well kept, and include a barbecue area, hot tub, and self-serve laundromat.

107 Main Rd. (on the west end of Sudderth Drive, 3 blocks from intersection with Mecham Drive). ☎ *800-441-4331 or 505-257-4886. Fax: 505-257-2000. Internet:* www. SMLruidoso.com. *Rack rates: Memorial Day–Oct 22 and holidays $109 double; Oct 23–Memorial Day $69–$84 double. Christmas holidays $119. Ski packages available. AE, DC, DISC, MC, V.*

Dining out

Unfortunately, in this resort town, you won't find the excellent food that a city like Santa Fe offers, but you can find a decent meal at some of the spots listed below.

Casa Blanca
$–$$ Ruidoso   NEW MEXICAN

Every town needs one: A south-of-the-border kind of place where people can float placidly on the waves of margaritas and chile and forget the rip-tides of the world. Don't say *olé* too fast, though. Here, you won't quite get the refined New Mexican flavors that you find in Albuquerque or Santa Fe, but you do find decent food served in a festive atmosphere. After complimentary chips and salsa, you can dine on chicken enchiladas with sour cream, or on beef or chicken fajitas. Kids enjoy the relaxed atmosphere and their own menu.

501 Mechem Dr. (¾ mile north of Sudderth Drive). ☎ *505-257-2495. Main courses: $5–$10. AE, MC, V. Open: Daily 11 a.m.–9 p.m., with later hours during the summer and winter holidays; closed Thanksgiving and Christmas.*

Cattle Baron Steak House
$$–$$$$ Ruidoso   STEAKS/SEAFOOD

Welcome to carnivoreland, where steaks are plentiful and guilt about eating them is checked at the door. A casually elegant restaurant with lots of brass and wood, this is often a busy place, where locals and travelers come to savor all manner of steaks as well as lighter fare, such as a turkey and avocado sandwich or chicken teriyaki kabob.

657 Sudderth Dr. (1 mile from the center of town). ☎ *505-257-9355. Main courses: $6–$10 lunch; $8–$19 dinner. AE, DC, DISC, MC, V. Open: Memorial Day–Labor Day Mon–Thur 11 a.m.–9:30 p.m., Fri–Sat 11 a.m.–10 p.m., Sun 11 a.m.–9 p.m. Rest of the year, Mon–Thurs 11:30 a.m.–9:30 p.m.; Fri–Sat 11:30 a.m.–10 p.m.; Sun 11 a.m.–9 p.m.*

Flying J Ranch
$$–$$$ Ruidoso   CHUCK WAGON

An enthusiastic canned Western experience, the Flying J Ranch serves up a chuck-wagon dinner, staged gunfights, and pony rides for kids. The spot offers a good family experience set in a Western village. While you eat barbecue beef or chicken and ranch fixins, the Flying J Wranglers present a fast-paced stage show with Western music and a world champion yodeler.

Billy the Kid

In the late 1800s, a young punk named Billy the Kid shot up some sheriffs and deputies in the Lincoln County War, escaped from the town of Lincoln, and became a Wild-West legend. He claimed to have killed 21 men, one for every year he lived, but some sources say he killed only four. Legendary lawman Pat Garrett tracked him down and arrested him. A judge sentenced the Kid to die by hanging in Lincoln. Less than a month before his hanging, he escaped, killing two guards and helping five other prisoners out of the Lincoln County Court House Jail. Garrett tracked him down again, this time in Fort Sumner, where he killed the Kid, only 21 years old.

If you're interested in tracking the Kid yourself, start in **Lincoln** (see "Discovering the top attractions" in this section), and then make your way northeast to the **Billy the Kid Museum** (☎ 505-355-2380), 1 mile east of downtown Fort Sumner on U.S. 60/84. The museum, which contains more than 60,000 relics of the Old West, including the Kid's rifle, is open daily year-round from 8:30 a.m. to 5 p.m., except in winter when Sunday hours shorten to 11 a.m. to 5 p.m. Admission is $4 for adults, $3.50 for seniors, and $2 for children. You can also visit the **Old Fort Sumner Museum** (☎ 505-355-2942) to see Old West artifacts, pictures, and documents. This private museum, which may not be worth the $3 admission, is open in summer from 8:30 a.m. to 5:30 p.m., in winter from 9 a.m. to 4 p.m. Behind the museum (you don't have to go through the building) is the grave of Billy the Kid.

Hwy. 48 (1 mile north of Alto). ☎ 505-336-4330. Reservations appreciated. $16 for ages 13 and up; $8 ages 4 through 12; free for age 3 and under. AE, DISC, MC, V. Open: May–Labor Day Mon–Sat 6 p.m. (one seating only).

La Lorraine
$$$–$$$$ Ruidoso   FRENCH

For a moment, you may think you're in an intimate cafe on the Left Bank. But alas, the Eiffel Tower is nowhere to be seen, nor is the Seine River. Guess you'll have to be content with some French provincial decor and *canard á l'orange* (duck in orange sauce) with rich mashed potatoes and green beans on the side. Or maybe the grilled rack of lamb served with *polenta* (a kind of mush made of cornmeal) will satisfy your Parisian appetite.

2523 Sudderth Dr. ☎ 505-257-2954. Reservations recommended. Main courses: $13–$29; lunch $6–$11. AE, DISC, DC, MC, V. Open: Wed–Sat 11:30 a.m.–2 p.m.; Tues–Sat 5:30–9 p.m.

Exploring Ruidoso and the Lincoln Loop

With a Wild-West village and a high-elevation ski area to investigate, you find plenty to do in this region.

Discovering the top attractions

Lincoln Loop

One of the best ways to get acquainted with this part of the world is by taking a drive around the Lincoln Loop. The one- or two-day 162-mile road trip takes you from Ruidoso to historic sites and natural wonders. Along the way you can do the following:

- ✔ **Play a little polo and view a little art.** Heading east from Ruidoso on U.S. 70, about 18 miles past Ruidoso Downs, is the small community of **San Patricio,** where you find (watch for signs) the **Hurd–La Rinconada Gallery** (☎ **505-653-4331**). The gallery shows and sells works by Peter Hurd, Henriette Wyeth, Michael Hurd, Andrew Wyeth, and N.C. Wyeth. Many of the works capture the ambience of the landscape in the San Patricio area, including the richness of a polo field that's used occasionally. The gallery is open Monday to Saturday from 9 a.m. to 5 p.m., and Sunday from 10 a.m. to 4 p.m. Several rooms and guesthouses are available by the night or for longer periods. From San Patricio, continue east on U.S. 70 for 4 miles to the community of Hondo, at the confluence of the Rio Hondo and Rio Bonito, and turn west onto U.S. 380. From here it's about 10 miles to **Lincoln,** a fascinating little town that is also a National Historic Landmark (see the listing for the Lincoln State Monument, earlier in this section).

- ✔ **Visit Smokey the Bear.** From Lincoln, continue west on U.S. 380 about a dozen miles to the town of **Capitan,** the home of **Smokey Bear Historical State Park,** 118 First St. (☎ **505-354-2748**). You know Smokey, the national symbol of forest fire prevention. Well, he was born near here and found as an orphaned cub by firefighters in the early 1950s. You can see exhibits about him and visit his grave. Open daily from 9 a.m. to 5 p.m. Admission is $1 for adults, 50¢ for children age 7 to 12, and free for children under age 7.

- ✔ **Eat one of New Mexico's best green chile cheeseburgers.** Heading west on U.S. 380 from Capitan about 20 miles takes you to **Carrizozo,** the Lincoln County seat since 1912. You can find one of the best green-chile cheeseburgers in the Southwest at the **Outpost** (☎ **505-648-9994**), 415 Central Ave. (in the center of town). It's served in a basket with homemade fries, if you like. Inside this dark, cool bar/restaurant, you find cowboys and farmers chowing under the plastic gaze of bison and deer heads. The Outpost is open Monday through Thursday from 11 a.m. to 10 p.m., Friday through Saturday from 11 a.m. to 11 p.m., and Sunday from noon to 10 p.m.

- ✔ **Explore a lava field.** Continue west on U.S. 380 for 4 miles to **Valley of Fires Recreation Area** (☎ **505-648-2241**), where you find what is considered one of the youngest and best-preserved lava fields in the United States. Among the black lava formations, a ¾-mile self-guided nature trail is well worth the walk. A small visitor center and bookstore is in the nearby campground. The area is open 24-hours year-round. Admission is $3 per person or $5 per car for day use.

✔ **Hunt for petroglyphs.** To continue the loop tour, return 4 miles to Carrizozo, turn south onto U.S. 54, and go about 28 miles to the turnoff to **Three Rivers Petroglyph National Recreation Area** (☎ 505-525-4300), which is about 5 miles east of the turnoff on a paved road. Here you find some 20,000 individual rock art images, carved by Mogollon peoples who lived in the area centuries ago. A ⅖-mile trail links many of the more interesting petroglyphs, while the view surrounding the area, with mountains to the east and White Sands National Monument to the southwest, may just give you goosebumps. The park also includes the partially excavated ruins of an ancient Native American village. The area is open daily, 24 hours. The day use or camping fee is $3 per vehicle.

✔ **Sip some vino.** From the recreation area, return 5 miles to U.S. 54 and continue south about 15 miles to **Tularosa Vineyards** (☎ 505-585-2260), which offers tours and tastings daily from noon until 5 p.m. Using all New Mexico grapes, the winery is especially known for its award-winning reds. You can purchase wines by the bottle, with prices ranging from $6 to $18.

✔ **Visit the Apaches and their mountain gods.** Continuing south from the winery, drive about 2 miles on U.S. 54 to Tularosa and turn east onto U.S. 70, which you take for about 16 miles to the village of **Mescalero** on the **Mescalero Apache Indian Reservation** (☎ 505-464-4494). Covering 719 square miles, it is home to about 2,800 members of the Mescalero, Chiricahua, and Lipan bands of Apaches. From U.S. 70, turn south onto Eagle Drive to get to the imposing **St. Joseph's Church** (☎ 505-464-4473), standing more than 100 feet tall to the tip of the cross, with stone walls up to 4 feet thick. The church is open Tuesday through Friday from 10 a.m. to 3 p.m. Admission is free. When you return to Ruidoso (about 19 miles on U.S. 70), you may want to check out the **Inn of the Mountain Gods,** a luxury year-round resort owned and operated by the tribe (see "Staying in style," earlier in this section). Throughout the year, the Mescalero Apaches host pow wows of colorful dancing and traditional drumming, open to the public and with unrestricted photography. Call the reservation for a schedule.

The Lincoln Loop heads east from Ruidoso on U.S. 70. At Hondo, turn west onto U.S. 380. Pass through Lincoln and continue on U.S. 380 to Capitan and on to Carrizozo and the Valley of Fires Recreation Area. Then return 4 miles to Carrizozo, turn south onto U.S. 54, which passes the turnoff for Three Rivers Petroglyph National Recreation Area, and on to Tularosa. Turn east onto U.S. 70, which goes through Mescalero en route back to Ruidoso.

Lincoln State Monument
Lincoln

Lincoln is one of the last historic, yet uncommercialized 19th-century towns remaining in the American West. Here you find lovely historic, adobe buildings — no fast-food joints, no convenience stores. Lincoln is best known as the place where Billy the Kid, that notorious 19th-century outlaw, was incarcerated and sentenced to hanging — one chapter in the history of the bloody Lincoln County War (see the "Billy the Kid" sidebar in this chapter). The war was fought between various ranching and merchant factions over the issue of beef contracts for Fort Stanton near Ruidoso. The entire town is a New Mexico State Monument and a National Historic Landmark. Begin your tour at the Lincoln Historical Center, where exhibits explain Lincoln's history. There you can pick up a brochure describing the self-guided walking tour of the town. The most important stop is the Lincoln County Court House, built in 1873–1874, where Billy the Kid killed two guards and escaped, leaving bullet holes in the wall. Youngsters love seeing these and following The Kid's footsteps through town.

37 miles northeast of Ruidoso on U.S. 380. ☎ *800-263-5929. Admission: $6 adults (includes entry to seven buildings) or $2.50 per building; children age 16 and under are free. Open: Year-round 8:30 a.m.–5 p.m.*

Finding more cool things to see and do

If you're looking for still more adventure, try one of the following activities:

- ✔ **Hit the slopes.** Yes, finding quality skiing in this desert environment is amazing, but it's no mirage. **Ski Apache** (☎ **505-257-9001** for snow report, or 505-336-4356 for information; Internet: www.skiapache.com), only 20 miles northwest of Ruidoso in the Mescalero Apache Reservation, has a gondola, two quad chairs, five triple chairs, and one double chair, servicing 55 trails (20% beginner, 35% intermediate, and 45% advanced). Though its location seems remote, many skiers fill this mountain during weekends and holidays. Your best bet is to ski during the week. The slopes are open daily Thanksgiving through Easter from 8:45 a.m. to 4 p.m. All-day lift tickets cost $43 to $46 for adults and $28 to $31 for children age 12 and under.

- ✔ **Horse around.** For those of you who can't get enough of equinimity, head to the **Hubbard Museum of the American West** (☎ **505-378-4142**), located at the famous **Ruidoso Downs Racetrack** (☎ **505-378-4431**), 2 miles east of Ruidoso on U.S. 70. Home to a collection of more than 10,000 horse-related items, the museum is open daily year-round (excluding Thanksgiving and Christmas) from 10 a.m. to 5 p.m. Admission is $6 for adults, $5 for seniors and military, $2 for ages 6 to 16, and free for children under age 6. The world's richest quarter-horse race, the $2.5 million All-American Futurity, is run each year on Labor Day at the racetrack. Many other days of quarter horse and thoroughbred racing lead up to the big one, beginning in May and running to Labor Day. Post time weekdays is 3:30 p.m. and weekends and holidays is 1 p.m. Grandstand admission is free. Call for reserved seating ($2.50 and up) plus box seating for four to six persons.

✔ **Entertain the family.** If you like the smell of cotton candy and the sound of high-pitched screaming, make tracks to **Funtrackers Family Fun Center,** 101 Carrizo Canyon Rd., in the center of Ruidoso (☎ **505-257-3275**). Spread out below a hill are go-cart courses for a variety of ages, bumper boats, a bull riding concession, and miniature golf. *Beware:* This place can be crammed with people mid-summer and on weekends. The center is open weekends and holidays year-round (call for hours) and daily from Memorial Day to Labor Day from 10 a.m. to 10 p.m. Each ride costs $4.

✔ **Take in some high-brow theater.** The **Spencer Theater for the Performing Arts** (☎ **888-818-7872** or 505-336-4800) is a $20 million theater where world-class artists perform; talents such as the Paul Taylor Dance Company and Marvin Hamlisch have performed in the past. The theater is on Sierra Blanca Airport Highway 220, 4½ miles east of Highway 48. Performances take place on weekends and occasionally on weekdays. The season runs year-round and tickets cost from $25 to $50.

Shopping 'til you drop

Though this area is galaxies away from Saks Fifth Avenue and Bloomingdale's, some notable shops and galleries are in the vicinity. In fact, you may be surprised to know that earlier in the 20th century, many noted artists made their homes in Ruidoso and the surrounding

The Long March

The ruins at **Fort Sumner State Monument** (☎ 505-355-2573) stand as a sad testament to the "Long March," during which the U.S. Government forced some Navajos to walk more than 400 miles to this site. They and many Mescalero Apaches (9,000 people) were imprisoned there under brutal conditions. Some 3,000 Native Americans died. A short walking tour takes you to various signposts explaining what was once on the land. The visitor center (open Wednesday to Monday from 8:30 a.m. to 5 p.m.) gives you a good background before you head out to the site. The monument is located 7 miles southeast of the town of Fort Sumner, via U.S. 60/84 and N.M. 272. Admission is $3 for adults, free for children age 17 and under.

Lincoln County, resulting in a proliferation of galleries in town. Most are open daily from 10 a.m. to 6 p.m. Among my favorites are **Casa Bonita,** 2330 Sudderth Dr. (☎ **505-257-5024**), which carries eclectic imported crosses, pewter dinnerware, and jewelry, and is great for wedding present shopping; **Crucis Art Bronze Foundry and Gallery,** 524 Sudderth Dr. (☎ **505-257-7186**), which shows nature and Western sculptures as well as gold and silver Southwestern and contemporary jewelry; and **Fenton's Gallery,** 2629 Sudderth Dr. (☎ **505-257-9738**), which has American, Western, and Native American originals and prints.

Quick Concierge: Ruidoso

Area Code

The area code is **505**. Although some area codes in the state may change in 2002, Ruidoso will most likely retain this one. For updates, contact the New Mexico Department of Tourism (☎ 800-733-6396; Internet: www.new mexico.org).

ATMs

You can find major banks with ATM machines along Sudderth Drive.

Emergencies

Call ☎ **911**.

Hospitals

Lincoln County Medical Center, 211 Sudderth Dr., on the east side of Ruidoso (☎ 505-257-7381), offers 24-hour emergency service.

Information

The folks at the Ruidoso Valley Chamber of Commerce and Visitor Center, 720 Sudderth Dr. (☎ 800-253-2255 or 505-257-7395; Internet: www.ruidoso.net) are quite helpful.

Internet Access

Head to the Postal Annex at 2814 Sudderth Dr. (☎ 505-257-5606).

Pharmacies

Walgreens, 138 Sudderth Dr., at the east end of Ruidoso (☎ 505-257-0054), is open daily from 8 a.m. to 10 p.m.

Police

In case of emergency, dial ☎ **911**. For other matters, call the Ruidoso Police Department (☎ 505-258-7365).

Post Office

Ruidoso has a new post office, located at 1090 Mechem Dr., 3 miles north of Sudderth Drive (☎ 505-257-7120).

Road Conditions

Call ☎ 800-432-4269.

Weather Updates

To get weather forecasts on the Internet, log on to www.accuweather.com and type in the Ruidoso zip code, 88345.

Spacing Out: White Sands National Monument, Alamogordo, and the Tularosa Valley

You would be hard-pressed to find another spot in the world where you can spend an afternoon learning about space (at the **New Mexican Museum of Space History** in Alamogordo) and then pretend you're actually on the moon (as you wander through the sweeping white expanse of undulating, talcum-powder-like gypsum that makes up the breathtaking **White Sands National Monument**).

Both attractions are just a few miles away from each other in the expansive **Tularosa Valley,** which stretches between the San Andres and Sacramento mountain ranges. As you cruise around, don't be surprised to see fighter pilots jetting overhead on training missions from Holloman Air Force Base; and, if you're really lucky, you just may spot a space shuttle gliding down to the White Sands Space Harbor (the shuttle's alternative landing site).

Looking to add a little intrigue to your Tularosa Valley trip? Pick up a paperback copy of *Tularosa* (WW Norton & Company) by Michael McGarrity. Set in the Tularosa Basin, the book is a thrilling mystery about the White Sands Missile Range and Spanish gold.

Getting there

From Albuquerque, the trip is about four hours: Take I-25 south 87 miles to San Antonio; turn east on U.S. 380, and head 66 miles to Carrizozo; then make your way south on U.S. 54 for 58 miles. From Las Cruces, take U.S. 70 northeast for about one and half hours. (*Note:* U.S. 70 may be closed for up to two hours during tests on the White Sands Missile Range; call ☎ 505-443-7199 for updates. Unfortunately, there's no alternative route, unless you take the *long* way around via El Paso, Texas.) From El Paso, take U.S. 54 north for about one and a half hours.

The nearest major airport is the **El Paso International Airport** (☎ 915-780-4700). The **Alamo Shuttle Service** (☎ 800-872-2701) operates a shuttle to Alamogordo from El Paso International for $31 one-way and $44 round-trip; call for schedules and discounts. The local airport, **Alamogordo–White Sands Regional Airport** (☎ 505-439-4110), is served by **Mesa Airlines** (☎ 800-637-2247 or 505-437-9111), which has daily flights from Albuquerque. Once at the airport, you can rent a car from **Avis** (☎ 800-831-2847 or 505-437-3140). **TNM&O Coaches** (☎ 505-437-3050) stops at the Alamogordo bus station, 601 N. White Sands Blvd.

Lay your head in the clouds

You can enjoy stunning views of the Tularosa Valley from the tiny mountain village of Cloudcroft, which sits 9,000 feet up in the Sacramento Mountains, about 20 miles east of Alamogordo via U.S. 82. The classic place to stay is **The Lodge at Cloudcroft** (\$\$\$–\$\$\$\$), 1 Corona Place (☎ **800-395-6343** or 505-682-2566; Internet: www.the lodgeresort.com), which is an atmospheric, antiques-filled throwback to the Victorian era. The lodge's restaurant, **Rebecca's (☎ 505-682-3131)**, is named after the resident ghost, believed to have been a chambermaid in the 1930s who was killed by her lumberjack lover. Amenities include a heated outdoor pool, tennis courts, bicycles and cross-country skis for rent, and nature trails. The lodge's nine-hole golf course is one of the nation's highest, with greens between 8,600 and 9,200 feet. For more information about Cloudcroft, contact the **Cloudcroft Chamber of Commerce,** located in a log cabin in the center of town on the south side of U.S. 82 (☎ **505-682-2733**).

Staying in style

The most memorable way to pass a night in the area is in a tent under the stars at **White Sands National Monument** (particularly when the moon is full), so you can best experience the lunar landscape of curvy dunes. The monument has no formal campground facilities, however, and only tents are allowed. If camping isn't an option, you can find a decent selection of lodgings in Alamogordo along White Sands Boulevard, the main drag through town.

Best Western Desert Aire
$ Alamogordo

This link in the Best Western chain is probably your best all-around option for lodging in the area. The recently renovated rooms are cozy, clean, and comfortable, and some have kitchenettes. If you go for a suite, you also get a whirlpool bath, which may be worth the splurge after a long drive. Other amenities include a nice outdoor heated pool (open year-round), as well as a sauna and hot tub. Your stay includes a continental breakfast.

1021 S. White Sands Blvd. ☎ 800-528-1234 or 505-437-2110. Fax: 505-437-1898. Rack rates: $68 double; $75 suite. AE, DC, DISC, MC, V.

Days Inn Alamogordo
$ Alamogordo

Although second best in every way to the Best Western, you still find clean, comfortable rooms here in this basic two-story motel. The medium-size rooms all have microwaves and mini-refrigerators. Outside is a swimming pool, but watch out: It ain't heated.

907 S. White Sands Blvd. ☎ 800-329-7466 or 505-437-5090. Fax: 505-434-5667. Rack rates: $75 double. AE, DC, DISC, MC, V.

Dining out

Plenty of fast food joints are along White Sands Boulevard, but if you want to sample the local grub, head to one of the options below.

Memories Restaurant
$$–$$$$ Alamogordo   AMERICAN

Old-fashioned Victorian elegance is the backdrop for the fine dining presented in this very popular, casual, comfortable restaurant. Try the 8-ounce filet mignon or the grilled pork chops, and save room for a slice of pie for dessert.

1223 New York Ave. ☎ 505-437-0077. Reservations recommended. Main courses: $7.95–$18.95. AE, DISC, MC, V. Open: Mon–Sat 11 a.m.–9 p.m.

Ramona's Restaurant
$–$$ Alamogordo   AMERICAN/MEXICAN

Come to this popular local hangout for the food and social scene, not for the dated '70s-style decor. Try Ramona's special: a *chile relleño* (stuffed pepper), chicken enchilada, and chicken *chimichanga* (a deep-fried burrito), topped with guacamole and sour cream, and served with beans and rice. You can also go for the chicken-fried steak.

2913 N. White Sands Blvd. ☎ 505-437-7616. Main courses: $5–$10. AE, MC, V. Open: Daily 6 a.m.–10 p.m.

Exploring White Sands, Alamogordo, and the Tularosa Valley

The nondescript town of Alamogordo is the hub for this area, but its lack of charm does little to take away from the captivating landscapes surrounding it.

Discovering the top attractions

New Mexican Museum of Space History
Alamogordo

This very cool museum, a kind of fantasy land for astrokids, contains both the International Space Hall of Fame and the Clyde W. Tombaugh IMAX Dome Theater. The *Golden Cube* (a five-story building with walls of golden glass) contains the Space Hall of Fame, where you can check out spacecraft and lunar exploration modules, as well as exhibits portraying the accomplishments of the first astronauts and cosmonauts from America's Apollo, Mercury, and Gemini programs and the early Soviet orbital flights. You also find displays about astronomy, missiles, rocketry, and satellites, as well as New Mexico's role in space exploration history. On the grounds outside, you can check out the *Sonic Wind No. 1* sled (which tested human endurance for space flights at speeds exceeding 600 m.p.h.) and various other space artifacts. At the Clyde W. Tombaugh Theater, the IMAX projection and Spitz 512 Planetarium Systems create earthly and cosmic experiences on a mind-boggling 2,700-square-foot dome.

At the top of N.M. Hwy. 2001, 2 miles east of U.S. 54. ☎ *877-333-6589 outside New Mexico, or 505-437-2840. Admission to Space Hall: $2.50 adults, $2.25 seniors (age 60 and older) and military, $2 teens (age 13–17) and youths (age 6–12), free for children age 5 and under. Admission to IMAX Theater: $5.50 adults, $5 seniors and military, $4.50 teens, $3.50 youths; free for children age 5 and under. Prices subject to change without notice. Open: Daily 9 a.m.–5 p.m.*

White Sands National Monument
Alamogordo

It may seem like a long way to drive just to see some sand, but the second you make your way into this stunning natural landscape of undulating, pure white gypsum, you'll feel a dramatic perception shift; to use hippie lingo, "it's trippy, man." White Sands National Monument contains most of the world's largest gypsum dune field (about 275 square miles), created over millions of years by rains and melting snows that dissolved the gypsum in the nearby mountains and carried it down to the area. The curvy, wind-shaped dunes roll on for miles and miles and are best seen at sunrise, at sunset, or by moonlight (best of all). The 16-mile **Dunes Drive** takes you through the heart of the sandy expanse, where the dunes are slowly moving northeast at the rate of about 20 feet a year. Playing in the sand is great fun, and you can even buy sleds at the visitors center, but don't tunnel into the sand (it can collapse), and be especially cautious with children, who will love playing man on the moon. You can find some short hiking trails, which keep you from getting lost, and hear nightly ranger talks and take sunset strolls in summer.

When driving near or in the monument, tune your radio to 1610 AM for information on what's happening.

The visitor center is 15 miles southwest of Alamogordo on U.S. 70/82. (Note: Due to missile testing on the adjacent White Sands Missile Range, this road is sometimes closed for up to two hours at a time.) ☎ *505-479-6124. Admission: $3 adults age 17 and over, kids free. Camping: Additional $3 for adults 17 and over, $1.50 for kids. Open: Memorial Day to Labor Day 8 a.m.–7 p.m. for the visitor center and 7 a.m.– 9 p.m. for Dunes Drive; rest of the year 8 a.m.–5 p.m. for the visitor center and 7 a.m. to sunset for Dunes Drive. Ranger talks and sunset strolls nightly from Memorial Day to Labor Day at 7 and 8:30 p.m.*

Finding more cool things to see and do

In this region you can hit the local trails or gain a new appreciation for toy trains and pistachio nuts. Here are my recommendations:

- ✔ **Go hiking.** Fifteen miles southeast of Alamogordo via U.S. 54 and Dog Canyon Road, you find well-marked hiking trails in the **Oliver Lee Memorial State Park,** which is tucked into the mouth of Dog Canyon. Various seeps and springs in the area support a wide variety of wildlife, as well as rare and endangered plant species.

- ✔ **Take a pistachio tour.** New Mexico's first and largest pistachio farm, **Eagle Ranch Pistachio Groves,** 7288 U.S. 54/70 (☎ 800-432-0999 or 505-434-0035), offers 45-minute tours Monday through Friday at 10 a.m. and 1:30 p.m. in summer, and 1:30 p.m. in winter. The tour offers a brief history of the pistachio grove, a walk-through of their shipping and receiving facility and salting and roasting department, and a stroll through the groves. Admission is free.

- ✔ **Choo-Choo-Chaboogie.** If you're into trains, put on your conductor's hat and head to the **Toy Train Depot,** 1991 N. White Sands Blvd. (☎ 505-437-2855). The three-room museum is housed in an 1898 railroad depot and celebrates the railroad's important presence in the area with toy trains chugging through miniature cities and landscapes. Hours are Wednesday through Sunday from noon to 4:30 p.m. Admission is $2.

Quick concierge: White Sands, Alamogordo, and the Tularosa Valley

Area Code

The area code is **505.** Although some area codes in the state may change, this area will most likely retain this one. For updates, contact the New Mexico Department of Tourism (☎ 800-733-6396; Internet: www.new mexico.org).

ATMs

You can find ATMs all over Alamogordo; Wells Fargo and 1st National Bank are two of the bigger banks in town.

Emergencies

Call ☎ **911.**

Hospitals

In case of an emergency, head to the emergency room at the Gerald Champion Regional Medical Center, 2669 North Scenic Dr., Alamogordo (☎ 505-439-6100).

Information

For information, call or stop by the Alamogordo Chamber of Commerce, 1301 N. White Sands Blvd. (☎ 800-826-0294 or 505-437-6120; Internet: www.alamogordo.com). You can pick up a map of Alamogordo and the Tularosa Basin here for $1. Hours are Monday through Friday from 8 a.m. to 5 p.m., Saturday from 9:30 a.m. to 3:30 p.m. Closed Sundays.

Internet Access

You can check your e-mail for free at the Alamogordo Public Library, 920 Oregon Ave. (☎ 505-439-4140). Hours are Monday through Thursday from 10 a.m. to 8 p.m., Friday from 10 a.m. to 5 p.m., Saturday and Sunday from 1 to 5 p.m.; closed holidays.

Pharmacies

In Alamogordo head to the Medical Arts Pharmacy, 1301 10th St. (☎ 505-437-5530). You can also try Walgreens, 895 White Sands Blvd. (☎ 505-434-4112), or Wal-Mart, 233 S. New York Ave. (☎ 505-434-5870).

Police

Call ☎ 911. For non-emergencies, call the Alamogordo Police Department (☎ 505-439-4300).

Post Office

You find the main branch of the Alamogordo Post Office at 930 East 12th St. (☎ 505-437-9390).

Road Conditions

The White Sands Missile Range sometimes closes roads due to missile testing; call ☎ 505-443-7199 for updates. For other road conditions, call ☎ 800-432-4269 or check the Internet at www.nmshtd.state.nm.us.

Weather Updates

For weather updates, call the National Weather Service in El Paso (☎ 505-589-4088). To get weather forecasts on the Internet, log on to www.accuweather.com and use the Alamogordo zip code, 88310.

Encountering Caves and Aliens: Carlsbad Caverns National Park and the Pecos River Valley

Named after the famous old spa in Bohemia, the tiny, bland city of **Carlsbad** (population 27,800) is best used as a base for exploring **Carlsbad Caverns National Park.** Aside from the nearby caves, the town is also well known for its pecans.

However, the caverns are the reason to come all the way down here, and you won't be the first to make the trip: More than 33 million visitors have toured the caves since the park opened in 1923. A privately-owned satellite community, Whites City, sits 20 miles south of Carlsbad at the park entrance junction and is a classic tourist trap of gift shops, motels, and restaurants, all enticingly located closer to the park than anything else. Staying in Carlsbad is cheaper, however.

Getting there

From Albuquerque, the drive takes about six hours; take I-40 east 59 miles to Clines Corners, turn south on U.S. 285, and drive 216 miles to Carlsbad via Roswell. From El Paso, take U.S. 62/180 east for about three hours.

Mesa Airlines (☎ 800-637-2247 or 505-885-0245) provides daily flights between Albuquerque and **Cavern City Air Terminal** (☎ 505-887-3060), which is located 4 miles south of the city via National Parks Highway (U.S. 62/180). You can rent a car at the airport from **Hertz** (☎ 800-654-3131 or 505-885-5236). The Greyhound bus station is located at 1000 S. Canyon (☎ 505-887-1108; Internet: www.greyhound.com).

Staying in style

You pay more and have fewer options if you stay near the caverns in Whites City rather than in Carlsbad, but then again, the additional 30 miles to Carlsbad makes Whites City a tempting location.

Best Western Cavern Inn
$$ Whites City

This complex of three hotels is the place to stay if you want to be close to the caverns. The best hotel here is the Guadalupe Inn, built around a courtyard with Southwestern-style rooms and a large pool in back. The Cavern Inn next door offers acceptable 1970s-style rooms, but try not to stay in the Walnut Canyon Inn unless you're really desperate. The Whites City Arcade, near the hotels, contains a post office, grocery store, gift shop, museum, and opera house. You also find hot tubs, a water park with two water slides, and tennis, volleyball, and basketball.

17 Carlsbad Cavern Hwy. at N.M. 7. ☎ 800-228-3767 or 505-785-2291. Fax: 505-785-2283. Rack rates: $90 double. AE, DC, DISC, MC, V.

Best Western Stevens Inn
$ Carlsbad

This hotel offers comfortable, spacious rooms with Southwestern motifs. The large outdoor pool is open seasonally, and a playground and self-service laundromat are also on site. The Flume restaurant (located on the premises) is one of the better restaurants in town.

1829 S. Canal St. ☎ 800-730-2851 or 505-887-2851. Fax: 505-887-6338. E-mail: BWStevensInn@carlsbadnm.com. Rack rates: $64 double; $79 suite. AE, DISC, MC, V.

Continental Inn
$ Carlsbad

This is a good choice for travelers on a budget. The rooms could use an upgrade, but they're clean and comfortable. On site is an outdoor heated swimming pool that's good-sized but has no shade. Services include dry cleaning, newspaper delivery, baby-sitting, and a courtesy car.

3820 National Parks Hwy. ☎ *505-887-0341. Fax: 505-885-1186. Rack rates: $75 double. AE, DC, DISC, MC, V.*

Holiday Inn
$$ Carlsbad

This spot is arguably the best hotel in Carlsbad, with handsome, well-lit rooms decorated with white wooden furniture and Southwestern prints. Amenities include a large swimming pool, sauna, whirlpool, playground, exercise room, and mist-cooled patio. A full breakfast comes with the room, and two restaurants, Ventanas and the Phenix Bar and Grill, are on the premises.

601 S. Canal St. ☎ *800-742-9586 or 505-885-8500. Fax: 505-887-5999. Rack rates: $115 double. AE, DC, DISC, MC, V.*

Dining out

Despite its size and location, Carlsbad has some good choices for dining out.

Blue House
$–$$ Carlsbad   CAFE/BAKERY

This hip hangout is the place to come for delicious coffee, fruit smoothies, muffins, scones, soups, and sandwiches. Try the grilled prosciutto and roasted red pepper sandwich.

609 N. Canyon St. ☎ *505-628-0555. Main courses: $5–$8. No credit cards. Open: Tues–Sat 7:30 a.m.–3:30 p.m.*

Firehouse Gourmet Grill & Club
$–$$$ Carlsbad   AMERICAN

Housed in a 1920s firehouse with a festive, jazzy atmosphere, this is Carlsbad's swinging hotspot for dinner. Try the prime rib or a steak, or the Caesar salad with grilled chicken if you want something lighter. After dinner, you can enjoy a drink at the **Fire Escape** club upstairs, which sometimes offers live music on Friday and Saturday nights.

222 W. Fox St. ☎ *505-234-1546. Reservations recommended. Main courses: $6–$16. AE, DISC, MC, V. Open: Mon–Sat 5–9 p.m., Sun noon–8 p.m.; nightclub Mon–Sat 5 p.m.–1:30 a.m.*

Lucy's
$–$$ Carlsbad   AMERICAN/MEXICAN

Home-cooked food is the main event in this busy restaurant named after its friendly owner. Many of Lucy's recipes reflect the requests of her regulars, such as "Barbara's Favorite Fix" (a beef enchilada and a *chile relleño*). Try the chicken fajita burrito or the combination plate. Families enjoy the cozy, relaxed atmosphere.

701 S. Canal St. ☎ 505-887-7714. Reservations recommended on weekends. Main courses: $3.95–$10.95. AE, DC, DISC, MC, V. Open: Mon–Sat 11 a.m.–9:30 p.m., Sun 11 a.m.–8 p.m.

Exploring Carlsbad Caverns National Park and the Pecos River Valley

Caves, caves, and more caves. Did I mention caves? Caves-R-Us should be the motto of Carlsbad, and when you think about it, it's kind of weird that much of the lifeblood of an economy can come from people spending money to wander around in holes. Aside from the cave-related souvenirs at the Carlsbad Caverns gift shop, this area doesn't offer much in the way of shopping, which means you can save it for food, lodging, gas, and entrance fees to . . . caves.

Discovering the top attractions

Carlsbad Caverns National Park
Whites City

This outstanding natural attraction comprises some 80 known caves (among the largest in the world), which snake their way through the porous limestone reef of the Guadalupe Mountains. In this subterranean universe, you find an extraordinary array of natural sculpture: from grand, operatic chambers to delicate miniature castles and frozen waterfalls. Two cave systems, Carlsbad Cavern and Slaughter Canyon Cave, are open to the public, and the National Park Service provides facilities, including elevators, to make it easy for everyone (including visitors in wheelchairs) to visit. Here's the rundown on tours and attractions:

> ✔ **Carlsbad Cavern** can be toured in three ways, depending on your time, interest, and level of ability. The easiest option is taking the elevator from the park's visitor center down 750 feet and following a self-guided tour of the spectacular 14-acre Big Room. The Big Room tour is 1¼ miles in length and takes about an hour. Vastly more rewarding, yet more difficult and time-consuming, is foregoing the elevator ride by taking a 1-mile self-guided tour along the Natural Entrance Route, which enters the cavern through the large historic natural entrance and follows the traditional explorer's route. The paved walkway through this entrance winds into the

depths of the cavern and leads through a series of underground rooms; the journey takes about an hour. At its lowest point, the trail reaches 750 feet below the surface, ending finally at an underground rest area. Visitors who take the elevator as well as those who take the Natural Entrance Route begin the self-guided tour of the Big Room near the rest area. The third option is a one and a half-hour ranger-guided Kings Palace tour, which also departs from the underground rest area. This tour descends to the deepest portion of the cavern open to the public. Reservations are required and an additional fee is charged for the guided tour.

✔ **Slaughter Canyon Cave** provides a less developed (and more strenuous) caving experience than Carlsbad Cavern. Slaughter Canyon Cave consists of an enormous, 1,140 foot long corridor with many side passageways. The lowest point is 250 feet below the surface, and the passage traversed by the ranger-guided tours is 1¾ miles long. The tour lasts about two and a half hours, and no more than 25 people may take part in it at once (by reservation only). You need to bring a flashlight, hiking boots or shoes, and a container of drinking water. You can reach Slaughter Canyon Cave via U.S. 180, 5 miles south of Whites City; look for a marked turnoff that leads 11 miles into a parking lot.

✔ **Other guided tours,** which visit the Left Hand Tunnel, Lower Cave, Hall of the White Giant, and Spider Cave, vary in degree of difficulty and adventure. Call in advance for tour times. All of these tours depart from the park's visitor center.

✔ **Bat flights:** Every sunset from early spring to October (the bats winter in Mexico), a crowd gathers at the natural entrance of Carlsbad Cavern to watch an estimated quarter-of-a-million bats spiral up into the evening sky to chow on the local bugs. Rangers offer a program around 7:30 p.m. (verify the time at the visitor center) at the outdoor Bat Flight Amphitheater overlooking the cave entrance.

Be sure to call in advance for schedules, because some tours occur only once a week.

For Carlsbad Cavern, take U.S. 62/180 23 miles southwest from Carlsbad or 150 miles east from El Paso, Texas. The scenic entrance road to the park is 7 miles long and originates at the park gate at Whites City. ☎ *800-967-2283; 505-785-2232, ext. 429 for tour reservations; 505-785-2107 for recorded information on guided tours. Admission: $6 for adults, $3 for children age 6–15, and free for children under age 6. Admission is good for three days and includes entry to the two self-guided walking tours. Guided tours: $6–$20 depending on the type of tour; reservations are required. Open: Daily Memorial Day–mid-Aug 8 a.m.–7 p.m.; rest of the year 8 a.m.–5:30 p.m.*

Finding more cool things to see and do

Aside from subterranean attractions, you can discover other hidden gems in the area. When you're ready to de-cave, check out the following outdoor activities, but don't forget your sunscreen and shades:

✔ **Cool off.** On those hot days, head to Carlsbad's **Riverwalk,** a 3½-mile promenade along the broad, shady banks of the Pecos River, beginning near the north end of Riverside Drive. Bring a picnic lunch, and tote along bathing apparel for the municipal beach at the north end (changing rooms and showers are available).

✔ **Frolic among the flora and fauna.** Had enough of the underground? Check out the **Living Desert Zoo and Gardens State Park,** 1504 Miehls Dr. (take Miehls Drive off U.S. 285 west of Carlsbad and proceed a little more than a mile; ☎ 505-887-5516). Situated within 1,200 acres of authentic Chihuahuan Desert, the park contains more than 50 species of desert mammals, birds, and reptiles, and almost 500 varieties of plants. You're likely to see lizards, golden eagles, great horned owls, deer, elk, bears, bobcats, and cougars. Kids especially love the prairie dog town. The zoo is open Memorial Day weekend through Labor Day, from 8 a.m. to 8 p.m.; last park entry by 6:30 p.m. The rest of the year, hours are from 9 a.m. to 5 p.m.; last park entry by 3:30 p.m. Admission is $4 for adults, $2 for children age 7–12, free for children age 6 and under.

Little green men

The infamous "Roswell Incident" of 1947 has been the subject of numerous books and films and, more than 50 years later, is still the most publicized UFO incident in the world. What really happened on July 8, 1947, when a local rancher named MacBrazel found unusual debris scattered across his property, is still under debate. The U.S. military initially released a statement saying the debris was wreckage from a spaceship crash, but a few hours later, the statement was retracted and replaced with a new claim that the debris was "only a weather balloon." Many in the local community (and points beyond) have never bought the weather balloon story, and eyewitnesses to the account maintain that the debris "was not of this world." There has also never been a satisfactory explanation given for the four "alien bodies" that were claimed to have been discovered among the debris. In 1997, two weeks before the 50th anniversary of the "crash," the U.S. Air Force asserted that the likely explanation for the unverified alien reports may be that people were simply remembering and misplacing in time a number of life-sized dummies dropped from the sky during a series of experiments in the 1950s. Hmm. See what you think after paying a visit to the friendly and informative **International UFO Museum and Research Center,** located in Roswell's old Plains Theater at 114 N. Main St. (☎ 505-625-9495). The museum is open daily in winter from 10 a.m. to 5 p.m., in summer from 9 a.m. to 5 p.m. Admission is free.

Quick concierge: Carlsbad

Area Code

The area code is **505**. Although some area codes in the state may change, Carlsbad will most likely retain this one. For updates, contact the New Mexico Department of Tourism (☎ 800-733-6396; Internet: www.newmexico.org).

ATMs

Carlsbad has several ATMs around town. The most well-known bank is Wells Fargo.

Emergencies

Call ☎ **911**.

Hospitals

In case of emergency, head to the emergency room at the Columbia Medical Center, 2430 West Pierce St. (☎ 505-887-4100).

Information

The Carlsbad Chamber of Commerce and the Carlsbad Convention and Visitors Bureau are both at 302 S. Canal St. (☎ 800-221-1224 or 505-887-6516; Internet: www.chamber@caverns.com) and are open Mondays from 9 a.m. to 5 p.m. and Tuesday through Friday from 8 a.m. to 5 p.m. From June through October, they're also open Saturday from 9 a.m. to 5 p.m. You can pick up a free copy of the official visitors guide, which includes a map of the area.

Internet Access

You can check your e-mail for free at the Carlsbad Public Library, 101 South Halagueno (☎ 505-885-6776). Hours are Monday through Thursday from 10 a.m. to 8 p.m., Friday and Saturday from 10 a.m. to 6 p.m., and Sunday from 2 to 6 p.m.; closed most holidays.

Pharmacies

Head to Walgreens, 902 W. Pierce St. (☎ 505-887-0572), or Wal-Mart, 2401 S. Canal St. (☎ 505-885-1029).

Police

Call ☎ **911**. For non-emergencies, call the Carlsbad Police Department (☎ 505-885-2111).

Post Office

You can find the main branch of the Carlsbad Post Office at 301 N. Canyon St. (☎ 505-885-5717).

Road Conditions

Call ☎ 800-432-4269 or check the Internet at www.nmshtd.state.nm.us.

Weather Updates

Call the National Weather Service in El Paso (☎ 505-589-4088). To get weather forecasts on the Internet, log on to www.accuweather.com and use the Carlsbad zip code, 88220.

Chapter 17

Southwestern New Mexico

. . . .

. . . .

As you make your way south from Albuquerque on I-25 toward Las Cruces, the surrounding landscape becomes emptier, drier, and dustier with every mile, and when the wind kicks up like a bronco, the sky often browns with airborne dirt. But just when you're thinking, "Shoot, there ain't nuthin' down here," thousands of birds swoop over on their way to the Bosque del Apache National Wildlife Refuge (just south of Socorro). The birds know the word on this part of the state — remote and rugged, the southwestern region has always been a great place to hide out (which may be why Billy the Kid and Geronimo both lived here).

East of the Bosque del Apache National Wildlife Refuge, the enormous white antennae dishes of the Very Large Array National Radio Astronomy Observatory spread across the sweeping San Augustin plains like props from a James Bond flick. Heading south, to the curiously named town of Truth or Consequences, you can soak your saddle-sore behind in the same hot springs where Geronimo once warmed his. And down in the low-slung, dusty town of Las Cruces (the state's second largest city with a population of 73,600), you get a taste of unpolished New Mexico — a refreshing counterpart to the image-conscious tourist towns up north.

However, the region is not all dust and desiccation, so before you saddle up a camel, take note that you can find green and cool spaces in one of the nation's largest and most spectacular wilderness areas, the 3.3-million-acre Gila National Forest. In the Gila wilderness and surrounding area (which includes Silver City), you can explore cliff dwellings, hot springs, and ghost towns, or hike for days alongside rivers slithering into the woods like rattlers.

Southwestern New Mexico

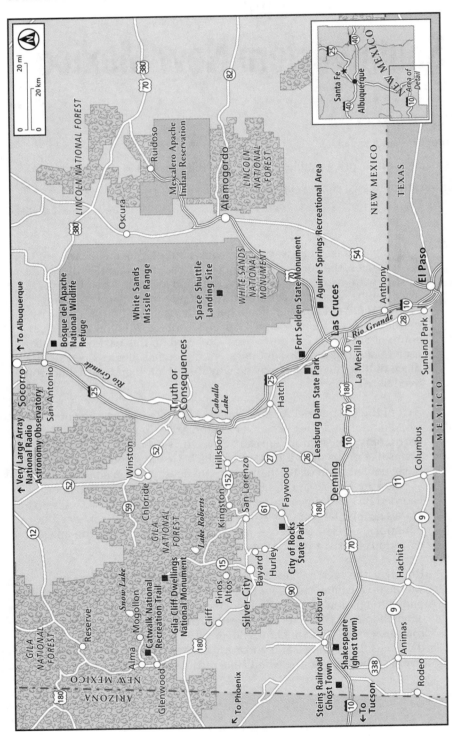

Because of a lack of public transportation in this region, you definitely need a car to get around here.

You can spend two or three days just driving around and hitting a couple of the major attractions, but you need about a week to really explore this area.

What's Where? Southwestern New Mexico and Its Major Attractions

This chapter highlights the attractions of three regions in this corner of New Mexico.

Socorro and nearby sights

You find huge antennae pointed into the skies here, as well as enormous numbers of migrating birds. The top sights include:

- ✔ **The Bosque del Apache National Wildlife Refuge.** More than 300 species of migratory birds make annual pit stops here.
- ✔ **Socorro.** This historic town (population 9,000) is where ranchers and miners mingle.
- ✔ **Very Large Array National Radio Astronomy Observatory.** Visit the largest radio telescope in the world, where part of the 1997 film *Contact* (starring Jodi Foster) was shot.

Las Cruces and Truth or Consequences

You discover another side of New Mexico in the dry, dusty plains of the south, including:

- ✔ **Las Cruces.** The second largest city in the state, Las Cruces is an agricultural center for chiles, cotton, and pecans.
- ✔ **Truth or Consequences.** Discover the truth about T or C (population 7,500) while soaking in one of the town's famous mineral baths.

Silver City and the surrounding attractions

Mines, cliff dwellings, ghost towns, and abundant nature identify this mountainous corner of the state, which features:

Electrifying art

Northwest of Gila National Forest, near Quemado, is the **Lightning Field,** an enormous sculpture by the American conceptual artist Walter De Maria. The sculpture consists of 400 stainless steel poles arranged in a rectangular grid one mile by one kilometer in size. The visiting season is May through October, and to walk around and look at the piece, you need to make a reservation far in advance (groups are limited to six or fewer). Visitors must spend the night in a pleasant cabin ($110–$135), where meals are prepared for you. The Lightning Field was commissioned and is maintained by the Dia Center for the Arts in New York City. For more information and reservations, call the Quemado office (☎ **505-773-4560**) or the Corrales office (☎ **505-898-3335**) of the Dia Center for the Arts. Online information is available at www.diacenter.org/ltproj/lf.

✔ **Ghost towns.** Time-travel to the Wild West in the many ghost towns sprinkled around these parts.

✔ **Gila Cliff Dwellings National Monument.** Peek into the past at these spectacular ruins of the ancient Mogollon people.

✔ **Silver City.** A historic mining town, Silver City is a good base of operations for surrounding explorations.

Searching the Ground and Sky: Socorro and Nearby Sights

Bird-watching, mining, and astronomy may seem like an incongruous mix, but hey, you're in New Mexico. The small town of Socorro, a former mining and ranching center, is the gateway for visits to the main attractions nearby — the Bosque del Apache National Wildlife Refuge and the Very Large Array National Radio Astronomy Observatory (VLA). Unless you plan to continue south, you can easily take in this region's major sights during a longish day trip from Albuquerque.

Getting there

From Albuquerque, follow I-25 south to Socorro, which takes about an hour and fifteen minutes. When you arrive in Socorro, you may want to spend an hour or so walking around its historic plaza, but save your time and energy for the attractions in the surrounding area.

Staying in style

You find a variety of chain motels and other lodgings along California Street (Socorro's main drag), as well as on the frontage road adjacent to I-25. Following is a list of the standouts.

Casa Blanca

$–$$ San Antonio

Okay, so this bed-and-breakfast is in the village of San Antonio (9 miles south of Socorro on I-25), but it's the closest lodging to the Bosque del Apache National Wildlife Refuge, which makes it a convenient base for predawn bird-watching expeditions. The cozy Victorian farmhouse is comfortable and well maintained, and it serves a great breakfast (included with the room).

505 E. La Plata St. ☎ 505-835-3027. Rack rates: $60–$90 double. MC, V. Closed: Memorial Day through Labor Day.

Holiday Inn Express

$$ Socorro

This chain has the basics and a few bonuses too. The clean, medium-size, Southwestern-style rooms each have a mini-refrigerator and a microwave. On site are an indoor pool, hot tubs, and two fitness rooms. A continental breakfast comes with the room.

1100 California Ave. NE. ☎ 505-838-0556. Fax: 505-838-0588. Rack rates: $89 double. AE, DC, DISC, MC, V.

Dining out

You wouldn't expect to find great food in Socorro, but this mining town has some hidden gems.

El Sombrero

$–$$ Socorro   NEW MEXICAN

Request a table near the fountain in the garden room, and feast on some of the best New Mexican food in the area. "The Hat" serves especially good chicken enchiladas, which come rolled with beans, rice, and a *sopaipilla* (a deep-fried, puffed pastry). Another good choice is the beef or chicken fajitas, served with rice, beans, tortillas, and guacamole. For dessert, try the *churro* (a cinnamon sugared pastry stick with vanilla ice cream).

210 Mesquite NE. ☎ *505-835-3945. Reservations accepted. Main courses: $4–$11. AE, DISC, MC, V. Open: Daily 11a.m.–9 p.m.*

Socorro Springs Brewing Company

$–$$ Socorro   PIZZA

Housed in a historic building dating from the late 1800s, this long, narrow eatery is often crowded with locals and students (from New Mexico Tech) downing pizzas from the wood-burning oven and washing them down with the suds brewed on site. Try the *bandido* pizza, with pepperoni, Italian sausage, proscuitto, and jalapeños.

115 Abeyta Ave. ☎ *505-838-0650. Reservations accepted. Main courses: $4.25–$6.75. AE, MC, V. Open: Daily 11:00 a.m.–10 p.m.*

Val Verde Steak House

$–$$$$ Socorro   STEAKS/SEAFOOD

This classic restaurant is housed in the former Val Verde Hotel, a National Historic Landmark (now apartments). The stars of the show here are the lobster tail and steak, although the beef stroganoff and pepper steak capri (in Madeira sauce) are the house specialties.

203 Manzanares Ave. (in the Val Verde Hotel). ☎ *505-835-3380. Reservations recommended. Main courses: $5.95–$18; $32.50 lobster tail and steak. AE, DC, DISC, MC, V. Open: Mon–Thurs 5–9:30 p.m.; Fri–Sat 5–10 p.m.; Sun noon–9 p.m.*

Exploring Socorro and the surrounding sights

The top attractions in this area involve watching the sky for birds and stars. Not known for its shopping, the region is generally easier on the wallet than other parts of the state.

Discovering the top attractions

Bosque del Apache National Wildlife Refuge

South of Socorro

This barren, inhospitable-looking landscape (the northernmost finger of the great Chihuahuan Desert) seems the very last place to stumble upon one of the most extraordinary wildlife spectacles in the entire Southwest. However, this 57,191-acre refuge, along a 25-mile stretch of the Rio Grande, supports an amazing diversity of critters, including amphibians, reptiles, and mammals, but most notably more than 300 species of birds — all a feast for the eyes for kids, big and small. The refuge is a major pit stop on the Central Flyway flight path of migratory birds, which come here each year from as far away as South America. From November through March, the refuge may harbor as many as 45,000 snow geese, 57,000 ducks of many different species, 18,000 sandhill cranes, and a very small number of rare whooping cranes. During the winter months, when activity is highest, you see huge numbers of birds going about their daily business. They are best seen at dawn as you slowly drive the 15-mile loop of the auto tour; the birds take off in huge numbers to eat breakfast in the nearby fields. The next best time to see them is at sunset, when they return. If you come in late summer and early fall, you may see one of the migratory American white pelicans (enormous birds with wingspans as broad as 9½ feet), which usually stop by for a visit. Allow two to three hours at sunrise or sunset.

The on-site **visitor center** has a small, free museum with interpretive displays.

State Hwy. 1 (Follow I-25 for 9 miles south of Socorro, and then take the San Antonio exit. At the main intersection of San Antonio, turn south onto State Hwy. 1. In 3 miles you arrive on refuge lands, and another 4 miles brings you to the visitor center.). ☎ *505-835-1828. Admission: $3 per vehicle. Refuge open: Year-round daily one hour before sunrise to one hour after sunset. Visitor center open: Mon–Fri 7:30 a.m.– 4 p.m., weekends 8 a.m.–4:30 p.m.*

Socorro Historic District

Downtown Socorro

Buildings from the mid-1800s, many of them on the National Register of Historic Places, dominate downtown Socorro. You can take a walking tour of the historic district. Tours begin at the **Socorro County Chamber of Commerce,** 101 Plaza (☎ **505-835-0424**), where you can also pick up a free map and guide. The highlight is the **Old San Miguel Mission,** 403 El Camino Real N.W. (2 blocks north of the plaza; ☎ **505-835-1620**), which was built from 1615 to 1626. The mission is open daily from 7 a.m. to 7 p.m., and admission is free. Allow an hour — two at most.

The historic district is located on and around the plaza.

Very Large Array National Radio Astronomy Observatory (VLA)

West of Socorro

If you saw the 1997 film *Contact,* starring Jodi Foster, you'll recognize the 27 gigantic white antennae dishes (82 feet each in diameter) that spread across the San Augustin plains and together form the world's most powerful radio telescope. Radio telescopes are sensitive to low-frequency radio waves, and they effectively "photograph" space by transforming the radio waves into pictures. You don't have to understand how it works to appreciate the bizarre sight of the gargantuan white antennae with tiny herds of cows grazing below them. The dishes look like satellite dishes pumped up on steroids, and they're moved around on railroad tracks. Begin your tour in the small visitor center, where you can view exhibits and a film about the VLA. A self-guided, outdoor walking tour allows for a closer look at the massive antennae. Allow an hour or two.

50 miles west of Socorro on U.S. 60. ☎ 505-835-7000. Admission: Free. Open: Daily 8:30 a.m. to sunset.

Finding more cool things to see and do

Just because it looks dry and barren in these here parts doesn't mean there aren't more points of interest. In this region, you can also:

- ✔ **Check in at Conrad Hilton's birthplace.** The tiny village of **San Antonio,** 9 miles south of Socorro via I-25, was the unlikely boyhood home of Conrad Hilton, founder of the luxury Hilton hotel empire. During the panic of 1907, his merchant father, Augustus Hilton, converted part of his store into a rooming house (only the ruins of which now remain), giving young Conrad his first exposure to the hospitality industry. The **Owl Bar and Cafe** ($), a friendly, low-slung adobe watering hole at the intersection of State Highway 1 and U.S. 380 (☎ **505-835-9946**), has long been considered *the* place to stop for a green chile cheeseburger ($3) in all of New Mexico.

- ✔ **Brave the ghost towns.** Two ghost towns are along U.S. 60 on the way to the Very Large Array (see listing earlier in the chapter). The historic mining and ranching town of **Magdalena,** 27 miles west of Socorro on U.S. 60, has become home to a growing number of artists in recent years. Three miles south of Magdalena is the old ghost town of **Kelly,** which produced more than $40 million worth of lead, zinc, copper, silver, and gold in the late 19th and early 20th centuries.

Quick concierge: Socorro

Area Code

The area code is **505.** Although some area codes in the state may change in 2002, Socorro will most likely retain this one. For updates, contact the New Mexico Department of Tourism (☎ 800-733-6396; Internet: www.newmexico.org).

ATMs

ATMs are located all over Socorro in shopping centers and banks, including Bank of America and Wells Fargo.

Emergencies

Dial ☎ **911.**

Hospital

Socorro General Hospital, 1202 Hwy. 60 West (☎ 505-835-1140), has an emergency room.

Information

The Socorro County Chamber of Commerce, 101 Plaza (☎ 505-835-0424), offers free printed guides and maps.

Internet Access

You can check your e-mail for free at the Socorro Public Library, 401 Park St. (☎ 505-835-1114). Library hours are Monday through Thursday from 9 a.m. to 7 p.m., Friday and Saturday from 9 a.m. to 5 p.m.; closed Sundays.

Pharmacies

Furr's Supermarket, 901 California St. (☎ 505-835-9495), has a pharmacy.

Police

In case of emergency, dial ☎ **911**. For other matters, call the Socorro Police Department at ☎ 505-835-1883.

Post Office

The Socorro Post Office is at 124 Plaza (☎ 505-835-0542).

Road Conditions

Call ☎ 800-432-4269 or check the Internet at www.nmshtd.state.nm.us.

Weather Updates

For weather updates, call the National Weather Service in Albuquerque (☎ 505-243-0702). To get weather forecasts on the Internet, log on to www.accuweather.com and use the Socorro zip code, 87801.

Encountering Hot Springs, Chile Peppers, and Other Wonders: Las Cruces

Roughly the same size as Santa Fe, Las Cruces is as unpretentious as the state capital is arty. You experience a different side of New Mexico in this university town (New Mexico State University is here) and agricultural center known for its chiles, cotton, and pecans. The Rio Grande slips alongside Las Cruces to the west, and the jagged Organ Mountains jut up in the east (when the setting sun turns them bright pink, the mountains look like a neon-colored aquarium reef). Founded in 1849, Las Cruces was named after the weathered wooden crosses that marked the graves of settlers murdered by the Apaches. Indeed, the town has a colorful history: Billy the Kid was sentenced to death in the old town of La Mesilla (southern New Mexico's major center for three centuries), which is now a cute historic village on the southwest side of Las Cruces. Pancho Villa (a turn-of-the-last-century Mexican revolutionary) also spent time here. Although lacking the polished ambience of Santa Fe or Taos, Las Cruces has a relaxed charm of its own, which may convince you to linger here for a couple of extra days.

Las Cruces works well as a hub for exploring White Sands, Alamogordo, Truth or Consequences, Silver City, and the Gila Wilderness.

Getting there

From Albuquerque, take I-25 south for about four hours. The **El Paso International Airport,** 47 miles south of Las Cruces (☎ **915-772-4271**),

has daily flights to and from Albuquerque on **Southwest Airlines**
(☎ **800-435-9792**). Most of the major car-rental chains have represen-
tatives at the airport (see the Appendix for their toll-free numbers), or
you can use the **Las Cruces Shuttle Service** (☎ **800-288-1784** or
505-525-1784), which travels between the El Paso International Airport
and Las Cruces for $28 one-way or $43 round-trip per person. The
Greyhound bus terminal is located at 490 North Valley Dr. (☎ **505-
524-8518**; Internet: www.greyhound.com).

Staying in style

Situated at the crossroads of I-10 and I-25, Las Cruces has a variety of
cheap chain motels that cater to the interstate crowd. A few other
interesting options, some of them quite nice, are also nearby. When
hotel-room hunting, you may want to consider a place with a swimming
pool because the weather here can be stinking hot.

Best Western Mission Inn

$ Las Cruces

This mission-style motel is a welcome refuge for the road weary. The
large, Southwestern rooms are decorated with cute touches, such as
hand-painted flowers on the walls and Mexican tile in the bathrooms. You
also find a pool in a courtyard and a good selection of choices on the
breakfast menu for pre-road refueling.

*1765 S. Main St. ☎ 800-390-1440 or 505-524-8591. Fax: 505-523-4740. Rack rates:
$59 double. AE, DC, DISC, MC, V.*

Hampton Inn

$ Las Cruces

This solid choice is clean, economical, and only five minutes from the
historic village of La Mesilla. The medium-size Southwestern-style rooms
each have large TVs, a coffeemaker, and a mini-refrigerator. A large
garden and a swimming pool are also on site.

*755 Avenida de Mesilla (I-10 Exit 140). ☎ 800-426-7866 or 505-526-8311. Fax::
505-527-2015. Rack rates: $57 double. AE, DC, DISC, MC, V.*

Las Cruces Hilton

$$ Las Cruces

The swank place to stay in Las Cruces has spacious south-of-the-border
style rooms and fantastic views of the Organ Mountains. Bonuses include
an inviting triangular pool shaded by palm trees, a whirlpool, and an exer-
cise room.

Feeling chile?

The tiny town of Hatch (39 miles north of Las Cruces on I-25), known as the "chile capital of the world," is the processing hub of a 22,000-acre agricultural belt where more chile is grown than anywhere else on earth. Every year on Labor Day, the annual **Hatch Chile Festival** celebrates the harvest. For more information, call the Hatch Chamber of Commerce (☎ **505-267-5050**).

705 S. Telshor Blvd. ☎ 800-284-0616 or 505-522-4300. Fax: 505-521-4707. Rack rates: $125 double. AE, DC, DISC, MC, V.

Lundeen's Inn of the Arts

$–$$ Las Cruces

This inn is housed in a rambling old adobe home from the late 1890s, and the very thoughtfully decorated guest rooms are each named after an artist (Frederic Remington and Maria Martinez, for example). On site is an art gallery, and you can arrange walking tours of nearby La Mesilla.

618 S. Alameda Blvd. ☎ 888-526-3326 or 505-526-3326. Fax: 505-647-1334. E-mail: lundeen@innofthearts.com. *Rack rates: $72–$77 double. AE, DC, DISC, MC, V.*

Dining out

Due, perhaps, to its proximity to Hatch (the "chile capital of the world"), Las Cruces has some of the most authentic New Mexican food in the state. However, when you just can't eat another chile relleño burrito, decent Sicilian cuisine, as well as surprisingly stylish continental dining, is also available.

Chope's

$–$$ South of La Mesilla   NEW MEXICAN

A 20-minute drive from La Mesilla, Chope's is where Las Cruceans go for a tasty country meal. The restaurant doesn't look like much from the outside, but the food is wonderful and the prices are cheap. Try the taco or *chile relleño* plates, served with rice and beans, or the red or green enchiladas.

On N.M. 28 (15 miles south of La Mesilla). ☎ 505-233-9976. Reservations not accepted. Main courses: $2–$7.50. No credit cards. Open: Tues–Sat 11:30 a.m.– 1:30 p.m. and 6:00–8:30 p.m.

Double Eagle

$$–$$$$ La Mesilla CONTINENTAL

You can feast on filet mignon and imported salmon in this magnificent 150-year-old hacienda in La Mesilla. On the National Register of Historic Places, Double Eagle also has a fantastic old bar done up with gold-leaf columns, and antique oil paintings of Rubenesque nudes adorn the walls.

2355 Calle de Guadalupe (on the east side of Old Mesilla Plaza). ☎ *505-523-6700. Reservations recommended. Main courses: $11.95–$26.95. AE, DC, DISC, MC, V. Open: Mon–Sat 11 a.m.–10 p.m., Sun 11 a.m.–9 p.m.*

Lorenzos

$$–$$$ La Mesilla SICILIAN

Not far from the Double Eagle, a taste trip to Sicily awaits you at Lorenzos. Rustic, flavorful Sicilian fare fills the menu here, mostly of the red-sauce-and-fresh-pasta variety. You can wash it all down with a glass of Chianti in an atmosphere that is usually lively.

2000 Hwy. 292 (Onate Plaza — a block from Old Mesilla Plaza). ☎ *505-525-3174. Reservations not accepted. Main courses: $7–$15. AE, DISC, MC, V. Open: Mon–Thu 11 a.m.–9:00 p.m.; Fri–Sat 11 a.m.–9:30 p.m.; Sun 11 a.m.–8:30 p.m.*

Nellie's

$–$$ Las Cruces NEW MEXICAN

This place rules, and just about anything you can order off the menu is excellent. The two-room cafe is always packed with eager-looking diners ordering everything from sopaipillas to *menudo* (beef tripe and hominy in red chile).

1226 W. Hadley. ☎ *505-524-9982. Main courses: $5.25–$7.75. No credit cards. Open: Mon–Sat 8 a.m.–4 p.m.*

Way Out West Restaurant

$$–$$$ Las Cruces TAPAS/NEW MEXICAN

This place with contemporary decor stands out as one of the hippest restaurants in Las Cruces. You can eat outside on the broad veranda or enjoy views of the Organ Mountains from inside. Try the enchiladas, burgers, or catch of the day.

1720 Avenida de Mesilla. ☎ *505-541-1969. Reservations accepted. Main courses: $7.50–$15. AE, DC, DISC, MC, V. Open: Sun–Thurs, 11:30 a.m.–9 p.m.; Fri–Sat, 11:30 a.m.–10 p.m.*

Exploring Las Cruces

The main attraction in Las Cruces is the cute historic village of La Mesilla on the southwest side of the city. Most of the other attractions mentioned in this section are just a short drive from town. Aside from several touristy boutiques around the old plaza in La Mesilla, Las Cruces isn't particularly interesting for shopping, so you can keep your wallet closed. You can save in other ways, too, because the town is quite inexpensive.

Discovering the top attractions

Fort Selden State Monument

North of Las Cruces

The eroded ruins of this old fort (founded in 1865, closed in 1891) were once home to the *Buffalo Soldiers,* the legendary black cavalry who protected settlers from raiding natives. This was also the boyhood home of General Douglas MacArthur, whose father, Arthur, was in charge of troops patrolling the U.S.–Mexican border in the 1880s. Displays in the visitor center illustrate Fort Selden's story, including childhood photos of General MacArthur.

On I-25 at Exit 19 and N.M. 185 (15 miles north of Las Cruces). ☎ *505-526-8911. Admission: $3 for adults, free for children age 16 and under. Open: Wed–Mon 8:30 a.m.–5 p.m.*

La Mesilla

Southwest side of Las Cruces

This picturesque village on the southwestern flank of Las Cruces was established in the late 1500s and became the crossroads of the El Camino Real (a trade route between Mexico City and Santa Fe) and the Butterfield Overland Stagecoach route. The Gadsden Purchase, which turned over land in extreme southern New Mexico and Arizona to the United States from Mexico, was signed here in 1854. The town's most notorious resident, Billy the Kid, was sentenced to death at the county courthouse (he escaped on his way to Lincoln to be hanged). La Mesilla's historic adobe buildings, which mostly house restaurants and shops, are gathered around the attractive, central Old Mesilla Plaza, which has a small bandstand in its middle. On the north side of the plaza, the **San Albino Church** (☎ **505-526-9349**) is a good place to begin a stroll about the area; it's open Monday through Saturday from 1 to 3 p.m., and admission is free. The church is one of the oldest in the Mesilla valley — built in 1906 on the foundation of the original church, which was constructed in 1851. Three blocks east of the plaza is the **Gadsden Museum,** 1875 Boutz St. (☎ **505-526-6293**). This small museum houses Indian and Civil War relics, as well as Old West artifacts. The highlight is a painting of the signing of the Gadsden Purchase. The museum is open Monday through Saturday from 9 to 11 a.m. and daily from 1 to 5p.m.; admission is $2 for adults, $1 for children age 6 to 12. Allow an hour to visit the town and its sights.

New Mexico Farm and Ranch Heritage Museum

Las Cruces

This 47-acre interactive museum uses effective displays to illustrate the 3,000-year history of farming and ranching in New Mexico. (This may not appeal to many aside from those tractor-heads who really dig farm and ranch equipment.) Aside from displays of farm equipment, you also find art exhibits on rotational display. The museum restaurant, **Purple Sage,** serves dressed-up Mexican dishes and burgers. Allow two hours.

4100 Dripping Springs Rd. ☎ 505-522-4100. Admission: $3 for adults, $2 for senior citizens age 60 and over, $1 for students age 6–17, free for children age 5 and under. Open: Tues–Sat 9 a.m.–5 p.m., Sun noon to 5 p.m.

The truth or consequences about Hot Springs

In 1950, the small spa town of Hot Springs (about two and a half hours south of Albuquerque on I-25) changed its moniker to Truth or Consequences, when the popular radio and television show by that name broadcast its 10th-anniversary program from the town in exchange for the honor. The hokey name has survived to this day, but the main attraction is still "taking the waters" of the town's original namesake. "T or C," as the town's called, sits over a table of hot, odorless mineral water, 98 to 115 degrees Fahrenheit, which bubbles up to the surface through wells or natural pools. The town has several bathhouses (most dating from the 1930s), which are generally open from morning to early evening, with baths of 20 minutes or longer starting at $3 per person. The **Artesian Bath House,** 312 Marr St. (☎ 505-894-2684), is cleaner than most, or you might try **Hay-Yo-Kay Hot Springs,** 300 Austin St. (☎ 505-894-2228), which was recently renovated and has nice, private tubs. Accommodation-filled Las Cruces is only an hour or so down the road, but if you get as limp as a noodle from soaking in the hot springs and want to spend the night, try the **Best Western Hot Springs Inn** ($), 2270 N. Date St. at I-25 Exit 79 (☎ 800-528-1234 or 505-894-6665). The best place in town to grab a bite is **Los Arcos Steak & Lobster** ($$–$$$$), 1400 Date St. (☎ 505-894-6200). The **Visitor Information Center** is located at the corner of Main Street (Business Loop 25) and Foch Street (☎ 800-831-9487 or 505-894-3536). If you want to go for a swim in cooler waters, head to Elephant Butte Lake State Park nearby.

Organ Mountains

Northeast of Las Cruces

They aren't named after kidneys, livers, or other body parts, but rather regular church organ pipes, and you can see them from almost anywhere in the area (the highest is Organ Peak at 9,119 feet). The Organs are just a short drive from Las Cruces, and you can find terrific hiking trails and campsites at **Aguirre Springs Recreation Area** off of U.S. 70 (☎ **505-525-4300**). The recreation area has camping and picnic sites, as well as hiking and horseback trails. The 6-mile (one-way) **Baylor Pass** trail crosses along the base of the Organ peaks and up through a pass — a worthwhile trip to reach a meadow with amazing views of the surrounding area. You can easily spend a morning or afternoon hiking here.

The Organ Mountains are 15 miles northwest from Las Cruces via U.S. 70.

Finding more cool things to see and do

If you're into pecans and war memorabilia, here are some fabulous attractions:

- ✔ **Pecans on parade.** The world's largest family-owned producer of pecans, **Stahmann Farms** (☎ 505-526-2453), is just 10 miles south of La Mesilla on N.M. 28 and has a **Country Store** (☎ 505-526-8974) that sells pecans and pecan candy. Hours are Monday through Saturday from 9 a.m. to 5:30 p.m. and Sunday from 11 a.m. to 5 p.m.

- ✔ **Wings of the past.** About 35 miles south of Las Cruces via I-10 is the **War Eagles Air Museum** (☎ 505-589-2000) at the Santa Teresa Airport. The museum has an amazing collection of historic aircraft from the Korean War and World War II, including a P-38 Lightning, P-51 Mustang, F-86 Sabre, and several Russian MIG-15s. Most of the museum's 28 planes are in flying condition and are kept inside an enormous, well-lit hangar. Admission is $5 for adults, $4 for senior citizens age 65 and over, and free for children under age 12. Hours are Tuesday through Sunday from 10 a.m. to 4 p.m.

Quick concierge: Las Cruces

Area Code

The area code is **505**. Although some area codes in the state may change in 2002, Las Cruces will most likely retain this one. For updates, contact the New Mexico Department of Tourism (☎ 800-733-6396; Internet: www.newmexico.org).

ATMs

ATMs are located all over town in shopping centers and at banks, including Bank of America and Wells Fargo.

Emergencies

Call ☎ **911.**

Hospital

Memorial Medical Center, 2450 South Telshore Blvd. (☎ 505-522-8641) has an emergency room.

Information

The Las Cruces Convention and Visitors Bureau, 211 N. Water St. (☎ 800-FIESTAS or 505-541-2444), offers free maps and printed guides.

Internet

You can check your e-mail for free at the Las Cruces Public Library, 200 East Picacho St. (☎ 505-528-4028). Hours are Monday through Saturday from noon to 5 p.m.

Pharmacy

Walgreens, 1300 El Paseo (☎ 505-525-8713), has a 24-hour pharmacy.

Police

Dial ☎ **911.** For non-emergencies call the Las Cruces Police department at 505-526-0795.

Post Office

The main branch of the Las Cruces Post Office is located at 201 East Las Cruces Ave. (☎ 505-524-2841).

Road Conditions

Call ☎ 800-432-4269 or check the Internet at www.nmshtd.state.nm.us.

Weather Updates

For weather updates, call the National Weather Service in El Paso (☎ 505-589-4088). To get weather forecasts on the Internet, log on to www.accuweather.com and use the Las Cruces zip code, 88001.

Checking Out Ghost Towns, Cliff Dwellings, and Forests: Silver City and Surrounding Attractions

West of the Rio Grande rise the Black Range and Mogollon Mountains in the stunning and expansive Gila National Forest. A thousand years ago, this was the homeland of the Mogollon Indians, and you can see some of their ruins preserved at Gila Cliff Dwellings National Monument. This was also the home of the fiercely independent Chiricahua Apaches in the 19th century (considered the last Native American Indians in North America to succumb to the whites; they counted Cochise and Geronimo among their leaders). The area has a long and colorful history of mining, from early Native Americans digging for turquoise and Spanish settlers mining copper to a boom when silver was discovered in 1870.

Historic Silver City (population 11,508) is the largest town in the area, but ghost towns reflecting the booms and busts of the mining industry over the past 140 years are all around. Silver City makes an excellent base for exploring the Gila Cliff Dwellings National Monument, the Gila National Forest, the nearby ghost towns of Mogollon and Pinos Altos, the City of Rocks State Park, and other attractions in the area.

Groovy ghost towns

Southwestern New Mexico is ghost town country, and two of the most interesting ones, **Hillsboro** and **Kingston,** are located along N.M. 152 between Truth or Consequences and Silver City. Hillsboro (32 miles from Truth or Consequences, via I-25 south to N.M. 152, and then west) has been recently invaded by artists and craftspeople, and it has a few antiques shops and galleries. In its heyday, after an 1877 gold strike nearby, the town produced $6 million in silver and gold. Kingston (9 miles west of Hillsboro on N.M. 152, just after you enter the Gila National Forest) once had the reputation of being one of the wildest mining towns in the region, with 7,000 people, 22 saloons, an opera house, and a notorious red-light district ironically located on Virtue Avenue.

Getting there

From Albuquerque, take I-25 south, 15 miles past Truth or Consequences; then go west on N.M. 152 and U.S. 180. The trip takes about five hours. From Las Cruces, the drive is about two hours: Take I-10 west to Deming, and then go north on U.S. 180. The **Las Cruces Shuttle Service** (☎ **800-288-1784**) runs several times daily from Silver City to the El Paso airport ($38 one-way, $60 round-trip) by way of Las Cruces and Deming.

Staying in style

You find several standard motels strung along U.S. 180 east of N.M. 90, but some of the more interesting accommodations, which I discuss in this section, are tucked away elsewhere.

Bear Mountain Lodge

$$–$$$ Silver City

The Nature Conservancy recently acquired and renovated this fantastic old lodge situated on 178 acres bordering the Gila National Forest, just 3½ miles northwest of downtown Silver City. If you like peace and quiet, and/or outdoorsy activities such as biking, hiking, and bird-watching, Bear Mountain Lodge is the place for you. An on-site naturalist is often on hand to inform visitors about the local flora and fauna and to conduct guided trips. The lodge's large guest rooms are pleasantly decorated and have maple floors, high ceilings, and French windows.

Cottage San Rd. (Turn north off U.S. 180 onto Alabama St., a half mile west of the N.M. 90 intersection. Proceed 2.8 miles — Alabama becomes Cottage San Rd. — to a dirt road turnoff to the left; the lodge is another ⁶⁄₁₀ miles on Cottage San Rd.) ☎ *877-620-BEAR. Internet:* www.bearmountainlodge.com. *Rack rates: $95–$175 double. Rates include breakfast. AE, MC, V.*

Casitas de Gila

$$–$$$ **Gila**

Remote and peaceful, set on a little bluff above Bear Creek (about a half hour from Silver City), this spot has five adobe-style *casitas* (little houses) handsomely done up in Southwestern style. The dwellings each offer a full kitchen as well as a *kiva fireplace* (a traditional rounded fireplace) and a small porch with a grill. You can find birding and hiking activities in the surrounding area, or you can just relax in the hot tub and enjoy the views.

310 Hooker Loop. ☎ *505-535-4455. Internet:* www.casitasdegila.com. *Rack rates: $110–$150 double. Price includes continental breakfast. AE, DISC, MC, V.*

Holiday Inn Motor Hotel

$ **Silver City**

A good bet on a budget, this motel has landscaped grounds, an inviting outdoor heated swimming pool, and medium-size, basic rooms. You also have a decent restaurant here and access to a nearby health club.

3420 U.S. 180 (3 miles east of downtown). ☎ *800-828-8291 or 505-538-3711. Fax: 505-538-3711. Rack rates: $55 double. AE, DC, DISC, MC, V.*

The Palace Hotel

$ **Silver City**

This small, clean, inexpensive hotel in the heart of the downtown historic district has a funky Wild West vibe with eclectic, uniquely decorated rooms. Its location right on Main Street means that the place is a little noisy on hot summer weekends when the lack of air-conditioning requires open windows.

106 W. Broadway. ☎ *505-388-1811. Internet:* www.zianet.com/palacehotel. *Rack rates: $32.50–$52.50 double. Rates include continental breakfast. AE, DC, DISC, MC, V.*

Dining out

Regular comfort food is the norm in the Silver City area, with your basic coffee shop enchilada being the tried-and-true standard, but a few hidden surprises also await you here.

Buckhorn Saloon and Opera House

$$–$$$$ **Pinos Altos**   **SEAFOOD/AMERICAN**

If you're in the mood for savoring a steak in an 1860s saloon, head 7 miles north of Silver City to this old-fashioned eatery in the cute little mountain town of Pinos Altos. The Buckhorn is noted for its burgers, Western-style steaks, seafood, homemade desserts, and excellent wine list. Try the New York strip with green chile and cheese, or the fried shrimp. They often feature live entertainment.

32 Main St. ☎ 505-538-9911. Reservations strongly recommended. Main courses: $6.25–$42.95. MC, V. Open: Mon–Sat 6–10 p.m.

Diane's Restaurant and Bakery

$$–$$$$ **Silver City**   **NEW AMERICAN**

This gourmet oasis reflects the refined tastes of a growing segment of the local populace. You can feast on dishes such as rack of lamb or slow-roasted duck breasts, but you also can't go wrong with the baked goods — the pies are particularly fabulous.

510 N. Bullard St. ☎ 505-538-8722. Main courses: $9–$22.95. AE, DISC, MC, V. Open: Wed–Sat 5:30–9 p.m.

Jalisco's

$–$$ **Silver City**   **NEW MEXICAN**

This cozy, well-kept restaurant in an old brick building in the historic district serves a solid plate of food and is a good spot for families (they have a kids' menu). Try a burger or one of the large combination plates, or go for the enchiladas.

103 S. Bullard St. ☎ 505-388-2060. Main courses: $5.39–$9.29. DISC, MC, V. Open: Mon–Sat 11 a.m.–8:30 p.m., Fri 11 a.m.–9 p.m.

Exploring Silver City and the surrounding attractions

Silver City and the surrounding area is a fun place to ramble around in, with lots of pretty, scenic drives that lead you to historic ghost towns, hiking trails, and ancient ruins. The great outdoors, rather than shopping or fine dining, draw most visitors.

Discovering the top attractions

Catwalk National Recreation Trail

Near Glenwood

This short trail, one of the most memorable you may ever hike, is especially thrilling for kids. The trail, a 250-foot metal catwalk, follows the route of a pipeline built in 1897 to carry water to the now-defunct town of Graham. The catwalk begins about a quarter mile above the parking area and clings to the sides of boulder-choked Whitewater Canyon, which is 20 feet wide and 250 feet deep in spots. Along the way, water pours through caves formed from boulders, and waterfalls spit from the cliffs. Farther up the canyon, a suspension bridge spans the chasm.

On N.M. 174 (68 miles north of Silver City on U.S. 180, and then 5 miles east of Glenwood via N.M. 174). ☎ *505-539-2481. Admission: $3 per vehicle. Open: Daily dawn to dusk.*

City of Rocks State Park

Southeast of Silver City

Did you pack your flowing white robe so you can worship like a druid? Too bad, because this is the place to don it. The park takes its name from the gigantic, fantastically-shaped volcanic rock formations which are reminiscent of Stonehenge. The park offers terrific camping and picnic sites and is a big spot for *bouldering* (a type of ropeless rock climbing).

Off N.M. 61 (25 miles south from Silver City via U.S. 180 and N.M. 61). ☎ *505-536-2800. Admission: $4 per vehicle; $10–$14 per campsite. Open: Park, daily 7 a.m.–9 p.m.; visitor center, daily 10 a.m.–4 p.m.*

Gila Cliff Dwellings National Monument

North of Silver City

About two hours away from Silver City, but much further back in time, lies the stunning remains of an ancient civilization abandoned for seven centuries. The Gila Cliff Dwellings are set in the mouths of six caves reached by a moderate, one-mile loop trail rising 175 feet from the canyon floor. The hike takes you into a narrow canyon, where you first spot the ruins perched 180 feet up the canyon wall. An ascent follows, and you continue up and up innumerable steps and rocks, until you're right there with the ancient ruins themselves. The cliff dwellings were first discovered by Anglo settlers in the early 1870s and offer an atmospheric glimpse into the lives of the Indians who lived here from the late 1270s through the early 1300s.

On N.M. 15 (from Silver City, take N.M. 15 north 44 miles). ☎ *505-536-9461. Internet:* www.nps.gov/gicl. *Admission: $3 per person, children age 8 and under free. Open: Cliff dwellings, Memorial Day–Labor Day 8 a.m.–6 p.m.; visitor center, 8 a.m.–5 p.m.; rest of the year, cliff dwellings, 9 a.m.–4 p.m. and visitor center, 8:00 a.m.–4:30 p.m.*

Gila National Forest

North of Silver City

The 3.3-million-acre Gila National Forest offers some of the most spectacular scenery in the Southwest and contains six out of seven *life zones* (an area defined by its animal and plant life). Here you can discover

Whitewater Baldy, the forest's highest peak at 10,892 feet, as well as nearly 400 miles of streams, a few small lakes, and 1,490 miles of trails for hiking, horseback riding, and cross-country skiing in winter. The wildlife is amazingly diverse — everything from elk, black bear, mule deer, antelope, mountain lion, and bighorn sheep, to trout, bass, and catfish. Several hiking trails tempt visitors, including the big daddy, the 41-mile Middle Fork Trail, which starts near the Gila Cliff Dwellings and takes about a week to complete. The West Fork of the Gila River offers the shorter, but perhaps even more beautiful, Middle Fork Loop hike (10½ miles round-trip). Trails are well marked, but routes along river bottoms have many wet crossings, so come prepared. Some of the best hikes in the area are the Frisco Box, Pueblo Creek, Whitewater Baldy, and Black Range Crest Trail.

On N.M. 15 (from Silver City, take N.M. 15 north 44 miles). For information on hiking, contact the U.S. Forest Service at ☎ 505-388-8201. Admission: Free.

Mogollon

North of Glenwood

This highly atmospheric little ghost town (the movie *My Name Is Nobody*, starring Henry Fonda, was filmed here) reflects the silver and gold mining booms that began in the late 19th century, and the disastrous effects of floods and fire in later years. The remains of its last operating mine, the Little Fanny (which ceased operation in the 1950s), are still visible, along with dozens of other old buildings, miners' shacks, and mining paraphernalia. An art gallery and museum are on the main drag.

Mogollon is 3½ miles north of Glenwood on U.S. 180, and then 9 miles east on N.M. 159, a narrow mountain road that takes a good 25 minutes to negotiate.

Pinos Altos

North of Silver City

You can still pan for gold in Pinos Altos, a cute little ghost town straddling the Continental Divide. Founded in the gold- and silver-rush era, the town contains the 1898 adobe Methodist–Episcopal Church, now home to the Grant County Art Guild. The Pinos Altos Museum displays a miniature reproduction of the Santa Rita del Cobre Fort and Trading Post, which was built in 1804 to protect the Santa Rita mine from the Apaches.

Pinos Altos is 6 miles north of Silver City on N.M. 15.

Silver City

In recent years, this pleasant little mining town has begun to attract both artists and urban refugees, drawn to the pastoral mountain setting and inexpensive cost of living. Founded in 1870, Silver City has many 19th-century brick buildings that look more like what you'd find in

Pennsylvania than New Mexico. In 1895, a raging flood washed out Main Street and created the Big Ditch, now a green park in the center of town. Billy the Kid lived here as a youth and waited tables at the Star Hotel (at Hudson Street and Broadway). You can see the site where the Kid's cabin once stood — a block north of the Broadway bridge, on the east side of the Big Ditch.

Silver City–Grant County Chamber of Commerce operates a visitor information center at 201 N. Hudson St. ☎ 800-548-9378.

Silver City Museum

Silver City

This well-conceived museum is lodged in the recently restored 1881 H.B. Ailman House, a former city hall and fire station. The displays relate to southwestern New Mexico's history and mining, and they include Native American pottery and early photographs. The main gallery features changing exhibits.

312 W. Broadway. ☎ 505-538-5921. Admission: Free. Open: Tues–Fri 9 a.m.– 4:30 p.m., Sat–Sun 10 a.m.–4 p.m.

More groovy ghost towns

A fun side trip that takes about an hour from Silver City introduces you to the ghost towns of Shakespeare and Stein near Lordsburg (population 3,010); take N.M. 90 to where it meets I-10. **Shakespeare (☎ 505-542-9034)** is a national historic site and was once home to 3,000 miners but had no church, newspaper, or local law. Since 1935, the town has been privately owned by the Hill family, which has kept six original buildings and two reconstructed buildings uncommercialized. Guided tours are offered on a limited basis. To get to Shakespeare from Lordsburg, drive 1³⁄₁₀ miles south from I-10 on Main Street. Just before the town cemetery, turn right, proceed ⁶⁄₁₀ of a mile and turn right again. Follow the dirt road ⁴⁄₁₀ of a mile into Shakespeare. Tours depart at 10 a.m. and 2 p.m. on the second full weekend of each month. Tours cost $3 for adults, $2 for children age 6 to 12.

Stein's Railroad Ghost Town (☎ 505-542-9791) started as a Butterfield Stage stop and was a railroad town of about 1,000 residents from 1880 to 1955. Twelve buildings remain today, with rooms filled with artifacts and furnishings from the 19th and early 20th centuries. You also find a petting zoo for kids. The town is located 19 miles west of Lordsburg off of I-10 (Exit 3). Hours are daily from 9 a.m. to dusk. Admission is $2.50 for those over age 12; kids under age 12 are admitted free.

For more information about both towns, contact the **Lordsburg/Hidalgo County Chamber of Commerce**, 117 E. 2nd St., Lordsburg (☎ 505-542-9864).

Western New Mexico University Museum

Silver City

The WNMU Museum has the largest permanent exhibit of prehistoric Mimbres pottery in the United States. (*Mimbres* is the final period of the Mogollon culture, dating from the 9th to the 13th century.) You also find displays of Casas Grandes Indian pottery, stone tools, ancient jewelry, historical photographs, and mining and military artifacts.

1000 W. College Ave. (Fleming Hall, WNMU). ☎ *505-538-6386. Admission by donation. Open: Mon–Fri 9 a.m.–4:30 p.m., Sat–Sun 10 a.m.–4 p.m.*

Finding more cool things to see and do

The great outdoors is at your disposal in this area — whether you're trotting across it, pedaling through it, or soaking in it. My recommendations include the following:

- **Peddle a mountain bike.** Gear heads can access quite a few trails in the **Gila National Forest** (☎ **505-388-8201**). Some to look for are the Pinos Altos Loop, the Cleveland Mine Trail, Silver City Loop, Fort Bayard Historical Trails, Continental Divide, Signal Peak, and Forest Trail 100. You can rent mountain bikes at Gila Hike and Bike, 103 East College Ave. (☎ **505-388-3222**). Bikes cost $20 for the first day, $15 for the second day, and $10 for each additional day after that.

- **Ride into the sunset.** If you're in the mood for saddling up, contact the **Double E Guest Ranch,** about a half hour from Silver City (☎ **505-535-2048**; Internet: www.doubleeranch.com), which offers authentic ranch riding across 30,000 acres adjoining the Gila National Forest.

- **Soak in some hot springs.** Near City of Rocks State Park is **Faywood Hotsprings** (☎ **505-536-9663**), where you can soak in outdoor pools (clothing is required in only one of the pools; massage and camping are available). **Lightfeather Hot Spring** is near the Gila Cliff Dwellings National Monument visitor center. For more information, call the visitor center at ☎ **505-536-9461.**

Quick concierge: Silver City

Area Code

The area code is **505.** Although some area codes in the state may change in 2002, Silver City will most likely retain this one. For updates, contact the New Mexico Department of Tourism (☎ 800-733-6396; Internet: www.newmexico.org).

ATMs

ATMs are located all over town at banks, including Bank of America and Wells Fargo.

Emergencies

Call ☎ **911.**

Hospital

Gila Regional Medical Center, 1313 East 32nd St. (☎ 505-538-4000), has an emergency room.

Information

The Silver City–Grant County Chamber of Commerce, 201 N. Hudson St. (☎ 800-548-9378 or 505-538-3785), offers a free map and printed guide, as well as many other useful tourist publications.

Internet Access

You can drop in and check your e-mail for free at the Silver City Public Library, 515 West College St. (☎ 505-538-3672). Hours are Monday and Thursday from 9 a.m. to 8 p.m., Tuesday and Wednesday from 9 a.m to 6 p.m., Friday from 9 a.m. to 5 p.m., and Saturday from 9 a.m. to 1 p.m. Closed Sundays.

Pharmacy

Wal-Mart, 2501 East Hwy. 180 (☎ 505-388-3113), has a pharmacy.

Police

In case of emergency, call ☎ **911**. For other matters, call the Silver City Police department at ☎ 505-538-3723.

Post Office

The Silver City Post Office is located at 500 North Hudson St. (☎ 505-538-2831).

Road Conditions

Call ☎ 800-432-4269 or check the Internet at www.nmshtd.state.nm.us.

Weather Updates

For weather updates, call the National Weather Service in El Paso (☎ 505-589-4088). To get weather forecasts on the Internet, log on to www.accuweather.com and use the Silver City zip code, 88061.

Chapter 18

Northeastern New Mexico

• •

In This Chapter

▶ Hiding out with the outlaws

▶ Hunting dinosaurs, volcanoes, and Folsom Man on the Santa Fe Trail

▶ Rediscovering New Mexico's stretch of the Mother Road

• •

*I*f the humdrum of contemporary life has you longing for the excitement of Wild-West shootouts, roaring dinosaurs, and exploding volcanoes, northeastern New Mexico will definitely get your adrenaline flowing. It's a place of wide-open plains once traversed by wagon trains on the Santa Fe Trail — a 19th-century trade route that ran from Missouri to Santa Fe. It's a place of historic poker games and gunfights headed by some of the West's most notorious characters: Butch Cassidy and Clay Allison, Black Jack Ketchum and Jesse James. The northeast is also a place where nature has played dramatic roles, leaving traces of its legacy in the form of dinosaur footprints and towering volcanoes.

This region, which is north of I-40 and east of the Sangre de Cristo Mountains, takes many hours of driving to traverse, so don't plan just a few hours here. Though you can skip over to Las Vegas (New Mexico, not Nevada) from Santa Fe as an afternoon outing, the rest of the region requires more time. I'd schedule two to three days if you want to see the major sites, more if you want to really taste the life of the cowboy or gunslinger. Your best bet is to stay on the move, planning a night in Las Vegas and another in either Cimmarron or Raton. If you travel through the region on I-40, you can easily experience the Route 66 part of it in Santa Rosa and Tucumcari, places you can cover well in a day.

Northeastern New Mexico

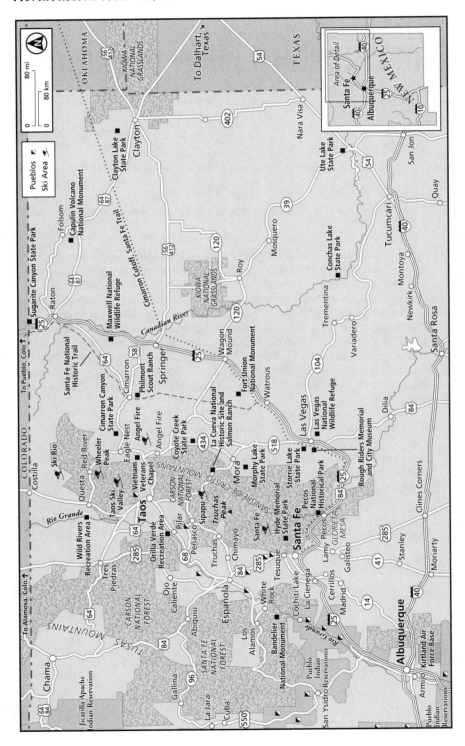

What's Where? Northeastern New Mexico and Its Major Attractions

This chapter covers three regions, each with its own highlights.

Las Vegas and environs

Named long before Nevada's Las Vegas, the Wild-West town of Las Vegas, New Mexico, housed such star players as Doc Holliday, Bat Masterson, and Wyatt Earp in the 1880s. Today the town contains some 900 historic properties. Here are some of the key sights in and around town:

- ✔ **Fort Union National Monument.** The ruins of the largest military institution in the Southwest during the 19th century tell a story of hardship along the Santa Fe Trail.

- ✔ **La Cueva National Historic Site and Salman Ranch.** Surrounding the picturesque rural village of Mora are a variety of historic sites, from an old mill to a cathedral surrounded by raspberry fields.

- ✔ **Las Vegas Plaza and Historic District** and the **Armand Hammer United World College** in the old Montezuma Hotel. Few places allow you to travel back in time the way Las Vegas, with its many historic gems, does.

- ✔ **Pecos National Monument.** A good stop on the road between Santa Fe and Las Vegas, this monument paints a vivid picture of life before, during, and after the Spanish conquest of the region.

Cimarron and Raton

Just outside the wild and wooly outpost towns of Cimarron and Raton (which are 40 miles apart), you can follow the Santa Fe Trail onto the high plains, where dinosaurs and ancient people once roamed a vast landscape punctuated by volcanoes. Along the journey, you encounter a number of noteworthy sites:

- ✔ **Capulin Volcano National Monument.** Active just 60,000 years ago, this huge cone sitting on the plains east of Raton is the perfect place from which to view the whole region, as well as to see the guts of a major explosive force.

- ✔ **Cimarron.** With the **St. James Hotel, Old Mill Museum,** and **Philmont Scout Ranch,** this is a place of great contrast. Bullet holes in the ceiling and tarnished ruins point to the raucous past of this 19th-century town, which today plays host to Boy Scouts.

✔ **Clayton Lake State Park Dinosaur Tracks.** In case Folsom man doesn't impress you with his longevity, try the impressions left 100 million years ago by dinosaurs. (Talk about a stick in the mud.)

✔ **Folsom.** You think you're getting old? Check out the history of Folsom man, whose remains have stuck around for 10,000 years in this area east of Raton.

✔ **Raton.** With its **Historic District** and the **Raton Museum,** this town is the gateway to New Mexico from the north.

Route 66 and the I-40 Corridor

Not a lot goes on in the sleepy highway towns near New Mexico's eastern border, but if you want a taste of Route 66 (much of which became obsolete after the construction of I-40) and some fairly bizarre small town exhibits, check out this area. You find good eats and some of the nicest folks this side of the Mississippi at places like the following:

✔ **Conchas Lake.** It's no mirage. This 25-mile long lake even has hidden coves and sun-drenched beaches. Powerboaters and fishers can't get enough of the place.

✔ **Santa Rosa.** Fine Route 66 signage, some excellent malts and chicken fried steak, and the **Blue Hole,** a sink hole deep enough for scuba diving, greet you in this highway-side town.

✔ **Tucumcari and its Mesalands Dinosaur Museum.** Though most of the exhibits here are made of bronze rather than bone, their stature is enough to remind you what scrawny creatures we humans are.

Living Like an Outlaw: Las Vegas and Environs

Imagining the many incarnations of frontier life is easy in **Las Vegas,** with its well-preserved plaza and scores of Victorian houses. Once a trading center on the Santa Fe Trail, and then a major stop for the Atchison, Topeka, and Santa Fe Railway in the late 1800s, this town on the plains could easily be a movie set. The area around Las Vegas is packed with historical jaunts, from the **Pecos National Historic Park** to **Fort Union National Monument.**

Of all the areas I detail in this chapter, Las Vegas works best as a day trip from Santa Fe. En route you can stop at **Pecos National Monument.** You can then explore the plaza in Las Vegas, have lunch, and return by evening. However, many local Santa Feans make an overnight trip to Las Vegas, where they stay in the historic Plaza Hotel, eat some good New Mexican food, and return to the city the next day.

Getting there

From Santa Fe, take I-25 north for one and a quarter hours; from Raton, take I-25 south for one and three-quarter hours; from Taos, follow N.M. 518 southeast 78 miles through Mora, which takes about two hours; from Tucumcari, follow N.M. 104 west for about two hours.

Las Vegas Municipal Airport handles private flights and charters. There is no regularly scheduled commercial service. You can take **Amtrak** (☎ **800-USA-RAIL;** Internet: www.amtrak.com) from Lamy (near Santa Fe) or Albuquerque. The ride is fun; however, because passenger trains run only occasionally, you may find yourself enslaved to the schedules. **Greyhound** (☎ **800-231-2222;** Internet: www.greyhound.com) runs buses between Santa Fe and Denver through Las Vegas.

Getting around

You definitely need wheels to tour the vast expanses on these plains, because there's no public transportation. However, after you arrive in town, you can tour Las Vegas's historic district on foot.

While in the area, you may hear people refer to East Las Vegas and West Las Vegas. In a sense the town is two towns, separated by the Gallinas River. The east side is the "newer" side, developed when the railroad rode to town in the late 1800s, while the west side contains an historic plaza, dating back to the 16th century.

Staying in style

Because it's one of the few cities between Denver and Albuquerque, Las Vegas has its share of chain motels, but if you want a more interesting experience, some good, non-chain options do exist.

Inn on the Santa Fe Trail

$–$$ Las Vegas

If you like to get your kicks in a Route 66 court-style motel, but you also want a clean, quiet stay, this is your spot. Built in the 1920s, this inn has been remodeled in a hacienda style with rooms looking out onto the central courtyard. Though not as historical as the Plaza Hotel (see the next listing), the rooms are a bit more up-to-date and functional, and you can park your car right outside. Kids love the pool and grassy courtyard. Be sure to read about the motel's restaurant, Blackjack's Grill, in "Dining out," later in this section.

1133 Grand Ave. (in the middle of town). ☎ **888-448-8438** *or 505-425-6791. Fax: 505-425-0417. Internet:* www.inonthesantafetrail.com. *Rack rates: $49–$79 double. Extra person $5. Rates include continental breakfast. AE, DISC, MC, V. Pets are permitted at an extra charge of $5.*

Plaza Hotel

$$–$$$ West Las Vegas

The Plaza Hotel is where the Sheriff and Miss Kitty would've stayed if they were actually living and breathing people. Built in 1882 in an elaborate Italianate style, the hotel was, in its heyday, a showcase for the railroad. While I was growing up in the area, the structure was a rundown, haunted building, but in 1992 (its 100-year birthday!) an energetic couple put a cool $2 million into it, making a stay here a fun sojourn into Las Vegas's history. Today, antiques fill the hotel, and although it doesn't have the elegance of the Ritz, it does have a frontier-style feel and luxuries such as turn-of-this-century plumbing, televisions, and coffeemakers in the rooms. The Landmark Grill serves good food, especially the New Mexican dishes.

230 Plaza (on West Las Vegas Plaza). ☎ *800-328-1882 or 505-425-3591. Fax: 505-425-9659. Internet:* www.worldplaces.com/plaza/. *Rack rates: $79–$139 double. Includes continental breakfast. AE, DC, DISC, MC, V.*

Star Hill Inn

$$–$$$ Northwest of Las Vegas

If you want to skip over to the Orion Spiral Arm of the Milky Way Galaxy for a few nights, you're in luck. In fact, you're already there. Confused? The owners of this star-gazing inn, 12 miles northwest of Las Vegas, can help you grasp your position in the cosmos *and* rent you a cottage. On 195 pine-covered acres at the base of the Sangre de Cristo Mountains, this large property has many cottages complete with fireplaces and comfortable beds.

Star Hill rents a variety of telescopes and offers one-hour "sky tours," which introduce visitors to the intricacies of the night sky, for $50 per hour including telescope rental.

Las Dispensas Rd., Sapello (for directions, request a map when you make reservations). ☎ *505-425-5605. Internet:* www.starhillinn.com. *Rack rates: $95–$150 double (cottage). $10 each additional guest over age 12. Minimum two-night stay. No credit cards.*

Dining out

You won't find baby beets from Pakistan or free-range petunia petals on the menu at restaurants here like you do in Santa Fe, but you do find good food, especially New Mexican. You also find some very atmospheric eateries, full of funky decor and lots of locals, so you can feast your eyes on dusty old cowboys and leather-clad Harley riders while feasting on an awesome enchilada.

Blackjack's Grill

$$–$$$$ East Las Vegas   NEW AMERICAN

This is the closest you can come to sophistication anywhere in northeastern New Mexico, so enjoy the baby greens and fresh seafood before heading into the hinterland. Decorated in brilliant colors with moody lighting, this New American restaurant serves steaks and seafood. I had an excellent halibut with a sesame seed crust here. Beer and wine are available.

1133 Grand Ave. (at the Inn on the Santa Fe Trail — see listing earlier in this chapter). ☎ *888-448-8438 or 505-425-6791. Reservations recommended. Main courses: $9.95–$18.95. AE, DC, MC, V. Open: Memorial Day–Labor Day Tues–Sun dinner; rest of the year, Thur–Sun dinner.*

El Rialto Restaurant & Lounge

$–$$$$ West Las Vegas   NEW MEXICAN

This restaurant's green chile is so good that you could smother a work boot in it and the boot would probably taste good. That's the secret to ordering here: Order anything you want, just make sure it's smothered. Families and old Hispanic farmers fill the place, which is a local's favorite. The chicken enchilada and the rellenos may help you forget about any woes you brought with you. A full bar and outdoor patio are on-site.

141 Bridge St. (1 block off the plaza). ☎ *505-454-0037. Reservations recommended. Main courses: $5–$23. Open: Mon–Sat lunch and dinner. AE, DC, DISC, MC, V.*

Hillcrest Restaurant

$$–$$$ East Las Vegas   AMERICAN/NEW MEXICAN

Looking for a diner-fest, complete with pancakes, hash browns, or maybe a chicken-fried steak or roast beef dinner? This is your place. You can also find a good selection of New Mexican food here. The dining room is open for lunch and dinner only; the coffee shop is busy all day. Kids enjoy the relaxed atmosphere and their own menu. The adjoining Trading Post Saloon offers a full bar.

1106 Grand Ave. ☎ *505-425-7211. Reservations accepted. Main courses: $7–$16. AE, DISC, MC, V. Open: Daily breakfast, lunch, and dinner.*

Exploring Las Vegas and environs

Las Vegas is a great place for strolling. Near the plaza are some good antiques shops and funky stores that sell coffee and fudge. The surrounding region, dotted with small Hispanic villages full of history, is also interesting.

Armand Hammer United World College

Las Vegas

You wouldn't think of Las Vegas as a host to some of the world's biggest wigs, but it has been. In the early 1980s, England's Prince Charles and philanthropist and past chair of the Occidental Petroleum Corporation, Armand Hammer, showed up to open this international school with students from more than 70 countries. Part of the school is housed in the former **Montezuma Hotel,** a luxury resort built by the Santa Fe Railroad in the 1880s and now an historic landmark. Also on the campus are the **Montezuma Hot Springs,** which have attracted health-seekers for more than 1,000 years. If you like to watch light play, visit the **Light Sanctuary** on campus. The creation of a "spectrum artist," this meditation/ceremonial space has walls embedded with prisms, which form rainbows throughout. Allow about two hours to see the hotel and Light Sanctuary.

N.M. 65, 5 miles west of Las Vegas. ☎ *505-454-4200. Admission: Free at press time. Open: Montezuma Hot Springs, daily 8 a.m. to midnight; Light Sanctuary, weekdays 8 a.m.–5 p.m.; call for tour schedule for Montezuma Hotel.*

Fort Union National Monument

Northeast of Las Vegas

Ever wish you lived in another time, back in the Santa Fe Trail days, perhaps, when life was simpler and less harried? Maybe you fancy yourself a 19th-century wagon traveler stopping for rest and supplies. A visit to this monument, once the largest military installation in the 19th-century Southwest, may just quash any romantic notions you have about frontier living. Life was darn hard back then, and here's a great place to get a taste of it. Though today the settlement is in ruins, you can see wagon train ruts from the Santa Fe trail, and take a 1⁹⁄₁₀-mile self-guided interpretive walking tour. Allow one hour to tour the ruins.

18 miles north of Las Vegas on I-25; take the Watrous exit, and then travel another 8 miles northwest on N.M. 161. ☎ *505-425-8025. Admission: $3 per person for adults ages 17 and older, free 16 and younger. Open: Memorial Day–Labor Day daily 8 a.m.–6 p.m.; the rest of the year, daily 8 a.m.–5 p.m. Closed: Christmas and New Year's Day.*

La Cueva National Historic Site and Salman Ranch

North of Las Vegas

This is a berry, berry nice place to visit, especially in the fall when the raspberries are ripe and the soft-serve ice cream is cold. Salman Ranch's history dates from the early 1800s when a man named Vicente Romero began farming and raising sheep here. He completed an elegant two-story Northern New Mexico home that still stands, and a mill that ground flour and supplied electricity for the area. Just north of these historic sites is the San Rafael Mission Church, with exquisite French Gothic windows. The trip through these sites is worth the time (allow one hour) during any season, but in the fall, you can buy raspberries by the basket or crate, as well as in jams and (of course) with ice cream.

N.M. 518, 25 miles north of Mora. ☎ *505-387-2900. Admission: Free. Open: June–Sept Mon–Sat 9 a.m.–5 p.m., Sun 10 a.m.–5 p.m.; Oct–May hours limited, call first.*

Las Vegas Plaza and Historic District

Las Vegas

Have a hankering for some wandering? Head to the **Las Vegas Plaza and Historic District** (including Bridge Street). The place is so quaint and well-preserved that you may feel the urge to look for a carriage rather than your car when you're done. You see evidence of the town's early Spanish history: Adobe buildings going back to the first Spanish settlements in the 16th century still stand alongside the ornate structures of the late 1800s. More than just picturesque architecture, however, the plaza is also the site of an important moment in the state's history: In 1846, General Stephen Kearny stood atop an adobe building and claimed the New Mexico territory as part of the United States.

TIP

Before embarking on your tour, stop in at the **Las Vegas/San Miguel Chamber of Commerce,** 513 6th St. (☎ **800-832-5947** or 505-425-8631; Internet: www.lasvegasnewmexico.com), to pick up a map of the self-guided historic district walking tour. Then, head next door to the **Rough Riders Memorial and City Museum** (see previous listing). Later, be sure to stop in at **Rough Rider Trading Company,** 158 Bridge St. (☎ **505-425-0246**), a good place to browse for Old West memorabilia, and **Plaza Antiques,** 1805 Plaza (☎ **505-454-9447**), a fun place to find antique clothing and kitchen tables. Allow about two hours to tour this area.

Pecos National Historical Park

East of Santa Fe

A great day trip from Santa Fe or a good stopover en route to Las Vegas, this monument gives you a sense of how hard it was for the Spanish conquistadors to conquer the Pueblo people. Here you see ruins of a 15th-century pueblo alongside those of 17th- and 18th-century missions. A 1½-mile loop trail begins at the visitor center and continues through Pecos Pueblo and the main mission. Allow one hour.

Head east on I-25 from Santa Fe for 20 miles to the Glorieta exit. Travel 8 miles on N.M. 50 to Pecos; turn right on N.M. 63 and travel for 2 miles. ☎ *505-757-6414. Admission: $3 per person; ages 16 and under are free. Open: Memorial Day–Labor Day daily, 8 a.m.–6 p.m.; rest of the year, daily 8 a.m.–5 p.m. Closed New Year's Day and Christmas.*

Checkin' in at the Harvey House

On your way to Las Vegas from I-25, you may want to check out the old Fred Harvey **Castañeda Hotel** at 510 Railroad Ave. "Harvey Houses," as these hotels were known, were fancy railroad hotels built from the 19th to the 20th century to lure travelers west. Built in 1898, the Castañeda Hotel is one of the early Harvey Houses built in the Mission Revival style. Although the building no longer contains a hotel, you can peek in the windows and have a beer at the dive bar near the tracks.

Rough Riders Memorial and City Museum

East Las Vegas

Call in the Cavalry! Nowhere in the United States is that exclamation more a part of a place's history than here in Las Vegas. The largest contingent of the First U.S. Volunteer Cavalry, also known as the Rough Riders, was recruited from New Mexico to fight in the 1898 Spanish–American War. This museum chronicles their contribution to U.S. history. Allow a half hour to see the museum.

727 Grand Ave. (in the center of east Las Vegas). ☎ *505-454-1401, ext. 283. Admission: Free. Open: Mon–Fri 9 a.m.–12 p.m. and 1–4 p.m.; May–Oct also open Sat 10 a.m.–3 p.m. and Sun 12–4 p.m.; closed holidays.*

Shopping 'til you drop

If you're looking for Saks and Banana Republic, you're way out of luck in this region. Your best bet for shopping is to visit the **Las Vegas Plaza and Historic District** (see the listing in the previous section) and check out some of the interesting antiques shops along the way. You also find books, fudge, and ice cream for sale on the plaza.

Quick concierge: Las Vegas

Area Code

The area code is **505**. Although some area codes in the state may change, Las Vegas will most likely retain this one. For updates, contact the New Mexico Department of Tourism (☎ 800-733-6396; Internet: www.newmexico.org).

ATMs

You find plenty of ATM machines in Las Vegas, particularly downtown in East Las Vegas.

Emergencies

Call ☎ 911.

Hospitals

In case of an emergency, go to Northeastern Regional Hospital on Eighth Street in Las Vegas (☎ 505-425-6751).

Information

The Las Vegas/San Miguel Chamber of Commerce, 513 6th St.

(☎ 800-832-5947 or 505-425-8631; Internet: www.lasvegasnew mexico.com), can provide information about the town as well as give you a map of the self-guided, historic district walking tour.

Internet Access

Access the Internet at Carnegie Library, 500 National Ave., at 6th Street (☎ 505-454-1403).

Pharmacies

Walgreens, 620 Mills Ave. (at the corner of Mills and 7th Street; ☎ 505-425-3303), is a full-service pharmacy on the north side of town. Hours are Monday through Saturday from 8 a.m. to 10 p.m. and Sunday from 9 a.m. to 9 p.m.

Police

If you have an emergency, call ☎ **911**. For less pressing problems, contact the Las Vegas Police Department (☎ 505-425-7504).

Post Office

Las Vegas Post Office, 1001 Douglas Ave. (at 10th Street; ☎ 505-425-9387), is open Monday through Friday from 8:30 a.m. to 5:30 p.m. and Saturday from 9 a.m. to 12 p.m.

Road Conditions

Call ☎ 800-432-4269.

Weather Updates

To get weather forecasts on the Internet, log on to www.accuweather.com and use the Las Vegas zip code, 87701.

Tracking Dinosaurs and Volcanoes on the Santa Fe Trail: Cimarron and Raton

Northeastern New Mexico is a place of vast open plains, where cattle graze and outlaws and dinosaurs once roamed. Towering above it all is the 8,182-foot Capulin Volcano, active 60,000 years ago — one of those amazing geologic wonders that makes you scratch your head and consider life's bigger questions. Springboards for these sights are Cimarron and Raton, two rough-and-ready outposts on the Santa Fe Trail.

Getting there

Cimarron is about 125 miles north of Santa Fe. You can either travel through Taos and take U.S. 64 east from there, or take I-25 north from Las Vegas, turning west on N.M. 58. Raton is another 42 miles north of Cimarron via U.S. 64.

Getting around

Neither Cimarron nor Raton have public transportation. You definitely need a car to get around this area, because most of the sights listed in the following sections are far from the town centers. Both Cimarron and Raton have fun walking tours worth checking out. Cimarron is such a small town that most of its activity takes place at the intersection of U.S. 64 and N.M. 58. Similarly, Raton has two major thoroughfares, Second Street, which runs north–south, and Clayton Road, which runs east–west.

Staying in style

Fans of chain hotels will find them here. A clean **Holiday Inn Express** (☎ **800-HOLIDAY**) is on the south end of Raton. The following listings are a few places that are a bit older but no less reliable.

Best Western Sands

$–$$ Raton

Get yours now; they're going fast. This could be the motto of this family-owned motel equidistant between downtown and the interstate, where rooms are so clean and spacious that reservations are a must during summer months. Decorated with Southwestern prints, all rooms have comfortable beds and plenty of amenities. A hot tub, family-style restaurant, playground, and seasonal outdoor heated swimming pool make this a great choice for travelers with children.

300 Clayton Hwy. (½ mile west of I-25). ☎ *800-518-2581, 800-528-1234, or 505-445-2737. Fax: 505-445-4053. Rack rates: $49–$99 double. Extra person $3. AE, DC, DISC, MC, V.*

Casa de Gavilan

$$–$$$ Cimarron

You can't get much farther into the country than this inn outside Cimarron. Easy to access, the inn is surrounded by meadows and *piñon trees* (low-growing pines) and looks out across the Philmont Scout Ranch. The sprawling adobe hacienda gives you a sense of what New Mexico luxury was like back around 1910, when it was built, but these days the place has comfortable beds and modern plumbing.

N.M. 21 (6 miles south of Cimarron). ☎ *800-GAVILAN or 505-376-2246. Fax: 505-376-2247. Internet:* www.casadelgavilan.com. *Rack rates: $75–$130 double. Rates include breakfast. AE, DISC, MC, V.*

St. James Hotel

$–$$ **Cimarron**

Looking for a little Old West in your night's stay? This is the place to find it. Built in 1873, the St. James was once a rare luxury hotel on the Santa Fe Trail, with a dining room, a saloon, gambling rooms, and lavish guest rooms outfitted with Victorian furniture. Today, little has changed except that there's no gambling. The rooms are still without TVs and phones — the better to evoke the days when famous guests such as Zane Grey, who wrote *Fighting Caravans* at the hotel, were residents. Annie Oakley's bed is here, and a glass case holds a register with the signatures of Buffalo Bill Cody and the notorious Jesse James. The hotel has a restaurant and coffee shop (see "Dining out," later in this section). Next door, in a separate bulding, the hotel has 12 small motel rooms with phones and televisions.

17th and Collinson St. (from U.S. 64, turn south on N.M. 21 and travel 4 blocks). ☎ *800-748-2694 or 505-376-2664. Fax: 505-376-2623. E-mail:* stjhotel@ringer coop.com. *Rack rates: Hotel $90 double, $120 suite; motel $60 double. AE, DISC, MC, V.*

Dining out

Down-home cooking is the order of the day in this ranchy region, which is a carnivore's paradise and a vegetarian's hell. All restaurants in the region close early, so you have to head out of your hotel room *before* watching that prime-time television show.

Though Raton has a fair selection of restaurants, Cimarron doesn't. I mention one option below, the **St. James Hotel,** but it sometimes closes for months at a time. If it is closed, head over to the **Kit Carson Motel** (☎ **505-376-2288**), at the junction of U.S. 64 and N.M. 58, where you can get decent grub at a reasonable price.

Oasis

$–$$ **Raton** **AMERICAN/NEW MEXICAN**

One of the best measures of a good restaurant is how many cars are parked outside during meal time. This family-style eatery wins hands-down in the parking category, with a full lot every meal. What's the draw? Home cooked everything, from hand-cut french fries to hand-patted tortillas. In business since 1954, the Oasis is a good place for breakfast, lunch, or dinner. You get all the basics here — eggs, burgers, steaks — as well as an awesome breakfast burrito, homemade soups and pies, and any number of specials.

1445 South Second St. (from Clayton Road, turn north). ☎ **505-445-2221.** *Reservations not needed. Main courses: $4.25–$12.95. Open: Daily breakfast, lunch, and dinner. DISC, MC, V.*

St. James Hotel

$–$$$$ Cimarron   NEW MEXICAN/AMERICAN

Set in a Santa Fe Trail hotel built in 1873, this restaurant serves up decent food with a side dish of history. The hotel has two restaurants serving from April to October: a casual cafe open daily and a more formal dining room open Fridays to Sundays. The cafe serves good New Mexican food and burgers, while the dining room serves more upscale food ranging from pasta primavera to filet mignon, as well as farm-raised wild game such as bison and venison.

17th and Collinson St. (from U.S. 64, turn south on N.M. 21 and travel 4 blocks).
☎ _800-748-2694 or 505-376-2664. Call to make sure the restaurant is open. Reservations are appreciated for dining room, not needed for cafe. Main courses: $5–$25. AE, DISC, MC, V. Open: Apr–Oct café, daily lunch and dinner; dining room, Fri–Sun dinner. (During busy times, the dining room is open for dinner seven days a week.)_

Exploring Cimarron and Raton

If I had very little time to spend in this region, I would do two things: visit Capulin Volcano (it's not a National Monument for nothin') and stroll through Cimarron. That said, plenty more awaits you if you have relatives here or really like to explore off the beaten track.

Cimarron has many creaky and evocative historic buildings, and a walking tour to see them only takes about a half hour. A tour map is included in a brochure available at the Old Mill Museum (see the listing in this section).

Discovering the top attractions

Capulin Volcano National Monument

Capulin

Looking for an explosive outdoor experience? Well, your imagination may have to wander back some 60,000 years to experience the eruptions of this volcano, but your senses will still have plenty to do here. You can drive a 2-mile road 600 feet up from the visitor center to the 8,182-foot peak, where two self-guiding trails leave from the parking area: a 1-mile hike around the crater rim and a 100-foot descent into the crater. Because of the elevation, wear light jackets in the summer and layers during the rest of the year. Be aware that the road up to the crater rim is frequently closed due to weather conditions. Plan on spending one to three hours at the volcano.

30 miles east of Raton via U.S. 64/87 and north 3 miles on N.M. 325. ☎ 505-278-2201. Admission: $5 per car or $3 per person for those hiking or riding a bicycle or motorcycle. Open: Memorial Day–Labor Day daily 7:30 a.m.–6:30 p.m.; the rest of the year, daily 8 a.m.–4 p.m.

Clayton Lake State Park

Clayton

I don't know about you, but for me, the notion of a footprint enduring more than 100 million years is beyond intriguing. At this modest lake on New Mexico's northeastern plains, not one, but many dinosaurs — eight species, in fact — left about 500 footprints in mud that later transformed into stone.

12 miles north of Clayton off N.M. 370. ☎ 505-374-8808. Admission: Day use $4. Open: Daily 24 hours.

Old Mill Museum

Cimarron

If stories of empires rising and falling strike your fancy, you definitely want to spend an hour in this country museum, all that's left of land baron Lucien Maxwell's 1.7-million-acre estate. The Donald Trump of the West, Maxwell founded Cimarron in 1848 as the base of operations for his **Maxwell Ranch,** which spread throughout northern New Mexico. Though today his once-opulent mansion is nothing but a foundation, you can visit his 1864 stone gristmill, built to supply flour to Fort Union. The grand, three-story structure houses early photos and lots of memorabilia, from a saddle that belonged to Kit Carson to dresses worn by Virginia Maxwell.

220 W. 17th St. (just west of St. James Hotel). ☎ 505-376-2417. Admission: $2 adults, $1 seniors and children. Open: Memorial Day–Labor Day, Fri–Sat and Mon–Wed 9 a.m.–5 p.m., Sun 1–5 p.m.; May and Sept, Sat 9–5 p.m. and Sun 1–5 p.m.

Wild-West watering hole

En route to Clayton Lake State Park (see the listing in this section), take a loop through **Clayton** (population 2,454), a ranching center just 9 miles west of the Texas and Oklahoma panhandle borders. Rich prairie grasses led to the town's founding in 1887 at the site of a longtime cowboy resting spot and watering hole. Clayton is best known as the location where notorious train robber Thomas "Black Jack" Ketchum was inadvertently decapitated while being hanged in 1901. (A doctor carefully reunited head and body before Ketchum was buried here.)

St. James Hotel

Cimarron

Frontier personalities including Kit Carson and Wyatt Earp, Buffalo Bill Cody and Annie Oakley, Bat Masterson and Doc Holliday, Butch Cassidy and Jesse James, painter Frederic Remington, and novelist Zane Grey all passed through and stayed in Cimarron — most of them at the St. James Hotel, which is still in business. Visitors can wander through the lobby, look at bullet holes on the dining room ceiling, and view a sample guest room at this hotel full of history. Plan on spending a half hour touring the hotel.

17th and Collinson St. (from U.S. 64, turn south on N.M. 21 and travel 4 blocks). ☎ *800-748-2694 or 505-376-2664. Admission: Free. Open for tours: Mon–Tues 7 a.m.–2 p.m.; Wed–Sun 7 a.m.–8 p.m.*

Finding more cool things to see and do

If you like to explore, this region has endless miles of interesting highways, rich with oddities (or is that odysseys?) and adventures. Here are a few:

- ✔ **Be trustworthy, loyal, helpful, friendly, and courteous.** At the **Philmont Scout Ranch** (☎ 505-376-2281), you can be as the Boy Scouts of America pledge to be, or just watch them being all those things and remain your usual grumpy self. It's your choice at this ranch, a 137,000-acre property, donated in pieces starting in 1938 to the Boy Scouts by Texas oilman Waite Phillips. Scouts from all over the world use the ranch for backcountry camping and leadership training from June to August and for conferences the remainder of the year. Even if you have no interest in scouting, you may want to tour the Villa or the other two museums on the ranch (dedicated to scouting and regional history). Each has its own schedule; call for hours and cost. To get here, travel 5 miles south of Cimarron on N.M. 21.

- ✔ **Walk through history.** Raton has a beautiful historic district with some 70 significant buildings; five blocks of the district are listed on the National Register of Historic Places. Exploring the historic district by foot is best. Allow one to two hours. Start at the **Raton Museum,** 216 S. First St. (☎ 505-445-8979), where you can pick up a walking tour map. The museum (open in summer Tuesday to Saturday from 9 a.m. to 5 p.m.; in winter Wednesday to Saturday from 10 a.m. to 4 p.m.) displays a wide variety of mining, railroad, and ranching items from the early days of the town.

Meet Folsom Man

In the mid-1920s, near the sleepy hamlet of Folsom, a cowboy named George McJunkin discovered a spear point embedded in an ancient bison bone and changed notions about natural history. The 10,000-year-old remains of "Folsom Man," excavated by the Denver Museum of Natural History in 1926, represented the first association of the artifacts of prehistoric people (spear points) with the fossil bones of extinct animals (a species of bison). (Gee, Wally, you mean cavemen really used spears to kill buffalo?)

The site of McJunkin's discovery is on private property and is closed to the public, but some artifacts (prehistoric as well as some from the 19th century) are displayed at the Folsom Museum, Main Street, Folsom (☎ **505-278-2122** in summer; 505-278-3616 in winter). The museum does not, however, contain any authentic Folsom spear points, only copies. Hours are from 10 a.m. to 5 p.m. daily from Memorial Day to Labor Day, winter by appointment. Open weekends only in May and September. Admission is $1 for adults, 50¢ for children age 6 to 12, and free for children under age 6. To get to Folsom, take N.M. 325 off the Clayton Highway (U.S. 64/87, which runs 83 miles east–southeast from Raton to Clayton) for 7 miles.

Quick concierge: Cimarron and Raton

Area Code

The area code is **505**. Although some area codes in the state may change, Cimarron and Raton will most likely retain this one. For updates, contact the New Mexico Department of Tourism (☎ 800-733-6396; Internet: www.newmexico.org).

ATMs

In Raton, look for the money-spitting beasts on Second Street or the Clayton Highway.

Emergencies

Call ☎ **911**.

Hospitals

In case of emergency, head to Miners Colfax Medical Center, 200 Hospital Dr. (☎ 505-445-3661).

Information

For Raton, the tourist information center is at the Raton Chamber and Economic Development Council, 100 Clayton Rd., at the corner of Second Street (☎ 800-638-6161 or 505-445-3689). For other help, the Cimarron Chamber of Commerce, 104 N. Lincoln Ave. at the corner of U.S. 64 (☎ 505-376-2417), has complete information on the region. In Clayton, you find information on area attractions, lodging, and dining, at the Clayton–Union County Chamber of Commerce, 1103 S. First St. (☎ 505-374-9253).

Internet Access

Log onto the Internet at the Arthur Johnson Memorial Library, 244 Cook Ave., at Second Street (☎ 505-445-9711).

Pharmacies

The region has two reliable places to get medications and other health goods: Horizon Pharmacy, 955 S. Second St., Raton (☎ 505-445-3131), open Monday through Friday from 8 a.m. to 6 p.m., Saturday from 8 a.m. to 5 p.m., Sunday from 9 a.m. to 2 p.m.; and the Medicine Shop, 1275 S. Second St., Raton (☎ 505-445-0075), open Monday through Fri from 9 a.m. to 6 p.m., and Saturday from 9:30 a.m. to 3 p.m.

Police

Call ☎ **911** for emergencies. For other matters, contact the Raton Police (☎ 505-445-2704).

Post Office

You find the Raton Post Office at 245 Park Ave. (☎ 505-445-2681).

Road Conditions

Call ☎ 800-432-4269.

Weather Updates

To get weather forecasts on the Internet, log on to www. accuweather.com and use the Raton zip code, 87740.

Gettin' Your Kicks on the Mother Road: Route 66 and the I-40 Corridor

Though not exactly a destination spot (Where are *you* going for spring break? I'm going to Tucumcari!), the eastern gateway to New Mexico hosts travelers en route to the heart of the Land of Enchantment. Like them, you may be rolling in on the Mother Road (Route 66) and wonder what's shakin' in Tucumcari and Santa Rosa. You find that the valleys of the Canadian River (Tucumcari is on its banks) and the Pecos River (site of Santa Rosa) have several attractions, including natural lakes and small-town museums.

Getting there

Travel time from Albuquerque to Tucumcari via I-40 is two hours, 40 minutes; to Santa Rosa, one hour, 45 minutes. No regularly scheduled commercial flights service Tucumcari or Santa Rosa. **Greyhound** (☎ **800-231-2222;** Internet: www.greyhound.com) runs buses along I-40 daily.

Getting around

No public transportation is available in either Tucumcari or Santa Rosa. In order to see this area where most of the sights are outside town, you definitely need your own car.

Staying in style

With some 2,000 beds in the area, you won't have trouble finding a room here. In fact, you can choose from among the major chain hotels, which are located at the I-40 interchanges in both Tucumcari and Santa Rosa. Smaller ma-and-pa motels are on Tucumcari Boulevard in Tucumcari and Will Rogers Drive in Santa Rosa. You can still find some Route 66–era spots along the towns' main streets, which were once segments of the legendary Road to Freedom.

Best Western Adobe Inn

$ Santa Rosa

Looking for a clean, quiet room near Route 66? This two-story adobe-colored stone building with turquoise trim may do the trick. Here you find spacious rooms with comfortable beds; a nice, outdoor pool (open seasonally); and restaurants nearby. What more could you want?

Reliving the heyday of Route 66

For true road warriors, Route 66 is far more than a ribbon of pavement traversing from Chicago to the promised land, California. This historic stretch is a state of being, a symbol of hope and freedom. These notions were created by the earliest roots of Route 66, dubbed the Mother Road, Road to Freedom, or Main Street, U.S.A. Built in the late 1920s and paved in 1937, the road was the artery of communities in eight states and served symbolically as the route away from the darkness of the Great Depression.

Parts of U.S. 66 still remain today, though finding them may be as hard as realizing the fantasies that the route conjures. Mostly, the highway has been replaced by interstates, but a few stretches remain where you can follow the white stripes to neon-studded diners and creaky court motels.

In Tucumcari, the Mother Road cruises through the center of town along what is today Tucumcari Boulevard. Santa Rosa's Will Rogers Drive is that city's 4-mile claim to the Road to Freedom. In Albuquerque, U.S. 66 makes a grand pass for 18 miles on Central Avenue.

West of Albuquerque, you can get a great feel for Main Street, U.S.A, along N.M. 124, which winds 25 miles from Mesita to Acoma. Pick up the Route again in Grants, along the 6-mile Santa Fe Avenue. Gallup has 9 miles of U.S. 66, and west of Gallup, the historic route continues to the Arizona border as N.M. 118.

For more information about Route 66, contact the **Grants/Cibola County Chamber of Commerce** (☎ 800-748-2142) or the **New Mexico Department of Tourism** (☎ 800-545-2040).

E. Business Loop 40 (at I-40). ☎ *800-528-1234 or 505-472-3446. Rack rates: May–Oct, $54–$65 double; Nov–Apr, $44–$58 double. Rates include continental breakfast. AE, DC, DISC, MC, V. Small pets are welcome.*

Best Western Discovery Inn

$ Tucumcari

If you're looking for a bit of an oasis in the vast, dry prairie lands, head to this pink mission-style motel near I-40. It has large, quiet rooms and amenities such as an outdoor pool (open seasonally) and an indoor hot tub surrounded by greenery. Next door, you can grab a steak or burger at K-Bob's restaurant.

200 E. Estrella Ave. (at Exit 332). ☎ *800-528-1234 or 505-461-4884. Fax: 505-461-2463. Internet:* www.bestwestern.com/discoveryinn. *Rack rates: May–Oct, $69–$74 double; Nov–Apr, $53–$58 double. AE, DC, DISC, MC, V. Pets accepted for an additional $5.*

Dining out

Though you won't find a lot of selection or sophistication out in this ranch country, you do find a few really good places to eat the basics, such as New Mexican food and steaks. Both restaurants I list here are fun Route 66 stops, open relatively late to accommodate weary travelers.

Del's Family Restaurant

$–$$$ Tucumcari   AMERICAN/NEW MEXICAN

Look for the big cow atop a neon sign and you'll find not only a Route 66 landmark, but some darn tasty roast beef, served with mashed potatoes. At this casual diner-style restaurant, big windows and plenty of plants lend a home-style atmosphere. You can also order a grilled chicken breast. The New Mexican food is good but not great. Del's is not licensed to serve alcoholic beverages.

1202 E. Tucumcari Blvd. (center of town). ☎ *505-461-1740. Reservations recommended. Main courses: $4–$15. MC, V. Open: Mon–Sat 6 a.m.–9 p.m.*

Joseph's Restaurant & Cantina

$–$$ Santa Rosa   AMERICAN

As you drive through Santa Rosa, you can't miss the neon with the smiling man on it, the symbol for a Route 66 tradition since 1956 — "Joe's." And you won't want to miss eating here either. The place has all the Mother-Road trappings, from comfortable window-side booths to vintage RC Cola posters. You can order up fresh salads and juicy burgers and wash them down with malts and shakes. You also find a bakery and full-service bar.

865 Will Rogers Dr. (on Route 66 in the center of town). ☎ 505-472-3361. Main courses: $4–$12. AE, DC, DISC, MC, V. Open: June–Aug daily 6 a.m.–10 p.m.; Sept–May daily 6 a.m.–9 p.m.

Exploring Route 66 and the I-40 Corridor

Road trippers delight in simply cruising the main drag of Route 66 as it slips through these two towns. They relish stopping in a diner for some true freedom food and daydreaming about such novelties as tent camps and motel courts. But those of you who actually want to see *sights* are in luck too.

Discovering the top attraction
Mesalands Dinosaur Museum

Tucumcari

Northeastern New Mexico is a Jurassic Park of sorts, only its reptilian giants are in the form of bone. For years, dinosaur hunters have tromped these lands, finding entire skeletons, which they excavated and carried away to distant lands. In 2000, the region laid claim to its piece of the Ice-Age-and-beyond pie, building this museum, which displays the largest collection of life-size bronze prehistoric skeletons in the world. Besides the bronzes, visitors can see a long-toothed monster, the only existing skeleton in the world of Torvosaurus, close cousin to the better-known Tyrannosaurus Rex — and equally frightening!

211 East Laughlin (½ block east off First Street). ☎ 505-461-3466. Internet: www.mesatc.cc.nm.us. Admission: $5 adults; $4 seniors 65 and older; $2.50 children ages 5–11. Open: Mar 15–Oct 15 Tues–Sat noon–8 p.m.; Oct 16–Mar 14 Tues–Sat noon–5 p.m. Closed: Thanksgiving, Christmas, and New Year's Day.

Finding more cool things to see and do

Though water may seem scarce on these dusty plains, you can find a few pools worth dipping into:

✔ **Go water-skiing, sailing, or fishing.** This is the land of lakes, so you have a number of options. Be aware, though, that shade is at a premium out here. To the northwest, 34 miles from Tucumcari on N.M. 104, is **Conchas Lake State Park** (☎ 505-868-2270), with a reservoir 25 miles long. This is *the* hot spot for northeastern New Mexicans to waterski, jet ski, and swim. A marina on the northern side provides facilities for boating, fishing, and waterskiing, while nearby are a store, cafe, RV park with hookups, and trailers available to rent. The park is open daily, 24 hours. Admission is $4 per vehicle. The south side of the lake, which is managed by the private concessionaire **Conchas Lodge and Resort** (☎ 505-868-2988), contains a lodge, campgrounds, and boat-launch facilities.

Door of the moon

Ten miles south of Santa Rosa via N.M. 91, the village of **Puerto de Luna** (Door of the Moon) is a 19th-century county seat with a mid-1800s courthouse and church, Nuestra Señora del Refugio. Francisco Vásquez de Coronado camped here as he traveled en route to Kansas. For insight into village life here, read Rudolfo Anaya's *Bless Me, Ultima,* a tale of growing up on the *llano* (plains, pronounced *ya*-no) of the area.

✔ **Try scuba diving.** That's right — scuba diving in the middle of the eastern plains. No, I don't have the bends in my brain. Santa Rosa calls itself "the city of natural lakes," and these bodies of water include **Blue Hole,** a crystal-clear, 81-foot-deep artesian well just east of downtown. Fed by a subterranean river that flows 3,000 gallons per minute at a constant 61°, the hole is a scuba diver's fish bowl, deep enough to merit open water certification (a permit is required). For those accustomed to diving in the ocean, these waters don't provide much room for exploration, but, out here in land-locked-ville, who has a choice? No permit is required for swimming or snorkeling; a bathhouse is on-site.

Quick Concierge: Route 66 and the I-40 Corridor

Area Code

The area code is **505.** Although some area codes in the state may change, Route 66 and the I-40 Corridor will most likely retain this one. For updates, contact the New Mexico Department of Tourism (☎ 800-733-6396; Internet: www.newmexico.org).

ATMs

Check out U.S. 66 in both Tucumcari and Santa Rosa for a few ATM options.

Emergencies

Call ☎ **911.**

Hospitals

In Tucumcari, go to Trigg Memorial Hospital, 301 E. Miel de Luna Ave., on the south end of town, off exit 332 (☎ 505-461-0141), which has 24-hour emergency service. In Santa Rosa, try Guadalupe County Hospital, 535 Lake Dr., off Business 42 (☎ 505-472-5909), which also offers 24-hour emergency service.

Information

Get informed at either Tucumcari–Quay County Chamber of Commerce, 404 W. Tucumcari Blvd. (☎ 505-461-1694), or Santa Rosa Chamber of Commerce, 486 Parker Ave. (☎ 505-472-3763).

Internet Access

Access the Internet in Tucumcari at the Tucumcari Public Library, 602 S. Second St. (between McGee Avenue and

Laughlin Avenue; ☎ 505-461-0295); and in Santa Rosa at the Moise Memorial Library, 205 Fifth St. (off Route 66; ☎ 505-472-3101).

Pharmacies

In Tucumcari, Bob's Budget Pharmacy, 511 S. Second (turn north off Tucumcari Boulevard; ☎ 505-461-1200), is open Monday through Friday from 8 a.m. to 6 p.m.; Saturday from 8 a.m. to 12 p.m. In Santa Rosa, La Botica, 143 S. Fourth St., at the corner of Business Route 66 (☎ 505-472-5666), is open Monday through Friday from 10 a.m. to 12:30 p.m. and from 1:30 to 5:30 p.m.

Police

In case of emergency, dial ☎ **911.** For other matters, contact the Tucumcari Police Department (☎ 505-461-2160) or Santa Rosa Police Department (☎ 505-472-3605).

Post Office

You find post offices at 221 South First St., Tucumcari (☎ 505-461-0370), and 120 Fifth St., Santa Rosa (☎ 505-472-3743).

Road Conditions

Call ☎ 800-432-4269.

Weather Updates

To get weather forecasts on the Internet, log on to www. accuweather.com and use the Tucumcari zip code, 88401.

Chapter 19

Northwestern New Mexico

● ●

In This Chapter

▶ Exploring ancient Acoma and outdoor wonders near Grants

▶ Kicking up your heels in Gallup

▶ Discovering the mysteries of the Four Corners region

▶ Riding the rails through Chama and the High Country

● ●

Get out your Navajo dictionary or your Puebloan culture guide, because you're headed to a foreign land. Actually, you can get around fine with the help of this book, but you may find yourself wondering: What country is this? In this part of the state, Pueblo, Navajo, and Apache cultures rule, or at least do their best to do so. As you travel from Acoma Pueblo's sky city (an ancient village perched precariously atop a mesa) to the ruins at Chaco Culture National Historic Park, you may feel as though you've slipped through a wormhole into a whole different time and place. A chug on the turn-of-last-century Cumbres and Toltec Scenic Railroad, the longest and highest narrow-gauge steam railroad in the country, will complete your other-worldly experience. So slip on your blue jeans, tighten your bolo tie, open your mind, and prepare to take a turn in the land that time forgot.

This land of jagged buttes and dusty roads takes some doing to penetrate. Sure you can enjoy a day trip from Albuquerque to Acoma or Chaco, but to see the region and get a feel for the cultures here, plan on spending two to three days. You can head west from Albuquerque on I-40 and take in Acoma, El Malpais, El Morrow, Chaco, and Gallup. Or, you can take U.S. 550 diagonally to the north and visit Chaco and the Four Corners region. You can also head north on U.S. 84 to Chama, where you can cool down in the highlands and ride the Cumbres and Toltec Scenic Railroad.

 The contemporary Puebloan tribes no longer want to use the word *Anasazi* to refer to the people who once inhabited the ruins of Chaco, Salmon, Aztec, Mesa Verde, and other pueblos. *Anasazi* is a Navajo word meaning "ancient ones," or possibly "ancient enemies." The Pueblo tribes, believed to be the descendents of the Anasazi, prefer the term *ancestral Puebloan people.*

Northwestern New Mexico

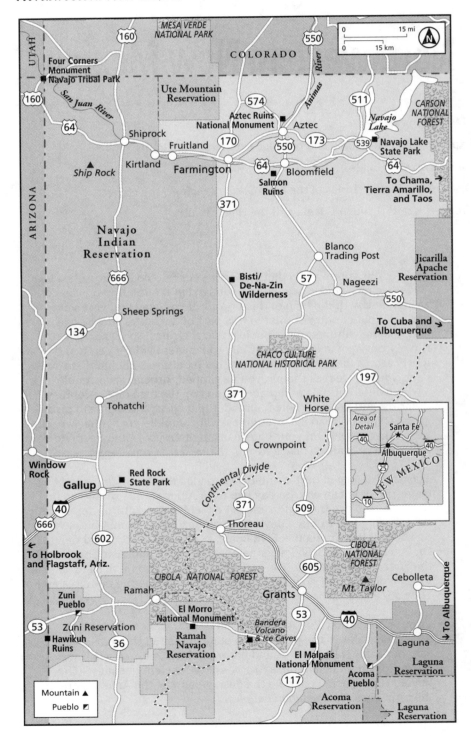

What's Where? Northwestern New Mexico and Its Major Attractions

Of all the regions in this book, northwestern New Mexico wins the Oscar for its scattered plot; the many sights to see here are spread across the land. Fortunately, a few clusters allow for less driving. But if you visit here, check your cruise control and fill your cooler; your odometer is going to get a workout. Following are the four major attraction clusters.

Grants and Acoma

If the notion of a sky city — a walled adobe village perched 367 feet above a valley — doesn't lure you, how about 115,000 acres of cinder cones and lava tubes? Or this country's first graffiti wall, with messages dating back to 1605? The highlights of this picturesque region include:

- **Acoma Pueblo.** Inhabited since at least the 11th century, this village is the longest continuously occupied community in the United States — and you can wander through it.

- **El Malpais National Monument.** You don't want to be caught without a map in these badlands that stretch 115,000 acres across western New Mexico. Spectacular overlooks, an arch, and miles and miles of lava draw amblers and serious hikers alike.

- **El Morro National Monument.** This 200-foot-high bluff — where travelers got in touch before the days of e-mail — holds some of the most captivating messages in North America, carved with steel points and stones.

Gallup

Home to many Native Americans, and with an unmistakable architectural presence from the days of Route 66, Gallup just doesn't seem to exist in this era. And that's the best thing about the place. History buffs enjoy the walking tours here, and power shoppers can flex their plastic while buying jewelry and other crafts. Some of the other places that give you a feel for this timeless place include:

- **Navajo Nation.** You may have trouble staying *off* the massive Navajo Reservation in this part of the state; a short jaunt west of Gallup can take you to its trading posts and headquarters.

- **Red Rock State Park.** If you're looking to get outside, this park has hiking and horseback trails. It also has a museum and amphitheater.

Chaco Canyon and the Four Corners Region

This region introduces you to the ancestral Puebloans, previously known as the Anasazi, who thrived here between A.D. 750 and 1300. The hub of the area is Farmington, which has a few interesting sites of its own. Standout attractions include:

- ✔ **Aztec Museum and Pioneer Village.** Populated by strangely ubiquitous mannequins, this village thrills with authentic displays and enactments.

- ✔ **Aztec Ruins National Monument.** These ruins aren't nearly as impressive as Chaco, but they do tell a story of their own and have an amazingly restored great *kiva* (a round ceremonial room).

- ✔ **Chaco Culture National Historical Park.** An important pilgrimage site for fans of ancient culture, this site boasts a stunning setting and well-preserved ruins.

- ✔ **Peaks and wilderness.** The region has incredible land monuments including **Shiprock Peak,** as well as one of the baddest of badlands, the **Bisti/De-Na-Zin Wilderness.**

- ✔ **Salmon Ruins.** Part of an archaeological research center, these ancestral Puebloan ruins sit on a lovely hillside near the San Juan River.

Chama and the High Country

The biggest draw to this region is the Cumbres and Toltec Scenic Railroad, which winds its way through valleys and mountain meadows for 64 miles into Colorado. But that's just the beginning of outdoor adventuring in this area. Other highlights include:

- ✔ **Los Ojos.** A town bent on preserving *Spanish churro sheep* (a long-haird sheep brought to the New World in 1598) as well as the lifestyle built around them, this village celebrates this feat at a store called **Tierra Wools.**

- ✔ **Outdoor adventuring.** Those who like to travel under their own steam find plenty to traverse here, from **El Vado** and **Heron Lakes** to the **Brazos Cliffs** and the bold and beautiful **Echo Canyon Amphitheater.**

Looking into the Past: Grants and Acoma

When the Spanish explorer Francisco Vásquez de Coronado came through this area in 1540 to 1542, he was looking for the legendary Seven Cities of Gold. He never found them, and nor will you, but you do find several unique surprises in this intriguing area. Residents still live without electricity and running water in the spectacular mesa-top pueblo of **Acoma Sky City,** and you can still follow the ancient Zuni–Acoma trail across the eerie lava beds of **El Malpais National Monument.**

You can easily visit the area on day trips from Albuquerque or Santa Fe, but for longer explorations, your best bet is to base yourself in the non-descript town of **Grants,** where the **New Mexico Museum of Mining** is well worth seeing.

Getting there

The attractions listed in this section are either located on I-40 or are fairly short drives from it. Grants is located 72 miles west of Albuquerque along I-40, at Exit 85. Take Exit 102 for Acoma Sky City, Exit 89 for El Malpais National Monument, and Exit 85 for El Morro National Monument.

Getting around

You definitely need wheels to move about this area, but the roads are well marked and it's a beautiful part of the state with which to get acquainted.

Staying in style

You won't be reading about Grants lodgings in glossy travel magazines anytime soon. Nevertheless, you can find some decent rooms competing for I-40 motorists. If you're just day tripping in the area, you may as well stay in Albuquerque (a little more than an hour's drive away) or in Santa Fe (about two and a half hours away by car).

Best Western Inn & Suites

$ **Grants**

You find Southwestern-style rooms and suites here, along with an indoor pool, sauna, and hot tub. A full buffet breakfast comes with the price of the room, and if you check into a suite, you also get a microwave, a wet bar, and a mini-refrigerator.

1501 E. Santa Fe Ave. (exit 85 from I-40). ☎ **800-528-1234** *or 505-287-7901. Fax: 505-285-5751. Rack rates: $61–$75 double; $68–$85 suite. AE, DC, DISC, MC, V.*

Holiday Inn Express

$–$$ Grants

This two-story chain motel has nice, largish, Southwestern-style rooms (most with microwaves and refrigerators) just off I-40. You also find a hot tub and an indoor pool, and rates include continental breakfast.

1496 E. Santa Fe Ave. (exit 85 from I-40). ☎ **800-465-4329** *or 505-285-4676. Fax: 505-285-6998. E-mail:* hexpress@7cities.net. *Rack rates: $59.95–$89.95 double. AE, DC, DISC, MC, V.*

Sands Motel

$ Grants

This older, family-owned hotel, a half block from old Route 66, isn't an obvious choice to lay your head until you consider the appealing location in the center of town (away from I-40) and its Mother-Road style — something you won't find at the chain establishments. The rooms can use an upgrade, but they're spacious and clean, and the price is right.

112 McArthur St. ☎ *800-424-7679 or 505-287-2996. Fax: 505-287-2107. Internet:* www.sandsmotelonroute66.com. *Rack rates: $36–$38 double. AE, DC, DISC, MC, V.*

Dining out

This area is even less well known for its dining than its lodging. Aside from the typical interstate chain restaurants, you can find a couple of acceptable choices in Grants.

Although you may find soft drinks and *fry bread* (fried dough) to snack on at the local pueblos, don't expect to find anything to eat or drink at the local national monuments. If you're just day tripping in the area from Albuquerque or Santa Fe, packing a picnic is a wise move.

La Ventana

$$$–$$$$ Grants NEW MEXICAN/SEAFOOD/STEAKS

This unremarkable-looking eatery serves the swankiest eats in Grants, including steaks, seafood, and New Mexican fare. In addition to filet mignon and deep-fried shrimp, you can also find pasta specials.

110½ Geis St. (at the Hillcrest Center). ☎ *505-287-9393. Reservations recommended. Main courses: $15–$30 dinner. AE, DC, DISC, MC, V. Open: Mon–Sat 11 a.m.–11 p.m.*

Monte Carlo Restaurant and Lounge

$$–$$$ Grants   NEW MEXICAN/STEAKS

This laidback place specializes in New Mexican specialties such as *huevos rancheros* (one egg on a corn tortilla, topped with chile and cheese) and *natillas* (frothy custard) for dessert. Otherwise, plenty of steak and seafood are on the menu.

721 W. Santa Fe Ave. ☎ 505-287-9250. Main courses: $6.95–$12.95. AE, DC, DISC, MC, V. Open: Daily 7 a.m.–10 p.m.

Exploring Acoma and sights near Grants

Aside from the town of Grants, this region remains remote, with little to do but visit the big attractions. Don't expect any nightlife, except some amazing stargazing, or much shopping, aside from that at Acoma Sky City, where you can buy pottery and other crafts.

Discovering the top attractions

Acoma Sky City

Acoma Pueblo

One of the outstanding attractions in the entire Southwest, the spectacular Acoma Sky City is situated on 70 acres atop a 367-foot-high mesa jutting from the floor of a dramatic valley. The natural stronghold is home to the longest continuously occupied community in the United States, dating at least from the 11th century — about four or five dozen Acoma live here year-round. Both Acoma Sky City and its fortress-like mission church, San Esteban del Rey (built in 1639), are National Historic Landmarks, but exploring them on your own is forbidden; you must join one of the guided, hour-long group tours that begin at the visitor's center at the foot of the mesa (where you also find a small museum). The Acomas are famous for their elegant pottery, and you are given several opportunities to buy pieces as you tour the village. Allow two hours — an hour for the tour and an hour to poke around.

From Grants, drive east 15 miles on I-40 to McCartys, and then south 13 miles on paved tribal roads to the visitor center. From Albuquerque, drive west 52 miles on I-40 to the Acoma Sky City exit, and then 12 miles southwest. ☎ 800-747-0181 or 505-469-1052. Admission: $9 for adults, $8 for seniors age 60 and over, $6 for children age 6–17, and free for children under age 6. Additional $10 charge to take still photographs. No digital cameras, videotaping, sketching, or painting allowed without special permission. Open: Daily May–Sept, 8 a.m.–7 p.m.; Oct–Apr, 8 a.m.–4 p.m.; often closed for feast days and other functions, so be sure to call ahead.

El Malpais National Monument

Between Route 117 and Route 53

Weird and wonderful, *El Malpais* (Spanish for "badlands") is one of the best examples of a volcanic landscape in the United States. The national monument contains 115,000 acres of lava flows, cinder cones, ice caves, lava tubes, natural bridges and arches, and ancient Native American trails. You can approach the park from I-40 or Route 53. Ten miles south of I-40 on Route 117, you come to the turnoff to **Sandstone Bluffs Overlook,** from which many volcanic craters are visible in the lava flow. Seventeen miles further south on Route 117 is **La Ventana Natural Arch,** the largest accessible natural arch in New Mexico. From Route 53, which heads south from I-40 just west of Grants, you can access the other-worldly **Zuni–Acoma Trail,** an ancient trade route crossing four major lava flows in a 7½-mile (one-way) hike. Twenty miles farther south on Route 53 is **El Calderon,** a trailhead for exploring more lava tubes, a cinder cone, and a bat cave. Allow two to three hours to explore El Malpais, or a full day to hike the Zuni–Acoma Trail.

The approach to the park from the I-40 side is mostly for sightseeing purposes. The largest number of hiking, backpacking, and caving opportunities are on the Route 53 side, where you also find the **visitor center** just off Route 53 between mile markers 63 and 64.

Route 117, which exits I-40 7 miles east of Grants. Route 53 exits I-40 at Grants. ☎ *505-783-4774. Internet:* www.nps.gov/elma. *Admission is free. Visitor center open: Daily 8:30 a.m.–4:30 p.m.*

El Morro National Monument

On Route 53

You may gain a new appreciation for e-mail after visiting *Inscription Rock,* a 200-foot sandstone bluff used as a message board for centuries, beginning with the ancestral Puebloan people around 1200. Much later, messages were carved into the rock with steel points by seemingly every conquistador, missionary, and pioneer who passed by between 1605 and 1906, when the rock was preserved by the National Park Service.

43 miles west of Grants along Route 53. ☎ *505-783-4226. Internet:* www.nps.gov/elmo. *Admission: $3 per person, ages 17 and under free with an adult. Open: May–Sept, daily 8 a.m.–7 p.m. (trails until 6 p.m.); Oct–Apr, daily 9 a.m.–5 p.m. (trails until 4 p.m.).*

Grants

On I-40

The seat of Cíbola County, Grants has been on a rollercoaster ride of booms and busts since the late 19th century when the railroad first arrived. Aside from an unlikely period of large-scale carrot-growing, the town didn't rebound until the 1950s, when a Navajo sheep rancher discovered uranium in the area, and the burg boomed again until the demand for uranium dropped in the early 1980s. Today, Grants functions mostly as a pit-stop for motorists traveling on I-40. Part of Route 66 runs through town, passing some cool old buildings. Allow an hour.

Finding more cool things to see and do

Some of the coolest (literally) attractions in this area are underground — from ice caves to mining exhibits. In this region you can:

- ✔ **Chill out.** When you're ready to take a break from the heat, head to the **Ice Caves Resort,** 25 miles south of I-40 on Route 53 (☎ **888-423-2283** or 505-783-4303; Internet: www.icecaves.com). This site is within El Malpais National Monument. For a fee of $8 for adults and $4 for children age 5 through 12, you can enter an ice cave (with a steady temperature of 31 degrees — so don't forget to bring warm clothes) and examine the space from a viewing platform. Afterward, you can hike a separate trail half way up inside the cinder cone of **Bandera Volcano,** the largest of all Malpais cinder cones. The resort is open daily from 8 a.m. to one hour before sunset, which means hikers can start out no later than 7 p.m. in summertime or 4 p.m. in mid-winter.

- ✔ **Don your hard hat.** If you think Grants is only a fizzled out mining town, head to **The New Mexico Museum of Mining,** 100 N. Iron Ave. (☎ **800-748-2142** or 505-287-4802) for a pleasant surprise. The only underground uranium-mining museum in the world expands your knowledge of the field through exhibits and a subterranean recreation of a mine reached by an elevator. The museum is open Monday through Saturday from 9 a.m. to 4 p.m. Admission is $3 for adults; $2 for seniors 60 and over and for kids age 7 to 18; free for children age 6 and under.

Quick concierge: Grants

Area Code

The area code is **505.** Although some area codes in the state may change in 2002, Grants will most likely retain this one. For updates, contact the New Mexico Department of Tourism (☎ 800-733-6396; Internet: www.newmexico.org).

ATMs

You can find several ATMs in Grants at Wells Fargo bank, Wal-Mart, and the Allsup's chain of convenience stores.

Emergencies

Call ☎ **911.**

Hospital

In case of emergency, head to the Cibola General Hospital, 1016 East Roosevelt Ave., Grants (☎ 505-287-4446).

Information

For information, call or stop by the Grants/Cíbola County Chamber of Commerce, 100 N. Iron Ave., Grants

(☎ 800-748-2142 or 505-287-4802; Internet: www.grants.org), in the same building as the mining museum. You can pick up a free city map and a list of accommodations. Hours are Monday through Saturday from 9 a.m. to 5 p.m.

Internet Access

You can check your e-mail at Mother Whiteside Library at the corner of High and Iron streets (☎ 505-287-4793). Call for hours.

Pharmacies

Two pharmacies you can try in Grants are Wal-Mart, 1624 East Santa Fe Ave. (☎ 505-285-3378), or Parkhurst Pharmacy, 1208 Bonita (☎ 505-287-4641).

Police

In case of emergency, dial ☎ **911**. For other matters, call the Grants Police Department: ☎ 505-287-4404.

Post Office

The Grants Post Office is at 816 West Santa Fe Ave. (☎ 505-287-3143).

Road Conditions

Call ☎ 800-432-4269, or check the Internet at www.nmshtd.state.nm.us.

Weather Updates

For weather updates, call the National Weather Service in Albuquerque, ☎ 505-243-0702. To get weather forecasts on the Internet, log on to www.accuweather.com and use the Grants zip code, 87020.

Heading into the Heart of Indian Country: Gallup

Although the setting isn't much, Gallup offers a feast for the eyes. But rather than the usual fare of pretty scenery or fancy clothes, you see rich culture. Gallup is no gussied up resort town, but a real place, a local center where rural people (mostly Native Americans) come to gas up, chomp down, and head back to their often unique lifestyles. The town did have its heyday, though: During the Route-66 era, moviemakers made this a home base, and remnants of those grand days still glitter here and there, though the shine has dimmed.

Getting there

From Albuquerque, take I-40 west (two and a half hours). From Farmington, take U.S. 64 west to Shiprock, and then U.S. 666 south (two and a half hours). From Flagstaff, Arizona, take I-40 east (three hours). **America West Express** (☎ 800-235-9292) and **Mesa Airlines** (☎ 800-637-2247 or 505-722-5404) serve **Gallup Municipal Airport,** West Highway 66 (☎ 505-722-4896), several times daily. Regular connections exist to and from Farmington and Phoenix, Arizona. **Greyhound** (☎ 800-231-1222; Internet: www.greyhound.com) also services the town with several buses daily, traveling east–west on I-40. **Amtrak** (☎ 800-872-7245) runs trains through daily.

Getting around

Gallup doesn't have public transportation. You really don't want to be here without wheels. But, if you find yourself afoot, you can call **Luna's Cab** (☎ 505-722-9777) or rent a car at the Gallup Municipal Airport from **Budget** (☎ 800-748-2540) or **Enterprise** (☎ 800-325-8007).

Once you have wheels under you, you'll find getting around easy. The city is bisected by north–south running U.S. 666 (also known as the Devil's Highway) and east–west running I-40, alongside which Route 66 runs through downtown. Most of the motels, restaurants, and attractions are along Route 66 or just a few blocks from it.

For years, residents of this region have attempted to change the name of U.S. 666. It's not just the numbers of the highway that give it the moniker "The Devil's Highway." The section of this U.S. highway from Gallup to Shiprock was named by *USA Today* as America's "most dangerous highway" because of the number of traffic deaths. Many believe that if the name were changed, the road might lose its curse. More likely, the high incidence of accidents is due to the high alcoholism rates in the area.

Staying in style

Don't expect fancy resorts or quaint bed-and-breakfasts in this very practical town. Your best bet here is a good solid chain hotel, with one exception: Gallup's historic El Rancho, "Home to the Movie Stars," delivers a Route 66 kind of stay and lets you rub elbows with many movie star ghosts. Virtually every accommodation in Gallup is somewhere along Route 66, either near the I-40 interchanges or on the highway through downtown.

Best Western Red Rock Inn

$–$$ **Gallup**

True to its Best Western lineage, this motel has the most reliable bunks in Gallup. Built in 1990, the pink stucco hotel has average-size rooms with firm beds and the added bonus of both corridor and motel-style access. Best of all are the indoor pool, hot tub, and weight room. This place doesn't allow pets, nor does it have a restaurant. If either of those are requisites for you, try the Best Western Inn & Suites (☎ 800-528-1234, 800-600-5221, or 505-287-7901) on the *west* side of town.

3010 E. Hwy. 66 (exit 26 from I-40; turn left and travel one mile). ☎ *800-528-1234 or 505-722-7600. Internet:* www.newmexico-lodging.com/. *Rack rates: $54–$99 double. Children under age 12 stay free in parent's room. AE, DC, DISC, MC, V.*

El Rancho: "Home to the Movie Stars"

Even if you don't stay at El Rancho Hotel, you definitely want to stroll through the lobby and maybe even have a drink in the bar, where John Wayne once rode in and ordered one for himself and one for his horse. Opened in 1937, the hotel, now on the National Register of Historic Places, was built by R.E. Griffith, brother of the movie magnate D.W. Griffith. From the 1940s to 1960s, a who's who of Hollywood slept in the hotel. Spencer Tracy and Katharine Hepburn stayed there during production of *The Sea of Grass;* Burt Lancaster and Lee Remick were guests when they made *The Hallelujah Trail.* The list goes on and on. Carefully restored, the hotel still holds some of the grandness of the old days of film.

El Rancho Hotel and Motel

$ Gallup

As you make your way down the broad circular staircase in the lobby of this "Home to the Movie Stars," the Norma Desmond in you may find fulfillment. Opened in 1937, the hotel served as a base for crews and stars on location in the Southwest until well into the 1960s (see the "El Rancho: Home to the Movie Stars" sidebar in this chapter). Most of the rooms are long and medium-size, with wagon-wheel headboards and heavy pine furniture stained dark. El Rancho has a lounge, full-service restaurant, and gift shop. Also on-site are a seasonal outdoor pool and guest laundromat.

1000 E. 66 Ave. (exit 22 from I-40, turn left). ☎ *800-543-6351 or 505-863-9311. Fax: 505-722-5917. Internet:* www.elranchohotel.com. *Rack rates: $47–$65 double. AE, DISC, MC, V. Pets are welcome.*

Dining out

You won't find anything flambéed or rotisserie cooked here. The food, except for grand plates smothered with New Mexico chile, is mediocre at best. But the local color in this most genuine of towns makes up for the lack of refined foods.

The Coffee House

$–$$ Gallup   BAKED GOODS/SANDWICHES

In search of a full-bodied Sumatra or rich French roast? This is the closest you'll come in the coffee wasteland of northwestern New Mexico. Set in a historic building in the center of town, the cafe serves up espresso and cappuccino, as well as scones, muffins, and sandwiches.

203 W. Coal Ave. (at the corner of Second Street). ☎ *505-726-0291. All menu items under $8. No credit cards. Open: Mon–Thurs 7 a.m.–9:30 p.m.; Fri 7 a.m.–11 p.m.; Sat 8 a.m.–11 p.m.*

Earl's

$–$$ Gallup   NEW MEXICAN/AMERICAN

With lots of Native American vendors buzzing about, this Denny's-style restaurant that has been around since 1947 can have a bit of a bazaar feel. Order the New Mexican dishes such as *huevos rancheros* or a smothered grande burrito. Kids have their own menu, as do folks with smaller appetites.

1400 E. 66 Ave. (2 miles east of downtown). ☎ *505-863-4201. Reservations accepted except Fri–Sat. Main courses $5–$10. AE, MC, V. Open: Mon–Sat 6 a.m.–9:30 p.m.; Sun 7 a.m.–9 p.m.*

Jerry's Café

$–$$ Gallup   NEW MEXICAN

You can't get more local than this narrow and cozy space, where Gallupites come to fill up on New Mexican fare. Usually, the cafe is packed with all manners of people chowing on big plates of food smothered in chile sauces. Try the flat enchiladas topped with an egg and served with a flour tortilla and *sopaipilla* (a deep-fried, puffed pastry). A children's menu, as well as burgers and basic sandwiches, are also available. They don't serve alcohol.

406 W. Coal Ave. (one block south of Route 66, between Fourth and Fifth streets). ☎ *505-772-6775. No reservations. Main courses: $6.50–$10. MC, V. Open: Mon–Sat 8 a.m.–9 p.m.*

Exploring the Gallup Area

Gallup is less a tourist mecca than a regular, unpretentious city. Because this city, known as the "Native American Capital of the World," has few attractions, it's mainly a base for exploring the region.

After all of your adventuring in the region, dusty ole Gallup just may take on a cosmopolitan air for you. Most of the activities here are low key, requiring a strolling or lulling-about mentality. The best options include:

 ✔ **Take a historic walking tour.** Gallup has 20 buildings that are either listed on, or have been nominated to, the National Register of Historic Places. Some hold trading posts worth visiting. Pick up a walking tour map and start your sojourn at the **Gallup–McKinley County Chamber of Commerce,** 103 W. Route 66 (☎ **505-722-2228**). Be sure to check "Shopping 'til you drop," later in this section, so you can hit some trading post hot spots along the way.

✔ **Watch Native Americans dance.** Every evening from Memorial Day to Labor Day, dancers from a variety of area tribes sing, drum, and twirl in a stunning display of ritual from 7 to 8 p.m. The dances take place at the **Gallup Cultural Center** (☎ 505-863-4131) on East 66 Avenue and Strong Street. Built in 1923 in modified mission style with heavy Spanish Pueblo revival–style massing, the building has been renovated into a museum and community transportation center, complete with a gift shop and diner. The center is open Monday to Friday from 9 a.m. to 5 p.m., often with extended hours in the summer. Admission to the center and dances is free.

✔ **Get outside.** You may see them as you drive in from east of Gallup — the stunning red stone cliffs and monoliths of **Red Rock State Park** (☎ 505-722-3839). Many call the area a mini Sedona (which is an Arizona city famous for its red rock and mystical sights). Though you may not find vortexes here, you do find hiking and horseback trails and a playground. This is a good place to stretch your legs after a long drive or to spend a morning or afternoon in the country. A museum is also on-site. The park, 6 miles east of downtown Gallup off I-40, is open daily from about 8 a.m. to 10 p.m. Admission is free.

Shopping 'til you drop

If you're looking for Navajo, Zuni, and Hopi arts and crafts, you won't find more selection and better prices anywhere, possibly in the world, than you'll find in Gallup. Here are some hot spots: **First American Traders,** 120 E. Route 66 (☎ 505-722-6601), is a warehouse-type place packed with *kachinas* (ceremonial dolls) and pottery. West of there, the **All Tribes Indian Center,** 100 W. Route 66 (☎ 505-722-6272) has some interesting stone carvings and jewelry. Also downtown is **Richardson's Trading Company,** 222 W. Highway 66 (☎ 505-722-4762), the place to buy and look at saddles, blankets, and rugs.

Crossing state lines: Navajoland

The best attractions of the 24,000-square-mile Navajo Reservation (☎ 520-871-6436) are nearby in Arizona. In **Window Rock,** Arizona (24 miles northwest of Gallup), you find the Navajo Nation Arts and Crafts Enterprise, the Navajo Museum, and Window Rock Tribal Park, which contains the natural red-rock arch after which the community is named. Nearby attractions include **Hubbell Trading Post National Historic Site** at Ganado (awesome shopping), 30 miles west of Window Rock, and **Canyon de Chelly National Monument** (major sight-seeing action), 39 miles north of Ganado. If you don't care to venture into Arizona (because you'd have to buy another guide book!), you can see some beautiful Navajo Nation land by driving U.S. 666 north from Gallup to Shiprock. From there you can head east to Farmington.

A taste of Gallup's living culture

If you like to mix culture and commerce, two events may interest you. Most notable is the **Crownpoint Rug Weavers Association** auction (☎ **505-786-5302**), which happens each month, normally on the third Friday evening. Hundreds of buyers and penniless wannabes like me show up for the auction at 7 p.m. The event takes place at the village of Crownpoint, 53 miles northeast of Gallup via I-40 and N.M. 371. Admission is free. ("We just want your money" the manager says.)

Lots of Native Americans come into Gallup on Saturdays to trade their crafts. Some set up shop at the **Flea Market,** located north of town just off U.S. 666. Here you can sample fry bread, Zuni bread, and Acoma bread, eat real mutton stew, and shop for anything from jewelry to underwear.

A short distance away from downtown, you find everything from pawn jewelry to Pendleton robes at **Ellis Tanner Trading Company,** Highway 602 Bypass (south from I-40 on Highway 602 about 2 miles) at the corner of Nizhoni Boulevard (☎ **505-863-4434**); and **Tobe Turpen's Indian Trading Company,** 1710 S. Second St. (☎ **505-722-3806**), a big brick building full of jewelry, rugs, kachinas, and pottery.

Quick concierge: Gallup

Area Code

The area code is **505.** Although some area codes in the state may change in 2002, Gallup will most likely retain this one. For updates, contact the New Mexico Department of Tourism (☎ 800-733-6396; Internet: www. newmexico.org).

ATMs

Gallup has a few of the major chain banks. Cruise Route 66 through town to find yours.

Emergencies

Dial ☎ **911.**

Hospital

For medical needs, contact Rehoboth McKinley Christian Health Care Services, 1901 Red Rock Dr., Gallup (☎ 505-863-7000).

Information

The Gallup Convention and Visitors Bureau, 701 East Montoya Blvd. (☎ 800-242-4282 or 505-863-3841; Internet: www.gallupnm.org), is conveniently located in Miyamura Park, just north of the main I-40 interchange for downtown Gallup. Or contact the Gallup–McKinley County Chamber of Commerce, 103 W. Route 66 (☎ 505-722-2228).

Internet Access

You can log on at Octavia Fellin Public Library, 115 West Hill St. (between First and Second streets.; ☎ 505-863-1291).

Pharmacy

Walgreens Pharmacy, 1626 E. Hwy. 66, Gallup (☎ 505-722-9499), is open Monday through Friday from 8 a.m. to 10 p.m., Saturday from 9 a.m. to 6 p.m., and Sunday from 10 a.m. to 6 p.m.

Police

In case of emergency, call ☎ **911**. For other matters, contact the Gallup Police Department (☎ 505-863-1319).

Post Office

The Gallup Post Office is at 950 W. Aztec St. (Exit 20 off I-40, head south on Muñoz and turn left on Aztec; ☎ 505-863-3491).

Road Conditions

Call ☎ 800-432-4269.

Weather Updates

To get weather forecasts on the Internet, log on to www.accuweather.com and use the Gallup zip code, 87305.

Visiting Man-Made and Natural Monuments: The Four Corners Region

Midwestern in its sensibility, the Farmington/Aztec/Bloomfield area mostly serves as a jumping-off point for large adventures. Explorations of Chaco Culture National Historical Park and the Aztec and Salmon ruins keep history buffs happily entrenched in the past, while outdoor lovers can hike in the Bisti/De-Na-Zin Wilderness, fly-fish the world-class waters of the San Juan River, or mountain bike in Lions Wilderness.

Because of its location in the corner of the state, you won't be able to just skip up to this area from Albuquerque for a day. Your best bet is to spend at least two days here, one to see Chaco and another to tour some of the other sites in the area. If you're headed on to Arizona, this area is a great stopover spot.

Getting there

From Albuquerque, take U.S. 550 (through Cuba), and then turn left (west) on U.S. 64 at Bloomfield; the trip takes three and a half hours. From Gallup, take U.S. 666 north to Shiprock, and then turn right (east) on U.S. 64; the drive is about two hours. From Taos, follow U.S. 64 all the way for three and a half hours.

All commercial flights arrive at busy **Four Corners Regional Airport,** just west of Farmington on West Navajo Drive (☎ **505-599-1395**). The principal carriers are **United Express** (☎ **800-241-6522**), with flights from Denver and other Colorado cities; and **America West Express** (☎ **800-235-9292**), with flights from Phoenix and other Arizona cities. **Mesa Airlines** (☎ **800-637-2247**) has flights from Albuquerque and Phoenix, and **Rio Grande Air** (☎ **877-435-9742**) has flights from Albuquerque. If you're looking to bus your way to the Four Corners, **TNM&O Coaches** (☎ **505-325-1009**) services the area.

Getting around

Farmington's **Road Apple Transit** (☎ 505-325-3409) does a good job of servicing the city with its Red and Green Lines that run daily from 7 a.m. to 5 p.m. and cost $1. Car-rental agencies at Four Corners airport include **Avis** (☎ 800-331-1212 or 505-327-9864) and **Budget** (☎ 800-748-2540 or 505-327-7304). **K.B. Cab Company** (☎ 505-325-2999) offers 24-hour service.

Staying in style

Accommodations run the gamut in this region from full-service hotels to small bed-and-breakfasts, so you have your pick. Your biggest decision, though, is picking the town in which to stay. If you're mainly here to see the ruins, you may want to stay in the sleepy town of Aztec.

Best Western Inn and Suites

$$ Farmington

For those who like what we New Mexicans call "the whole enchilada" (meaning a hotel, restaurant, lounge, and year-round pool, all rolled into one), this quadrangle-shaped two-story inn definitely delivers. Rooms are spacious, clean, and comfortable.

700 Scott Ave. (at the corner of Broadway and Scott). ☎ *800-528-1234, 800-600-5221, or 505-327-5221. Fax: 505-327-1565. Internet:* www.newmexico/ innandsuites.com. *Rack rates: $79–$89 double. AE, DC, DISC, MC, V. Pets are welcome for a $10 fee.*

Casa Blanca

$–$$$ Farmington

This adobe B&B supplies a touch of 1940s elegance with modern plumbing. Located within a residential neighborhood just a few blocks from the shops and restaurants of Main Street, Casa Blanca has spacious rooms decorated with antiques. Breakfasts include such delicacies as peach–melba waffles and eggs Benedict.

505 E. La Plata St. (½ mile from downtown). ☎ *505-327-6503. Fax: 505-326-5680. Internet:* www.farmington-nm-lodging.com. *Rack rates: $68–$150 double. AE, DISC, MC, V.*

Step Back Inn

$ Aztec

A fun place to "step back" into history, this modern Victorian-style inn recalls the region's early pioneers by naming rooms after them. But the

---

Bedrock revisited: Cave dwelling

The Flintstones would've found bliss at this one-room inn nestled into a sandstone cliff a few miles outside Farmington, and so can you. The brainchild of a retired (and bored?) geologist, who paid some out-of-work miners to dynamite away, **Kokopelli's Cave** (☎ **505-325-7855**; Internet: www.bbonline.com/nm/ kokopelli) is a luxury accommodation, complete with queen bed, a kitchen, and a bathtub with a waterfall and jetted flagstone tub. A night in the place isn't cheap but is well worth the thrill of standing on the balcony and looking down toward the distant lights of Bedrock. (Rack rates: $200 double; $240 3–4 people. Closed Dec–Feb. AE, MC, V.)

---

real draw is the very contemporary level of service (thanks to a completely dedicated innkeeper) and design (thanks to the architect who designed the notable Inn of the Anasazi in Santa Fe, see Chapter 13).

103 W. Aztec Blvd. (at U.S. 550). ☎ ***800-334-1255*** *or 505-334-1200. Internet:* www. aztecnm.com. *Rack rates: May 15–Nov 1 $68–$72 double; Nov 2–May 14 $58–$62 double. Rates include cinnamon Danish, juice, and coffee. AE, MC, V.*

Dining out

For a primarily rural area, the Four Corners region has surprisingly sophisticated food — at least at a few spots. You'll want to eat early in these small towns, because restaurants close their doors shortly after nightfall.

3 Rivers Eatery & Brewhouse

$–$$$$ Farmington   AMERICAN

With brew names such as Badlands Pale Ale and Arroyo Amber Ale, you have to figure somebody at this restaurant/brewery has a good imagination. The owners are definitely good enough to brew beers that match the caliber of their names, and to concoct outstanding dishes as well. Try the pecan encrusted salmon or smoked Thai chicken. The burgers are good too.

101 E. Main St. (at Orchard Avenue). ☎ ***505-324-2187***. *Reservations recommended. Main courses: $5–$17. AE, MC, V. Open: Mon–Sat 10 a.m.–10 p.m.; Sun 10 a.m.–8 p.m.*

Atomic Espresso Bistro

$–$$ Aztec   CAFE/BAKERY

Though you may think finding a good cup of coffee is as easy as walking to the corner or driving to the mall, locating one out here in Folgers-land is not so easy. Well, here's the place for Joe — and fortunately, the blues musicians who own the bistro are good cooks too. You find home-baked muffins and veggie sandwiches, as well as specials such as an awesome artichoke and feta quiche. If you need a buzz, try a double chocolate latte or a chocolate/cream cheese brownie for dessert.

122 N. Main St. (at the center of town). ☎ *505-334-0109. Reservations not necessary. Main courses: $5–$8. AE, DISC, MC, V. Open: Mon–Fri 7 a.m.–3 p.m.; Sat and (in summer) Sun 8 a.m.–3 p.m.*

Exploring the Four Corners

You may spend very little time within the towns of Farmington and Aztec, but you'll see them ripping by as you head from Four Corners National Monument to Aztec Ruins and other outlying places. So fasten your seatbelt and slip in a CD; exploring here means cruising through ancient history.

Discovering the top attractions

Aztec Museum and Pioneer Village

Aztec

Populated by strangely ubiquitous mannequins, this museum/village transports visitors back a full century. You can walk through a 1912 jail and sheriff's office (where a stuffed Andy of Mayberry look-alike sits lethargically), and trip through a blacksmith shop and a bank run by attentive mannequin women. From Labor Day through Memorial Day, Monday through Saturday, volunteers perform a high-noon shootout. Allow one hour.

125 N. Main St. (in the center of town). ☎ *505-334-9829. Admission: $2 for adults, $1 for children age 11–17; free for children 10 and under. Open: June–Aug Mon–Sat 9 a.m.–5 p.m.; Sept–May Mon–Sat 10 a.m.–4 p.m.*

Aztec Ruins National Monument

Aztec

With this monument's history — it has been misnamed, abandoned, remodeled, and abandoned again — you may wonder if these ruins are worthwhile. Believe me: They're a fascinating piece of history, with one big bonus. Named for Mexico's Aztec Indians (who lived much later and never in this area), the ruins of this 450-room pueblo were built and then abandoned by the Chacoans and later the Mesa Verdeans, all between 1100 and the late 1200s. What's most striking here is the *Great Kiva,* the only completely reconstructed ancestral Puebloan Great Kiva in existence. Allow about one hour for a stop at the museum and a walk around the self-guided loop.

Chaco Culture National Historical Park

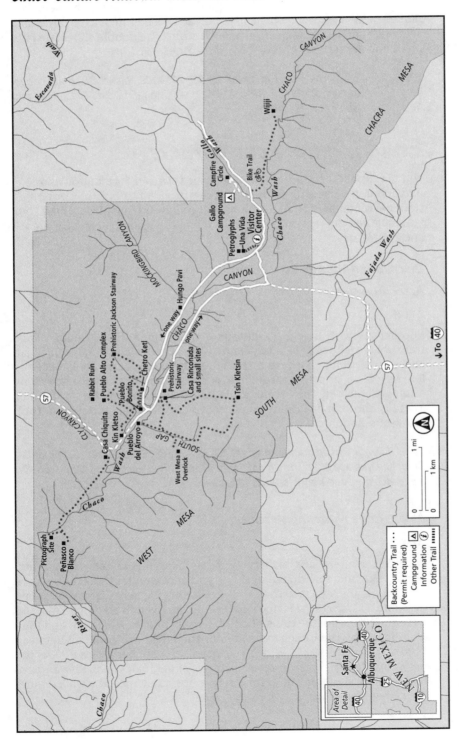

Half a mile north of U.S. 550 on Ruins Road (County Road 2900) on the north edge of the town of Aztec. ☎ *505-334-6174, ext. 30. Admission: $4 for adults; free for children under age 17. Open: Memorial Day–Labor Day daily 8 a.m.–6 p.m.; rest of the year daily 8 a.m.–5 p.m. Closed: Thanksgiving, Christmas, and New Year's Day.*

Chaco Culture National Historical Park

South of Nageezi

As you leave the highway and make your way along the dirt back roads to Chaco Canyon, you leave the U.S. behind and enter the center of an ancient civilization, which was the economic center of the San Juan Basin by A.D. 1000. As many as 5,000 people may have lived in some 400 settlements in and around Chaco, but these days you find little more than ruins, some with well-constructed masonry walls rising more than four stories high. At one time, the Chacoans' trade network stretched from California to Texas and south into Mexico. Scientists disagree over why the site was abandoned and where the Chacoans went, but their departure seems to have coincided with a drought in the San Juan Basin between A.D. 1130 and 1180. The pueblo ruins stand within 5 or 6 miles of each other in a broad canyon floor; the most outstanding one is **Pueblo Bonito,** the largest prehistoric Southwest Native American dwelling ever excavated, which contains giant kivas and 800 rooms covering more than 3 acres. To explore the area and learn about its history, check out the ranger-guided walks and campfire talks available in summer at the **visitor center.** Allow a morning or afternoon for a visit.

Chaco Culture National Historical Park is an isolated area with no food, gas, or lodging, so be sure to stock up on provisions before entering the park. If you need help, call the 24-hour emergency number (☎ **505-786-7060**), which connects directly to the homes of law-enforcement rangers in the park.

Coming from Farmington or Santa Fe, U.S. 550 takes you as far as the Nageezi Trading Post (the last stop for food, gas, or lodging). The final 26 miles to the park are graded dirt roads that can become treacherous when wet. To inquire about road conditions, call (☎ **505-786-7014**).

The two park entrances are on N.M. 57 and San Juan County Road 7900. From Santa Fe (a four-hour trip), take I-25 south to Bernalillo, and then U.S. 550 northwest through Cuba. Three miles before Nageezi, turn left on County Road 7950. You drive on pavement for 7 miles and then on a dirt road for 16 miles before reaching Chaco Canyon. From Farmington (a one-and-a-half-hour trip), the nearest population center, take U.S. 64 east to Bloomfield, head south on U.S. 550 to 3 miles past Nageezi, where you turn right on County Road 7950. From Grants (a two-hour trip), take I-40 west to N.M. 371 north to N.M. 57 north (with the final 19 miles graded dirt). ☎ *505-786-7014. Internet:* www.nps.gov/chcu. *Admission: $8 per car. Campsites: $10 per night. Open: Memorial Day–Labor Day daily 8 a.m.–6 p.m.; the rest of the year, daily 8 a.m.–5 p.m. Trails open from sunrise to sunset.*

Salmon Ruin and San Juan County Archaeological Research Center

Bloomfield

Location, location, location — these ancestral Puebloans had Park Place on the Four Corners Monopoly board. Set on a hillside surrounded by lush San Juan River forest, the site has 150 well-preserved rooms. You start in the museum and then take a self-guided tour through ruins with two strong architectural influences: the Chacoan and Mesa Verdean. Also on-site is **Heritage Park,** a series of reconstructed ancient and historic dwellings representing the area's cultures. Kids young and old can enter the re-creations. Allow about one hour.

6131 U.S. Hwy. 64 (11 miles west of Farmington near Bloomfield). ☎ **505-632-2013.** *Internet:* www.more2it.com/salmon. *Admission: $3 for adults, $1 for children age 6–16, $2 seniors. Open: June–Aug daily 9 a.m.–5 p.m.; Sept–May Mon–Sat 9 a.m.–5 p.m., Sun noon to 5 p.m.*

Finding more cool things to see and do

As well as intriguing ruins and museums, this region has awesome natural attractions. You definitely want to wear sturdy walking or hiking shoes and bring a good sun hat, a big bottle of water, and your camera. The best options include:

- ✔ **Peruse some awesome natural architecture.** Though you can't climb on or around **Shiprock,** the distinctive ship-shaped landmark visible from much of the area, you can gawk at it. The rock is located on the Navajo Indian Reservation southwest of the town of Shiprock, 29 miles west of Farmington via U.S. 64. Known to the Navajo as the "Rock with wings," it rises 1,700 feet off the desert floor to an elevation of 7,178 feet. Viewpoints are off U.S. 666, 6 to 7 miles south of the town of Shiprock. The town named after the rock is a gateway to the Navajo reservation and the Four Corners region and has a tribal visitor center.

- ✔ **Stand in four states at once.** At **Four Corners Monument Navajo Tribal Park** (☎ 520/871-6647), a cartographic wonder delineates the only point in the U.S. where four states meet: New Mexico, Colorado, Utah, and Arizona. You even find a marked concrete slab, which helps make the boundaries seem more real. To get there from Shiprock, drive 26 miles west on U.S. 64 to Teec Nos Pos, Arizona, and then north 5 miles on U.S. 160. You find a visitor center and crafts and food booths. The monument is open daily from 8 a.m. to 5 p.m. at a cost of $2 per person.

✔ **Fish world-class waters.** If fly-fishers had a paradise, it would be the **San Juan River** (☎ **505-632-2278**) below the dam, a pastoral spot bordered by green hills, where huge rainbow, brown, and cutthroat trout live in a relative population explosion — but are a challenge to catch. Much of the water is designated "catch and release," which is why these fish are so wily; they're attuned to the best tricks, drawing expert anglers from all over the world. Some fly-fishers, however, find the river too crowded. Just above these trout waters is **Navajo Lake** (also ☎ **505-632-2278**), northwestern New Mexico's camping, fishing, and boating destination, with 15,000 acres.

✔ **Hike in a bonafide badlands:** Often referred to as the Bisti (pronounced bist-*eye*) Badlands, the **Bisti/De-Na-Zin Wilderness** (☎ **505-599-8900**) is a fairyland of mushroom and animal-shaped rocks in a painted-desert array of color. Along with the spires and fanciful rock shapes, hikers may find petrified wood and fossils throughout the area, but be aware that removing them is prohibited. Although the park does not have designated trails, you can't go wrong following the *arroyos* (dry waterways) that cut through the badlands. Bikes and motorized vehicles are prohibited, and the park has no water or significant shade. Primitive camping is allowed, but bring plenty of water and other supplies. The wilderness is located just off N.M. 371, 37 miles south of Farmington.

Shopping 'til you drop

In this land of trading posts, major credit-card friction can happen. Don't sweat it, though. You get more for your dollar (er, swipe) here than you do in Santa Fe. **Foutz Indian Room,** 301 W. Main St., Farmington (☎ **505-325-9413**), has some affordable jewelry as well as whimsical Navajo folk art. At **Navajo Trading Company,** 126 E. Main St., Farmington (☎ **505-325-1685**), a real pawnshop with lots of exquisite old jewelry, you can peruse bracelets and necklaces while listening to clerks speaking Navajo.

Quick concierge: Four Corners

Area Code

The area code is **505.** Although some area codes in the state may change in 2002, the Four Corners will most likely retain this one. For updates, contact the New Mexico Department of Tourism (☎ 800-733-6396; Internet: www.newmexico.org).

ATMs

Farmington has national banks, most with ATM machines.

Emergencies

Call ☎ **911.**

Hospital

San Juan Regional Medical Center, 801 W. Maple St., Farmington (☎ 505-325-5011), offers 24-hour service.

Information

The Farmington Convention and Visitors Bureau, 3041 E. Main St. (☎ 800-448-1240 or 505-326-7602), is the clearinghouse for tourist information for the Four Corners region. Another outlet is the Farmington Chamber of Commerce, 105 N. Orchard (☎ 888-325-0279 or 505-325-0279). The Aztec Chamber of Commerce, 110 N. Ash St. (☎ 505-334-9551; Internet: www.aztecnm.com), is a friendly place with a wealth of information about the area.

Internet Access

You can log on at the Farmington Public Library, 100 W. Broadway St., at Orchard Avenue (☎ 505-599-1270).

Pharmacy

Walgreens is at 4221 E. Main St. (☎ 505- 325-1749 or 505-564-2652), 4 miles east of downtown Farmington.

Police

In case of emergency, dial ☎ 911. For other matters, call the Farmington Police Department (☎ 505-334-6622).

Post Office

The Farmington Post Office is at 2301 E. 20th St. (☎ 505-325-5047), on the east side of town (from Main Street, take Fairview to 20th Street).

Road Conditions

Call ☎ 800-432-4269.

Weather Updates

To get weather forecasts on the Internet, log on to www.accuweather.com and use the Farmington zip code, 87401.

Chugging Through the Past: Chama

If you're one of those folks who likes mountains and rivers better than shopping malls and sidewalks, you'll be right at home in the Chama area, where outdoor adventuring is a way of life. This pioneer village of 1,250 people at the base of the 10,000-foot Cumbres Pass is best known for America's longest and highest narrow-gauge coal-fired steam line, the Cumbres and Toltec Scenic Railroad (called the C&T Railroad), which winds through valleys and mountain meadows 64 miles between Chama and Antonito, Colorado.

If you just plan to sightsee in the area and ride the railroad, you may want to spend two days and one night here. However, if you decide to take in some of the more rigorous adventures, allow two to three days to experience this pristine country.

Getting there

From Santa Fe, take U.S. 84 north for two hours. From Taos, take U.S. 64 west for two and a half hours. From Farmington, take U.S. 64 east for two and a quarter hours.

You can neither travel by rail nor bus to Chama (except from Antonito, Colorado). This is strictly a driving place, where you want to have wheels to see the many outlying sites.

Getting around

Public transportation is not available in Chama. Though the sights in the Chama area are spread out, the town itself allows for some nice strolling to its few small shops and restaurants. Most everything in Chama is referenced by its proximity to "the Y," which refers to the junction of U.S. 64/84 and N.M. 17.

Staying in style

Chain hotels have yet to find this little hamlet, so if you like the kind of consistency that they offer, you're out of luck. Some interesting accommodations are in Chama, though, most with a little rustic frontier charm. Most are located on N.M. 17 or south of the U.S. 64/84 junction known as the "Y."

Gandy Dancer

$$ Chama

For a full-on turn-of-the-19th-century experience, stay in this inn and ride the C&T Railroad. You get lots of old-world feel with new-world amenities. Located in a 1912 two-story Victorian, the rooms are medium-size, well equipped, and quite functional, including VCRs (great for zoning out after a long day on the train). Plants surround an outdoor hot tub. The large breakfast holds you until dinner.

299 Maple Ave. (from Terrace Avenue, turn west on Third Street and travel one block). ☎ *800-424-6702 or 505-756-2191. Internet:* www.gandydancerbb.com. *Rack rates: $85–$115 double, with special winter rates. Rates include breakfast. AE, CB, DC, DISC, MC, V.*

The Timbers at Chama

$$–$$$ Tierra Amarilla

This luxury lodge, set on 400 acres of meadow, has comfortable Montana ranch-style rooms, views, and lots of trophy animal heads on the Great Room wall (tender hearts beware!). Outside is a broad deck with a hot tub and outdoor fireplace overlooking a little pond. Hunting and fishing guides are available, as are horses for guests to ride, all for an additional charge.

Off N.M. 512 en route to the Brazos Cliffs. ☎ *505-588-7950. Fax: 505-588-7051. Internet:* www.thetimbersatchama.com. *Rack rates: $100–$175 double. Rates include breakfast. MC, V.*

Dining out

Though Chama doesn't offer a lot of variety in the way of food, what you find here is good — not gourmet good, but down-home good, with big portions, fresh ingredients, and friendly wait people. Go early, though, because this place shuts down early.

High Country Restaurant and Saloon

$$–$$$$ Chama   AMERICAN/NEW MEXICAN

There's nothin' like country cookin' to make you feel at home on the road. That's what you get at this casual all-purpose restaurant, where Chama-ites linger. Big sellers here are the St. Louis–style pork ribs sold with the tantalizing monikers of "full slab" or "half slab." The half-chicken is rubbed with spices and herbs and smoked with mesquite. The attached saloon has a full bar and bustles with people eating peanuts and throwing the shells on the floor.

On N.M. 17. (¹⁄₁₀ mile north of the "Y"). ☎ 505-756-2384. Reservations not accepted. Main courses: $6–$20. AE, DISC, MC, V. Open: Daily 11 a.m.–10 p.m. Closed: Thanksgiving, Christmas, and Easter.

Viva Vera's Mexican Kitchen

$–$$ Chama   NEW MEXICAN

If you can handle tasty sauces over rich enchiladas and burritos, followed by fluffy sopaipillas soaked with honey, you'll be happy at this restaurant run by Vera herself. Some complain that the chile is too hot, but for me, I say bring it on. The setting is pastoral, with fields of gazing horses stretching to the river. You can relax on the porch — *the* place to sit on warmer days. They serve beer and wine, but the favorite seems to be wine margaritas, frothy and frozen, served in big glasses.

2202 Hwy. 17 (at the Y). ☎ 505-756-2557. Main courses: breakfast $4–$7; lunch and dinner $4–$12.50. AE, DC, DISC, MC, V. Open: Daily June–Sept 8 a.m.–9 p.m.; Oct–May daily 8 a.m.—8 p.m. May be closed during Easter week.

Exploring the Chama area

Though Chama doesn't have many attractions per se, the main one, the train ride, really ranks and is easy to arrange. Other pastimes require a little more gusto when planning.

Discovering the top attractions

Cumbres and Toltec Scenic Railroad

Chama

Even if you didn't spend your youth tinkering with toy train engines, you'll likely get a kick out of a ride on this gem. America's longest and highest narrow-gauge steam railroad (circa 1880) takes passengers on a 64-mile trek between Chama and Antonito, Colorado, passing through pine and aspen forests, past striking rock formations, and over the 10,015-foot Cumbres Pass, the highest in the U.S. used by scheduled passenger trains. When scheduling your trip, you have two options: You may take the train to Osier, Colorado, have a picnic, and return home by train, or you may go all the way to Antonito and return by van. Be aware that either option makes for a long day with lots of sitting, with the latter option being the longest.

500 Terrace Ave. (in the center of town). ☎ *505-756-2151. Fax: 505-756-2694. Internet:* www.cumbrestoltec.com. *Round-trip by train to Osier: Adults $40, children age 2–11 $20. One-way trip by train to Antonito and return by van (or to Antonito by van, return by train): Adults $60, children age 2–11 $30. Reservations highly recommended. AE, DC, DISC, MC, V. Memorial Day to mid-Oct trains leave Chama daily at 10 a.m.*

Finding more cool things to see and do

Beyond riding the rails, this area offers plenty more to do, from touring quaint villages full of history to checking out natural wonders. The top options include:

- ✔ **Shop in a traditional Hispanic village.** A cool little stop-off en route from Chama to Santa Fe is the village of Los Ojos (just off U.S. 84, 12 miles south of Chama), where **Tierra Wools** (☎ **505-588-7231**) sells one-of-a-kind blankets and men's and women's apparel. Shop hours are Monday through Saturday from 9 a.m. to 6 p.m. in summer and from 10 a.m. to 5 p.m. in winter.

- ✔ **Explore the outdoors.** Just north of the village of Los Ojos, N.M. 512 heads east 7½ miles up the **Brazos Box Canyon.** High cliffs rising from the valley floor give it a Yosemite-like appearance — which is even more apparent from an overlook on U.S. 64, 18 miles east of Tierra Amarilla en route to Taos. Several resort lodges are in the area (check out The Timbers at Chama, listed earlier in this section under "Staying in style").

  About 37 miles south of Tierra Amarilla on U.S. 84 and 3 miles north of Ghost Ranch, is **Echo Canyon Amphitheater** (☎ **505-684-2486**), a U.S. Forest Service campground and picnic area. This natural theater was hollowed out of boldly colored sandstone. The walls send back eerie echoes and even clips of conversations. The amphitheater is just a ten-minute walk from the parking area.

Quick concierge: Chama

Area Code

The area code is **505**. Although some area codes in the state may change in 2002, Chama will most likely retain this one. For updates, contact the New Mexico Department of Tourism (☎ 800-733-6396; Internet: www.newmexico.org).

ATMs

You can find two ATMs in Chama, one in the center of town and the other at the junction of U.S. 64/84 and N.M. 17.

Emergencies

Call ☎ **911.**

Hospital

La Clinica, 15 miles south of Chama on Highway 84 in Tierra Amarilla (☎ 505-588-7252), offers 24-hour emergency service, but you must call first.

Information

The Chama Visitor Center (☎ 505-756-2235) is at the south end of town, at the junction of U.S. 64/84 and N.M. 17. Hours are daily from 8 a.m. to 6 p.m. in summer, 8 a.m. to 5 p.m. in winter. For complete local information, contact the Chama Valley Chamber of Commerce, Cumbres Mall, 463 Terrace Ave. (☎ 800-477-0149 or 505-756-2306).

Internet Access

Log on at the Eleanor Daggett Memorial Library, 299 Fourth St., at Pine Street (☎ 505-756-2388).

Pharmacy

Rio Drugs of Chama, 587 S. Terrace Ave. (in the middle of Chama; ☎ 505-756-2131), is open Monday through Friday from 9 a.m. to 6 p.m. and Saturday from 9 a.m. to 5 p.m.

Police

In case of emergency, dial ☎ **911.** There is no police department in Chama, but you can contact the New Mexico State Police Department (☎ 505-753-2277).

Post Office

The Chama Post office is at 199 W. Fifth St. in Chama just off Terrance Avenue (☎ 505-756-2240).

Road Conditions

Call ☎ 800-432-4269.

Weather Updates

To get weather forecasts on the Internet, log on to www.accuweather.com and use the Chama zip code, 87520.

Part V

The Part of Tens

The 5th Wave By Rich Tennant

In this part . . .

*I*f the rest of this book is the road map of how to make your way through New Mexico, this part contains the street signs, clueing you in on when and how to stop, yield, cruise, or race through this lovely state, so that you can avoid any, er, accidents and enjoy as much scenery and adventure as possible. This part explores three topics — local quirks, Native American etiquette, and arts and crafts — presented in a top ten format. So, ladies and gentlemen, start your engines.

Chapter 20

The Top Ten Ways to Act Like a New Mexican

*Y*ou don't have to give up any of your unique identity in order to fit into New Mexico. In fact, the more quirky you are, the *more* you may fit in with all the eccentrics who were born here and have moved here over the years. (New Mexico has long held a reputation for being *the* place that East Coast families send their misfit kids to get them out of the way.) So, you'll be fine here even if you like to wear mismatched socks or put your elbows on the table during dinner. However, if you're looking for a smooth transition into the Land of Enchantment, you may want to pay attention to a few of the state's own quirks.

Driving a Truck

Sometimes it seems as if everyone drives a truck in New Mexico — from rusty, 1950s Studebakers to factory-fresh Toyotas. What they all have in common is that no one ever washes them (the dirtier, the better, in fact), and they all have cracked windshields from traveling along the many dirt roads of the state. A clean truck is the sign of a newcomer, a tourist, or someone who's just plain *loco* (weird). What's more, you must also *accessorize* your truck — a Virgen de Guadalupe gearshift knob, a pair of Yosemite Sam "Back Off!" mudflaps, and two or three peeling bumper stickers displaying slogans should do the trick. Don't forget the mud.

Owning at Least One Dog

Of course, no truck is complete without at least one canine (typically a mutt) road-surfing in back. There's no doubt about it: New Mexicans are dog nuts. First-time visitors to the state are often struck by how many dogs reside here, and how large a part they play in people's lives. Certainly, dogs seem to be everywhere, and sometimes it seems as if everyone has at least one at the end of a leash. Every year in Santa Fe, the **Pet Parade** occurs during September's Santa Fe Fiesta (☎ **575-988-7575**), and every winter the **Barkin' Ball** (most recently hosted by actress Ali McGraw) raises money for the Santa Fe Animal Shelter & Humane Society (☎ **575-983-4309**). Aside from dogs, you also find plenty of cats, and don't be surprised to see goats or llamas in people's back yards.

Habla-ing a Little Español

Spanish history in New Mexico dates back some 400 years to the days when Francisco Vásquez de Coronado found many cities of mud and stone here instead of the Seven Cities of Gold that he was seeking. His descendants and the many generations of Spaniards that followed left a lot of the Latin-rooted language in the state. In order to get along well here, you definitely want to clear out the cobwebs woven since your high school Spanish class.

Sure, your weekly trips to your local Mexican restaurant may have you prepped for linguistic adventures such as ordering nachos, enchiladas, and flan. But even in New Mexico's restaurants, you may need a little help, because this state has its own unique variety of food. (See the primer on New Mexico food on the Cheat Sheet at the front of this book.)

Your biggest challenge may be navigating *around* New Mexico. Most streets, towns, buildings, mountains, and rivers have Spanish names. Even if you don't know what the words mean, by listening to locals, you can very quickly become accustomed to pronouncing names such as Rio Grande (R-*io Grand*-ay), New Mexico's "big river," or Sangre de Cristo Mountains (*San*-grey day *Cris*-tow), which means "blood of Christ." Don't get carried away with pronouncing words with a Spanish accent, however. A friend once called me in distress; he was lost north of Santa Fe. I asked him where he was and he said o-*pair*-a. "Wow," I replied, "I have no idea where that is." After some negotiating, we figured out he was at the Santa Fe *Opera*.

Keep in mind a few basics:

✔ If you're looking at a Spanish word, *j*'s are usually pronounced "h" if at the beginning of the word, as in *juez* (*hu*-ez), meaning "judge," a word you may need when you red-line that rental car and get a speeding ticket.

✔ *G's* are also often pronounced like an "h," as in *gila* (*hee*-la) monster, but not as in *gringo* (*gring*-go), pronounced with a hard "g" and meaning "darned foreigner" (a possible name for you if you don't get your Spanish right).

✔ You want to trill your double *r*'s as well as you can, especially when ordering such treats as *churros* (*choo*-ros), just so the waitperson doesn't get your order wrong.

✔ Some *n*'s have tildes on top of them (so the *n* is pronounced "ny") as in *mañana* (mahn-*yahn*-ah), meaning "tomorrow," a word you'd better get used to while in the Land of Enchantment. The pace is so relaxed, you may just have to lull in the shade one more day and put off your plans until tomorrow.

Being Late for Everything

You don't need a new watch battery — everyone's just late around here. The clock on the wall may look the same as everywhere else, but a New Mexican's internal clock is set at least 20 minutes slower than normal. The local saying, *mañana* (tomorrow), gives you an idea of what to expect, and there's no point in fighting the system. It's just the way it is. If you want a local to meet you on time, always tell that person a half hour or so earlier than when you intend to be there yourself. This logic also applies to home improvement projects, car repairs, orders at restaurants, and so on.

Joining the New Age

Don't be shy about adopting a so-called alternative lifestyle while in New Mexico. In fact, you'll fit in better if you do. Workshops abound on every type of alternative therapy you can possibly imagine, and then some. If you believe in UFOs, past-life regressions, psychic surgery, crystal massage, high colonics, tantric sex, or that your pet has an aura, you don't have to worry about belonging. Otherwise, start getting with it by brushing up on your astrology. The '70s have been dead and buried everywhere but in New Mexico, so "what's your sign" is a typical conversation starter in these here parts.

Becoming an Artist

Devotees of the New Age aren't the only folks who come to New Mexico for the light. This state is absolutely crawling with artists. Everyone seems to be a painter or a writer here, so you may as well pick up whatever supplies you need and join the ranks. Now, if your stuff really stinks, no worries — the hypercritical bite of New York has been slow to reach this part of the country. Just wander through a few Santa Fe galleries, and you'll see. . . .

Dressing the Part

Part of acting like an artist requires looking like an artist. In fact, many of New Mexico's so-called artists are much better at looking like an artistic creation than actually creating the art itself. Think Fleetwood Mac. Remember the album cover of *Rumors?* That's the look you want. Another handy fashion tip is to load yourself down with as much heavy silver and turquoise jewelry as you possibly can. Gaudy, gigantic concha belts, earrings, necklaces, and rings will all combine to help you both fit in and drop a few pounds from lugging around the sheer weight of it all.

Saying Chile, Not Chili

New Mexicans don't generally eat *chili,* that tomato, bean, and meat concoction especially loved by Texans. Instead we eat *chile,* a delectable red or green sauce containing fresh chiles and served over enchiladas, burritos, and other foods, as well as in a bowl on its own with a tortilla on the side. Chile uses the Spanish spelling of the word, which in New Mexico is considered the only true spelling — no matter what your dictionary may say.

New Mexicans have such a personal attachment to this small agricultural gem that in 1983 we directed our senior U.S. senator, Pete Domenici, to enter New Mexico's official position on the spelling of chile into the *Congressional Record.* That's taking your chiles seriously.

Chiles are grown throughout the state, in a perfect climate for cultivating and drying the small but powerful red and green New Mexican varieties. The most notable location is the town of Hatch, which bills itself as the "Chile Capital of the World." Regardless of where you travel in the state, chiles appear on the menu. Virtually anything you order in a restaurant may be topped with a chile sauce. You even find novelties here such as green chile jelly and green chile ice cream.

If you're not accustomed to spicy foods, certain varieties of red or green chiles will make your eyes water, your sinuses drain, and your palate feel as if it's on fire — all after just one forkful. *Warning:* No amount of water or beer will alleviate the sting. Drink milk or shovel in a *sopaipilla* (a deep-fried, puffed pastry) drizzled with honey to cool down.

But don't let these words of caution scare you away from genuine New Mexico chiles. The pleasure of eating them far outweighs the pain. Start slow, with salsas and chile sauces first, perhaps *relleños* (stuffed peppers) next, followed by *rajas* (roasted peeled chiles cut into strips). Before long, you'll be buying *chile ristras* (chiles strung on rope) and hanging them up for decoration. Perhaps you'll be so smitten that you'll purchase bags of chile powder or a chile plant to take home. These souvenirs will certainly remain a piquant reminder of the difference between chile and chili.

Doing Drive-Thru Everything

New Mexicans have been known to form unnatural attachments to their vehicles and show a general reluctance to leave them, so many businesses offer drive-thru services. Quite often, you find much longer lines in the drive-thru area of an establishment than inside the actual business itself. Although drive-thru liquor shops were outlawed several years ago (a good thing), you can still do your banking, buy a green-chile cheeseburger, snap up some gourmet coffee, or pay your utility bill at drive-thru establishments around the state.

Acknowledging Your Fellow Drivers

As you start driving around New Mexico, you soon notice your fellow motorists either nodding at you or raising a finger or two from the top of their steering wheels and making a sort of mini-wave in your direction. It would be tempting at first to think that either everyone is mistaking you for their best friend, or that they actually recognize you, but this is not the case — folks are just generally friendlier around here.

Chapter 21

The Top Ten Ways to Be Friendly with the Native Americans

• •

In This Chapter

▶ Understanding the terms and history

▶ Following pueblo etiquette and law

▶ Enjoying Native American rituals

• •

*W*ith your extensive wit and charm, you can probably get along
fine in New Mexico. However, even the most winsome characters
need to know a few rules. Although rules are scarce in this renegade
land of wide-open deserts and rambunctious mountain ranges, these
few will help you get along with the locals, particularly with the Native
Americans, who lead unique lives and have distinct customs. Follow
these pointers and you'll no doubt feel welcome wherever you turn in
the Land of Enchantment.

Know the History and a Few Terms

While visiting New Mexico, keep in mind that the Native Americans
who inhabit the state have been here longer than you have. (After all,
you just got here.) Also recall that they've lived in this land called the
United States longer than the country's first settlers — the Native
Americans have been here for more than a millennium, probably
longer, while the Spaniards arrived about 400 years ago and the
Pilgrims arrived 100 years after that!

In order to honor their longevity here, it may help to understand a few
Native American terms.

✔ **Ceremonial dances:** During various times of year, various pueblos perform dances to commemorate seasons or elements in nature important to their survival, such as corn, buffalo, eagle, elk, and deer.

✔ **Feast day:** On feast day, a pueblo's tribal members commemorate the saint related to their village, usually by performing ceremonial dances.

✔ **Kiva:** A kiva is a sacred ceremonial room, usually round and underground.

✔ **Pueblo:** Literally, *pueblo* is the Spanish word for "town." Early Spaniards began calling the Native American villages this, and the name stuck not only to define *where* the tribes live but also *who* they are. Thus, the Pueblo people.

Follow Pueblo Etiquette

Many of New Mexico's pueblos welcome visitors, but you have to remember that you're treading on foreign turf here (technically, Native American reservations are sovereign nations), so the usual codes of conduct don't always apply. If you don't follow their codes, you'll likely be asked to leave.

While on a Native American reservation, remember:

✔ Stay out of sacred places such as cemeteries and ceremonial rooms.

✔ Don't wander into people's yards or homes.

✔ Get a permit from the tribal office to take pictures or videos, or to sketch or paint.

✔ If you're on a guided tour, stay with the tour.

✔ Be respectful of ceremonial dances. Do not speak during them, and don't applaud at the end — the dancers aren't performing for your amusement; they're dancing as part of their ceremony.

In short, be respectful and courteous, and don't do anything you wouldn't do in your own mother's house.

Understand Who's Who in Indian Country

Travelers to New Mexico often assume that all the Native Americans hearken from related tribes. Guess again. Two very distinct lineages inhabit this state. Arizona's Hopi Indians, New Mexico's Zunis, and all the tribes along the Rio Grande share the same Puebloan roots, a lineage traced back over a millennium to ruins at places such as Arizona's Keet Seel and New Mexico's Chaco Culture National Historic Park. In contrast, the Navajos, like their linguistic cousins the Apaches, belong to the large family of Athabaskan Indians found across Alaska and northwestern Canada and in parts of the Northern California coast. The Navajos and Apaches probably migrated to the Southwest around the 14th century. Despite their need to share these lands, over the centuries the two groups have not exactly been chummy.

Say "Ancestral Puebloan"

Be careful of using the commonly used term "Anasazi" to refer to the people who once inhabited places such as Chaco Culture National Historic Park and Bandelier National Monument. The Navajo word *anasazi* means "ancient ones" and "ancient enemies." The Pueblo tribes prefer the name *ancestral Puebloans* for those people who have proven to be their relatives.

Say "Petroglyph"

Don't go around calling those lovely ancient images etched in stone "rock art," at least not in front of rangers at, say, Petroglyph National Monument in Albuquerque. The politically correct police have determined that "rock art" demeans the images, which are sacred to the descendents of those who drew them. The preferred word is *petroglyphs*. (Of course, U.S. culture is one of the few that separates art from the sacred, but alas, that's the United States for you.)

Ask Before Shooting

Though you may be tempted to point your camera at that lovely Puebloan woman wearing a purple velvet blouse and turquoise chunk necklace, stop before you do. Most Native Americans prefer not to have their pictures taken. I've heard that they believe it harms their souls. Whatever the reason, *always* ask before you point and shoot. Sometimes, the Native American may request some money or ask that you buy some crafts for the privilege of taking a picture.

Walk Around the Walls

On your sojourn in the Land of Enchantment, you may find yourself at some point standing among lovely timeworn walls of an ancient pueblo. Maybe the structure is round and sunken in the ground, the remains of a sacred ceremonial kiva. Though you may feel a great rush of childlike joy pour through your heart, avoid the temptation of alighting on the ruin walls and climbing around, or jumping up and down within the fragile domains. Instead, contain your enthusiasm until you get back to the parking lot; then jump up and down on the hood of your car, if that suits you.

Leave the Artifacts

Who knows whether it's fact or fable, but word has it that if you discretely (or indiscreetly) place in your pocket that lovely arrowhead or potshard you find on reservation land, you'll be haunted *forever.* Bad luck may assail you, but what may hurt worse is getting caught; the police will make you pay a hefty fine. Your best bet is to pick up the prime piece of history, examine it, and then set it back on the ground — so others can enjoy it and so the voodoo doesn't get you.

Avoid Saying "Ya Ta Hey" and "How"

Although you may think that the glorious 20th-century teacher, the television, has given you ample lessons in how to speak to Native Americans, think again. Most of what you've been fed over the years about Native Americans' lives is wrong, from the notion that they all speak the same stilted, simplistic language that Tonto spoke, to the notion that they all have some deep, secret knowledge about life that we should revere. Native Americans are people, each tribe with a different language, and each individual with a world as varied as yours and mine. However, many also live lives very separate from ours and have beliefs that we can't fathom (but should respect). Your best bet is to simply say, "Hello."

Take a Sweat

Although most Native Americans couldn't care less whether or not you *take a sweat,* you may want to try this oh-so-chic pastime. Some spas offer up the rite as a spiritual and physical cleansing. Basically, you sit within a very small tent where hot rocks are continually placed until you're so out-of-your-mind uncomfortable that you can't help but surrender. To what? That's your choice. Some people have visions after such an experience. Others simply have clean pores.

Chapter 22

The Top Ten New Mexico Arts and Crafts

*L*ots of folks come to New Mexico just to shop for Hispanic and Native American arts and crafts — from folksy Spanish Colonial–style hammered tinwork to elegantly woven Navajo rugs. The quality and price of these items covers a lot of territory — from cheap souvenirs to extremely expensive collector's items. Although you don't have to be an art aficionado or spend an arm and a leg to purchase something nice, being as knowledgeable as you can certainly helps prevent your cash from turning into trash.

First off, do your homework. Three useful books to check out are *The Field Guide to Southwest Indian Arts and Crafts* (Treasure Chest Books) by Susanne Page and Jake Page; *Spanish New Mexico: The Spanish Colonial Arts Society Collection* (Museum of New Mexico Press) by the Spanish Colonial Arts Society; and *The Trading Post Guidebook: Where to Find the Trading Posts, Galleries, Auctions, Artists, and Museums of the Four Corners Region* (Canyonlands Publishing) by Patrick Eddington and Susan Makov.

If you're a serious collector or thinking about becoming one, time your New Mexico trip to coincide with either **Traditional Spanish Market** (Internet: www.spanishcolonial.org) or **Indian Market** (Internet: www.swaia.org), both in Santa Fe. Many artists save their best efforts for these two annual summer events, which draw huge crowds.

In general, if you want to be sure that a Hispanic or Native American craft is genuine rather than a cheap knockoff, look for the name of the artisan on the item, or better yet, buy directly from the artist.

New Mexican art is a broad and rich topic; I could easily fill another book on the subject. But knowing that you just want the highlights, I cover just the top ten buys in this chapter, divided neatly into Spanish Colonial and Native American genres.

Searching for Spanish Colonial Treasures

New Mexico is world-famous for its Spanish Colonial art and crafts. Over the centuries, local artisans have put stateside twists on old world classics.

Bultos

The beautifully carved and painted wooden *santos* (saints) and religious figures you see in New Mexican country churches are called *bultos*. They are typically carved from local woods such as cottonwood or aspen, and they have been made in New Mexico since the 16th century. You quite often see bultos in New Mexican homes, tucked away in little *nichos* (small coves in a wall). They aren't all serious, however. In recent years, artists such as Nicholas Herrera have been bringing whimsy and humor to their carvings.

Retablos

These paintings on wooden panels (usually pine) typically depict religious figures and are often used to form altar screens in churches or shrines in people's homes. The imagery in the paintings is typically rooted in traditional Spanish Catholic iconography, but over the centuries, New Mexican twists have been added, and a style has emerged that is unique to New Mexico.

Wooden furniture

Stately and handsome, but not always comfortable, Spanish Colonial–style furniture is typically constructed from local pine using mortise and tenon joints and is usually either left unpainted or stained a shade of brown. Designs for contemporary furniture are still based on prototypes for chairs, chests, tables, benches, and *trasteros* (armoires) that were brought to the New World in the 16th century from Spain. But, this being New Mexico, various elements have been added over the centuries to create a truly New Mexican style of furniture.

Textiles

Weaving began in the Southwest at the end of the 16th century, when the Spaniard Juan de Oñate brought thousands of sheep with him to New Mexico. Contemporary weavings are still based on traditional Spanish designs, and natural, vegetable dyes are also still used. Chimayo is the best place in New Mexico to find traditional Hispanic weavings.

Tinwork

In northern New Mexico in particular, you often see religious and utilitarian objects made from cut and punched tin. New Mexican tinwork is known as the "poor man's silver," because objects can be made from readily available cans. Traditional tinwork items include frames for pictures and mirrors and lampshades.

Hunting for Native American Crafts

For more than a millennium, Native Americans have perfected their crafts in the Southwest. Today, you can find a broad range of treasures, from ancient pots to contemporary earrings.

Silver and turquoise jewelry

Everywhere you go in the Land of Enchantment, you see wonderful jewelry. The intricate Zuni style has patterns of inlaid stones. The Navajo version is made of large stones, often with silver, cast in elaborate patterns. Hopi jewelry usually is without stones and has darkened motifs incised into the top layer of silver. Whatever style you choose, you want to make sure that the jewelry is well made and consists of quality materials.

Make sure that the silver has clean lines, a general harmony of design, and finely executed soldering. If what you seek is jewelry made with New Mexico's most emblematic stone, turquoise, you want to watch for some important details. Turquoise is considered of higher quality when its color is deepest, but try to find out if it has been color-treated. Quite often, turquoise is soaked in resin and baked for stabilization, which makes the stone more durable and prevents it from changing color with age and contact with body oils. Although this process has advantages, color treatment prevents the turquoise from improving with age, as untreated stones tend to do. Also, beware of reconstituted turquoise, where the stone is disassembled and reassembled, which gives it an unnatural-looking uniformly blue color.

Some of the most desirable jewelry items are *concho belts* (leather belts strung with conchos, which are round or oblong silver plates, often set with turquoise stones), turquoise strings, bolo ties, hatbands, and silver and turquoise bracelets, rings, and earrings. You can find these at craft shops all over New Mexico. One of the best places to shop is along the plazas in Santa Fe and Albuquerque, where Native Americans display items for sale on blankets.

Navajo rugs

The Navajo are world-famous for their extraordinary weavings and are known as much for their design skills as for their superb craftsmanship. As a rule, Navajo rugs are appraised according to their tightness and evenness of weave, their symmetry of design, and whether commercial or natural dyes have been used. Traditional Navajo designs to look out for include *Chief's Blanket* and *Two Gray Hills.*

Pottery

Native American pottery is traditionally made of natural, hand-coiled clay which is hand polished with a stone, hand painted, and then fired in an outdoor oven (usually an open fire pit). Look for an even shape; clean, accurate painting; a high polish (if the piece is polished); and an artist's signature. Maria Martinez of San Ildefonso Pueblo was the most famous potter in New Mexico; now deceased, she was known for making black pots, which are still available. The potters at Acoma create exquisitely thin, beautifully painted pots with intricate geometric designs.

Fetishes — gifts of power

For generations, while wandering across their lands in western New Mexico, Zuni Indians found stones shaped like particular animals. The Zunis and other Native Americans believe that many such stones are the remains of long-lost animals that still contain their soul or last breath.

In many shops in New Mexico, you too can pick up a carved animal figure, called a *fetish.* According to some beliefs, the owner of the fetish is able to absorb the power of that creature. Many fetishes were long ago used for protection and strength in the hunt. Today, people own fetishes for many reasons. Someone may carry a carved bear for health and strength, or an eagle for keen perspective. A mole may be placed in a home's foundation for protection from elements underground, a frog buried with crops for fertility and rain, or a ram carried in the purse for prosperity. For love, some people recommend pairs of fetishes — often foxes or coyotes carved from a single piece of stone.

Fetishes can be carved from a variety of mediums; most common are turquoise, alabaster, lapis, jet, and quartz. Some fetishes come arranged with bundles on top attached with thread made of tendon. These additions serve as an offering to the animal spirit that resides within the stone. When shopping for the treasures, take time to appreciate the difference between clumsily carved ones and more gracefully executed ones. A good fetish is not necessarily one that is meticulously carved; some are barely carved at all, because the original shape of the stone already contains the form of the animal. When you have a sense of the quality and elegance available, decide which animal (and power) suits you best. Native Americans caution, however, that the fetish won't impart an attribute you don't already possess. Instead, the fetish helps elicit the power that already resides within you.

Locating fetishes is easy throughout New Mexico, particularly in many crafts shops in Santa Fe. However, the best selection is at **Pueblo of Zuni Arts and Crafts (☎ 505-782-5531)**, south of Gallup.

Pawn

While shopping in the Gallup area and other parts of New Mexico, you may likely come across *pawn*. Unlike in other parts of the United States, this word doesn't refer to junk sold in desperation. Real pawn is some of the best crafts you can find. Why? Historically, pawnbrokers are the Fort Knoxes of the area. Native American artisans bring their blankets, jewelry, and pottery to these dudes who have major safes in which to keep them — a much safer prospect than stashing them under the bed in the old hogan or pueblo house. The pawnbroker or trader holds onto an item for months or even years before deeming it dead and putting it up for sale. Less than 5% of items ever go unredeemed, but when they do, you're in luck. Some of the shops you enter may simply be craft shops, but others will be pawnshops, which can be distinguished by their noticeable security. Take a look around. You may hear some Navajo, Tiwa, and Tewa spoken, and you may very well find some timeless treasures.

Appendix

Quick Concierge

• •

Fast Facts

Ambulance

Call ☎ **911**. This call is free from pay phones.

American Automobile Association (AAA)

For roadside assistance, dial ☎ 800-222-4357 or 505-291-6600. Offices are in Albuquerque at 10501 Montgomery Blvd. NE at Morris Street (☎ 505-291-6688), and in Santa Fe at 1644 St. Michael's Dr. (☎ 505-471-6620).

American Express

You can find an American Express Travel Service office at Atlas Travel and Cruise, 1301 Wyoming Blvd. in Albuquerque (☎ 505-291-6575). To report lost credit cards, call ☎ 800-528-2122.

Area Codes

The area code for all of New Mexico is **505**, although at press time plans were rumbling to add new ones in the state. For updates, contact the New Mexico Department of Tourism (☎ 800-733-6396; Internet: www.newmexico.org).

ATMs

ATMs are widely available throughout all cities at banks, on the street, and in convenience stores and supermarkets.

Baby-sitting

Check with your hotel's front desk or concierge for suggestions. In Albuquerque, call Professional Nannies of New Mexico (☎ 505-299-6181; Internet: www.jfsabq.org). In Santa Fe, try Magical Happenings (☎ 505-982-9327).

Camera Repair

In Albuquerque, try Kurt's Camera Corral, 3417 Central Ave. NE (☎ 505-296-4888) near the University of New Mexico; in downtown Santa Fe, head to Camera and Darkroom, 216 Galisteo St. (☎ 505-983-2948).

Convention Centers

Centers include the Albuquerque Convention Center at 20 First Plaza NW, Suite 601 (☎ 800-733-9918; Internet: www.abqcvb.org), and Sweeney Convention Center in Santa Fe at 201 W. Marcy St. (☎ 800-777-CITY or 505-955-6200; Internet: www.santafe.org).

Credit Cards

For lost or stolen cards, contact the following: Visa (☎ 800-847-2911), MasterCard (☎ 800-307-7309), or American Express (☎ 800-668-2639).

Dentists

Check with the front desk or concierge at your hotel, or try the Emergency Dental Referral Service in Albuquerque (☎ 505-260-7333), or Dr. Leslie E. La Kind in Santa Fe (☎ 505-988-3500).

Doctors

Check with the front desk or concierge at your hotel, or try a referral service. Call the St. Joseph Hospital referral service (☎ 505-727-7778) in Albuquerque. In Santa Fe, contact Lovelace Health Care (☎ 505-955-2400). Each city and regional chapter in this book lists a hospital where you can obtain a referral. Before seeking medical treatment, be sure you understand your insurance carrier's policy on emergency care and preapproval.

Emergencies

Call ☎ **911** for the police, an ambulance, or in case of fire. This call is free from pay phones.

Hospitals

In Albuquerque, the major facilities are Presbyterian Hospital, 1100 Central Ave. SE (☎ 505-841-1234 or 505-841-1111 for emergency services); and University of New Mexico Hospital, 2211 Lomas Blvd. NE (☎ 505-272-2111 or 505-272-2411 for emergency services). In Santa Fe, head to St. Vincent's Hospital, 455 St. Michael's Dr. (☎ 505-820-5250). Check the "Quick Concierge" sections in each city and regional chapter for the hospital closest to you.

Hotlines

Crisis centers include Agora Crisis Center (☎ 505-277-3013), University of New Mexico Mental Health Center (☎ 505-272-1700), and Santa Fe Crisis Response Center (☎ 888-920-6333).

Information

Contact the New Mexico Department of Tourism in Santa Fe, 491 Old Santa Fe Trail (☎ 800-733-6396 or 505-827-7400; Internet: www.nnewmexico.org); the Albuquerque Convention and Visitors Bureau, 20 First Plaza NW (☎ 800-284-2282 or 505-842-9918; Internet: www.abqcvb.org); or the Santa Fe Convention and Visitors Bureau, 201 W. Marcy St. (☎ 800-777-2489 or 505-955-6200; Internet: www.santafe.org or www.visitsantafe.com). Each city and regional chapter in this book lists info sources in the "Quick Concierge" section. For telephone directory assistance, call ☎ 411. (Also see "Where to Get More Information," later in this Appendix.)

Internet Access

Kinko's provides high-speed Internet access at five locations throughout Albuquerque. Two convenient ones are: 6220 San Mateo Blvd. NE, at Academy Blvd. (☎ 505-821-2222), and 2706 Central Ave. SE, at Princeton Blvd. (☎ 505-255-9673). In Santa Fe, you can enjoy an espresso with your e-mail at the Aztec Café, 317 Aztec St. (☎ 505-983-9464), or retrieve your e-mail at Kinko's, 301 N. Guadalupe St. (☎ 505-473-7303). Each city and regional chapter in this book lists Internet log-on sights in the "Quick Concierge" section.

Liquor Laws

The drinking age is 21. Monday through Saturday, bars close at 2 a.m.; on Sunday bars may be open only between noon and midnight. Wine, beer, and spirits are sold at licensed supermarkets and liquor stores. A special allowance must be granted for liquor to be dispensed in proximity to any church. Transporting liquor through most Indian reservations is illegal.

Maps

Most gas stations, convenience stores, and supermarkets sell maps, which tend to be better than the ones you can get at the local tourist offices — although those from the tourist offices often indicate the popular sights. If you're a member of AAA, you can also get excellent maps in advance at your local AAA office. The Internet site Mapquest (www.mapquest.com) will plot a route from point A to point B; this is a good resource if you know exactly where you're coming from and where you're going.

Newspapers/Alternative Weeklies

The *Santa Fe New Mexican,* the *Albuquerque Journal,* and the *Albuquerque Tribune* are the state's most important daily papers. In Albuquerque, the free *Weekly Alibi,* and in Santa Fe, the free weekly *Reporter* carry arts coverage, entertainment, and restaurant listings for their respective cities; you can find them in newspaper boxes around town. (See "Information on the Web" later in this Appendix for Web site information.)

Pharmacies

Most towns have a Wal-Mart with a pharmacy. Other chains to look for include Walgreens and Sav-On Drugs.

Photography

Because New Mexico is typically sunny, you'll get the best all-around results with 100-speed film. If your camera accepts filters, use a polarizing one to bring out the blue.

Police

Throughout the state, call ☎ **911** for emergencies.

Radio Stations

KUNM-FM (89.9), broadcast from the University of New Mexico in Albuquerque, is the local National Public Radio affiliate.

Restrooms

You can find clean public restrooms along the interstates, but when you're on the smaller roads, they can be hard to find. Luckily, most gas stations and country stores have restrooms you can use. Public restrooms are few and far between in the cities, but many restaurants, hotels, and coffee shops will let you use their facilities.

Road Conditions

For regular updates on New Mexico's road conditions, call ☎ 800-432-4269 or check the Internet at www.nmshtd.state.nm.us.

Safety

You need to take the same common-sense precautions for your personal safety and that of your belongings that you would take anywhere else in the United States. (See Chapter 9 for information about what to do if your

money gets lost or stolen.) But in New Mexico, you also have to think about the road – and the elements. (See Chapter 7 for details about driving around New Mexico.)

Smoking

There is a statewide ban on smoking in all public buildings, and many restaurants also prohibit smoking. However, many restaurants also have bars where smoking is permitted.

Taxes

A gross receipts tax, which varies from town to town but is usually between 5% and 7%, is applied to purchases including hotel bills. On top of this, local governments add their own lodging tax, which varies throughout the state.

Time Zone

New Mexico is in the Mountain time zone — one hour ahead of the West Coast and two hours behind the East Coast. Daylight saving time is in effect from April through October.

Tipping

The average tip for most service providers, including waiters and cab drivers, is 15%, rising to 20% for particularly good service. Tip bellhops $1 or $2 per bag, hotel housekeepers at least $1 per person per day, and valet parking and coat-check attendants $1 to $2.

Weather Updates

For weather updates in most of the state, call the National Weather Service in Albuquerque (☎ 505-243-0702). However, in some of the southernmost regions, you need to call the National Weather Service in El Paso (☎ 505-589-4088). To get weather forecasts on the Internet, log on to www.accuweather.com, and use the local zip code.

Toll-Free Numbers and Web Sites

Major North-American carriers

Aeromexico
☎ 800-237-6639
www.aeromexico.com

America West Airlines and America West Express
☎ 800-235-9292
www.americawest.com

American Airlines
☎ 800-433-7300
www.im.aa.com

Continental Airlines
☎ 800-525-0280
www.continental.com

Delta Air Lines
☎ 800-221-1212
www.delta.com

Frontier Airlines
☎ 800-432-1359
www.frontierairlines.com

Mesa Airlines
☎ 800-637-2247
www.mesa-air.com

Northwest Airlines
☎ 800-225-2525
www.nwa.com

Rio Grande Air
☎ 877-I-FLY-RGA
www.iflyrga.com

Southwest Airlines
☎ 800-435-9792
www.southwest.com

Trans World Airlines (TWA)
☎ 800-221-2000
www.twa.com

United Airlines and United Express
☎ 800-241-6522
www.united.com

US Airways
☎ 800-428-4322
www.usairways.com

Car-rental agencies

Alamo
☎ 800-327-9633
www.goalamo.com

Avis
☎ 800-331-1212 in Continental U.S.
☎ 800-TRY-AVIS in Canada
www.avis.com

Budget
☎ 800-527-0700
www.budgetrentacar.com

Dollar
☎ 800-800-4000
www.dollar.com

Enterprise
☎ 800-325-8007
www.enterprise.com

Hertz
☎ 800-654-3131
www.hertz.com

National
☎ 800-CAR-RENT
www.nationalcar.com

Rent-A-Wreck
☎ 800-535-1391
www.rent-a-wreck.com

Thrifty
☎ 800-367-2277
www.thrifty.com

Major hotel and motel chains

Best Western International
☎ 800-528-1234
www.bestwestern.com

Clarion Hotels
☎ 800-CLARION
www.clarionhotel.com or
www.hotelchoice.com

Comfort Inn
☎ 800-228-5150
www.comfortinn.com or www.
hotelchoice.com

Courtyard by Marriott
☎ 800-321-2211
www.courtyard.com

Crowne Plaza Hotel
☎ 800-227-6963
www.CrownePlaza.com

Days Inn
☎ 800-325-2525
www.daysinn.com

Doubletree Hotels
☎ 800-222-TREE
www.doubletree.com

Econo Lodge
☎ 800-55-ECONO
www.hotelchoice.com

Fairfield Inn by Marriott
☎ 800-228-2800
www.fairfieldinn.com

Hampton Inn
☎ 800-HAMPTON
www.hampton-inn.com

Hilton Hotels
☎ 800-HILTONS
www.hilton.com

Holiday Inn
☎ 800-HOLIDAY
www.basshotels.com

Howard Johnson
☎ 800-654-2000
www.hojo.com

Hyatt Hotels & Resorts
☎ 800-228-9000
www.hyatt.com

Marriott Hotel
☎ 800-228-9290
www.marriott.com

Quality Inn
☎ 800-228-5151
www.hotelchoice.com

Radisson Hotels International
☎ 800-333-3333
www.radisson.com

Ramada Inn
☎ 800-2-RAMADA
www.ramada.com

Residence Inn by Marriott
☎ 800-331-3131
www.residenceinn.com

Sheraton Hotels & Resorts
☎ 800-325-3535
www.sheraton.com

Super 8 Motel
☎ 800-800-8000
www.super8.com

Travelodge
☎ 800-255-3050
www.travelodge.com

Westin Hotels & Resorts
☎ 800-937-8461
www.westin.com

Wyndham Hotels & Resorts
☎ 800-822-4200
www.wyndham.com

Where to Get More Information

Some of your best sources of information are tourist agencies. This section describes the primary ones within the state.

Tourist information

You can request a free New Mexico guide, which includes a comprehensive calendar of events and a description of each of the state's regions and pueblos, from the **New Mexico Department of Tourism,** 491 Old Santa Fe Trail, Santa Fe, NM 87501 (☎ 800-733-6396 or 505-827-7400; Internet: www.nnewmexico.org). The office has a helpful staff and enough brochures to wallpaper your house.

The **Albuquerque Convention and Visitors Bureau,** 20 First Plaza NW (☎ 800-284-2282 or 505-842-9918; Internet: www.abqcvb.org), offers free guides to Albuquerque. The colorful publication includes a map and a number of good tours within and outside the city.

The free Santa Fe visitors guide, available from the **Santa Fe Convention and Visitors Bureau,** 201 W. Marcy St. (☎ 800-777-2489 or 505-955-6200; Internet: www.santafe.org or www.visitsantafe.com), has decent articles about the region as well as a map, lodging guide, and colorful photographs.

Information on the Web

If you're Web-wise, you can explore the following Internet sites while planning your trip:

- ✔ **www.santafenewmexican.com.** This Web site, for the oldest newspaper in the West, is packed with news, classifieds, entertainment listings, and other useful information about the Santa Fe area.

- ✔ **www.ABQjournal.com.** This useful site about Albuquerque and New Mexico in general is packed with news, classifieds, entertainment listings, and other useful information about the Albuquerque area.

- ✔ **www.weeklywire.com.** This funky Web site for the *Weekly Alibi* (Albuquerque's alternative weekly) offers abundant arts and entertainment coverage, including listings and reviews.

- ✔ **www.newmexico.org.** The official Web site of the New Mexico Department of Tourism, this site is packed with information about the state and has many useful links for planning a trip.

- ✔ **www.santafeinformation.com**. If you can't wait to see it in person, you can visit the Santa Fe Plaza virtually by clicking onto this site's Santa Fe Plaza Web cam.

Information in print

If you prefer to gather your information the old-fashioned way — reading from the printed page — you may want to check out some of these books and magazines:

- ✔ **Frommer's New Mexico** (Hungry Minds, Inc.). This guide takes a comprehensive look at the entire state and includes more lodging, dining, and attraction listings than this book can accommodate.

- ✔ **Frommer's Santa Fe, Taos & Albuquerque** (Hungry Minds, Inc.). This publication offers a more focused view of the state's three notable cities.

- ✔ **Frommer's Great Outdoor Guide to Arizona & New Mexico** (Hungry Minds, Inc.). This guide for outdoor lovers outlines the best places to hike, bike, climb, ski, and stroll (and pursue other pastimes as well) in these two Southwestern states.

- ✔ **New Mexico Magazine.** This slick monthly covers the state's arts, entertainment, culture, and scenery, as well as small-town oddities. You can also check it out online at www.nmmagazine.com.

- ✔ **The Santa Fean.** A very glossy magazine, *The Santa Fean* is published ten times a year and covers Santa Fe arts, entertainment, culture, shopping, homes, and celebrities. You can check it out online at www.santafean.com.

Making Dollars and Sense of It

Expense	Amount
Airfare	
Car Rental	
Lodging	
Parking	
Breakfast	
Lunch	
Dinner	
Babysitting	
Attractions	
Transportation	
Souvenirs	
Tips	
Grand Total	

Notes

Fare Game: Choosing an Airline

Travel Agency: _____ Phone: _____

Agent's Name: _____ Quoted Fare: _____

Departure Schedule & Flight Information

Airline: _____ Airport: _____

Flight #: _____ Date: _____ Time: _____ a.m./p.m.

Arrives in: _____ Time: _____ a.m./p.m.

Connecting Flight (if any)

Amount of time between flights: _____ hours/mins

Airline: _____ Airport: _____

Flight #: _____ Date: _____ Time: _____ a.m./p.m.

Arrives in: _____ Time: _____ a.m./p.m.

Return Trip Schedule & Flight Information

Airline: _____ Airport: _____

Flight #: _____ Date: _____ Time: _____ a.m./p.m.

Arrives in: _____ Time: _____ a.m./p.m.

Connecting Flight (if any)

Amount of time between flights: _____ hours/mins

Airline: _____ Airport: _____

Flight #: _____ Date: _____ Time: _____ a.m./p.m.

Arrives in: _____ Time: _____ a.m./p.m.

Notes

Sweet Dreams: Choosing Your Hotel

Enter the hotels where you'd prefer to stay based on location and price. Then use the worksheet below to plan your itinerary.

Hotel	Location	Price per night

Menus & Venues

Enter the restaurants where you'd most like to dine. Then use the worksheet below to plan your itinerary.

Name	Address/Phone	Cuisine/Price

Places to Go, People to See, Things to Do

Enter the attractions you would most like to see. Then use the worksheet below to plan your itinerary.

Attractions	Amount of time you expect to spend there	Best day and time to go

Going "My" Way

Itinerary #1

- ☐ _____
- ☐ _____
- ☐ _____
- ☐ _____

Itinerary #2

- ☐ _____
- ☐ _____
- ☐ _____
- ☐ _____

Itinerary #3

- ☐ _____
- ☐ _____
- ☐ _____
- ☐ _____

Itinerary #4

- ☐ _____
- ☐ _____
- ☐ _____
- ☐ _____

Itinerary #5

- ☐ _____
- ☐ _____
- ☐ _____
- ☐ _____

Itinerary #6

☐ _____
☐ _____
☐ _____
☐ _____

Itinerary #7

☐ _____
☐ _____
☐ _____
☐ _____

Itinerary #8

☐ _____
☐ _____
☐ _____
☐ _____

Itinerary #9

☐ _____
☐ _____
☐ _____
☐ _____

Itinerary #10

☐ _____
☐ _____
☐ _____
☐ _____

Notes

Index

• C •